❖

THE ZIEGFELD TOUCH

❖

THE LIFE AND TIMES OF FLORENZ ZIEGFELD, JR.

THE ZIEGFELD TOUCH

THE LIFE AND TIMES OF FLORENZ ZIEGFELD, JR.

RICHARD AND PAULETTE ZIEGFELD

FOREWORD BY PATRICIA ZIEGFELD STEPHENSON

HARRY N. ABRAMS, INC., PUBLISHERS

EDITOR:
BEVERLY FAZIO
DESIGNER:
RAYMOND P. HOOPER

Library of Congress Cataloging-in-Publication Data

Ziegfeld, Richard E.
The Ziegfeld touch: the life and times of Florenz Ziegfeld, Jr. /
Richard and Paulette Ziegfeld; with a foreword by Patricia Ziegfeld
Stephenson.
p.   cm.
Includes bibliographical references and index.
ISBN 0–8109–3966–5
1. Ziegfeld, Flo, 1869–1932.   2. Theatrical producers and
directors—United States—Biography.   I. Ziegfeld, Paulette, 1948–.
II. Title.
PN2287.Z5Z54   1992
792'.0232'092—dc20

[B]   92–4546
CIP

Published in 1993 by Harry N. Abrams, Incorporated, New York
A Times Mirror Company

Printed and bound in Japan

❖ CONTENTS ❖

❖
FOREWORD
❖

PATRICIA ZIEGFELD STEPHENSON

When Richard Ziegfeld, a distant cousin whom I had never met, telephoned one day in 1987 to say that he was planning a book about my father and would like to discuss it with me, I had the usual reservations. Since my father had died in 1932, many books, movies, and magazine articles had been produced about "The Great Ziegfeld" (there had even been an ill-fated musical based on his life), but none, I felt, had captured the complex, contradictory, strong-willed, and loving spirit of the man I knew as Daddy. Would Richard, who was born sixteen years after my Father died, do any better? It was with considerable hesitation and doubts that I approached our first meeting.

That initial conversation grew into more than a year of interviews, during which we gradually felt our way to a mutually respectful literary relationship. Our goals were originally different. Richard was committed to a documented biography of Florenz Ziegfeld's life and career. I was more concerned with making sure that my father's human side would receive adequate attention and that his private self—his humor, his loyalty and his love of family—would be presented as fairly and completely as his public persona. As time went on, Richard and I each began to learn from the other. I gained a new, more objective perspective on my father's life. Richard, I think, came to see the man behind the image and the complexities of the theater world.

To the outside world, my life as the daughter of the great impresario Ziegfeld and the celebrated comedienne Billie Burke must have seemed too good to be true—with the opening nights and private railroad cars and yachts and country estates. But that was only part of my world. Both my father and mother had very high standards and strict rules to live by, learned from their own parents. Gramma Burke, a thwarted actress, was a demanding woman, and my mother bowed to her every wish, knowing the sacrifices that Gramma had made to give her dancing and singing lessons. Grandpa Ziegfeld, or "Opa" as we called him, was also a strong disciplinarian who stood for no nonsense from anyone, especially his son Florenz. Both grandparents had great influence on their children and ultimately on me.

My parents were determined that I have a normal childhood and not grow up a spoiled brat. At Burkeley Crest, our home in Hastings-on-Hudson, New York, I had to report to my father in his bedroom before I went to school, no matter how late he had come home the night before. If I missed a morning, or was late for school, there would be a note waiting for me when I came home. He would correct my spelling, saying there was no excuse for not knowing how to spell correctly: "Look it up in the dictionary; that's what dictionaries are for." He noticed if I hadn't brushed my hair properly, or if I needed a shampoo, or if my teeth could stand extra polishing.

Mother was even tougher in some ways. When we were up at Camp Patricia (on Billie Burke Island), our summer place in the Laurentian Mountains north of Quebec, Daddy would sometimes relax his discipline a little, but never Mother, especially when it came to table manners and dirty nails. Daddy would say, "Oh, come on, Bill; fingers were made before forks." Mother never relented, though. And I grew up knowing that three things were forbidden: telling lies, whining, and bad sportsmanship.

For all of the discipline, my parents were amusing and fun to be with. Somehow, too, my father and mother were able to shield me from the glare of publicity in which they lived and from the occasional scandals that swirled around them. When a school friend made a cutting remark about Anna Held (Daddy's first wife), for instance, I had no idea whom she was talking about.

Now, more than half a century after his death, I think I see my father in a clearer light than ever before. Others have commemorated his great taste, his extraordinary sense of color, his flair for the dramatic. What is difficult for most people to believe is that he was as much at home out-of-doors as he was inside a theater. He loved nature in all its aspects. He knew flowers and just where to plant them in our garden to achieve the effect he wanted. He grew his favorite foods in profusion—country-gentleman corn, white raspberries, and concord grapes—and had a prize mint bed.

He loved animals, so we were always surrounded by no fewer than five or six dogs, not to mention parrots, a cockatoo, an imported bullfinch from Germany, and, for one memorable period, a beautiful black squirrel named "Nicky." We raised all our own chickens and, from time to time, turkeys and pheasants.

Daddy was an active outdoor sportsman: fishing, hunting, golf, sailing, ice skating—he excelled in them all. He made sure that I had sound training in them, too.

However, he left the household management entirely in Mother's competent hands. He might make a suggestion once in a while or try his hand at a recipe—yes, he could cook a little—but only once do I remember him ever entering the realm of homemaking. While Mother and I were in Palm Beach one year, he secretly hired Elsie Sloan Farley, one of the popular interior decorators of the time, to redecorate the entire house. It was a gamble, but it paid off: Mother loved it.

Neither Father nor Mother was business-oriented. Though they had the usual complement of business managers and accountants, they were never able to save much money. They were an ideal couple when it came to spending: what one did not think of, the other did. The chemistry between these two strong-willed individuals could have been disastrous, but somehow they made their marriage work. Mother created so pleasurable an environment for Daddy that no temptation, and there were many, would prompt him to leave it. She worshiped the ground he walked on, but she recognized his frailties and somehow knew exactly how to deal with them. Actually, she had as many men falling at her feet as he had women falling at his. The fact that they were each so desirable to others may have been a factor that kept their marriage intact.

I was not quite sixteen when Daddy died—virtually bankrupt. To make ends meet, Mother went back to acting more frequently, this time as a character actress rather than a leading lady. The years that followed were not easy ones. Even in the most difficult days, though, she spoke of Daddy with pride and affection. Toward the end of her life, she often remarked that she missed my father more in her later years than she did right after his death.

Florenz Ziegfeld was envied, praised, censured, even hated, but he was also very much loved.

Now, half a century later, that past has suddenly been brought back to life by Richard and Paulette's masterful recreation of my father's career. He would have been utterly amazed to realize he had produced all those shows, fought with all those people, and enjoyed so much of life. For me, reading this book has been like sitting in the audience watching the lights go up on a darkened stage and seeing one's own life, and that of one's loved ones, played out in fascinating detail, like a tapestry woven in myriads of color. It has been an emotionally exciting, sometimes exhausting, but always rewarding experience.

I should not have been surprised. During all those hours I spent with Richard, I learned to recognize—and respect—his insatiable curiosity about all aspects of the task before him, his unflagging determination to do the best job possible within his capabilities, and his almost fierce dedication. And I realized that these very qualities—which are often summed up in that one word "drive"—were the same ones that explained much of my father's extraordinary success.

Perhaps "the Ziegfeld touch" runs in the family.

PREFACE AND ACKNOWLEDGMENTS

Richard grew up knowing that Florenz Ziegfeld, Jr., his cousin, was a major figure on Broadway, but he had never taken a serious interest in the fact. As he grew older, Richard started reading books on Ziegfeld, each useful in its own right, but located no complete overview on the man or his career. We also began to check resources, discovering this: for the first third of Ziegfeld's life, there was a dearth of information, and for the last third, there was a glut of facts. Overall, though, virtually no information on his personal reaction to any event was available, and analytical commentary was scarce. Moreover, because Ziegfeld was known for light theater fare, scholars paid little attention, with the notable exception of *Show Boat*. Thus, even traditional sources of information were limited.

This fact created a substantial research challenge. The key to this book was Patty Ziegfeld Stephenson's full cooperation. Through dozens of letters and phone calls and more than ninety hours of interview, Patty has generously shared her knowledge.

While she provided a wealth of insight, this was only one person's viewpoint. The difficult task was to locate written source material, given that the major research center, the New York Public Library Theater Collection, is rich on photos and published materials but has few unpublished documents. After determining that Ziegfeld's corpus was nearly twice as large as previously believed (eighty-three productions rather than forty-five), we discovered that most material we needed lurked in nontraditional locations. This required working with more than 150 people during thirty-five road trips to thirty-four archives or private collections. Previously untapped Ziegfeld materials included collections belonging the these individuals or institutions: Patricia Ziegfeld Stephenson—extensive personal collection; Liane Carrera—materials relating to Anna Held and the Ziegfeld family; the New York Public Library—uncatalogued Robert Baral and Ziegfeld Club collection; Norma Terris—unpublished autobiography and memorabilia; John Harkrider—unpublished autobiography; Chicago Musical College at Roosevelt University—ledgers and papers; the Lorimar Picture Research Library—photos of Ziegfeld shows.

This discovery process about the Ziegfeld family and the source material occupied two of us for three years, allowing us to bring home twenty linear feet of research material. More important than the volume of data was the intensity of the experience. This project has been unquestionably the most trying and yet satisfying one we have undertaken. Trying because the trail to the information and the personality involved has been so elusive. Satisfying because the search has been so personal and because at long last we felt as though we had begun to understand the man, his accomplishment, and his era.

This book has two threads: Ziegfeld's life and a history of his theatrical productions—including more than one hundred profiles on his actors and production staff. Richard wrote the biographical material on Ziegfeld, and Paulette handled the history of the productions. Some shows we cite were Ziegfeld co-productions. In several instances, we listed Ziegfeld shows that did not reach Broadway but that were historically significant. Also, in two cases, Ziegfeld is not listed as the producer, but he contributed artistically.

We discuss productions in chronological order so readers can see Ziegfeld's work develop. Not all his shows succeeded; however, those mentioned all provide historical insight. Readers can gauge the variety and volume of Ziegfeld's work and observe how he progressed from simple revivals of comic farces such as *A Parlor Match* to complex, dramatic musicals, including *Show Boat*.

We have cited dates for the Broadway runs, not the number of performances, because there are so many discrepancies in the counting methods and so much confusion about the *Follies* chronology in the mid-1920s. Instead we carefully worked the newspapers and trade magazines to determine when shows opened and closed. Most Ziegfeld shows toured the East Coast and Midwest. Some did not have long Broadway runs but succeeded on tour. We have not included details about road engagements.

One editorial practice warrants a note. To make telegrams readable, we standardized capitalization, punctuation, and spelling. The rationale: Western Union often introduced errors and routinely omitted most punctuation, making it impossible to determine who generated the idiosyncrasies. However, when quoting letters, we retained the idiosyncrasies because they reveal character.

We are indebted to many people, especially Paul Gottlieb, Beverly Fazio, and Mark Greenberg at Abrams. We also thank Richard Newman, Michael Roach, and John Wright.

Richard's day job with Sverdrup Technology supported us while we wrote the book: we especially thank David Benner, Wendell Norman, and Lee Petrie for their cooperation.

These people granted interviews and gave generously of their time: Marilyn Baker; Lina Basquette; William Block; Henry Buhl (deceased); Natalie Clary; Matilda Clough (deceased); Charles, Doris, and

Joseph Eaton; Ronald J. Fields; Evelyn Freeman; Nona Friedman; Felix Ganz (deceased); Alexander Hegedus; James Knott; Muriel Merrill; Ector Munn; Chet O'Brien; Dana O'Connell; Annabelle Reals; Jimmy Rogers; Gloria Rudes; Anna Sosenko; Evelyn Smith; Norma Terris (deceased); Donald Thurber; Rosemarie Vulcano; Lucile Zinman.

Many dedicated librarians helped out—especially the staff at New York Public Library—Theater. Other libraries include these: Academy of Motion Picture Arts and Sciences, Bettmann Archive, Chicago Historical Society, Chicago Public, Cleveland Public, Columbia University, Harvard University, Hastings Historical Society, Historical Society of Palm Beach, Lorimar Picture Research, Movietone News Archive, Museum of the City of New York, Newberry, New York State Surrogate Court (Westchester County), Roosevelt University, Shubert Archive, Society of the Four Arts, Theatre Historical Society, UCLA, University of South Carolina, University of Southern California, University of Texas, University of Wisconsin, Wisconsin Historical Society, Will Rogers Memorial.

Help on research, computers, photos, and manuscript review came from Joe Adamson, Gerald Bordman, Randolph Carter, Cecily Collins, Barbara Cohen-Stratyner, Joyce Compton, Chip Cooper, Robert Cushman, Donald Draganski, Al Fedor, Albert Firestone, Jane Fuglister, Herb Goldman, Connie Hamilton, Jerol Hanlon, Nils Hanson, Michael Hiatt, Charles Higham, Mike Jaros, David A. Jasen, Stephen Johnson, Rennie Kane, Hillary Knight, Miles Kreuger, Elisabeth Lamont, Gene London, Rosalie McDonald, Geraldine Maschio, Barry Paris, Jim Patrick, William Paxton, Burton Raffel, Peter Russell, Quentin Schwinn, Miles Solle, Rosaline Stone, Ben Thompson, Richard Thompson, Gretl Urban, Danguole Variakojis, Jonathan Wallen, Arthur Wertheim, and Ben Yagoda.

We also thank people who made travel more pleasant: Bob and Harriet Baker, Eric Hanson and Sharon Kreder, Ina Hark, Richard and Carl Lanham, Ed and Jeanne Semler.

Last, Adam Ziegfeld, our son, showed the patience and humor of an adult, while *both* of his parents pursued this quest, so he deserves several big hugs.

Richard and Paulette Ziegfeld
September 1992

Above: Florenz Ziegfeld, Jr., about age three. Top, left to right: Brown School in Chicago, where Ziegfeld received his elementary education; the four Ziegfeld children about 1881: (left to right) Carl, Louise, Flo (standing), and William; Florenz Ziegfeld, Sr.

CHAPTER 1

❖

THE CHICAGO YEARS

❖

The things Flo cherished as a showman were color, music, spectacle, and fun. . . . His genius was his towering ability to play one against the other, matching his palette to his music, his comedy to his spectacle, stirring and mixing the whole until he produced out of the utter conflict that unique work of art, a great musical comedy. No one, indeed, ever knew how he accomplished it.

Billie Burke Ziegfeld

Everyone who writes about Florenz Ziegfeld, Jr., feels compelled to portray the man with superlatives. Broadway's greatest showman. Impresario extraordinaire. Perfectionist. Eccentric. Glorifier of the American girl. Heartless womanizer. Talent scout supreme. Compulsive gambler. These descriptions, each accurate in its context, have been repeated countless times, but taken individually or even in aggregate, the list misses the crucial point. Above all else, Ziegfeld was an artist.

The superlatives derive from this fundamental point. Sooner or later readers find themselves asking: "Why would he do something so foolish, so expensive, so cruel?" The answer is that he was driven by a vision of beauty. He once told his first wife, Anna Held, that he was compelled by a dream of "demolishing all the current methods of staging shows." Nothing less. What made this dream all the more interesting was that he accomplished it in theatrical realms not noted in his day for their artistry—the revue and the musical comedy. His theatrical genius lay in transforming popular but plebeian dramatic forms into art without losing their mass appeal. That was the "Ziegfeld touch."

The origins of the Ziegfeld touch lie in Chicago, during the 1860s and 1870s.

Left: William F. "Buffalo Bill" Cody brought his "Wild West Show" to Chicago in 1885. Right: Flo Ziegfeld, Jr., as a young man

The Chicago in which Florenz, Jr., grew up was a potent combination of rough-and-tumble frontier town and sophisticated cultural activity.

Florenz Ziegfeld, Sr., the showman's father, son of yet another "Florenz," moved to Chicago in 1863. (The family tree is littered with a confusing array of men and women carrying that given name.) Florenz, Sr., was born June 10, 1841, in Jever, a village in northern Germany. His father and mother, Louise Kirchoff, were both Lutherans. Florenz, Sr.'s father was the town mayor and an official in the court of the grand duke of Oldenburg. He loved music and conveyed that passion to his son.

A precocious student, Florenz, Sr., started music lessons at age six, with the celebrated Carl Stiehl. The boy soon became a skillful pianist and performed successfully in public and private concerts. In 1859, of college age, he studied at the Leipzig Conservatory, then the most prestigious music institute in Germany, where he completed his degree in 1863. His work had been so good that he received an offer to direct a Russian conservatory, but he chose the United States instead. He stopped in New York City before settling in Chicago, where by 1865 he had joined W. W. Kimball (of piano fame) and George Root in a music-publishing business. He had also opened his first educational institution, the Chicago Conservatorium of Music, with seven faculty members. It failed within a year or two.

Meanwhile, Florenz, Sr., married Rosalie de Hez on May 17, 1865. She was seven years younger than he and was Catholic; because Ziegfeld was not Catholic, the ceremony was performed by Father Roles in Roles's home. Rosalie was the grand niece of General Etienne Gérard, Napoleon's marshal of France; her granddaughter Patty says that Rosalie was of Belgian extraction. Rosalie arrived in Chicago before Ziegfeld, but there is no precise information about when her family emigrated.

After the initial music college failed, Florenz, Sr., made another attempt to establish himself in the commercial music business with Ziegfeld, Gerard, & Co., a firm that published music and sold instruments. He does not seem to have played or taught professionally that year.

During the latter half of the 1860s, the Ziegfelds moved several times. The house at 298 East Chicago Street was where their first child, Florenz Edward, Jr., was born on March 21, 1867. Florenz, Jr., was baptized Catholic, with the Right Reverend Edward Soren, founder of Notre Dame University, acting as godfather and Mother Angela, Mother Superior of St. Mary's Academy, South Bend, Indiana, as god-mother. The Ziegfeld knack for establishing useful social contacts was already evident.

The family's ecumenical attitude became evident when Flo's brothers, Carl (born in 1869) and William (1873), were baptized Lutheran and his sister, Louise (1875), was christened in the Methodist Episcopal Church. Florenz, Sr., a Lutheran, played the organ at the Catholic Holy Name Cathedral.

After Florenz, Jr., was born, the peripatetic family continued to change locations in Chicago's downtown area, later known as the Loop. Florenz, Sr., opened another conservatory, the Chicago Musical Academy, in 1867. Because the institution has survived more than 125 years, it is easy to overlook the fact that opening a musical college in Chicago in the mid-nineteenth century took some courage. Nevertheless, Chicago was a reasonable location for an ambitious artist to take a risk because it was growing rapidly, almost doubling from 179,000 residents in 1865 to 334,000 by 1871, just six years later.

The year 1871 was a pivotal one for the Ziegfeld family and for Chicago. Their home and the school building, along with the greater portion of the Loop, were destroyed during the great fire on October 8. The downtown section was almost completely ruined: the fire destroyed 17,450 buildings in an area covering 2,124 acres. Property damage was estimated at $200 million. The Ziegfeld home was in the midst of the conflagration that wiped out a section thirty-six blocks north and eight blocks west.

Florenz, Sr., relocated the college to an office at 610 Michigan. Then he transferred it to 800 Wabash; finally, he was forced to operate it from his home at 493 Wabash. Despite the devastating setback, he placed prominent advertisements within days of the fire, announcing that he had reopened his business.

That same year, Florenz, Sr., took eleven of his pupils to Germany, where they visited the important musical sites. Franz Liszt, himself, invited them to one of his Sunday-morning concerts and arranged a dinner in their honor. A year later, Florenz, Sr., received yet another professional distinction. He was asked to assist with the Boston Peace Jubilee, June 17 to July 4, 1872. Fifty thousand people attended. Ziegfeld persuaded Johann Strauss to participate in the festival, no mean feat given that Strauss had a deep and well-justified fear of ocean travel. The elder Ziegfeld's ability to entice the great musicians of Europe to participate set an example for Flo, Jr.

During 1872, the school changed its name to the Chicago Musical College and underwent a reorganization that made Dr. George Root president instead of Florenz, Sr., who was named director. Flo, Sr., returned to the position of president by 1876 and retained it until 1916—an impressive forty years. Meanwhile, the school grew significantly, so that as early as 1872, it already had nine hundred pupils.

Between 1876 and 1878, as the Chicago Musical College expanded, classes were held at various sites, including 493 Wabash, 297 West Madison, and 333 North Market, as well as in faculty homes. Florenz, Sr., then consolidated the Madison and Market Street sites at 44 Loomis Street, which was the fifth Ziegfeld home. He was at this time still actively teaching piano, harmony, and composition. The school also offered

Cover from the 1892–93 Chicago
Musical College catalogue

elocution, languages (German, French, Italian), deportment for young ladies, and a little dance instruction. Its catalogue claimed that the Chicago Musical College was attracting young people from practically every state in the Union. The board of directors included numerous well-known Chicagoans, as the college had become a fashionable place for the elite to send their daughters.

In 1878, Florenz, Sr., assumed the title of "Doctor." No evidence suggests that Ziegfeld earned his doctorate—or that he was honored with one—and no one attempted to explain why the educator felt compelled to assume the title. His colleagues and the Chicago press never questioned the designation.

Around 1882, the Ziegfelds moved into their sixth and last home, at 1448 West Adams. It was a tall, narrow brownstone: one room wide and three stories high plus a half-level for the cellar and kitchen. The kitchen and dining room were a bit below street level, with high windows for light and ventilation. The attic—a true attic in which you could not stand except in the middle—was the site for one of the more remarkable anecdotes about Ziegfeld's childhood. His daughter, Patty, vividly recalls seeing bullet holes in the walls when she was small. Ziegfeld explained that he had maintained a flock of pigeons, which he would release from time to time, and that he had used a .22 rifle for pigeon target practice—in the attic itself. If this tale is to be believed, it substantially belies the popular notion that Ziegfeld's father was a stern disciplinarian. It may, of course, simply be Ziegfeld's whimsical retelling of his childhood.

Flo, Jr., received his early education at the Brown Elementary School at 1758 Warren Boulevard, a public, neighborhood school with an outstanding reputation. He was not a particularly good student, although he managed to avoid failing any subjects. Brown's reputation lay partly in its academic regimen, but it also developed because many people who eventually became famous attended the school: Lillian Russell, Mrs. Potter Palmer, Eddie Foy, and Edgar Rice Burroughs, among others. So even in his Chicago grammar-school days, Flo was influenced by stories about prominent people.

Flo, Jr.'s second wife, Billie Burke, captured Ziegfeld's attitude toward formal education when she noted that "he always flattered himself he never even went to school, but bless his heart, if he didn't he was pretty well self-educated. I remember his father used to have to lock him in to make him practice piano, but even then he found a way out, through making up to the cook, I believe."

As a boy, Ziegfeld was close to his mother, who was gentle but firm. She encouraged him in his activities and protected him from the senior Ziegfeld when he got into mischief. An outstanding cook with lots of family recipes for sauces, Rosalie loved to prepare "strudels and soups, pot roasts, fritters and pastries" for Flo, Jr., who grew up appreciating this rich European cuisine.

After Florenz, Jr., finished Brown Elementary School, he attended Ogden High (probably from 1881 to 1885). None of his school records survive. While still in high school, he started working for his father at the Chicago Musical College (about 1882), earning a modest but regular salary that increased from $3 to $5 a week between 1883 and 1885.

Flo, Sr., was by now well established at the college. His booming voice and commanding presence prompted many writers to draw a narrow stereotype, almost a caricature, of a rigid Prussian autocrat, but Louis Falk's recollections round out the portrait of Dr. Ziegfeld's character when he describes the camaraderie he shared with Ziegfeld and another of Chicago's dominant music figures, Theodore Thomas. With Thomas in the lead and Ziegfeld assisting, this group eventually established the renowned Chicago Symphony Orchestra. Falk, who was on the Chicago Musical College faculty, notes that "it was our custom to gather around a table after closing hours at the College . . . eating our sandwiches . . . and drinking beer or strong coffee. . . . The "Ziegfeld Club" . . . met once a month for dinner, program, and a general good time. . . . It was considered quite the thing to be invited to one of these affairs, for there one met many really famous artists of that day."

While the Ziegfelds were safely ensconced in a comfortable world of fine-art and beer-hall friendships, popular entertainment was beginning to emerge in new forms. In New York Rudolph Aronson was building the Casino in 1882, the first roof garden—an open-air site that offered food, drinks, and popular entertainment. Eventually nine gardens would operate above New York theaters.

In July 1883, when he was sixteen, Ziegfeld's parents sent him to a cattle ranch in Wyoming. Along the way, he had gained shooting expertise from his father, an expert marksman in the Illinois National Guard. While he was in high school, Flo became intrigued by Buffalo Bill's Wild West Show, an appealing entertainment that drew huge audiences. A feature in the *Chicago Daily News* (May 30, 1885) dramatically described Buffalo Bill (William Cody) and his companion, Major Frank Powell: "By their look and carriage, they appeared to belong to that wild, untamed order of society which knows no restraint except the law of nature." This was the stuff of captivating adventure for a teenaged boy. It clashed starkly with the European values represented by Dr. Ziegfeld and his musical college.

Several stories have arisen about Ziegfeld and the Wild West Show. One source has Ziegfeld successfully challenging Annie Oakley in a shooting match in 1880. According to this story, Buffalo Bill then hired Florenz, Jr., prompting him to run away from home for three weeks until his father caught up with him and dragged him back. Another source has Ziegfeld outshooting Buffalo Bill himself. Yet another version dates the experience precisely—May 28, 1883—and has Ziegfeld shooting against Oakley. Since Annie Oakley did not join Buffalo Bill until 1885, Ziegfeld could not have outshot her in 1880 or 1883, so the story is probably apocryphal. Nevertheless, the tale remains important because Ziegfeld mentioned it years later in explaining how he became interested in popular entertainment. In a preface to a book on the revue as a dramatic form, Ziegfeld recalls adventures "beginning with my running away with Buffalo Bill's Wild West Show." Something about the Buffalo Bill phenomenon captured his imagination, and by the early 1880s, young Ziegfeld had become fascinated with "low" culture.

Buffalo Bill's show epitomized the New World, American style, a style at odds with the European values of Dr. Ziegfeld's Chicago, where the demanding standard of high culture was dominant, the social hierarchy prevailed, and the bourgeois ethic was never far away. But the Chicago to which Flo, Jr., gravitated was a wide-open city with a bawdy nightlife replete with liquor, women, and gambling. A red-light district was located within a mile of the Ziegfeld house. As Flo, Jr., was growing up, several dozen classy gambling houses were run openly on Chicago's near West Side, fairly close to 1448 West Adams.

Florenz, Jr., came of age in a transitional world that straddled both cultures. As Ziegfeld finished high school, he may not have accepted his father's values completely, but it would take nearly a decade for him to break away. During the interlude, he served an apprenticeship under his father.

In 1885, Florenz, Jr., began working full-time at the Chicago Musical College as assistant treasurer. We have little information about his activities there for the next seven years, but it appears that he did well because his father promoted him quickly to positions with more responsibility. Within one year Florenz, Jr., became treasurer and was made a member of the board of directors.

While Ziegfeld was serving his apprenticeship at the Chicago Musical College, his heart was elsewhere. His great passion was dancing. He became so expert at this pastime that he even won contests during these years and was a leader of Chicago cotillions. Outside of work Flo was getting around town a bit; according to Billie Burke, he "was a great favorite in Chicago society in his twenties, squiring among others the daughters of the fabulously wealthy Pullman family." He was also participating in small-time show business enterprises. Some sources, not verifiable, refer to the incident of "The Dancing Ducks of Denmark," which landed Ziegfeld in trouble with the Society for the Prevention of Cruelty to Animals for inducing the ducks to dance by heating their feet over a gas flame. In addition, he managed amateur shows at the Farragut Boat Club, the first of many exclusive clubs to which he would belong.

Because so much of the commentary about Ziegfeld has emphasized the strain in his relationship with his father, it is relevant to note some lessons that Flo, Jr., learned during the ten years that he worked at the Chicago Musical College, years that other commentators have cast aside as "lost" time.

The flair that Flo, Jr., showed for publicity has been thoroughly documented. The senior Ziegfeld was not quite so flamboyant in this area, but he did have a talent for it. Florenz, Sr., advertised his business steadily. In 1888, the annual promotion budget was around $1,000; three years later it had expanded sharply, to around $3,700. Clearly this was more than inflation; other influences were coming to bear. He also created a series of special touches that made the institution appeal to wealthier families. Each year Florenz, Sr., awarded the best students expensive diamond pins and gold and silver medals; an interesting aside is that Dr. Ziegfeld eventually began soliciting these and other gifts from wealthy donors. Flo, Jr., watched his father "working" these patrons and persuading them to back him. The college incorporated two other new features: a telephone line and a hansom cab to pick up arriving pupils—for free—at the train station. Which Ziegfeld came up with these ideas is not clear, but they appeared in 1891, around the time that Flo, Jr., at age twenty-four, was emerging from his apprenticeship. The key point of these services is that they made the students and their parents feel special.

In 1891, when Theodore Thomas organized the Chicago Symphony Orchestra, Dr. Ziegfeld assisted him. Thomas had organized the New York Philharmonic, but he left New York City to found the Chicago Symphony because he felt that Chicago supported him more strongly. The symphony's favorable reception contributed to Dr. Ziegfeld's and the college's reputation.

Florenz, Jr., worked intimately with and had to have absorbed the values of men such as Thomas and his father, who believed passionately, almost obsessively, in their artistic visions. He watched his father nurture a lifelong dream—to create *the* dominant music college in the United States—until that vision became a reality and saw Thomas adhere to his ideals, even though they led him into serious financial straits and made him unpopular with powerful musicians and important politicians. He also observed the reverence these men had for artistic talent, and he saw firsthand what was required to deal with that temperament.

These, too, were valuable lessons for the future showman.

In March 1892, the Ziegfelds celebrated the Chicago Musical College's twenty-fifth anniversary with a glittering evening that "attracted a large and brilliant audience" and featured the Chicago Symphony. In an advertisement for the gala, Flo, Jr., was cited as the manager of the Central Music Hall, where the event took place. Outside testimonials came from a variety of sources. Probably most meaningful to Ziegfeld was the praise offered by Theodore Thomas and quoted prominently in the *Chicago Tribune*. Thomas said of Florenz, Sr.: "From the first he aimed high, placed his ideal of culture high. . . . The musical life of the city has been quickened and elevated; and today the Chicago Musical College is one of the largest and best in America and its great work is fully confessed in Europe."

The anniversary celebration must have attracted many new students, because the 1892–93 Chicago Musical College ledgers show this to have been one of the most successful years in the school's history. Annual profit until this point had been between $2,500 and $3,500: this year it was approximately $10,000. Flo, Sr., took an income draw of $9,660 against college equity; Flo, Jr., $3,368; and Carl $1,200. When combined with college profit, this yields a total income of nearly $25,000, which translates into a 1992 value of $450,000. Profit was unusually good in 1892, but during the decade that Flo, Jr., worked at the college, the salary draws remained fairly stable. Hence, typical family income would have been the equivalent of at least $325,000 annually—at a time when the rent on the West Adams Street house remained $15 a month, less than one percent of the family's income. Dr. Ziegfeld's thriving business allowed his son to come of age in very comfortable circumstances.

Hosting a World's Fair, though rarely profitable, was a much sought-after opportunity. The two leading contenders for the right to host the 1893 event, Chicago and New York City, competed head-to-head for the plum, and Chicago won. Theodore Thomas and Flo, Sr., were both elected to the board of commissioners for the international congress of musicians at the World's Fair. On November 18, 1891, Thomas agreed to become music director for the Columbian Exposition (the Fair was named in honor of the four-hundredth anniversary of Columbus's voyage). The appointment was especially significant for the Ziegfelds because their friendship with Thomas ensured them a central role in the event's music.

Once the World's Fair site, Jackson Park, was selected, exhibitors started building as early as the beginning of 1892. People dubbed Chicago "The White City" because the Fair buildings, which "resembled ancient Greece more than late nineteenth-century America," were stark white. The design artfully combined escapist and formal elements to create a fantasy land for Fair patrons.

Thomas and Ziegfeld devised grandiose plans for the Fair's music program. They had two primary goals: to show the world the progress in American music and to introduce Americans to foreign music.

The Fair's music was ambitious, as could be expected of any effort that Thomas supported. The program offered Wagner's music in May, Russian musicians and Handel's *Messiah* in June, the German-American Women's Chorus in July, the German Liederkranz of New York City, and the Junge Männerchor of Philadelphia. Local newspapers praised the musical intentions, but one noted that the plan "proved to be impracticable and luxuriously expensive." Only the pop concerts and children's choruses were well received.

The Fair as a whole, however, was a resounding success. More than 21 million people paid admission with a weekly attendance that ranged from 110,000 to 138,000. A Fair retrospective noted that the Cairo exhibit (a lowbrow offering) was the most popular, with more than 2.25 million paid admissions. The Chicago Fair took in $14 million in admissions and concession fees, much better than the Paris Exposition of 1889, where the total was $8.3 million. Since it drew substantially better than Paris, which was then considered the center of the civilized world, Chicago took its place as a world-class city.

Although numerous writers have said that Dr. Ziegfeld was director of music for the Fair, his official function, as Chicago newspapers clearly indicated, was to act as the Chairman of the Jury of Piano and Organ awards. He also assisted Thomas by booking some of the European acts, which reflected Thomas's lofty goal of educating Americans about musical developments outside this country.

While the Ziegfelds participated in Thomas's high-minded vision, another development was afoot in 1892. Florenz, Sr., created a nightclub with popular music called The International Temple of Music. The temple's building, the Trocadero, was first located at the old First Regiment Armory (Michigan Avenue and Sixteenth Street) and later at Battery D (Michigan and Monroe), just north of the Art Institute of Chicago. This downtown location, near the Loop, was miles from the city's South Side, where the Fair was held.

Previous accounts of Ziegfeld's life have perpetuated a good deal of confusion about the relationship between the Trocadero and the World's Fair. Florenz, Sr., set up the Trocadero as an independent, for-profit operation that had no official tie to the Fair. At the outset, he booked European bands for the club (in addition to those for the Fair) with help from his son. Financial figures on the Trocadero indicate that initially it was run on a shoestring budget. Even after the Fair opened and the crowds were in town, it did not attract a large number of patrons.

Events of 1892 and 1893—the Chicago Musical College's twenty-fifth anniversary, Fair preparations, creation of the Trocadero—set the stage for Flo, Jr., to emerge from his father's shadow.

Above left: The Trocadero and surrounding area about 1892, just before Ziegfeld began managing the theatre. The large building in front of the Trocadero (center of photo) is the Art Institute of Chicago. Above right: Bertha Palmer, socialite wife of Potter Palmer, owner of Chicago's Palmer House

CHAPTER 2

❖

THE PERFECT MAN

❖

F lorenz, Sr.'s first venture into popular entertainment opened shortly before huge crowds arrived in Chicago over the summer of 1893. Flo, Jr., acted as foreign representative, his crucial break in show business. As he was returning from Europe, he received a telegram informing him that the Trocadero building had burned down. The Ziegfelds were forced to relocate the club to the National Guard's Battery D Building. This location, even farther away from the Fair, was decidedly less attractive.

Trocadero ads appeared prior to the Fair, and by May 1 the private enterprise was set to run the duration of the Fair. The club's initial bill was a peculiar mix of popular acts and light classical material: Voros Miska's Hungarian Orchestra; Iwanoff's Russian Singers and Dancers; Cyrene, "an eccentric English lady dancer"; and "a couple of minor concert singers." The program for May 3 included Gounod's *Faust* and Strauss's "Blue Danube" waltz. Clearly, Flo, Sr., had not yet mastered popular programming. Flo, Jr., was soon named manager (in August), but his father was still cited prominently as president of the board.

The Trocadero show did not succeed financially. Even a fifty-cent admission was too much. In an early example of his lifelong penchant for taking the big risk, Flo, Jr., offered to assume responsibility for the show's contracts. He obtained the rights at "advantageous terms" and immediately juggled the acts to liven the program. But the hapless adventure continued to lose significant sums, while Lillian Russell and Buffalo Bill were making money effortlessly just outside the Fair gate.

Sometime during 1893, Florenz, Jr., visited Rudolph Aronson's Casino Theatre in New York. As early as 1883, the Casino specialized in presenting operetta, and by the end of the 1880s it enjoyed an international reputation as the "pre-eminent operetta house." By this time, the Casino Roof Garden was presenting vaudeville, burlesque, and popular French acts, as well as light opera and musical comedies. To make the variety shows more appealing, the owners tried to introduce a sophisticated European flavor.

Aronson had booked Eugene Sandow, a strongman, to perform at the Casino. Ziegfeld arrived at the propitious moment: Sandow was drawing $500 per week but wanted double that amount. Ziegfeld had $5,000 intended for advertising. He could not afford a headliner, so he offered Sandow 10 percent of the gross to play the Trocadero. In another move that would characterize his career, he gambled the $5,000 on Sandow. Ziegfeld negotiated a deal for Sandow's services for the duration of the Fair, either directly or through the strongman's manager, a man named Abbey.

The strongman was born in 1867 in Königsberg, Germany. At age ten, Sandow was a "pale, frail, delicate, even weakly" child, but at eighteen, he had exercised so hard that he was in "perfect health and strength." After knocking around Europe a bit, he got his break in November 1889, when he bested another strongman, "Samson," before a packed house in London.

Chicago was in a circus mood, so Ziegfeld gave Sandow a billing that P. T. Barnum would have admired. The August 1 notice in the *Chicago Tribune* said that the Trocadero was presenting the "greatest vaudeville performance ever offered in America." Highly aware of the roof-garden phenomenon, Ziegfeld asserted that his club was "better than a roof garden" and "cooler than a roof garden."

At the opening, Ziegfeld's name appeared above those of his performers. Ziegfeld never gave star billing to individual performers in those early days. Nevertheless, he devised a tremendous buildup for Sandow, prominently advertising the strongman's physical prowess: even though he was only five feet, eight inches tall, he could expand his chest to at least 58 inches. To generate more publicity, Flo, Jr., called in reporters and physicians to ask if Sandow were not the perfect physical specimen. The doctors concurred. His feats were notable for their ingenuity. He would set a man on the palm of his hand and lift him up, wrestle three men at one time, and let three horses walk across a plank on his chest.

The Trocadero program also included an array of other performers, called the Trocadero Vaudevilles. Eventually the troupe incorporated acts such as Jules Levy, the cornetist; Marie Collins, the pop singer; and Tartajada, a Spanish dancer.

Even at this stage in his career, Ziegfeld had access to the right people. On the opening night of Sandow's run, August 1, 1893, Flo, Jr., invited several society ladies he knew, including Mrs. George M. Pullman and Mrs. Potter Palmer, to meet Sandow in his dressing room. Partly owing to the panache provided by the women, Amy Leslie wrote a rave review in the next day's *Chicago Daily News,* calling Sandow "a dangerously handsome young man."

Leslie's review and the publicity about the society ladies' backstage visit affected business immediately. Ziegfeld issued invitations to one hundred persons nightly to visit Sandow's dressing room, and the first

GRAND OPERA HOUSE

ELM PLACE near FULTON ST.

Week Commencing Monday, Dec. 23
1896

WEDNESDAY — MATINEES — SATURDAY

Direct from the Chicago Auditorium,

THE TROCADERO VAUDEVILLES

10—EUROPEAN NOVELTIES—10

Headed by the Peerless **SANDOW** His Farewell!

Presenting a refined vaudeville and athletic entertainment, patronized by the best class of theatre-goers in America and recognized by press and public as a performance without a peer in number, quality and variety of acts, and special individual features.

Congress of World-Famous Artists and Athletes.
Greatest Physical Lesson of the Age.

Conceived, Organized and Promoted by
F. ZIEGFELD, JR.

PROGRAMME

Descriptive Piece—"A Hunting Scene.".................P. Bucalosi
Description of the morning break. Calm and Peaceful. The Huntsman prepare for the pleasure of the Chase. Our Brutsman sounds a merry blast. Echo. The Parties join. A Hunting we will go. Barking of dogs. Tally-Ho. Full Cry. The Death. We return home. A Hunting we will go.
March—"The Real Thing."..........................H. W. Petrie

HERR AUGUST DEWELL
The Eminent Scandinavian Gymnast.

THE LUCIFERS
Grotesque from the Alhambra, London. Mr. Lucifer, champion combined high kicker and jumper of the world. Mr. Lucifer's muscular development has been attained in one year under Sandow's System of Physical Culture.

STACK and LATELL
Premier Triple Bar Performers. First Appearance.

N. E. KAUFMANN
The champion bicycle trick rider of the world and holder of every existing championship and who has appeared before most of the crowned heads of Europe. Mr. Kaufmann is ready to defend his title at any time against all comers for any amount at two to one. He originated all his novel feats and odd wheels.

MONS O'GUST
The Eminent French Clown, from the Follies Bergere, Paris, presenting his marvelous imitations. His first appearance in America. Mons. O'Gust enjoys the distinction of being only French artist who has ever appeared before the Emperor of Germany. Many have tried to equal his Trombone Solo-imitation, but pale into insignificance beside this great artist.

5—THE FIVE JORDANS—5
Misses Mamie, Rosey, Nelly, Messrs. Lewis and August. Performing the most graceful and daring aerial acts ever witnessed.
Mr. Ziegfeld requests the indulgence of the audience for the short delay necessary in placing the net, which entirely precludes the possibility of any accident befalling the performers.

INTERMISSION FIVE MINUTES.

THE GREAT AMANN
Europe's greatest impersonator, introducing life-like reproductions of world-famous men, including America's greatest statesmen. The management desires to call attention to the remarkable work of this truly great artist. Having devoted a life-time to the study of character impersonations, he is able to produce life-like representations of the world's most famous men. The inspired look of the poet, the thoughtful mien of the statesman and the determined countenance of the vivo long warrior, are given with such stating fidelity that it is difficult to realize it is all the face of one man. Special attention is called to Amann's impersonation of Svengali, without the aid of any artifice except wig and beard. Mr. Amann makes up for this character in less than half a minute, the time required by Mr. Leon Lackaye being two hours, and his portrayal of this character has astonished all artists.

BILLY VAN
Comedian.

Curtain will drop one minute to allow for setting the stage for Sandow.

Performance concluding with

!! SANDOW !!
THE MONARCH OF MUSCLE.

Mr. Ziegfeld offers $10,000 to any athlete duplicating Sandow's Performance. Mr. Sandow will select his programme from the following superhuman feats:

Physically perfect. Acknowledged by anatomists to be the strongest man in the world. History does not record among the great gladiators of ancient Rome a man with such muscular development as Sandow.

His 400 wonderfully developed muscles are exhibited in the following manner:
Muscular repose (all the muscles relaxed.)
Muscular tension (all muscles firm as steel.)
Abdominal muscles when tense, producing the wonderful checker-board arrangement of fibers, existence of which modern anatomists deny, being plainly visible at a distance of 300 feet.
The Biceps (muscles of the upper arm), the Triceps (muscles of the back of arm), the Deltoid (muscles of the shoulders), the Trapezius (muscles which raise the shoulders.)
The muscles of the back showing plainly all three layers.
The action and uses of the different muscles.
The chest expansion; Sandow's chest measurement is 47 inches, expanded it is 61 inches, an expansion of 14 inches. The greatest expansion known at the Olympian Games in Rome was 6 inches.
Sandow will exhibit his extraordinary command over his entire muscular system by making his muscles dance.

NEW.   NEW.   NEW.

The world's greatest acrobats have found it almost impossible to turn somersaults landing on the same spot they spring from, and only a few have accomplished it, and to perform this feat with weights has never been attempted. Mr. Sandow stands alone in accomplishing this feat with 56 pounds in each hand.
The audience will hardly realize what the announcement that Mr. Sandow will turn a complete somersault from the knees means, and it is only his enormous and unequalled strength that enables him to perform this feat with 56 pounds in each hand.

Lifting with one Finger 750 Pounds Dead Weight from the Ground.
The Muscle Dance still further demonstrates the absolute control Mr. Sandow has of his muscular system, and the enormous strength in his individual muscles. He will compel his Biceps to drop 90 pounds attached to each Bicep.
Resisting the dropping of 90 pounds attached to chain from each thumb, arms extended, weight doubling at the drop of each foot.

Holding Out at Arm's Length, Mounted Bicyclist in each Hand.
Resting only on neck and heels and holding four men on body. Those who do not appreciate how difficult this feat is, can easily convince themselves by attempting it without any weight resting on the body.

Mr. Sandow's performance concluding with his new feat entitled,

TOMB OF HERCULES.

SANDOW bearing upon his body a weight of 3200 pounds, composed of all the paraphernalia used in his performance with his attendants thereon.

"To Mr. Henry E. Abbey, of New York, and Mr. F. Ziegfeld, Jr., of Chicago, great credit is due for providing the American public with such entertaining and valuable stimulant to encourage physical development as Sandow's performance produces."—Inter-Ocean, Chicago, October 8th.

EXECUTIVE STAFF FOR MR. F. ZIEGFELD, Jr.

E. D. Stults...............................Representative
G. Salde ina............................Musical Director
August Fewel..........................Stage Director
Ed. Maxwell...........................Stage Manager
Frank Wickward......................Master of Properties
Harry Jordan..........................Machinist
Martin Hajack.........................Master of Properties for Sandow

Program from the December 23, 1895, performance at the Grand Opera House in Rochester, New York. Although the year 1896 is written in, the 23rd was on a Monday in 1895, not 1896. By early 1896, Sandow's tour had ended. Sandow and the Trocadero Vaudevilles performed in at least nine theatres around the country that were named the "Grand Opera House."

week's receipts were $32,000. Ziegfeld's advertisement on August 6, 1893, said that the Trocadero was "packed to the doors." Several newspaper features on Sandow followed over the next three months. The *Chicago Tribune* reported that "under Manager F. Ziegfeld, Jr. the Trocadero has accomplished in a comparatively short space of time what it has taken New York...many years to achieve—namely: the securing of a high class of patronage for a refined vaudeville and music hall amusement enterprise."

Ziegfeld's choice for a headliner and his promotion of this act reveal an ability to gauge public taste. Who else would think of enticing society ladies backstage to feel a strongman's muscles? The key to understanding Flo's accomplishment is to imagine how much conviction it must have taken for a scion of a prominent educator to overcome class restraints. Flo, Jr., took up vaudeville when it was considered risqué and was patronized only by people whom the Chicago society of that era would have scorned.

As the Fair closed, Ziegfeld's plans were uncertain. He was trying to make the Trocadero a permanent establishment, adding John Philip Sousa's band to the bill and attempting to persuade Sandow, who was still under Abbey's management, to extend his engagement. But the strongman suddenly returned to Europe on family business. Ziegfeld's setbacks continued, as he lost his lease on the Battery D building.

Meanwhile, Florenz, Sr., having apparently focused most of his energy on the Fair, had been seriously neglecting the Chicago Musical College. While the college had a profitable year, Dr. Ziegfeld made only $3,500, compared with $10,000 the previous year. Florenz, Jr., who was more interested in managing the Trocadero, had ceded most of his responsibilities at the college to his brother Carl.

In late 1893, the American economy slumped. Chicago was especially hard hit because jobs from the Fair disappeared. Perhaps as a result of the depression, something also went terribly wrong at the college. The ledger appears to have been done hastily, but figures indicate that tuition income was down drastically.

In November 1893, despite his youth and relative inexperience, Ziegfeld somehow persuaded Sandow to terminate his contract with Abbey and sign with him. The time was right for Florenz, Jr., to test himself in New York and on the road. When Ziegfeld resigned from the Chicago Musical College, his differences with his father became exacerbated. Surely from Dr. Ziegfeld's perspective, this phase was apostasy, despite the enormous financial success. But no matter how great the tension between father and son, there was never a complete break; Ziegfeld received both his parents' deep support as he left Chicago.

With Flo, Jr., gone from the college, his father turned to Carl and William. Carl took over as secretary-treasurer and business manager, and William became assistant manager in 1894. Carl earned substantially less money than Flo had, and neither brother progressed as quickly as Flo at the college. About

Left, above: Ziegfeld (standing, second from right) at Eugene Sandow's wedding, c. 1893. Left, below: Flo Ziegfeld and Anna Held in New York Harbor on Held's arrival in the United States (1896)

this time, Dr. Ziegfeld received international recognition of his accomplishments in music education. In September 1894, he was awarded a gold medal and diploma from the Italian Royal Academy of Letters and Art. Over the next few years, his sterling reputation also allowed the college to recover its financial health, affording Dr. Ziegfeld nearly $10,000 a year in salary and about $9,000 in business profit.

Ziegfeld took Sandow to Koster & Bial's in New York for approximately three months following the World's Fair. Koster & Bial's was one of New York's vibrant night spots—famous or infamous, depending on the viewer's perspective—with a "sporting" crowd that enjoyed popular entertainment.

The New York run must have been successful because Sandow next appeared in San Francisco, where he played between March and May, at the Orpheum, the Vienna Prater, the Midwinter Fair, and Stockwell's. During this run, Colonel Daniel Boone was promoting a fight between a lion and a bear. Seats were selling for $50 each until police interfered, and even the prospect of the event prompted editorials denouncing the contest. The stage was set for the next major move in Ziegfeld's career.

Ziegfeld seized the opportunity and challenged the owner of the lion to a contest between the animal and Sandow. The *San Francisco Chronicle,* with assistance from budding publicist F. Ziegfeld, Jr., provided superb advance billing, noting that Ziegfeld had given Boone his word that Sandow would not hurt the lion.

The buildup succeeded; later accounts suggested that forty thousand people attended. A contemporary account in the *Chronicle* cites a more modest number—three thousand. The actual contest proved disappointing. Nevertheless, it was billed as the "event of the century," and according to the *Chronicle,* "in some respects it was. Nothing like it has been witnessed in this or any other century." The *Chronicle's* account records the event:

> The German athlete won the match. He couldn't help it, because the . . . monarch of the African jungles buried his head in the sawdust of the arena and imagined himself hid while Sandow wrestled. Commodore [the lion] . . . refused to go on . . . even when Sandow pulled his whiskers. . . .
>
> Before the . . . struggle . . . had progressed two minutes some of the spectators yelled "fake." This was really unkind, to say the least, for the thrill of horror and anticipation which convulsed one every time the lion roared in his cage outside the tent more than made up for the lack of wrestling ability displayed by the brute.

Ziegfeld and Sandow may, indeed, have fixed the contest. Hostile viewers and historians remarked that Commodore was hampered by the six-ounce mittens over his paws (to make it purely a contest of strength) and possibly a stiff dose of chloroform. Sandow, Ziegfeld, and Colonel Boone vigorously denied having slipped Commodore a Mickey Finn, however. Sixteen years later, Sandow offered an explanation of the difficulty. In his 1910 account, the strongman contended that the lion was "a particularly fierce animal, and only a week before he had enjoyed a dish that was not on the menu—his keeper." Not interested in repeating the keeper's mistake, Sandow claimed, he decided to rehearse with Commodore. The five-hundred-pound beast was up for a real contest on rehearsal day, for as soon as Sandow came into the cage, Commodore attacked him. Sandow says: "I gripped his head, then caught him firmly by the neck and in one motion shot him clean over my head. . . . He lay where he fell, dazed." Despite the suspicious details, the contest seems to have had little negative effect on either man's career.

After San Francisco, Ziegfeld and Sandow went on an extended road tour, during which Ziegfeld began to indulge his weakness for gambling. Sandow's autobiography describes two gambling episodes. In the first, Sandow and his cohorts were left penniless; each man lost hundreds of dollars.

> During the next part of the journey we heard that there was another gambling house . . . [connected] with that at which we had just lost our money, and no doubt the manager would be informed . . . of the easy manner in which we had been duped. . . . At the beginning . . . each of us had a few hundred dollars to the good. Then of a sudden our luck began to turn. . . . There was six or seven minutes to spare before the train started, and the manager and his friends said "You have lots of time, gentlemen." . . . Much to their astonishment, however, we insisted on leaving. . . . On this occasion we had turned the tables successfully.

At this point, Ziegfeld's gambling was controlled enough that he escaped while he was still ahead.

During 1894, Florenz, Jr., allowed Sandow to pose for a kinetoscope at Thomas Edison's New Jersey studio. One of Edison's first films, it consisted of a single-camera shot of Sandow flexing his muscles and doing a backflip. Given his later public statements decrying the film industry's influence, it is ironic that Ziegfeld was one of the first theatrical producers to become involved with the film medium.

After relaxing over the summer, Ziegfeld and the Trocadero Vaudevilles, with Sandow as the star, resumed the road circuit from October 1, 1894, to May 18, 1895. The troupe had grown sufficiently that Ziegfeld had a staff of ten, including treasurer, musical director, stage director, and electrician. They hit thirty-two cities in seven and a half months, including the major vaudeville stops—Philadelphia, Washington, Baltimore, Pittsburgh, St. Louis, Kansas City, Chicago, Cleveland, Detroit, New York City, and Boston. The longest engagements were a week, with lots of one-, two-, or three-day stands. During the 1894–95 season, Sandow became a nationally known figure. The *Cleveland Plain Dealer* said: "Sandow is par excellence the athlete of the century and is undoubtedly the most famous man in this respect that the world has ever known. Probably no man of our times has been so much talked and written about."

The 1895–96 season began on September 23, 1895. The only significant variation in the itinerary was that there were stops in several Canadian cities. Sandow remained as the headliner, but Ziegfeld reorganized the Trocadero troupe to include acts such as "O'Gust, a French clown and mimic; . . . the five Jordans, trapeze performers; and Miss Josephine Subel, vocalist." Clearly, Ziegfeld was learning a largely visual circus style that required rapid-fire pacing and large casts. At the time, the connection between the circus and vaudeville was intimate, with much cross-fertilization of form and content.

For Ziegfeld, the tour was extremely successful in both financial and professional terms. Before he was thirty years old, he had made nearly $250,000 (about $5 million today). But he lost most of it to gambling, beginning a lifelong pattern of tumultuous swings between wealth and insolvency.

Initially the best of friends, Ziegfeld and Sandow later drifted apart, Ziegfeld often ending up alone while his star socialized with others. It is not clear why the two ended their partnership, but Sandow last performed for Ziegfeld on February 29, nearly three months before the normal conclusion of the season.

Despite the spectacular start, Ziegfeld was adrift in early 1896. He landed in New York, where he frequented establishments such as Rector's, Tony Pastor's, and Koster & Bial's. Rector's, which became one of Ziegfeld's favorite lobster palaces, had an "air of naughtiness," offering what historian Lewis Erenberg called "escape from the stifling formality of the exclusive circles." Outstanding food, plenty of liquor and young women, and an opportunity to gamble attracted a broad cross section, including men of society. Well-to-do businessmen, who lived with their wives on Fifth Avenue, also visited private rooms at Rector's, some of which featured gambling parties, while others were places to meet their mistresses.

Presumably, it was in one of these New York night spots, about 1896, that Ziegfeld met the first in a long line of wealthy backers. James Brady, better known as "Diamond Jim," made his money in the railroad equipment business. This very hefty man, who weighed approximately three hundred pounds, was inarticulate and none too handsome. He developed a well-deserved reputation as a big spender with an enormous appetite for food and women. The close tie between wealthy "characters" such as Brady and celebrated theater people was to become a crucial element in Ziegfeld's theatrical enterprises.

Even more serendipitous was Ziegfeld's meeting Charles Evans at Rector's. Evans had staged *A Parlor Match*, a well-written comedy with good lines and a compelling plot, in Chicago during the World's Fair. The show had made Evans and co-author William Hoey very wealthy during a run that lasted an astounding 2,550 performances. As testimony to his powers of persuasion, Ziegfeld convinced Evans to revive *A Parlor Match*, even though both authors had grown weary of the show. In preparation for the revival, Ziegfeld and Evans traveled to Europe in 1896, seeking a woman to play the part of Lucille. While they were in England, Teddy Marks, a man of the theater, suggested that they go see a young performer named Anna Held who was appearing at the Palace in London.

Anna Held was born on March 18, 1873. She was the last of ten or twelve children (reports vary) and the only one to survive infancy. Held's father died about 1881, and her pampered childhood ended. She began singing in the streets of Paris, but soon she and her mother went to London, where when she was sixteen, she performed at the Princess Theatre. Her mentor was Jacob Adler, director of a Yiddish theater company. Held toured Europe with Adler for five years. Later, Held appeared at the Théâtre des Variétés in Paris, where she had a leading role in *La Poupée*. She also performed in Germany and Russia.

In the spring of 1894, Anna Held married Maximo Carrera, a wealthy Spaniard whose family had emigrated to Uruguay. Like Ziegfeld, Carrera was a gambler. When his relatives discovered that Maximo had married Held and that a child was on the way, the family elders radically reduced his allowance. Gambling soon bankrupted him, and later that year when their daughter, Liane, was born, he was unable to support his wife and child. Anna was thus all too susceptible to Ziegfeld's lure.

Flo was infatuated with Anna. Despite having no cash, he offered her $1,500 a week to appear in *A Parlor Match*. When she finally agreed, she mentioned one minor obstacle: she had a contract to perform in the *Folies Bergère* that coming winter. When the owner of the *Folies Bergère* found out about her "treason," he insisted on receiving a $1,500 penalty fee to break her contract. Ziegfeld rose to the challenge by locating a backer, Jim Brady, who wired him the money to sign Held.

Perhaps the best insight into why Ziegfeld was able to woo Held comes from a description of his hold over women: "Ziegfeld could find little things to do for a woman that would never occur to any other man. . . . He understood better than anyone what it is that pleases women most." Within two years, Anna had left Maximo and had "deposited" Liane in a French convent.

Ziegfeld was now prepared for his second attempt to create a star, this time Anna Held, and to make his debut as a Broadway producer.

Left: Anna Held replaced a life-sized puppet in *La Poupée* (1897). Right: Anna Held and Flo Ziegfeld in the auto that Held used in *Papa's Wife* (1899)

Below: Lillian Russell was a close friend of Ziegfeld and Anna Held. Bottom: Sam Kingston and Flo Ziegfeld in the late 1890s. Kingston had worked for a Chicago newspaper before becoming a business manager. He worked for Ziegfeld on and off from the mid-1890s until he died in 1929.

CHAPTER 3

❖

BROADWAY BEGINNINGS

❖

When Ziegfeld made his Broadway debut with *A Parlor Match* (September 21, 1896), he had a number of things going for him. First, he was reviving a solid hit. Second, his two leads, Charles Evans and William Hoey, had appeared in the original run. It is also noteworthy that Sam Kingston, whom Ziegfeld had known from his days in Chicago, was business manager for *A Parlor Match*. As he gathered employees for his organization, Ziegfeld often turned to people he trusted, and he prized loyalty. This led to continuity among his staff, which, in turn, contributed to the quality of his shows.

Over the years, some reviewers criticized Ziegfeld for not having displayed much distinction in originating outstanding songs. Whatever his deficiencies in finding new tunes for his own shows, he had a talent for recognizing popular numbers that he could reuse. In *A Parlor Match* he interpolated a song that is still sometimes sung today—"Daisy Bell," better known as "A Bicycle Built for Two."

Anna Held was twenty-three years old when she appeared in *A Parlor Match*. Ziegfeld had enough experience to know that she was not yet ready for a lead role, so he had her sing her trademark song, "Won't You Come and Play with Me?" After one verse and chorus, the audience did not know how to react. The applause was so light that Hoey came onstage and sat down. Ziegfeld's friends clapped desperately, and Held tried one more verse, turning to Hoey at "Won't you come . . . ." According to *Dance Magazine*, he picked up on the cue and "called out 'In a minute' jumping out of the chair with a funny motion. After Held finished, there was a gasp, the audience laughed, and sustained applause broke out." Although Held's voice was not strong, she had a captivating stage presence.

During the run of *A Parlor Match*, Ziegfeld devised the first of his legendary publicity stunts by duping the press into believing that Held was taking milk baths. The newspapers reported that on October 9, 1896, a milkman named Wallace filed suit against Held for not paying a $64 tab on forty gallons of milk. Ziegfeld,

the story said, refused to pay because the milk was sour. Reporters jumped on the item when they heard Held's reasons for wanting the milk, which they recounted by transcribing her heavy French accent: "Ett eez for to take zee beauty bath." Before long, beauty-conscious women across the country were bathing in milk. Only later did the press learn that Ziegfeld had taken it for a ride.

Meanwhile, Ziegfeld had fallen in love with his petite, full-figured star, establishing a pattern of involvement with his leading ladies that would be repeated often over the next thirty-five years. Flo lavished attention on Anna, spending substantial time with her in private, visiting Coney Island, and frequenting such popular spots as Luchow's Restaurant and Tony Pastor's. Neither Anna nor Flo entered this relationship as a naïf, he being twenty-nine years old and she twenty-three and widely traveled when they met. Anna's European attitudes and charm attracted Flo, and she exposed him to French taste and standards. He, in turn, made her an international star and a household name.

When Held divorced Carrera in 1897, she and Ziegfeld began to live together as a married couple. An unofficial "marriage ceremony" was held in the spring of 1897 at the New Netherlands Hotel. Among the witnesses at their "wedding" were Jim Brady and Lillian Russell.

Beginning in 1897, Flo and Anna traveled in Europe each year, partly because she was extremely homesick. Flo often left Anna for weeks at a time to go on gambling escapades. Eventually he began to exhibit what Billie Burke referred to as that "withdrawn quality" she herself would experience as his second wife. Burke also thought that Held, being "frugal, domestic, and maternal," seemed inhibiting to Flo, who "lived in a dream-world in which petty bank accounts . . . and domestic economy were wretched bores."

For the 1897–98 season, Ziegfeld teamed with Oscar Hammerstein to produce *La Poupée*. When the show opened, reviewers described the music as unremarkable and the dialogue as dull. Although Held's singing and her mispronunciation of English charmed the crowd, the show played only one week.

Ziegfeld discovered very quickly that he did not much care for a partner. He and Hammerstein developed a mutual antipathy and ended up suing each other for damages. Ziegfeld always chafed at the limitations imposed by having to satisfy a fellow producer.

Despite the experience with Hammerstein, Ziegfeld found it necessary again to work with a partner because he lacked the capital to finance his own production. This time it was William A. Brady, who shared the cost of the lease on the Manhattan Theatre with Ziegfeld.

Later in the season (February 21, 1898), Ziegfeld and Brady staged *A Gay Deceiver*. The two men had a traveling troupe that toured the country. New York's Harlem Opera House, where they booked this show, was considered part of the tour. This theater bill had three separate elements: the farce *A Gay*

Above, from left: Anna Held and Flo Ziegfeld (second row) with unidentified friends on a fishing trip around the turn of the century. Anna Held performs a number with the assistance of an attached mannequin, year unknown. The four International Girls and diplomats in a scene from *The Red Feather* (1903)

In a scene from *Mam'selle Napoleon* (1903), Anna Held dresses as the great leader.

Playbill from *Mlle. Fifi* (1899) co-produced by William Brady and Ziegfeld

Deceiver; "The Cat and the Cherub," a one-act play by Chester Bailey Fernald about Chinese life in San Francisco; and songs by Anna Held from her "animated song sheet," a huge sheet of music that was set up behind her. While Held sang, the heads of black singers popped up one at a time from the black notes on the song's score; at each chorus the heads appeared simultaneously and accompanied Held. The animated song sheet was a fairly simple device, but it shows how early Ziegfeld began to experiment with the kind of staging techniques that eventually made his reputation.

While the newspapers did not mention Held's being in *A Gay Deceiver*, one biographical account asserts that Ziegfeld interpolated Held's songs into the last act of the farce. It is quite likely that Ziegfeld made changes to liven the show as it toured. When the troupe reached Chicago, the newspapers there did not mention *A Gay Deceiver*—just Anna Held and "The Cat and the Cherub."

That summer, in June 1898, Flo and Anna returned to Europe, where she performed without salary for one month at the *Folies Bergère*. This was part of the settlement that the nightclub's manager had demanded when Anna broke her contract with him to join Flo.

In the fall of 1898, Ziegfeld again worked with Brady, this time on a production of *The Turtle*. This show had played for two years in Paris, but when it opened in New York, it shocked some members of the audience. In one scene actress Sadie Martinot began to disrobe in her bedroom. After removing her bodice, she took off her skirt and her stays and then moved behind a glass-paneled screen to remove the rest of her clothes. The theater program claimed that neither the theme nor the artistic interpretation was unwholesome, and the *New York Herald* agreed that the scene was not vulgar but artistic; nevertheless, Ziegfeld's detractors dubbed this "the most vicious play of its time."

Above left: Anna Held (center) with the Swiss Guide Chorus in *Higgledy-Piggledy*. Top: Ziegfeld most likely had this business card made in late 1904 when he and Joe Weber were co-producing *Higgledy-Piggledy*. Above: Anna Held and her dog

The Broadway revival of *The French Maid,* produced by Brady and Ziegfeld, opened September 12, just three weeks after *The Turtle.* Ziegfeld took over the show during its last week. Newspaper ads announced that Anna Held would appear for the final eight performances in the lead role. Beginning on September 26, 1898, Held added new songs and wore a new wardrobe costing a reported $30,000. While *The French Maid* did not run long in New York, it gave Held a vehicle to take on the road, where most of the money was to be made.

Ziegfeld's next production, *Mlle. Fifi,* did fairly well. To compensate for a lifeless plot, Ziegfeld spiced this production, as he did *The Turtle,* with some show of flesh, modest by today's standards but sufficient to prompt a few critics to fault it for indecency. Reviewers referred to a "disgusting" and "vulgar" incident in the show in which Mlle. Fifi tries to entice her former lover by lying on a sofa and showing her legs—which were covered by black tights. Despite the critics, the show drew a good crowd.

The latter part of April 1899 was busy as Ziegfeld moved *The Turtle* from Broadway to the Grand Opera House (April 23–29) and *Mlle. Fifi* to the Harlem Opera House on April 24. On that same date, he and Brady opened another Broadway show, *The Manicure,* at the Manhattan Theatre. This farce was inferior to Ziegfeld's previous pair of shows. *The New York Times* said that while the actors tried their best, the show was simply dull. The producers closed it after one performance and brought in a comedy called *By the Sad Sea Waves* (not a Brady-Ziegfeld production) that had been playing at the Fourteenth Street Theatre. *By the Sad Sea Waves* starred a comedy team known as Matthews and Bulger; as an added attraction, Anna Held appeared in a specialty act. This bill played out the week (through April 29).

During the 1899–1900 season, Ziegfeld worked alone and slowed his pace significantly, as he produced only one show, *Papa's Wife,* one of the first shows in which the female chorus was a significant production element. The sixteen chorus girls were beautiful, and they wore gorgeous clothes. Anna Held's gowns and jewels were especially magnificent, and the scenery was elaborate. In one scene, Held exited the stage in an automobile. Her song "I Really Wish I Wasn't but I Am" captivated the audience; however, reviews on her acting were mixed. Because it had a fairly successful New York run, Ziegfeld took the show on the road. His advertisement called attention to the show's success on Broadway—"Organization direct from its capacity run of 200 Nights in New York City." Chicago's reaction to the hometown boy and *Papa's Wife* was not very kind: the *Chicago Tribune* noted that Anna Held's only virtue was "the illusion of her innocence." This tone was typical of the Chicago response to Ziegfeld through the early years.

By 1900, Flo and Anna had established a comfortable pattern. In the fall, they opened a new show for a limited run. Then they took it on the road, passing through Chicago for a family visit. After the run, they went to Paris to locate a show for the next season. Later they toured Europe, where Ziegfeld customarily lost a small fortune at the gaming tables. In September, they were back in New York.

During the summer theater hiatus, Anna visited Liane in France. Despite their divorce, Maximo Carrera always remained loyal to Held, meeting her in Paris when she visited her daughter. His constancy was a comforting antidote to Ziegfeld's distance. In Ziegfeld, Anna found a man who was never quite satisfied with their relationship, so she always had to struggle to keep him interested in her.

The fall of 1901 saw Ziegfeld producing independently, this time a show involving writer Harry B. Smith: a production of *The Little Duchess*. The program referred, interestingly enough, to the F. Ziegfeld, Jr., Musical Comedy Company. Apparently the dream of "empire" was alive this early in Ziegfeld's career.

The Little Duchess was well mounted and had beautiful scenic effects but was skimpy on plot: it was essentially a vaudeville presentation starring Held. Ziegfeld continued flirting with the bounds of propriety when he staged a bathing scene that again prompted talk about vulgarity.

After a four-month run, *The Little Duchess* went on the road. Ziegfeld already had the rudiments of his later success well in hand: he knew that a beautiful chorus attracted male patrons and that European fashion would draw society women. When *The Little Duchess* returned to New York after its tour, the plot was virtually eliminated to accommodate the many musical numbers.

Ziegfeld was gaining a reputation for mounting beautiful shows, but his artistry did not ensure hits. In 1902 he produced no show and in 1903 two shows, *The Red Feather* and *Mam'selle Napoleon,* both with disappointing results. *The Red Feather,* which opened on November 9, 1903, contained over thirty musical numbers and received excellent reviews, both in New York and on the road. One reviewer noted that although Ziegfeld was a relative newcomer to Broadway, he was beginning to make his mark, but the show's New York run was brief and business on the road inconsistent.

Mam'selle Napoleon opened on December 8 at the Knickerbocker Theatre; Ziegfeld's most extravagant production thus far, it cost $175,000. Anna Held sang her famous "Won't You Come and Play with Me?" as her face peered out from a black costume and her arms and legs danced like a doll's. As an excuse to show off colorful costumes, Ziegfeld placed a ball scene in Act Three that had nothing to do with the story. Despite favorable reviews, the show ran only five weeks. Jake Fields, a Wall Street financier, gave Ziegfeld $20,000 on opening night to keep the show afloat, but the project still lost money. The show toured the first half of 1904. Again, *The Chicago Record-Herald* carried a short, cutting review: "Dresses, ditties, dances....No more vulgar sidelight of the present state of our stage could be desired."

Later that year Ziegfeld joined forces with Joseph M. Weber to form the Weber and Ziegfeld Stock

Company, operating out of Weber Music Hall beginning in September. Weber wanted to star Anna Held in his upcoming show, *Higgledy-Piggledy,* and reluctantly teamed with Ziegfeld to obtain her services. On October 20, 1904, Ziegfeld and Weber opened *Higgledy-Piggledy,* Ziegfeld's only show that season. Weber played a wealthy American mustard merchant touring Europe with his rich friend (Harry Morris). Weber's character brought along his daughter (Marie Dressler), while Morris's brought along his friend Mimi (Held). Dressler was an immediate hit singing "A Great Big Girl Like Me." A prominent vaudeville and burlesque singer, Dressler says in her autobiography that after numerous press reports that she was stealing the show, Anna Held decided to leave the cast. One night after the show, Held came to Dressler's dressing room and told Dressler that she was leaving because there was not room for both of them in the same show.

If Ziegfeld felt that Dressler's performance was overshadowing Held's, he had good reason to take his star elsewhere. However, there is evidence that basic problems in the Weber and Ziegfeld partnership caused it to dissolve. Weber was very thrifty, so he and the free-spending Flo clashed almost immediately. According to a report in *Dance Magazine,* "Ziegfeld startled the burlesque-minded Weber with his elaborate plans for girls and gowns and ballets and the association was hastily broken off." By the time *Higgledy-Piggledy* began its tour, after the Broadway run ended March 25, 1905, Weber was the sole producer, and Trixie Friganza had replaced Anna Held. Before the arrangement collapsed, Weber and Ziegfeld had tried to mount another joint production. *The College Widow,* a musical satire, was set to open in January 1905, but Held quit before then because Weber cut her role to twenty lines.

Flo was now in his late thirties, and his prospects seemed bleak. Although he knew how to produce the kind of show that would make him a legend, he had not yet discovered the right combination of vehicle, star, and financial backing that would let him exhibit his talent fully. He and Anna "retired" from the theater during 1905, lived in Europe, and spent a year and a half driving all around the Continent. Ziegfeld went to Monte Carlo, Paris, Nice, Biarritz, and Trouville, where he won and lost fortunes at the gaming tables. He reportedly won 1.5 million francs in January but lost 2.5 million francs in June and was unable to pay it. He gave up titles to property and signed promissory notes. As French law made a wife responsible for her husband's debts, the authorities placed a lien on Held's property. She eluded the problem, though, when a lawyer pointed out that because theirs was a common-law marriage, not recognized in France, she was not, in fact, legally responsible. This did little to assuage her fury about Flo's ongoing habit.

Between 1896 and 1906, Ziegfeld's gambling habit developed into a full-blown obsession, one that seriously affected both his career and his relationship with Held. Meteoric swings between wealth and privation had begun. When Ziegfeld returned to New York in 1905, he was broke.

As he reengaged himself professionally in late 1905, Ziegfeld's character seemed to have changed. While he had staged a dozen shows on Broadway, he had had his occasional disagreements, but he was not litigious. Yet within one year after his return he got involved in legal disputes with Max Hoffmann over the music in *The Parisian Model* and the Shuberts over a business deal that went sour.

The wrangle with the Shuberts was a major event that was to affect Ziegfeld for the remainder of his career. He and Sam Shubert had become involved professionally in March 1905, when they signed a contract for an equal partnership on *La Belle Marseilles*. Ziegfeld was to control cast selection. Production and booking were to be in mutually agreeable venues except where Shubert houses were available. The Shuberts paid Ziegfeld's expenses for a recruiting trip. When Ziegfeld returned from Europe, he booked Anna Held with Marc Klaw and Abe Erlanger, who ran what was known as the Syndicate, a group that controlled bookings for about forty theaters. Since the Shuberts were trying to break the Syndicate's influence, Ziegfeld placed himself in a risky situation: if things had not worked out with Erlanger, the Shuberts would probably have blackballed him on Broadway, thereby running him out of New York.

Ziegfeld's accomplishments between 1907 and 1910 were tied directly to the Syndicate. This organization started casually in 1889, but the principals formalized the relationship by August 1896. That month, Marc Klaw, Abe Erlanger, J. F. Zimmerman, Alf Hayman, S. F. Nixon, and Charles Frohman formed what they called "the Theatre Trust" to combat the chaos in the booking industry. Bookings were handled on street corners and canceled capriciously. Producers seldom knew anyone else's plans, and when they did know, they devoted their energy to undermining the competitor's design. From the outset, Erlanger dominated the Syndicate. By 1906, the group controlled the American theater business: the theaters, the stars, and the successful scripts. Despite the risk Ziegfeld took when he defied the Shuberts, he was now in a strong position. He had two powerful theater groups competing for his star.

Cables between Ziegfeld and the Shuberts dated March through May 1906 indicate a dispute centering on the conditions for giving Ziegfeld $1,000. Ziegfeld claimed that they had given him a $1,000 advance on the following premise: if Ziegfeld and the Shuberts did not sign a contract, the Shuberts would pay Ziegfeld's expenses; if they signed a contract, they would split the expenses. The whole story is somewhat murky, but essentially the Shuberts argued that they already had a contract, and Ziegfeld disagreed. The case dragged on for years and took numerous turns, until 1909 when the Appellate Division Court ruled that Ziegfeld owed Lee Shubert $1,299. Ultimately, neither side won because the dispute initiated a rancorous, bitter competition that persisted for decades.

In the fall, Ziegfeld returned to Broadway with *The Parisian Model.* Anna Held sang "It's Delightful to Be Married" and "I Just Can't Make My Eyes Behave," both interpolations. In what was considered a daring number, Gertrude Hoffmann and sixteen chorus girls lay on a revolving platform. When they kicked their legs in the air, bells tied to their ankles chimed with the orchestra. Hoffmann also did imitations, including one of Anna Held singing the kissing song. She received six encores. Additionally, Hoffmann "produced what was at that time a unique dance number. . . . Clothed as a boy, she danced a Maxie with Anna Held which brought out a clamor of protest because of its alleged suggestiveness."

During tryouts in Chicago, the newspapers noted that the extraordinary costumes from Ziegfeld's earlier shows were commonplace compared with those in *The Parisian Model.* The women wore green and rose velvet as well as sable and ermine. In one number, Anna Held changed her gown eight times, wearing a different dress for each verse of a song. After modeling a gown, Held changed it onstage, with only the chorus girls as a screen. Charles Bigelow, a regular in Ziegfeld's shows, also changed costumes frequently in his comic role. The entire show was extravagant, with each scene seeming to outdo the last, until the finale where all the principals appeared in a brightly lit roller-skating rink.

The naughtiness of *The Parisian Model* prompted censorship in Pittsburgh and a succinct, brutal dismissal from the *Chicago Record-Herald,* which described it as "vulgar rubbish." Still, it ran thirty-three weeks in New York and then toured—Ziegfeld's most successful show thus far. With it, he proved he could create a vehicle that could run the whole season.

As Ziegfeld gained technical experience, he also broadened his range in advertising. He was getting even more innovative in this arena. The Chicago ad for *The Parisian Model* reproduced a photograph of a cross-eyed woman, playing on the notoriety of Anna's hit song "I Just Can't Make My Eyes Behave."

While *The Parisian Model* was on its tryout tour in the fall of 1906, Anna Held's jewelry was stolen—on the night of October 21 or the next morning—from the train between Harrisburg, Pennsylvania, and Cleveland. Initially, the police considered the circumstances suspicious and accused Ziegfeld of staging a publicity stunt, but eventually they decided that the incident had substance, and they launched an investigation. Estimates on the value of items in Anna's "black satchel" varied: the police report said that more than thirty pieces of jewelry, ranging in value from several hundred dollars to $35,000, were missing. Apparently Anna was so devastated by the incident that she had difficulty performing.

One news item focused on Flo and Anna's standards for realism. Held was quoted as saying: "Nossing is too good for my audience. My silks are real . . . my jewels are real. People say, 'How foolish of zis Anna Held to wear real gems when ze paste do quite as well.' Zey do not know me."

Within a few days, on October 31, a report surfaced that police had recovered her jewels from two thieves in Painesville, Ohio, and that a Detective Myers from Toledo took the satchel, saying that he would return it to Miss Held. Unfortunately, there was no such officer in Toledo. The mystery continued when Held, now in Detroit, wrote a dramatic note: "It's a lie. The jewels have not been recovered."

Detroit police had been investigating a jewel theft involving Mrs. Halsey Corwin, who was in the cast of *The Parisian Model*. The police suspected her of staging the Held theft to collect insurance money. Anna had seen Corwin speaking with two men—one big with gray hair and a small man "who looked like a ferret." Corwin and the two men fled. All three were later arrested, but none was ever tried for the theft.

Liane Carrera's version, in her book *Anna Held and Flo Ziegfeld*, claimed that Ziegfeld engineered the theft to obtain money for his next production. Allegedly, he went off for four days to an unnamed location, where he paid the thieves $11,800 for the jewels. Carrera's version is suspect because it is highly unlikely that Ziegfeld could disappear for four days right in the middle of a tour. Also, Carrera's account places the incident about November 5–9, by which point the tour was leaving Detroit. While the Held party was in Detroit, the local papers placed Ziegfeld in town to issue Held's denial that the jewels had been returned.

According to Carrera, the event destroyed her mother's faith in Ziegfeld. That certainly is possible. But Carrera's book is flawed with regard to the facts of this incident. She says, for example, that the reward was $11,800, when newspaper accounts fix it at $16,800, and claims that for the first time in her life Held failed to make her stage appearance due to the distress connected with the theft; in reality, Held appeared onstage within fifteen minutes of the normal curtain time.

Because Ziegfeld's relationship with Held was so stormy and was eventually overshadowed by his second marriage, many writers have underestimated Anna's influence on his career development. In fact, she helped introduce him to European culture, and her abiding love of fashion taught him to appreciate fine gowns, jewelry, and elegant surroundings. Ziegfeld had always had a refined flair for fashion, but Held extended the range of his fashion sense, particularly when it came to understanding what captivates women. Moreover, in those days Anna Held was the public figure—it was she who drew the headlines.

When Ziegfeld closed *The Parisian Model* and began searching for his next production, he had assimilated the best of two seemingly divergent cultures: a refined European sense of style and the American frontier spirit. As 1906 came to a close, Ziegfeld had the right ingredients for a major development in his career: the talent, public-relations experience, knowledge of elegant costume design, and maturity in managing popular entertainment acts. All he lacked was the opportunity in the ideal theatrical form.

Opposite, clockwise from left: A deaf Julian Mitchell giving instructions during rehearsal, c. 1907. Mlle. Genée and the fox hunters in a scene from *The Soul Kiss* (1908). Anna Held and daughter, Liane Carrera. The Hotel Ansonia, where Ziegfeld lived for a decade or more—first with Anna Held and later with Billie Burke. His daughter was also born there.

Above: This 1909 photograph from the *New York Star* shows Ziegfeld's long-time partners, Abe Erlanger (right) and Marc Klaw. Top left: The opening scene in Act Two of the *Follies of 1907*. Top right: The original Anna Held Girls. There were supposed to be as many as fifty Anna Held Girls in the first *Follies*, but fewer than half that many are shown here.

❖

CHAPTER 4

ART TRIUMPHS

❖

Florenz Ziegfeld's dramatic recovery from theatrical oblivion between 1907 and 1910 was made possible by his connection with the Syndicate and its powerful leader, Abe Erlanger. After he and Marc Klaw started their booking agency (with $250 in cash and notes for $4,000), Erlanger transformed the theater business. First, he guaranteed top bookings and developed a circuit that covered whole sections of the country; then he fashioned a monopoly that forced the touring companies to use Syndicate houses if they were to avoid long, costly "hops" in the itinerary. Second, he and Klaw wrote legally binding agreements that withstood court challenges. Theater owners, producers, and actors who wanted to play in the major houses came through the Syndicate for bookings. Erlanger did so well that eventually he started acquiring theaters on his own—by the time that he died, he personally owned or controlled almost fifty.

Marc Klaw was born May 29, 1858. As quiet as Erlanger was outspoken, he was a lawyer and became interested in the theater from his legal work for Daniel and Charles Frohman, prominent Broadway producers. By 1888, he had moved to New York and begun working with Erlanger. Klaw and Erlanger earned their share of enemies due to their stranglehold on the booking world and for their efforts to stymie Actors Equity at its inception and then to break the union. Nevertheless, by 1907, they were *the* dominant force on Broadway, and the Syndicate controlled the bookings in seven hundred theaters across the country.

Nothing is known about Ziegfeld's first meeting with Erlanger. However, by May 27, 1907, Ziegfeld was producing vaudeville acts for Erlanger and Klaw at the New York Theatre Roof's Jardin de Paris. The program included W. C. Fields (an "eccentric juggler") and Charlie Chaplin as the "inarticulate drunk."

In the move that launched his legendary rise on Broadway, Ziegfeld produced the *Follies of 1907*, beginning July 8, 1907, at the Jardin de Paris. Erlanger, Frank McKee, and Jerry Siegel each had a one-third interest in the show. Ziegfeld was still a salaried employee, earning $200 a week.

The New York Theatre Roof, where the *Follies* debuted, was an oblong area made of corrugated iron

with a cement floor covered by a green rug. The sides were open for ventilation or curtained when the weather was inclement. The audience sat on folding chairs, and behind them was a promenade on which the band of drummer girls (first-act finale) paraded. Refreshments were sold in a corner.

Ziegfeld noted that

> when Mr. Erlanger told me that a show was needed for this roof garden which he had on his hands I had just come back, broke, from a residence . . . in Paris. There I had seen many *revues,* and since New York had never had a real *revue* I thought to avoid competition by entering this field. . . . The stage of the New York Roof being so shallow and so placed that you could not see the side of the stage upon which you were sitting, no elaborate scenery could possibly be used. . . . Because of this cramped condition in the early shows, we spilled our attraction a good deal over the theater. This was something of an innovation then and was much commented upon.

Actually, Anna Held suggested the revue-style format (so popular in France) for the *Follies.* Harry B. Smith, author of this year's *Follies,* came up with the show's name, which was inspired by the title of his newspaper column, "Follies of the Day." Ziegfeld liked the title because it had thirteen characters, and he considered thirteen his lucky number in those days.

A careless tone surrounded the effort. This was a summer "filler" between the end of the 1906–7 season and the beginning of the 1907–8 season. The 1907 script opened with a character list that read "in the disorder of their appearance." The whimsical tone also appears in a stage description for one scene: "Small building with a sign 'Palace Hotel—Rooms $100.00 a day. Beds extra.'" Humor in this edition was "direct and boisterous." The principals included Harry Watson, Jr., and his partner, George Bickel; Grace LaRue; Mlle. Dazie; Grace Leigh; Dave Lewis; and May Leslie. Originally, Ziegfeld brought over six French dancing girls for the 1907 show, but he sent them back. He also booked the Lilliputians, a midget act, but he did not like them either, so he reduced their act until their six-week contract ended.

In this era before air-conditioning, shows virtually never ran over the summer. Usually theaters closed between June 1 and Labor Day, although occasionally a production would continue after a summer break. The *Follies* was the first Broadway show to play the entire summer. While it did not receive much critical attention, the public liked it immediately. Patrons were attracted by a chorus called the Anna Held Girls. Most of the women had appeared in *The Parisian Model* with Held.

The plot of the *Follies* centered on a reincarnated Captain John Smith and Pocahontas visiting New York. There was just enough story to hold the acts together. In fact, a news article said Ziegfeld threatened

Clockwise from top: To promote *Miss Innocence,* Anna Held (first on left) appeared in a Seattle Press Club auto. Jack Norworth and Nora Bayes sang "I'm Glad I'm a Boy and I'm Glad I'm a Girl" in 1909—before they left the *Follies* and were sued by Ziegfeld. Fannie Brice with second husband, Nicky Arnstein, to whom she was married from 1918 to 1927. Brice was in seven editions of the *Follies,* between 1910 and 1923, while Ziegfeld was alive; after his death she was in two *Ziegfeld Follies* produced by the Shuberts. Lillian Lorraine, a principal in four editions of the *Follies,* became one of that revue's first stars.

Left to right: Ziegfeld and Lillian Lorraine, with whom he had a long-term relationship. Sophie Tucker did not last the entire run with the 1909 *Follies*, but she was a hit while she appeared. Anna Held wearing her coat of 110 Russian sable skins; with her is her dog "Chubby."

Harry B. Smith with a suit for damages if "by some mistake a plot was unearthed." The show's comedy and satire were aimed at well-known persons and current events, with a heavy dose of puns. During its run, Ziegfeld advertised weekly changes, adding and dropping entertainers and numbers at will.

Although Ziegfeld implied that he introduced the revue to New York, the form had been on Broadway for several years. Ziegfeld drew attention to the revue form and significantly enhanced its popularity. The *Follies* became New York's most popular revue because Ziegfeld featured more talented and well-known stars and better music. And, with Julian Mitchell's help, he introduced the chorus of beautiful women for which revues became famous in the 1920s.

At the end of the summer, Ziegfeld wanted the show to continue indoors, and Erlanger finally agreed to move it to the street-level Liberty Theatre; unfortunately, the production was identified as summer entertainment, and receipts immediately plummeted. Ziegfeld then booked the show for one week each in Washington, D.C., where it took in $22,000, and Baltimore ($18,000) before proceeding to Chicago. In general the *Follies* tour was successful, but Ziegfeld did not fare as well as he might have hoped with critics from his hometown. The *Chicago Tribune* said: "It is just raw, common, and noisy."

To round out the 1907–8 season, Ziegfeld produced *The Soul Kiss* in January, a Harry B. Smith show that filled the gap until the 1908 edition of the *Follies* began in June. He brought the dancer Adeline Genée from England to star in this show. *The New York Times* described Genée's movements as a "ball of thistledown dancing in a breeze" and her dancing as like the "flight of a bird." To publicize the production, Ziegfeld announced that he had insured Genée's feet for $100,000, "or ten thousand dollars a toe."

Ziegfeld was also solidifying his reputation for extravagance because of his lavish costumes and sets. The final scene, set in an autumn wood and dale, opened with a pack of hounds rushing across the stage. Then a bugle call heralded the appearance of women in white hunting outfits. Finally, Mlle. Genée came onstage in a riding skirt and patent leather hat and boots.

Ziegfeld's skill was now fully evident. The precedent lay, it appears, in his father's accomplishments as a "talent scout" at the Chicago Musical College, where the elder Ziegfeld recruited internationally famous musicians such as Rudolph Ganz, Felix Borowski, and Leopold Auer.

Toward the end of *The Soul Kiss* run, Maximo Carrera died, on April 23, 1908, prompting Anna to bring Liane, then thirteen, to New York. Liane left the impression that while Maximo was alive, Ziegfeld had tried to bring her together with her mother permanently. With Maximo gone, Ziegfeld could have adopted her. He did not. Instead, Held took Liane back to Paris. Letters addressed to Liane at the Hotel Ansonia some years later suggest that she visited Held and Ziegfeld in their New York apartment, but the child received her education at convent schools in France and England.

Held had been concealing Liane's existence from the press. She was thirty-five years old in 1908, in an era when a woman over thirty would have had difficulties sustaining herself as a chanteuse. To acknowledge that she was the mother of a teenager would have destroyed the public image she had worked so hard to develop.

Ziegfeld opened the *Follies of 1908* on June 15, just three weeks after *The Soul Kiss* closed its Broadway run. Satire on current events (for example, the Chicago convention and a prizefight), a major theme of the 1907 edition, continued in this revue. Like many reviews of later *Follies*, the *Times* noted that, even with several funny scenes, the comedy was inferior to the show's musical and visual elements. The costumes were elaborate, and the ensemble dancing was more beautiful and novel than that of the typical Broadway show. Nora Bayes and Jack Norworth were main attractions; other principal performers were Lucy Weston, Billie Reeves, Arthur Deagon, William Schrode, Seymour Brown, and Mae Murray. Bickel and Watson, Grace LaRue, William Powers, and Mlle. Dazie returned from the previous year's show.

When the *Follies of 1908* reached Chicago late in the year, noted theater critic Burns Mantle gave the show a positive review, although he warned against its burlesque "of the better class, and the female form adorned with as scant covering as the law allows."

Ziegfeld's talent for generating publicity, particularly about his spending habits, continued unabated. A *New York Telegraph* news article reported Ziegfeld was depressed because he had inadvertently given an actor a $1,000 bill that he had been carrying in his trouser pocket. Ziegfeld thought that he was giving away a $1 bill. When asked how Ziegfeld knew that it was not a $1 million bill, he replied: "Because I always carry those in an inside pocket."

A story of Anna's complicated private life with Flo was published in what purported to be Held's memoirs: *Anna Held and Flo Ziegfeld*. This version claims that when Anna became pregnant, threatening the fate of *Miss Innocence* in 1908, Ziegfeld and a seedy doctor overpowered Held and aborted the male fetus she was carrying. The difficulty is that the Held "memoir" is fundamentally a hoax: it is actually Carrera's account of her mother's story. A thorough search of Carrera's estate turned up no evidence of any memoir in Anna Held's hand. What did surface were numerous manuscript versions of the book, in Liane's hand and typed versions, in both French and English. This woman, who discarded nothing, nevertheless had no original memoir by Held. Furthermore, Carrera had cut and pasted the manuscript (through numerous editions) and published the book in both first- and third-person versions—not the usual practice in editing authentic memoirs.

The situation is further complicated by evidence from Carrera's longtime friend, personal physician, and estate executor, Dr. Alexander Hegedus, who has said that Liane did not have an objective perspective on Ziegfeld. Despite virulent animosity toward Ziegfeld in her account of Anna's relationship with him, when Carrera died in 1988, nearly sixty years after Ziegfeld's passing, she had only two photographs on her living-room wall—one of a former lover and one of Flo Ziegfeld.

Asked specifically about the forced abortion, Dr. Hegedus mentioned that Carrera said she herself at one time became pregnant and subsequently aborted a male fetus. Hegedus wondered if Carrera were projecting that event backward onto her stepfather and her mother in the "memoirs."

There is no question that Ziegfeld was a tough producer who stood to lose lots of money if Held were pregnant. However, Carrera's claim of overt physical cruelty to a woman simply does not fit Ziegfeld's reputation for being soft-spoken and gallant with women. While there are numerous accounts of him shouting at men and riding them in public for professional failings, every single woman interviewed for this biography insisted that he was always extremely gentle when he delivered criticism. The abortion incident could have occurred, but external evidence makes Carrera's claim highly suspect.

Whatever the circumstances of Held's health, Ziegfeld produced *Miss Innocence* for her in 1908. Ziegfeld generated immense advance publicity for Anna and the production. A huge electric sign—eighty by forty-five feet—on the theater carried Held's name and got a lot of attention from the press.

Ziegfeld's personal relationship with Anna Held was crumbling rapidly, a situation that was further complicated by his introduction of Lillian Lorraine into the cast of *Miss Innocence*. Ziegfeld had discovered

In 1910 Bert Williams made his first *Follies* appearance; he was in seven other editions. Williams was the only black to appear in the *Follies* until 1931, when the team of Buck and Bubbles performed.

Lorraine the previous year at a performance of *The Tourists* at the Majestic Theatre. He later recalled: "A dark haired chorus girl seemed to me to have that elusive thing we call personality. She was only a minor member of the chorus, a slender slip of a girl, but she had traces of a peculiar beauty. I found out her name [and] sent for her. . . . That girl was Lillian Lorraine."

Thus began Ziegfeld's long-lasting, tortured relationship with Lorraine. Something about her touched Ziegfeld deeply, and she haunted him for the rest of his life. Her vulnerability evoked his protective instinct. The press billed her as "the most beautiful woman in the world." In private, another perspective emerged: Flo later told his daughter that she was "also the dumbest," more than likely a reference to her self-destructive behavior rather than to her intelligence.

Ziegfeld's infatuation with Lorraine naturally created serious problems with Held. When the show closed in May 1909, Anna returned to Paris by herself.

During 1909, Ziegfeld became bogged down in several legal hassles, among them a suit brought by the Biarritz gambling house. Ziegfeld countersued, saying that the French casino had no jurisdiction to collect from him in the United States. Ziegfeld admitted signing a note for his debt but testified that he had paid $200,000 the day he signed the bill of exchange. The Biarritz management claimed he owed $20,000 more. Anna Held testified that Ziegfeld seriously entangled her finances with his gambling debts.

Ziegfeld often became obsessed with a dream or would get involved in his gambling and would let nothing, particularly not pesky concerns about money, stand in his way. He would ignore the claim until someone became sufficiently exasperated to sue him. If that failed, his lawyers would dispute the debt by introducing technicalities. In the process Ziegfeld wore down many of his creditors, who simply gave up. When the creditor was persistent, Ziegfeld often lost the case in court and was forced to pay.

The *Follies* had been sufficiently successful that Ziegfeld, Klaw, and Erlanger continued the series in the summer of 1909. The roof was now enclosed by windows and had ceiling fans to circulate the air. Lillian Lorraine had replaced Anna Held as Ziegfeld's theatrical passion and made her *Follies* debut. Nora Bayes, accompanied by Jack Norworth, was the big star. Billie Reeves, William Bonelli, Arthur Deagon, Harry Pilcer, Sophie Tucker, Mae Murray, and Rosie Green were also on hand.

The script for the *Follies of 1909* reveals several ingredients of Ziegfeld's success. The cast of characters features prominent business and social figures including Theodore Roosevelt, Averell Harriman, Andrew Carnegie, and John D. Rockefeller. Ziegfeld understood early in his career that invoking the names of people who were in the audience or who were likely to be there is very appealing, not only to the individuals named but also to the audience. In this case, Roosevelt actually was in the opening night audience.

Ironically, the appeal in Ziegfeld's productions derived, even at the very beginning, from his ability to meld the best of both high and low cultures. He rejected serious content and classic dramatic works in favor of popular forms, but he presented even the lowly revue with all of the class that patrons associate with legitimate theater. He used wonderful music, the best performers available, and realistic sets, even when that meant spending astounding sums of money. His costumes, backdrops, even the artwork for some of his public-relations materials were rendered by designers who were eventually recognized as world-class artists.

Ziegfeld hired Eva Tanguay in July 1909, to replace Nora Bayes, who had been added to the show, for one week. When the week was up, Bayes and her husband, Jack Norworth, got into a dispute with Ziegfeld over working conditions and refused to return to the cast. Ziegfeld sought an injunction preventing them from appearing under other management until their contract expired. He claimed that the Norworths tried to run the rehearsal and that Bayes refused to sing her assigned songs and vowed to fight in court to "find out if they have a right to dictate what they shall do in my employ." In April 1910, before the New York Supreme Court, Bayes argued that Ziegfeld wanted her to wear flesh-colored tights and sit on an elephant and that she refused to do so. Ziegfeld contended that Bayes refused to sing certain verses of her songs. Bayes retorted that she left Ziegfeld's employ because the noise of the roof garden's electric fans disturbed her singing and the continual activity of the waiters serving drinks made her nervous.

In late January 1911, the court ruled in Ziegfeld's favor; he got $128, the cost of advertising Bayes and Norworth, and a restraining order preventing them from acting or singing until their contract expired on February 25, 1911. Consequently, the Norworths had to leave vaudeville, where they were earning $2,500 a week, and learned the hard way how much control producers had at that time.

This dispute provides insight into the circumstances that usually prompted Ziegfeld to take someone to court. He seldom sued over money; usually the issue was artistic control over the production. Ziegfeld seemed willing to brook differences of opinion from respected colleagues, so long as they were presented before or during rehearsals. Anyone who seriously believed, though, that this producer would tolerate defiance of his authority once his show opened was in for a rude shock.

Ziegfeld's personal relationships were no less tumultuous. Shortly after the Hotel Ansonia was built on the Upper West Side of Manhattan, he and Held took a thirteen-room apartment (about 1908 or 1909) in that luxurious residential hotel, which eventually became one of New York's most famous apartment buildings, fabled for its illustrious residents. In the fall of 1909, Held discovered upon her return from Europe that Ziegfeld had established Lillian Lorraine in the Hotel Ansonia, on another floor, in an exact replica of their apartment. Ziegfeld never said publicly why he did something so risky and hurtful. It certainly fit a larger pattern in his life: asked why he gambled so recklessly, he once explained that he needed the thrill of the danger and went on to draw a connection between gambling and the hazard of mounting a show on Broadway, which he said was just as chancy as rolling the dice.

By September 1909, the *Follies* started its road tour. According to *Dance Magazine,* Ziegfeld then put Adeline Genée, star of his *Soul Kiss,* into a Klaw and Erlanger musical titled *The Silver Star.* The article implies that Ziegfeld either had a contract to manage Genée or that he had some voice in the production of the show; however, there is no specific information to document these suppositions. Newspaper reports about the upcoming production do not mention Ziegfeld at all but say that Klaw and Erlanger were Genée's managers. And while several people who had worked for Ziegfeld in the past also worked on *The Silver Star* (Julian Mitchell, Sam Harrison, Harry B. Smith, and Bickel and Watson), Ziegfeld's name is not listed in program credits or reviews of the show, suggesting that *if* he had a role, it was very slight.

The *Follies of 1910* opened on June 20. This year's show was significant for the debut of two of Ziegfeld's biggest stars: Bert Williams and Fannie Brice, the smash hit of the show. Not only did Ziegfeld know how to spot talent, he sometimes overcame enormous resistance to snare or retain stars—in these cases, Williams because he was black and Brice because she was brash and not that attractive. Fannie Brice may have lacked the beauty common to most of Ziegfeld's female stars, but she made up for it in talent. Besides being an excellent comedian, known for her facial expressions and onstage antics, she was a good singer. Brice was one of Ziegfeld's most loyal stars; she performed in seven *Follies* between 1910 and 1923 and also appeared in several editions of the *Midnight Frolic.*

After months of longing to be in the *Follies,* Fannie almost missed her chance because Abe Erlanger did not like the way she sang "Lovey Joe." When Brice sang for Ziegfeld, the cast burst into applause. But during rehearsal before the Atlantic City opening, Erlanger told Brice that when she said "mo" for "more," it sounded too burlesque and was unacceptable for the *Follies.* Brice replied that she was singing a "coon" song (a burlesque on blacks) and could not sing it any other way. Erlanger promptly fired her.

Ziegfeld would not look at Brice as she walked out of the theater. Later he found her and asked why she had to argue with Erlanger, why could she not just sing "more" now and "mo" later. Brice said she wouldn't argue anymore. Ziegfeld put her back in the show but told her to stay out of Erlanger's sight and away from the theater until the Atlantic City opening. He even made her sit in the ladies' room on the train.

When the show opened, Brice breezed by Erlanger, who was standing in the wings in his trademark pink satin shirt and straw hat. She sang the song her way—facial expressions and all—and stopped the show. After the last encore, Brice left the stage to find Erlanger waiting for her. There are two versions of what happened next. One says that Erlanger had crumpled his straw hat when he became so excited over Brice's performance. Another claims that he repeatedly hit her on the head with the hat, saying, "good, good, good," until his hat broke. He told her she owed him a new one; she insisted he owed her an apology.

Ziegfeld took a real chance in hiring Bert Williams. Williams's appearance in the 1910 *Follies* marked the first time a black performer starred with white actors in a major Broadway musical. To avoid any impropriety, Williams insisted that his contract stipulate that he would not have to appear onstage with a female cast member. Ziegfeld in turn promised that the *Follies* would not tour Southern cities. (He knew Williams did not appear south of the Mason-Dixon line.) However, some *Follies* cast members were not as color-blind as Ziegfeld. According to historian Douglas Gilbert, Ziegfeld had a major part written for Williams in the 1910 show. The cast threatened to strike rather than act with a Negro, however, so Ziegfeld eliminated the part and had Williams perform his vaudeville act. When Williams was a hit, the cut material was restored. Ziegfeld said later that even though several performers initially objected to working with Williams, "they quickly got over that when they found out what an artist he was."

Ziegfeld's courage in backing actors whom he considered great and his devotion to furthering their careers generated remarkable loyalty in a field not noted for much trust between producers and actors. Williams's case is a good example. After Bert became a hit, producer David Belasco tried to lure him with a feature role in a play, but the actor turned him down because he wanted to honor his contract with Ziegfeld.

Successful as his career was at this juncture, Ziegfeld's personal life was in shambles. Although he had tired of Anna Held, they were still living together. Her sense of economy irked Ziegfeld, probably because it smacked of the "constraints" that he so detested. He had begun to earn some independence professionally with Erlanger and did not like being reminded that he could not have everything. Held was not particularly strong about standing up to Ziegfeld in their domestic life. She fell apart under stress, as in the jewel theft incident, and he often had to support her both emotionally and professionally.

Ziegfeld's passionate affair with Lillian Lorraine continued, but she was in obvious ways a troubled woman. Almost from the start her drunken scenes and promiscuity began to ruin their relationship. For all her physical beauty and sex appeal, she was reported to be a crude drunk who consorted with some fairly unsavory characters. Ziegfeld was deeply in love with her, but she certainly could not hold him over the long haul. At age forty-three, Ziegfeld had not yet found a woman he could respect—a woman who could genuinely engage his imagination, let alone sweep him away emotionally.

Above: Charles Dillingham, musical-comedy producer and theater manager, co-produced several shows with Ziegfeld. Top left: In the ice skating scene from *A Winsome Widow* (1912), the widows wore black and lavender, the show girls appeared in bright red and silver, and the ice dancers wore blue and silver as they skated on real ice. Top right: Ziegfeld's long-time employee and right-hand man, Gene Buck (left), with comedian Leon Errol

❖

CHAPTER 5

THE ONE WOMAN IN ALL THE WORLD

❖

Z iegfeld's success with the *Follies* earned him an increasingly larger role in the Klaw and Erlanger organization. When it was time to produce *The Pink Lady*, Ziegfeld participated in auditioning the cast, attended rehearsals, and had significant artistic input in the show. (In 1937, the Ziegfeld estate listed *The Pink Lady* among the many productions in which Ziegfeld had a financial interest.)

The Pink Lady opened on March 13, 1911, at the New Amsterdam Theatre. According to Hazel Dawn, when she finished auditioning, Erlanger ran up to her and said, "Talk about apple blossoms. You're just a little pink lady, aren't you?" Then he snapped his fingers and said, "That's the title of our play." Thus, *The Gay Claudine* (the show's original title) became *The Pink Lady,* and Dawn got the lead role.

This musical farce was a smash hit, running 312 performances. Critics praised it because it actually had a plot as well as clever lyrics and a melodious score. Moreover, the songs were related to the action. One ensemble number, "Donny Did, Donny Didn't," nearly stopped the show. "The Kiss Waltz" and other numbers were popular as well. Naturally there were also a beautiful chorus and splendid scenery.

Just before the *Follies* opened in 1911, Ziegfeld's tempestuous relationship with Lillian Lorraine reached a major crisis. In May 1911, the *New York Review* erroneously linked Lorraine to a murder in Denver (where the 1910 *Follies* was touring). Frank Henwood shot Tony Von Phul during a fight in which he accused Von Phul of blackmail. Both men were known to be acquaintances of Lorraine, but murder-trial documents did not implicate her. Six weeks later Lorraine's publicity problems worsened when she and Fanny Brice got into a row backstage during a *Follies* performance—allegedly over Frederick Gresheimer, a rich kid from Chicago. Fannie Brice was reported to have ripped off Lillian's costume without "waiting to unbutton buttons, or unhook eyes." Neither incident was the kind of publicity Ziegfeld wanted for his stars.

The *Follies* opened on June 26, 1911, at the Jardin de Paris. In a reflection of the times, this was primarily a dancing show. The Dolly Sisters, George White, Vera Maxwell, Tom Dingle, Bessie McCoy, Leon Errol, and Stella Chatelaine all contributed dance numbers; Bert Williams sang three songs and provided bits of comedy. A burlesque of *The Pink Lady* and a cabaret scene, in which Fannie Brice sang, provided some lighter moments. Counteracting this frivolity was "Everywife," described in the program as a "symbolic play," a long (forty-five minutes) and rather serious undertaking for the *Follies*.

That summer Ziegfeld hired two men who would become instrumental to his shows, Gene Buck on the production side and Leon Errol as comedian and actor. Both would become big names while working for him. Buck eventually made his reputation as a lyricist, but he also wrote sketches and scouted talent.

Buck went to Ziegfeld with some ideas for the *Follies,* and Ziegfeld was impressed with his aggressiveness and enthusiasm. One of Buck's ideas was to include a scene portraying two sweethearts from their youth to old age. Lillian Lorraine was to be the heroine, but her unprofessional behavior—continual tardiness for rehearsal and slowness in changing costumes—caused Erlanger, who disliked her intensely, to fire her. Erlanger also dropped Buck's scene, which he also did not particularly like.

Buck said later that he was "stunned when this happened." He fought the decision, mentioning that Ziegfeld had already spent $5,000 on the number. Nothing happened: odd as it seems, Ziegfeld would seldom defy Erlanger. Clearly, even though Flo was gaining stature, Erlanger still controlled the show.

In Chicago later that year, Percy Hammond finally acknowledged in his *Follies* review that Ziegfeld was the best in his business. "No other complaint is available, since Mr. Ziegfeld in this manifestation of his genius remains supreme as our most expert of frivolous showmen. No other producer is so lavish with his dress and so sophisticated in his instructions to his librettist." Hammond, though, could not persuade himself to drop the "cuts" about morality: "Often has he presented quick satires on things which needed satire, only to have them spoiled by little details not fit for observation by mother and the girls, to whom satire is as much of a beneficence as to any one else."

During the latter half of the 1911–12 season, Ziegfeld produced two shows with Charles Dillingham: *Over the River* and *A Winsome Widow.* Dillingham was born a year later than Ziegfeld (May 30, 1868) in Hartford, Connecticut. He started out as a reporter on newspapers in Hartford, Chicago, and New York. The two met as young men after Dillingham began working in Chicago in 1889 on the *Chicago Times.* Ziegfeld's relationship with Dillingham was never exceedingly close, but the two men maintained cordial relations and avoided the serious differences that characterized so many of Ziegfeld's business associations.

Above left: The Dolly Sisters were just two of the many dancers in the 1911 *Follies*. In this scene they appear with Vera Maxwell. In another number they were Siamese twins who shared a single skirt while dancing. Above right: Eddie Foy and the chorus in the *Over the River* (1912). Below: Billie Burke's mother, Blanche, with her dogs "Tutti" and "Frutti," shortly after the purchase of Burkeley Crest

They started running into one another again after Dillingham moved to New York and became interested in producing shows. In 1910, Dillingham took over management of the Hippodrome, a huge theater in the Times Square area that seated five thousand patrons; that same year, he also opened the Globe Theatre on Sixth Avenue between Forty-third and Forty-fourth streets.

Over the River enjoyed a decent run of three-and-a-half months, but it did little to enhance Ziegfeld's reputation. One review said this musical farce was vulgar but that Eddie Foy was very funny in the main role. Lillian Lorraine (who had some of the best musical numbers) and a group of women wore Chinese costumes for the "Chop Stick Rag" dance. Jean Schwartz, the song's composer, accompanied the women on the piano. The Marvelous Millers (from vaudeville) performed very popular contortionist dances. Elsie Janis composed the song "For de Lawd's Sake, Play a Waltz."

A Winsome Widow was a reworked version of Charles Hoyt's *A Trip to Chinatown* (1891). Ziegfeld even managed to entice Mae West into this show, where she was a hit. Earlier, West had declined to appear in the *Follies* because the theater was not intimate enough, but she agreed to be the baby vamp (La Petite Daffy) in *A Winsome Widow* and attracted the critics' attention.

The show's outstanding feature was the colorful costumes, particularly those found in two scenes—the masquerade carnival and the inside of the ice palace. According to *The New York Times,* the carnival was "full of glowing color and beauty seldom excelled." However, its beauty *was* excelled, in the ice-palace scene—where skaters wore "glittering attire" and provided a "wonderful medley of changing color."

The dancing and singing were also especially good; several reviewers commented on the acrobatic ability of the dancers, particularly Cathleen Clifford's and George Kirner's skating. However, some critics mentioned that the "interludes of plot" seemed dull when compared with the fast-paced dancing and songs.

Ziegfeld opened the *Ziegfeld Follies of 1912* late in October instead of the usual June. The production team had begun to stabilize as Julian Mitchell returned for a sixth year to stage the show, "Pop" Rosenbaum started managing the road tours, and William C. Schrode became stage manager. Schrode had been a *Follies* cast member from 1908 to 1911 and was stage manager in 1912 and again from 1915 to 1926. Lillian Lorraine, Elizabeth Brice, Rae Samuels, Vera Maxwell, and Josie Sadler were the principal female performers; Bert Williams, Leon Errol, and newcomer Bernard Granville were the leading male entertainers.

As usual, the women and the sets were the big draws in 1912, although critics also praised the comedy sketches involving Williams and Errol. When the show reached Chicago, it received admiration, with no serious qualifications: "The best of the series. By 'best' is meant the biggest, cleanest, most colorful, and almost the funniest of the spectacular shows."

New Amsterdam Theatre box office when *Follies* tickets were on sale

Even though the personal relationship between Flo and Anna had seriously degenerated, Held continued working in Ziegfeld shows, touring as late as November 1911, in a road version of *Miss Innocence*. But finally on April 10, 1912, Anna sued for divorce. Although theirs was a common-law marriage, New York law made such arrangements legally binding after seven years, so formal divorce proceedings were necessary. Justice Bischoff appointed Edward J. Whitaker the referee to take testimony in the suit. Held named several corespondents, including Lillian Lorraine. In the summer of 1912 their marital differences became acrimonious when Held sued Ziegfeld for $2,700 outstanding on a $10,000 loan from two years earlier. However, once the divorce papers were filed, Ziegfeld and Held wavered interminably over whether to remain married. In truth, she still loved him and thought that a threat of divorce would bring him around. And as late as December 27, 1912, Ziegfeld was still telling reporters that a reconciliation was possible.

Ziegfeld's ongoing affair with Lorraine must have sharpened Held's resolve, especially since the affair was so messy and public. Although Elsie Johnson, Lorraine's secretary/companion, claimed that Flo never even came near Lillian's room when she accompanied him on his camping trips to Canada, the couple were not especially discreet at other times; they visited Theodore Roosevelt's Long Island home together on several occasions, for example.

In March 1912, Lillian married Freddie Gresheimer. The ever-melodramatic *New York Review* reported that Flo fainted at news of the wedding. A bizarre series of events followed. First, Lillian deserted her role in Ziegfeld's *Over the River*. Soon another Mrs. Gresheimer surfaced, claiming no knowledge of a divorce. Days later, newspapers reported that Lorraine returned to Ziegfeld's show, having given up on marriage. Gresheimer's lawyer said that his client's divorce was pending and that Gresheimer had never married Lorraine. Finally, on April 25, Lorraine and Gresheimer "remarried."

Anna Held eventually obtained a divorce on January 9, 1913. Held did not request alimony. She was shocked and ultimately devastated when Flo gave her the divorce that she didn't really want.

Lillian's marriage to Gresheimer had not proven terribly beneficial, so she continued her liaison with Ziegfeld. The seamy situation reached an embarrassing culmination when Gresheimer caught Ziegfeld and Lorraine leaving Louis Martin's restaurant together. Gresheimer promptly crowned Flo with a cane and then punched him. The incident precipitated another round of unwelcome publicity.

Ziegfeld's professional life was going more smoothly. In 1913, Erlanger booked the *Follies* into the New Amsterdam Theatre, indicating that the *Follies* had "arrived." This theater was New York's theatrical jewel, referred to as the "Grandest in the World." Built in 1903 for about $2 million, it was the most beautiful Art Nouveau theater in the United States. Elaborate wood friezes lent it a dignified, rich air.

The building had two major elements: the theater proper (seating 1,702) and the tower that housed production offices (lower floors) and the rooftop theater (ninth and tenth floors). Patrons reached the roof via two elevators, which transported fifty people each. The dressing room complex accommodated five hundred cast members. The theater fronted on Forty-second Street, with the most famous stage door in Broadway history opening on Forty-first Street.

Ziegfeld's office at the New Amsterdam was tiny. It was painted in a neutral creamy/tan color and had yellow oak furniture. Ziegfeld decorated it with theater memorabilia, highlighted by pictures of showgirls.

In describing the New Amsterdam's cultural significance to New York City, writer Tom Prideaux said that this "two-theater complex had a pioneer importance.... Ziegfeld created exactly the kind of healthy theater plant that many of the nation's new repertory troupes are trying to emulate today."

This magnificent theater was the *Follies'* regular home for the next fifteen years. Between 1913 and 1927, thirteen editions of the *Follies* (1913–20, 1922–25, and 1927) opened there. The remaining two opened at the Globe Theatre because two popular shows—Ziegfeld's *Sally* (1920) and Dillingham's *Sunny* (1925)—were still playing at the New Amsterdam. The New Amsterdam would also be the site of two successful Ziegfeld musicals, and the theater's roof garden hosted seventeen editions of the *Ziegfeld Frolic*.

The *Ziegfeld Follies of 1913* opened at the New Amsterdam on June 16. Its loose plot concerned the frivolities of white men as seen by a group of American Indians looking down at Manhattan. Satan came into the plot because he wanted to sample some of the earth's "follies" before returning to his own realm. The most important addition to the cast was dancer Ann Pennington, who remained a popular attraction throughout her tenure with Ziegfeld. Jose Collins, Martin Brown, Stella Chatelaine, Frank Tinney, Leon Errol, and Ethel Amorita Kelly were other principals.

On New Years's Eve, 1913, Ziegfeld attended a memorable masquerade ball at the Astor Hotel's elegant Sixty Club. Anna Held was there, costumed as the Empress Josephine, with Lillian Russell and Jim Brady. Ziegfeld escorted Lillian Lorraine, but they had yet another quarrel, and he left temporarily. He returned after changing from his trademark tramp costume into evening clothes. Around 3 A.M., now January 1, 1914, Billie Burke made her grand entrance on the arm of Somerset Maugham. She was beautiful, with all the charisma of a true star. Also present was Marilyn Miller, who would one day become close to Ziegfeld. The four most important women in his life were in the same room on the same night.

Burke was starring in Maugham's *Land of Promise*. Following a late dinner party, Maugham suggested celebrating the New Year by toddling over to the Astor's ball. When the "Paul Jones" started, Burke found herself opposite Ziegfeld but did not recognize him.

Left: Kay Laurell achieved *Follies* fame by wearing few clothes on stage. Here she appears as September Morn in the 1914 edition. Right: Olive Thomas was sixteen or seventeen when she joined the *Follies* in 1915. She died just five years later.

A sketch depicting "The Skyscraper" scene that featured Bert Williams and Leon Errol in 1914

When Burke discovered she had been dancing with Ziegfeld, she "fled the ballroom," because she realized that it was a case of love at first sight. Ziegfeld, too, was immediately drawn to Billie.

Billie was born Mary William Ethelbert Appleton Burke in Washington, D.C., on August 7, 1884, the only child of Billy Burke and Blanche Hodkinson. Her father was a famous singing clown who traveled internationally with the circus, particularly in Europe; her mother, who had already raised four children by her first husband, was employed by the Treasury Department in Washington. Until Billie was eight, the family lived in New York and Washington, with her father touring constantly. Around 1892, after her father had suffered professional setbacks, the Burkes went to London. In England, Mr. Burke was successful, so the family settled there for a while. Blanche Burke decided while Billie was still young that her daughter would become an actress. Though Billie did not share those ambitions, she trained in elocution and singing, pursuits that often interrupted her formal schooling.

Billie Burke began her stage career in 1899 singing "coon songs." Her career was charmed from the outset. In her first legitimate stage role, in *The School Girl* (1903), Burke sang the hit number "Mamie, I Have a Little Canoe." This show, which ran for two years, made her a celebrity when she was only eighteen and linked her to a very powerful mentor, Charles Frohman, *The School Girl*'s co-producer. During these heady years, Billie became the darling of British society, even performing before King Edward. Her triumph was marred only by the death of her father on October 5, 1906. In August 1907, Frohman persuaded her to return to the United States, where she made her Broadway debut in *My Wife*, at $500 per week. This production, also starring John Drew, made her a hit in America as well.

Frohman did not believe in flashy press-agent tricks, so he sheltered Burke from the limelight. Instead he quietly introduced her to the Broadway theater elite (Maude Adams, the Barrymores, and Maxine Elliott), prominent literary figures such as Mark Twain, and members of New York society (the Astors, the Goulds). She gathered a large following among these groups and became known nationally as well. Frohman was one of the most important producers in the world. Burke described him as her "manager, friend, protector, adviser, and my absolute boss for seven years." He controlled half a dozen theaters in New York and another half dozen in London and was one of the founding members of the Syndicate.

Billie's myriad professional achievements did not rob her of the human touch. When one of her good friends in the theater, Mrs. Thomas Watson, died suddenly of pneumonia in 1909, leaving her daughter, Cherry, alone, Billie adopted the girl and made her a companion and protégée.

On January 24, 1912, at Blanche's urging, Billie bought the estate they named Burkeley Crest in

Hastings-on-Hudson, New York, about twenty miles north of the city. She and Blanche did not move in until the spring, but this purchase, which was a good investment, was a sign of how closely Blanche watched over her daughter's financial well-being. Billie was not one to exercise much fiscal discipline, but Blanche, according to her granddaughter Patty, was "very careful with a nickel."

When Ziegfeld and Burke first danced together that New Year's Day 1914, despite the notable difference in their ages (he was forty-six and she twenty-nine), each was a potent force in New York theater circles. Interestingly enough, although both had been on Broadway since 1907, they had never before met.

Ziegfeld embarked on a new relationship with his usual enthusiasm, pressing his case with flowers, notes, phone calls, gifts, and a dizzying profusion of romantic touches. Shortly after his first rush, Burke backed off, asking him not to see her anymore. She sensed the emotional risk and knew his reputation with women. She was also concerned about professional implications: her five-year contract precluded marriage while she worked for Frohman. Still, Billie and Flo seemed drawn into this relationship inexorably, as though neither was completely in control of what was happening, moths drawn to the flame.

Billie crystallized the drama in the courtship: "Of course I knew Flo Ziegfeld was a dangerous man . . . I felt the impact of his threat and his charm at once. But even if I had known then precisely what tortures and frustrations were in store for me during the next eighteen years because of this man, I should have kept right on falling in love."

He, in turn, had discovered the woman who had the beauty, the élan, the successful career, and, most important, the strength to challenge him as no woman before had been able to do. He, too, had his obstacles to overcome. Lillian Lorraine opposed the relationship and tried, in her inimitable way, to break it up. In a highly publicized incident she pursued Ziegfeld to the New Amsterdam roof wearing only a fur coat, threatening to open the coat there in the restaurant if he did not agree to stop seeing Burke.

Frohman's office intercepted Ziegfeld's letters because Frohman was afraid that his rival would deny him a "good meal ticket." Finally Ziegfeld enticed Victor Kiraly, the manager of Billie's current show, to run the *Midnight Frolic*. Ziegfeld then used Kiraly to pass notes. During this era, a manager could dominate an actress with a thoroughness that would be unacceptable today. This placed Billie in a difficult situation. Legally, Frohman was in a position to make things very unpleasant. Moreover, he could ruin her career simply by passing word to his associates that she was not reliable. Apparently, he threatened to do so.

Ziegfeld realized that the key to his goal was to win over Billie's mother. He courted Blanche almost as assiduously as he did her daughter. During the run of *The Land of Promise* (January and February 1914), Billie and Blanche often had Saturday dinner at the Ansonia. Ziegfeld attended to Blanche carefully, with small grace notes. He took her to the theater while Billie was working and sent her gifts such as out-of-season fruit and pink champagne. Blanche told her daughter that she would have to choose between the two producers and that she thought Ziegfeld would advance her career faster than Frohman.

Ziegfeld continued pursuing Billie with all of the flair he could muster. In one of his fabled ploys to make Billie feel special, when she complained that she could not reach him, he installed a direct, private line to his office in New York City: Billie did not need to call any number; she just picked up and there was Alice at the switchboard.

Frohman was so intent on breaking up the relationship that Billie and Flo resorted to sneaking around like teenagers. Billie recalled in her memoir that they sometimes met at Grant's Tomb: "There would be Flo impatiently stomping up and down inside the chilly rendezvous, glaring because he was sure Frohman's henchmen were lurking in the bushes." Apparently their subterfuge was not successful, as one day Frohman and Alf Hayman came to Burkeley Crest demanding that Billie stop seeing Ziegfeld. Their high-pressure tactics hastened her decision: she realized, she said later, "how deeply I wanted Flo Ziegfeld." Despite her feelings, however, she tried once again to break off the relationship.

In one of the few surviving letters that reflects Ziegfeld's own perspective on the relationship, Flo dramatically pressed Billie in April 1914, to make a decision about marrying him. This note seems to have helped tip the scales. On Friday, April 10, Flo and Billie decided to marry. According to *Dance Magazine*, "after parting from Miss Burke that afternoon he very shrewdly disappeared for twenty-four hours. He suspected that she would attempt to recall the appointment and he made sure that she would be unable to reach him. His suspicions were correct. She did try to break the elopement date but there was no one with whom to break it." After the Saturday matinée, Burke met Ziegfeld at Forty-fourth Street and Fifth Avenue. They took a car to Hoboken, New Jersey, where they were married on April 11, 1914.

The ceremony was brief. The wedding party included Flo's parents and Billie's mother. Ziegfeld and Burke were married "in the little back room of a parsonage." There was an amusing moment when Conrad Engelden, the minister, turned to Billie when referring to Florenz and to Ziegfeld for Billie.

The newlyweds returned to Manhattan by 6:00 P.M. and celebrated at the Brevoort Hotel before Billie performed that evening. They honeymooned at Long Beach, New York—with their parents in tow.

News of the wedding broke in the newspapers two days later. Frohman was furious, and inevitably Burke's relationship with him became extremely uncomfortable. The stress caused by Frohman's reaction set the tone for the next eighteen years. This relationship was to provide the newlyweds with more highs and lows than either imagined, as they became one of New York's best-known couples—charmed but tormented. Flo and Billie came to represent the spirit of the Jazz Age.

Initially the couple was happy with the new marriage and with country life at Burkeley Crest. As Billie became better acquainted with the man behind the public image, she learned Ziegfeld's foibles. Flo was so meticulous about his personal hygiene that his family often joked about what a production his toilette was.

He stocked enormous bottles, and then cases, of Guerlain eau de cologne that people frequently mistook for bootleg liquor. He also had several idiosyncrasies in his dress. Despite his fashionable clothes, even under pajamas he wore long underwear, "interwoven with silk, to be certain, of a delicate shade of peach, but woollies they were nevertheless." When Billie replaced them with shorts, "he was sure that he would freeze to death."

Flo sustained rough knocks shortly after his marriage when two of his most reliable organization people—Harry B. Smith and Julian Mitchell—broke with him. Ziegfeld had neglected Smith's royalty payments, causing his first serious breach with an author. Ziegfeld paid his actors very well by standards of the day and rarely failed to make timely payments; for some reason, though, he hated making royalty payments to authors and composers. Over the years many a relationship went sour as a result. This particular instance of nonpayment was noteworthy for the ingenuity of Smith's response: allegedly he had a process server interrupt Ziegfeld's honeymoon to serve papers on $4,330 in royalties for *Miss Innocence*.

The split with Mitchell was significant because it gave Leon Errol his first experience staging a Ziegfeld show. Ziegfeld rehearsals were always chaotic, but the changeover this year seemed to have made things even worse than usual. A "scouting" letter from J. V. Foley to one of the Shuberts, probably Lee, described preparation: "Although Abe Erlanger, Pat Casey, Leon Errol and Ziegfeld himself had been hammering, drilling, and fuming over the production almost continually for sixty hours before the curtain rose, it was still far from being in that presentable condition necessary to insure metropolitan success." The furtive Shubert "reviewer" doubted that a New York opening on June 1 was possible. Of course, he underestimated Ziegfeld's manic fury when he was under pressure to stage an opening.

Somehow Ziegfeld and company managed to open the *Ziegfeld Follies of 1914* on time. While comedy was no longer being woven into the plot—there was no plot—via the parodies of earlier editions, humor was very much evident in the sketches involving Bert Williams and Leon Errol. Williams was, in fact, this year's big star. Comedian Ed Wynn joined the cast and was also a hit. Among the other principals were Ann Pennington, Rita Gould, Kay Laurell, and Bernard Granville.

Ziegfeld's extravagance and artistic temperament were always a factor in the show's final shape. After this show opened, Ziegfeld was dissatisfied with a scene that had cost $18,000; he discarded the costumes and sets for the entire number.

This year's edition was criticized by several reviewers for being too much like the earlier shows. Although critics found Leon Errol and Stella Chatelaine funny doing an eccentric tango, the number was similar to their 1913 scene featuring the turkey trot. The costumes this year were said to be especially outstanding, particularly Ann Pennington's dress and Vera Michelena's Satan outfit. In general, the women wore more clothes than in previous years. Some reviewers suggested this was due to Billie Burke's presence at the show's opening.

After Southern blacks began moving to New York in large numbers around 1910, several theaters for Negro stock companies opened in Harlem. In 1913, downtown audiences went to Harlem to attend J. Leubrie Hill's *Darktown Follies*. After seeing the show himself, Ziegfeld bought the rights to several numbers for his own *Follies*. One of them was added to the revue in August 1914—"At the Ball That's All," a number based on the dance "Balling the Jack." Ziegfeld engaged black performers to teach the dance to whites, but he did not hire any blacks for the show. Hill was very disappointed because he had thought Ziegfeld was planning to break the color barrier for black chorus members on Broadway.

In a 1914 interview about how he put shows together, Ziegfeld said that he was involved in all aspects:

Too many managers let their details run down after the first week or two of success. They think minor parts and little bits of business or costume don't matter. . . . Details are what makes a show's "personality." . . . I hunt for chances of putting in a laugh or taking out a slow bit. I . . . keep [the show] combed, brushed, polished and groomed.

Ziegfeld's perceptiveness here proves that his success derived mainly from the fact that he had an artist's sensibility and not that of a mere producer. He tirelessly addressed all facets until his vision came to life. It could even be argued he fulfilled his vision *through* this passionate attention to the particulars.

Another interview during 1914 provided more insight into his working methods and his tastes. The article noted that "year after year he begins rehearsals without any definite knowledge of the main structure of the play. He is sure to have an idea or two about settings, many designs of costumes, and a chorus of the most dazzlingly beautiful young women in America. The plot and the unities may wait." He studied each girl "to bring out her individual beauty," saying: "I have a natural knack of knowing what costume will be most becoming to each girl. I am able to design my own costumes and the girls learn that they attract more attention in my shows than in some others." He may have presented seventy-five to one hundred women in his choruses, but his goal was to make each woman's stage presence distinctive.

To coincide with the launching of the 1914 *Follies,* Ziegfeld opened the New Amsterdam Roof for dancing each evening after the show. The "Danse de Follies" was not in itself particularly important for Ziegfeld's theater career, but it proved so successful that it eventually evolved into the *Midnight Frolic* production. One possible explanation for its popularity is that the World War raging in Europe caused wealthy Americans who might otherwise have been traveling to stay home.

The 1914 *Follies* was fairly successful financially. The show's ledger indicates that this edition netted a profit of $176,071. Ziegfeld's share came to nearly $90,000, which is equivalent to $1.5 million in today's terms. (Additionally, he was still drawing his salary of $200 per week, or $10,400 a year.)

The ledger also provides an interesting overview on the vicissitudes that arise even for successful Broadway productions. The *Follies* lost nearly $1,700 during the week in Atlantic City but then managed three very strong weeks in New York City with profits from $5,700 to $6,700 per week. Profits decreased steadily thereafter; the show netted $5,100 for the first week of July but by the closing week, it lost more than $2,000. Expenses ranged from $10,000 to $11,000 each week. The road tour overhead ran substantially lower, costing $5,000 to $7,000 weekly, while the profit pendulum swung wildly. The St. Louis engagement earned $9,518, while the closing week of the tour, in Milwaukee, saw a $2,465 loss.

The *Follies* usually started to tour in September, following the same basic route each year, always playing in Pittsburgh during Thanksgiving week. Typically the troupe did not go west of Kansas City because train fare for such a large cast was so expensive, but in 1914 the *Follies* toured the West Coast. After the Atlantic City previews and the New York engagement, the show played the following cities in this order: Philadelphia; Boston; Washington, D.C.; Pittsburgh; Chicago; Cleveland; Detroit; Cincinnati; Columbus/ Springfield/Dayton (one week total); Indianapolis; St. Louis; Kansas City; Denver; Los Angeles; San Francisco; Oakland/Portland; Seattle; Duluth; St. Paul; and Milwaukee. The tour ended in May.

The fluctuation in Ziegfeld's finances, though, were modest compared to the turbulence in his personal life. Frohman, still upset with Billie for marrying Flo, punished his star by sending her current show, *Jerry*, on tour prematurely. The separation caused by the road trip and her subsequent work in films (*Gloria's Romance* and *Peggy*) wrought havoc with Billie and Flo's relationship. It gave Ziegfeld an opportunity to get involved with Olive Thomas, a *Follies* cast member who was his latest infatuation.

When she learned about the Olive Thomas affair, Billie called Ziegfeld long-distance. He replied that he was leaving for California at once. In a few days he arrived. What Billie saw in his face made her tremble with anxiety. She was not explicit about what she observed, but the implication was that his face betrayed a deep fascination with Thomas. Despite his extramarital romances, Ziegfeld seems in his own way to have been quite committed to Billie. He had many opportunities to leave her for other women, but he stayed.

Ziegfeld appears to have been subject to wide mood swings—with periods of intense activity followed by prolonged periods of inertia. He was legendary for marathon rehearsals that would sometimes last nearly twenty-four hours or would involve several consecutive workdays of eighteen to twenty hours. When he believed the cause important, he was capable of driving himself well beyond the normal limits. Once the show opened, though, according to his daughter, he would suffer a "bilious" attack brought on by the sheer exhaustion of "eating at odd hours, not getting enough sleep, yelling at people, trying to get things together." Then he would say, "to hell with it," and collapse for two or three days, taking to his bed.

Billie offered Flo a steadiness that no other woman, or person for that matter, had provided. She was strong as he swung from one mood extreme to the other. While the early years, when he was so flagrantly unfaithful, must have been excruciating for her, Billie learned how to cope and helped him rise above personality traits that could have been devastating had he lived with someone less stable.

Surviving telegrams from Billie to Flo demonstrate just how devoted she was to him, but they also reveal the first evidence of an interesting series of role shifts. They were in daily contact when she was away, sometimes more than once a day. At times Billie was almost like a child, signing telegrams "Baby" and talking about how strict her husband was with her: "Morning, Liebling. Twenty four hours here on puff puff to my boy. Poor sweetheart, hope not suffering such pain. Been so lonesome these four days. Please are you loving me lots? Can hardly compose wire. Busy counting words. My husband very strict with me. One word left for 'love'." Or again on the same day comes this note: "Poor precious heart, good night. My gums just ache for my darling. Hope better." The next day, though, when she offered the perspective of a theater professional, roles had reversed, despite the closing from "Baby," and she referred to him as "old son": "Review full of your plans with Gene Buck. Your next *Follies* sound promising with he writing book and lyrics. Congratulations, old son. I am proud of you. Love, Baby."

Even though Billie was dismayed by news of Ziegfeld's involvement with Olive Thomas, she paused long enough to remember that of the four months they had been married they had spent only one together; the rest of the time she was traveling with her company or working on films. When this realization dawned on her, she sat Flo down for a frank talk that alleviated some of the tension. Seeing that he loved her alone, she decided to devote herself more to the marriage by working less.

The basic patterns of Ziegfeld's life were well set by 1914. He had proved that he had both the drive and the vision to produce stunning, successful shows and had already left his mark on Broadway. Gambling was a deeply established habit, whether the stakes involved theatrical productions or money on a casino table; his compulsive attraction to women, was likewise entrenched.

People who knew Ziegfeld assert that he was in love with Olive Thomas and other women. Though he seems to have been attracted to them physically and to have cared about them on a certain level, a far more plausible explanation, in psychological terms, is that Ziegfeld was able, for good or ill, to distinguish in his own mind between love for a woman whom he considered primary and his affairs with other women. Incidents that occur later reinforce this sense that he compartmentalized his relationships, but it is clear that he loved Billie deeply even while he was causing her substantial grief.

Above: Flo Ziegfeld wore one of the Balloon Girl costumes, including high heels, to a Palm Beach costume party in the mid-1920s. It looks as though he may have lost a couple of balloons to the lighted cigarette held by his friend Bill Averell. At right is Gladys Thaw. Top left: Sybil Carmen in her balloon costume. Carmen and the Balloon Girls were so popular that they appeared in the first four editions of the *Midnight Frolic*. Top right: Ford Dabney (standing center) and his Syncopated Orchestra, shown here in 1920, provided dance music for most editions of the *Frolic*. Dabney composed many of the songs he played.

CHAPTER 6

❖

JUST GIRLS: THE MIDNIGHT FROLIC

❖

Ever astute in knowing what the public wanted, Flo Ziegfeld, Jr., initiated the *Ziegfeld Midnight Frolic* in 1915 not only to entertain wealthy patrons but also to satisfy the public's craving for dance music. In the 1890s the public had wanted songs for singing around the home piano, but about 1910 a dance craze swept the country. On June 1, 1914, Ziegfeld opened the Danse de Follies atop the New Amsterdam Theatre so that patrons had a convenient place to dance (and drink) after they left the *Follies* around midnight. The Danse de Follies was so successful that Gene Buck suggested combining dinner and entertainment. Ziegfeld liked the idea and hired designer/architect Joseph Urban (who was well known in Europe) to redecorate the roof so a floor show could be presented. With the inauguration of the *Ziegfeld Midnight Frolic* on January 5, 1915, the Danse de Follies stayed open all year round. Ziegfeld engaged bandleader Ford Dabney and his orchestra to provide dance music (one-steps, waltzes, fox-trots, and tangos) before and after the *Frolic* and during intermission. Alcohol was available at these times but not during the show. The entertainment, a combination of vaudeville and musical comedy, attracted socialites and businessmen who were out for a night on the town, and it became the hit of New York high society.

The roof where the *Frolic* was presented could seat 480 people on the floor and 280 in the balcony. There was no traditional stage, but the west end of the room contained background scenery designed by Urban. Patrons sat at tables around the dance floor while the entertainers performed in the center. The atmosphere was intimate, and patrons even participated in some numbers. After a few editions, a four-foot-high platform with wide steps was added to the scenery. Entertainers descended the steps to the dance floor. A backdrop with a large circular opening—from which the cast emerged—was also added.

Ziegfeld hired choreographer/director Ned Wayburn to stage the first *Frolic*. Wayburn eventually

Left: Caricature of the January 1915 *Frolic*. The dresses worn by the women parading across the glass walkway were strips of material that were easily blown about. Right: Four women wearing various styles of lingerie stepped through drawings in a scene called "A Girl's Trousseau" (January 1916).

directed eleven *Frolics* as well as five *Follies* (beginning in 1916) and other Ziegfeld shows. In December 1917, Wayburn introduced a telescopic stage in the *Frolic*. Like the platform it abutted, the stage was four feet tall and had steps to the dance floor. It could be rolled out on rubber wheels until it covered the central dance floor, separating the performers from the audience when desired. The stage also elevated cast members so they could be seen. When the telescopic stage was added, the platform in back of it was deepened and the circular backdrop was replaced by an arch. Tableaux could be presented on the platform while other scenes and numbers unfolded on the stage or the dance floor.

The regular *Frolic* series consisted of sixteen shows between 1915 and 1921—typically two editions a year. The *Frolic*'s cast and numbers changed often; stars and chorus girls might leave the roof show to be in the *Follies*, and new talent would replace them. But within an edition, major numbers and stars were retained. Popular numbers were carried over into the next edition, but generally a new edition meant new numbers.

In 1918, Ziegfeld introduced a double *Frolic*. Ziegfeld opened the earlier show to capitalize on the popularity of the *Midnight Frolic* and to compete with Broadway shows until his new *Follies* opened. He considered the nine o'clock shows part of the *Frolic* series, as evidenced by his numbering system. The *Midnight Frolic* of November 1921 was number sixteen, although it was the thirteenth midnight production. The three nine o'clock shows (December 1918; March 1920; and February 1921) brought the series total to sixteen.

For the inaugural *Frolic*, Ziegfeld suspended a plate-glass walkway with colored lights just below the balcony and directly over the first row of tables. As the chorus girls danced on the floor, their reflections in the glass walkway gave the illusion that they were dancing on their heads. Additionally, Ziegfeld provided little wooden hammers for each table. Patrons used the hammers—which created quite a racket—to request an encore immediately after the first number. Ziegfeld also engaged a comedy juggler from vaudeville; dressed as a waiter, the juggler performed bits of his act during the show.

The attractive Sybil Carmen, accompanied by the Balloon Girls, sang "I Want Someone to Make a Fuss over Me." The women's costumes included helium-filled balloons attached to their gowns and headpieces. As they walked around the dance floor, invariably some of the men's lighted cigars touched and burst the balloons. Occasionally a balloon came loose and floated to the ceiling. The number was a big hit. The hammers and the bursting balloons set the tone for the entire series of *Frolics*. Audience members could be more boisterous than at a regular show; they also became personally involved in the production.

A wire from Billie, who was on the road when the *Frolic* opened, crystallizes the reaction to the show. It also indicates how enthusiastic she was in supporting her husband's efforts:

Will Rogers was one of Ziegfeld's biggest stars—of both the *Midnight Frolic* and the *Follies*. Rogers was the only star who never had a written contract with Ziegfeld.

Left: Chorus girls practice fishing from the glass walkway in the October 1916 *Frolic*. Right: Bee Palmer did a shimmy dance and sang in the 1918 editions of the *Frolic* and *Follies*.

Aerial artist Bird Millman appeared in one *Follies* and nine editions of the *Midnight Frolic*. She was also a vaudeville and circus star.

Oh, darling, I am so glad you scored so heavily and showed them they didn't know anything about putting on a show. I tell you, darling, you are an artist standing alone. I am crazy for you to get more productions going and make use of that clever brain of yours. How I should love to have been there. . . . The numbers are so wonderfully put on with such taste and beauty. They can't go up against them. Oh; I am so happy, darling; all the love and adoration of your, Baby 5:15 PM.

According to *Variety*, Ziegfeld initially lost money: his weekly salary outlay was $1,900, he purchased expensive costumes, and his ban on serving alcohol during the *Frolic* left only two hours to make money from liquor sales. But the *Frolic* was so popular that the first-night admission price of $1 was raised to $2 the second night for dance-floor seating (balcony seating was $1). A few months later, the admission price went up to $3. Despite the original operating loss, the show was profitable overall for seven years.

The *Frolic* entertainment was a hit, but Ziegfeld initially had his share of problems, as a letter to a friend indicates: "I am nearly off my nut trying to get this roof show right—looks rotten—Can't find a girl to sing songs in a cute way." Ziegfeld had problems in other areas as well. Wayburn and Urban became embroiled in a dispute over whether to focus the lighting on the scenery or the chorus girls. Wayburn devised a compromise that became a standard staging technique: spotlighting the women from the corners of the room. This allowed them to stand out without interfering with Urban's color and lighting.

Another creative collaboration led to the famed "Ziegfeld Girl strut." Ziegfeld and Wayburn were concerned that the intimacy of the roof and the proximity to beautiful, partially clad women would tempt the male patrons more than was appropriate. To create a sense of aloofness and to sustain decorum, Wayburn "taught the girls to hold their chins high when they paraded. . . . It succeeded."

Later that year, on August 23, 1915, Ziegfeld presented his second *Frolic*, titled "Just Girls." Comedian Will Rogers began a long-term professional relationship with Ziegfeld in this show, but his *Frolic* debut was inauspicious. Gene Buck had seen Rogers at another theater and persuaded Ziegfeld to hire him. However, Ziegfeld did not like Rogers's act, which consisted of twirling his lariat and telling jokes, and told Buck to fire him; possibly Ziegfeld did not think that Rogers was sophisticated enough for his shows. On the day that Buck had finally decided to let him go, Rogers asked for a $50-a-week raise and told Buck that Mrs. Rogers thought he should change his act and talk about what he read in the papers. Although Buck was afraid that Rogers's remarks could prompt a lawsuit, Rogers managed to convince him. The new act was a big hit.

Ziegfeld had been out of town the week Rogers revised his act; when he returned, he asked Buck how

Left: The "Beautiful Birds" number from the 1919 *Frolic*. Right, top to bottom: Anna Held in her white peacock outfit from *Follow Me* (1916). Dolores as the white peacock in the 1919 *Frolic*. Gladys Loftus was a tropical bird called "the Paradisier" in the 1919 *Frolic*.

Rogers had taken the firing. Buck told Ziegfeld that Rogers was still in the *Frolic* and suggested that Ziegfeld see him. Ziegfeld remained impassive during Rogers's monologue, but he could see that the audience liked Rogers, so he decided to keep him another week. Two weeks later Ziegfeld raised Rogers's salary to $225 a week. Rogers later found out how close he had come to being fired. His talent had won out and his friendship with Ziegfeld flourished, enduring for the remainder of Ziegfeld's life.

The third show in the series opened on January 24, 1916, with the usual variety of acts. In the number "A Girl's Trousseau," a singing lingerie salesman showed the audience a series of drawings in which the women wore progressively less lingerie. As the salesman sang, live models dressed in garments identical to those in the drawings stepped through the pictures one by one. Before the nude model was to appear the audience eagerly positioned for a better look. But instead of a beautiful nude woman, Will Rogers, as the masked marvel, stepped through the drawing.

On October 2, 1916, a new *Frolic* debuted. Frances White appeared as a barefoot, ragged urchin sitting on the glass walkway and singing "Every Girl Is Fishing" (about ways of catching lobsters). The chorus girls also fished from the runway, but with a different catch in mind; their hooks caught the outstretched sleeves of the first-nighters sitting below. William Rock performed a different dance with each of eight beautifully dressed women. Each woman represented a specific dance (minuet, polka, waltz, tango, fox-trot, etc.). At the end of the number, Rock and Frances White did a medley of all the other dances. The most spectacular number in the show, however, was the last scene, "The Melting Pot." As Lawrence Haynes sang, eight women dressed to represent eight countries descended one by one into a large golden pot. After the last woman disappeared, out stepped the beautiful Midnight Frolic Girl—Olive Thomas.

In the *Midnight Frolic* that opened April 24, 1917, the balloon girls of the first two seasons were replaced by women with miniature zeppelins attached to their costumes. The women were caught in a cross fire of searchlights as Sybil Carmen sang "The Midnight Zepps." Like the balloons from previous years, the zeppelins burst if touched by a lighted cigar or cigarette. Later, the chorus girls walked around dressed as clocks and switchboards, and patrons sitting at the right tables (i.e., those reached by the girls' telephone wires) could talk to them by telephone.

Just before the year ended, on December 29, the sixth *Frolic* opened. This edition had more than the usual opening-night cliff-hangers. Two days before its premiere, a fire destroyed most of the costumes. Then cold weather delayed the scenery from Boston; it arrived two hours before show time. As a final blow, cold-weather demand for cabs was so great that people couldn't get to the theater on time.

On opening night, the audience was asked to vote for the most beautiful chorus girl. The woman who

Left: Menu from the dinner that Ziegfeld gave on March 7, 1920, for the cast of the *Nine O'Clock Revue*. The revue opened the next evening. Right: Annette Bade (standing with telephone) was in "The Telephone Doll" number in 1922.

Bessie McCoy Davis appearing as the "Dancing Somnambulist" in the 1918 *Nine O'Clock Frolic*

received the most votes during the show's run was to have her salary doubled.

In 1916, Joseph Urban had designed huge pillars of crystal-like beads that changed colors for the various scenes. This year (1917), he provided an arch opening to blue sky. Across the back of the stage was a balustrade with a classic statue on either side.

April 24, 1918, was the opening date for the first of three *Frolics* that year. Eddie Cantor and Will Rogers offered a humorous imitation of Ziegfeld and his partner Charles Dillingham before and after leasing the Century Theatre. Rogers also impersonated Gene Buck, while Cantor did Ned Wayburn. Ben Ali Haggin contributed a beautiful tableau, "The Road to Victory," featuring women dressed to represent the Allied nations. This was just one of the show's several patriotic numbers.

On December 9, 1918, a double *Frolic* was presented for the first time. The *Ziegfeld Nine O'Clock Frolic* was followed by the *Ziegfeld Midnight Frolic*. Tickets for the two shows cost from $4.80 to $6.60. The earlier show featured Bee Palmer doing the shimmy and Bessie McCoy Davis in "The Dancing Somnambulist." Also appearing were Lillian Leitzel on her dangling rope and Lillian Lorraine singing "Tipperary Mary." The latter number included four real scrubwomen and was an audience favorite. The first show started late (9:30) and had a half-hour intermission for dancing and refreshments. When it ended at 11:00, patrons danced until the midnight show commenced.

The second show included Bert Williams, Fannie Brice in a burlesque of a vampire, Bee Palmer again, and Bird Millman in her high wire act. Although the nine o'clock show ran only a few months, the midnight show ran until August 1919, when it closed because of the Actors Equity strike.

Although only one new *Frolic* opened in 1919, and then not until October 2, the wait was worthwhile. In one of the most beautiful scenes Ziegfeld ever presented, twelve women were dressed as tropical birds with gorgeous plumes. The women paraded across the stage as Arthur Uttry sang "Beautiful Birds." The elegant Dolores was the famed white peacock. Her costume, created by Pascaud of Paris, had a ten-foot-long train consisting of sheer white embroidery with blue, green, and pink paillettes and bugle beads. When Dolores pulled the attached sequined ropes, the train was raised via pulleys to become a beautiful tail. Interestingly, Dolores's outfit was remarkably similar to the last outfit that Anna Held wore onstage, a white peacock costume with embroidery on the spread-out tail. Held wore the costume in the finale of *Follow Me!* (1916). Her costume had also been created in Paris from her sketch.

This *Frolic* contained several lovely numbers and was thought to be every bit as lavish and entertaining as the *Follies*. In fact, the "Tropical Birds" scene was so popular that it was carried over into the 1920 *Nine O'Clock Revue*. The number could easily have been a success in the *Follies* downstairs. However, according

Far left: Maurice Chevalier starred in the final *Midnight Frolic* for four weeks beginning in February 1929. Left: In "The Little Love Mill" from the 1921 *Frolic*, the Fairbanks Twins sit on the steps in front of Eleanor Griffith (the windmill).

to theater critic Robert Baral, when Gene Buck was asked why the number was never added to the *Follies,* he replied that Ziegfeld wouldn't hear of it—people might think he was trying to save money. Although Ziegfeld did not use that particular number in the *Follies,* he used similar numbers. Bird costumes recur in his shows: his very first *Follies* had the Peacock Girls, both the 1925 and 1926 revues featured beautiful bird numbers, and the 1927 *Follies* featured Claire Luce in ostrich feathers doing an "ostrich dance."

On March 8, 1920, the *Frolic* entitled "Ziegfeld Girls of 1920" opened. Notable stars included Kathlene Martyn, Fannie Brice, Allyn King, W. C. Fields, Mary Hay, Sybil Carmen, and Vanda Hoff. A Ouija board the size of a library table made funny remarks, and a blindfolded Indian princess read the thoughts of people in the audience. Dinner was served at 7:00 P.M.—before watching the show—and supper was served at 11:00.

The next edition opened on March 15, 1920. "In the Theatre" was a scene that re-created a complete auditorium on the stage. The principals, chorus, and audience watched the real audience as it came in late and got up at the wrong times. There was even a parody of a drama critic who made loud remarks.

Dancer Carl Randall was back, this time with a new partner, Andree Spinelli, who was also added to the nine o'clock show. Fannie Brice, Mary Eaton (in her only *Frolic* appearance), Frisco, Kathlene Martyn, and Charles Winninger were also cast members. Brandon Tynan did his first public imitation of theatrical producer David Belasco. Belasco was prominent on Broadway and easily recognizable by his white hair and clerical clothing, including a Roman collar. However, despite his ministerial appearance, it was rumored that he had a "casting couch" in his office. In the skit, which was written by Tynan and Gene Buck, an aspiring actress came to Belasco looking for a job. Belasco's alleged approach to casting was satirized. The skit was particularly effective because of Tynan's uncanny resemblance to Belasco.

September 2, 1920, was the date of the year's second midnight show. The "Summertime" number effectively presented women depicting a dozen sports from horseback riding, tennis, and polo to skating. Other features included performances by the following people: William and Gordon Dooley in a burlesque number, Jack Hanley juggling, John Steele singing, and the Rath Brothers performing acrobatic feats. Ben Ali Haggin had another outstanding tableau—"Le Trousseau."

February 8, 1921, marked the opening of another *Nine O'Clock Frolic,* this one featuring many dancers—the Fairbanks Twins, Princess White Deer, and Frank Harnum. But the costumes were the main attraction; they seemed to get lovelier with each scene until the stunning finale: young women engaged in winter sports in the Alps at St. Moritz.

The next evening, February 9, Ziegfeld opened yet another *Frolic.* Although it was billed as a new edition, many numbers had been carried over from the 1920 show. One new number featured Eleanor Griffith in a windmill costume accompanied by two dozen pretty Dutch maids as she sang "The Little Love Mill." A dance by the Fairbanks Twins in front of a lifelike Urban windmill concluded the scene.

A program from February 21, 1921, shows that by this date, Ziegfeld had taken the most popular numbers from both *Frolics* and combined them into one midnight show. When this production closed, the roof remained quiet for six months, until a lavish new *Midnight Frolic* opened on November 17. Will Rogers starred in the new *Frolic*; so did Leon Errol, as a tottering drunk. Carl Randall performed his acrobatic dancing wearing a derby hat. Muriel Stryker did an Oriental dance, while Mary Lewis (who later became an opera singer) sang several songs.

The presence of alcohol at the roof shows helped patrons to forget work and made them less inhibited. After the Volstead Act took effect in January 1920, the profits of the *Frolic* and similar entertainments began to decline. The sixteenth *Frolic* closed on April 9, 1922, and in 1923, the roof of the New Amsterdam Theatre was converted into a traditional 700-seat theater.

When Prohibition dampened the popularity of the *Frolic* in New York, Ziegfeld decided to take his popular show on the road. He probably felt that the lack of liquor would not be a drawback because the *Frolic* would be presented in legitimate theaters. The show that opened on January 10, 1922, at the Garrick Theatre in Philadelphia was the only *Ziegfeld Frolic* that toured and the only one never presented on the New Amsterdam roof. The *Frolic* toured for approximately four months, usually spending one week in big cities until its last stop—Chicago—where it remained about a month before closing in May.

The 1922 *Frolic* was atypical, as it used numbers and costumes from previous editions of the *Frolic*; most of the numbers originated in the 1919, 1920, or 1921 shows. Naturally a revue that toured in theaters could not provide the intimate atmosphere and audience participation that identified *Frolic* roof shows.

After a break of nearly seven years, the *Ziegfeld Midnight Frolic* reappeared on December 29, 1928. *The New York Times* reported that Ziegfeld spent $75,000 to refurbish the New Amsterdam for the *Frolic's* revival, although a financial statement indicates that the scenery, props, electrical work, and costumes totaled just over $65,000. When the redecoration was complete, nearly three hundred people could be seated. John Harkrider and Charles LeMaire designed the costumes; Joseph Urban decorated the walls and dome above the dance floor with a motif of butterflies and elephants.

The show itself featured "Stars from Ziegfeld Shows" and Paul Whiteman and his orchestra. Helen Morgan and Paul Gregory sang, and the Balloon Girls, so popular the first two seasons, were back. One review said that Eddie Cantor appeared in the opening-night show. (Later programs do not list him.)

Although this *Frolic* had no Ben Ali Haggin tableau, Haggin showed up to watch the opening-night performance. Mayor Walker and Marshall Field were also in the audience, just as in the old days. Unfortunately, the 1928 production did not capture the spirit of the earlier shows. Instead of introducing new material, it relied on many numbers from Ziegfeld's successful book shows. Dissatisfied with the show, Ziegfeld closed it around the end of January to make revisions.

The *Frolic* reopened February 6. New songs and special numbers were written by Dorothy Fields and James McHugh, with Sammy Lee directing the ensemble numbers. The newspapers mentioned fifty glorified girls, quite a few for a roof show.

On February 18, 1929, Maurice Chevalier made his American debut in the *Frolic* and became the show's star. Jesse Lasky of Paramount Studio had seen Chevalier in Paris and signed him to a five-year contract. The night after the French singer arrived in New York, a gala reception-banquet was held at the Ritz-Carlton in his honor. Flo Ziegfeld attended and the next day begged Lasky to let Chevalier sing in his show. Lasky demanded $5,000 a week. Flo agreed, and according to Lasky, his gratitude was "touching." The movie producer had not told Ziegfeld that he'd just learned Chevalier's film would be delayed at least six weeks. Instead of losing $1,500 (Chevalier's weekly salary), Paramount made $3,500 per week. Moreover, the studio got outstanding publicity—for free. Chevalier appeared in the *Frolic* for four weeks, until March 16, 1929.

The old days could not be revived, though, and neither could this midnight diversion—for long. The once-popular entertainment had lost its appeal, and on April 25, the *Frolic* closed, and the series ended permanently. That same night, Chevalier's first American film, *Innocents of Paris*, premiered in New York.

During most of its long run, however, the *Midnight Frolic* shows were an unqualified success. They were fast-paced and energetic: in some cases, performers entered and exited simultaneously or an entertainer performed in the audience between numbers. The shows emphasized escape from the drudgery of work and, for women, the isolation of home life. Patrons left the New Amsterdam feeling they had participated in the fast life available only in the city. In a continuation of a *Follies* theme, the city was a place of freedom and pleasure.

The roof, just as other cabaret-style entertainment did, let respectable people try out new values. As the barriers between men and women were being lowered, both sexes learned new life-styles. The chorus girl was a symbol of the single urban working woman. Money enabled her to lead an independent life. She symbolized the modern woman who could enjoy big-city freedom but could also attract and hold a man. The *Frolic* let her meet a variety of men. Likewise, it allowed stage-door Johnnies to meet chorus girls without creating a public scandal.

The restaurant crowd wanted women—youthful and attractive women. Chorus girls moved among the first rows of tables, close to the audience. The smiling women invited the patrons to project their fantasies upon them. Audience-participation numbers enticed male patrons to interact with the women. However, it was up to the men to take an active role. The men's role consisted of performing a task such as tossing a ring or holding knitting yarn. Since the men's actions were merely an extension of their traditional role—working and earning money—their values were not threatened. Men were quick to participate, because the chorus girls never criticized them; the men could remain in charge.

Women could enjoy the entertainment with their husbands because they did not feel threatened by the chorus girl. Most chorus girls were attractive and exciting but were not taken seriously. They were often viewed as too stupid to be a real threat. Moreover, although individual chorus girls moved among the tables, they always returned to the group. Because the chorus girls retreated, the wives felt safe and the men felt as though they controlled these beautiful women.

The *Midnight Frolic* was known not only for its beautiful women, but also for its gorgeous costumes. Some reviewers thought the costumes worn in the *Frolic* were more striking than those worn in the theater below. Charles LeMaire, who later won Academy Awards for his movie costumes, designed his first number for a *Midnight Frolic*. For both men and women, the reward and meaning of success was high-class glamour represented by expensive clothes. The costly fashions worn by women in the *Frolic* conveyed excitement, novelty, and glamour; they also signified that the women wearing the expensive frocks were ladies.

Although chorus girls were the primary focus of the *Frolic*, Ziegfeld required that all his shows contain some substance and talent. He engaged most of his big *Follies* stars (Fannie Brice, Bert Williams, W. C. Fields, Leon Errol, Ann Pennington, among them) to appear in one or more editions of the *Frolic*. Often these stars performed in both shows concurrently. Many *Follies* principals, as well as showgirls and chorus girls, appeared on the roof first before moving downstairs to the more prestigious *Follies*. In fact, Ziegfeld's most famous comedians (Eddie Cantor, Will Rogers, Joe Frisco) started in the *Frolic*.

The *Follies* and the *Midnight Frolic* were both musical revues, but the entertainment upstairs could be more innovative and daring than that downstairs. It was for the *Midnight Frolic* that Ben Ali Haggin created his first tableau. The series also contained many vaudeville acts, such as acrobats, jugglers, aerial artists, solo musicians, and animal acts (especially dogs and birds), not found in the more traditional *Follies*.

People flocked to the *Frolic* to dance, be with friends, and enjoy a funny show. One attractive aspect of the show for society people was the satire aimed at them. Will Rogers's monologues were legendary for "roasting" people in the audience. If the person mentioned wasn't present, his friends often were. Even those who weren't personally acquainted with the people being satirized could watch the subjects react.

On one occasion Eddie Cantor involved prominent patrons in his act. As Cantor described it:

This was the supper club of the Four Hundred, where menus were printed on silk. . . . Here were Mr. Ziegfeld and Billie Burke . . . with friends. . . . I whipped out a deck of cards and shuffled them. . . . Then, gravely, I approached several guests and asked if they would help me with the act. They were to stand and hold the cards high over their heads. . . . I didn't even know who the men were. I picked the first because he was so tall—William Randolph Hearst. Another was Diamond Jim Brady. A third, Charles B. Dillingham. They held up the cards, and ignoring them completely, I started to sing, "Oh How She Could Yacki, Hicki, Wicki Wacki Woo. She had the hula hula yacka bula in her walk. . . ." The men stood there holding the cards, and the audience began to howl, realizing that the cards had nothing to do with the act. . . . I'd taken a big chance; it'd worked.

For most Broadway shows, a patron sees the production once or twice but rarely a third time. The genius of the *Midnight Frolic* was that the intimacy of the setting, the audience's involvement in the show, and especially the changing acts kept bringing people back for repeat visits. The changes not only attracted repeat customers but also allowed Ziegfeld to cater to the tastes of his backers and to try out new talent.

A subtle but significant secondary gain from the *Frolic*'s popularity with New York's beautiful people is that it gave Ziegfeld direct, informal access to people who could back his shows. It is likely that Ziegfeld was able to break away from Abe Erlanger's financial and professional influence only after the *Frolic* opened and Ziegfeld cultivated friendships that offered him the luxury of independent "angels."

While many people have dismissed the *Midnight Frolic* as frivolous nightclub fare, it was definitely an important sidelight in Ziegfeld's career. The shows were a major draw for wealthy theatergoers and demonstrated how broad Ziegfeld's talents were in providing appealing entertainment.

Above: Ned Wayburn of the "Follies" baseball team talks to Raymond Hitchcock of the "Hitchy-Koo" team. The baseball teams played each other twice in 1917; money raised from the games was used to buy tobacco for American soldiers. Wayburn staged six editions of the *Follies* and twelve editions of *Frolic*. Hitchcock was in the 1921 *Follies*. Above middle: This shot of Mary and Joe Urban on camels was taken in February 1931. Urban worked for Ziegfeld from 1914 until 1931. Above right: Billie Burke (center) putting her okay on scenes from her 1915 movie *Peggy*

CHAPTER 7

❖

A COMPANY OF ARTISTS

❖

By 1915, Ziegfeld was beginning to be recognized as one of Broadway's great producers. While he was busy solidifying his reputation, Billie was on the road for her marathon tour, an experience that severely strained her relationship with Frohman. Then tragedy struck: a German submarine sank the *Lusitania* on May 7, 1915, taking Frohman to his death. The man who had launched her career and had been her mentor for more than a decade was gone, with the difficulties of their relationship left unresolved.

Billie was so devastated after Flo gave her the news that she faltered onstage and then collapsed in the wings. Charles Frohman, for all his peculiar possessiveness, occupied a special place in Billie's heart.

Ten days later, on May 17, 1915, Dr. Ziegfeld and Rosalie celebrated their fiftieth wedding anniversary. The event prompted a large family gala in Chicago, replete with a photograph of the elder Ziegfelds wearing crowns. Less than one year later, in April 1916, Dr. Ziegfeld retired to the position of President Emeritus at Chicago Musical College, after nearly forty-nine years as its leader. Clearly, the Ziegfeld family exhibited a strong sense of loyalty that served Flo well, given the transience that prevailed on Broadway.

The years 1915 and 1916 proved to be a turning point in Ziegfeld's career as well, as he developed his most significant professional relationships—with Gene Buck, Joseph Urban, Ned Wayburn, and major stars, including Will Rogers and Eddie Cantor. Although most of these men had been hired for the *Midnight Frolic*, it was the *Follies* that they helped raise to a nearly perfect revue form.

Joseph Urban's daughter, Gretl, says that when Ziegfeld and her father first met, Urban told Ziegfeld he would never compromise his artistic standards or "demean himself to work on a 'girlie' show. Flo put a check for $10,000 on the table and said: 'This is a retainer with the promise that I will never interfere with your work or ask you to lower your standards. It is the high caliber of your work I want.' He remained true to his word and, incidentally, his check on this occasion did not bounce."

Urban's work on the *Ziegfeld Follies of 1915* transformed the series and Broadway. Gretl Urban said

Left: In this scene from the 1915 *Follies*, each woman represented a different month of the year. Right: Lucille, or Lady Duff-Gordon, was one of several distinguished designers who created costumes for Ziegfeld's shows. She worked for Ziegfeld from 1915 to 1921, during which time she designed gowns for seven *Follies*, many editions of the *Frolic*, and three of his other shows.

of her father's settings: "They hardly surprised us, but the gasp of the audience, which had never seen anything like them, was startling." Ziegfeld, she added, "never allowed opulence to satiate. If, for example, one or all of the *Follies* girls appear with bosoms artistically bare, it is only for a fleeting second. Where other producers present, Ziegfeld suggests. . . . He steers a shrewd course of bringing sophistication and innocence into sudden, violent, and hence effective collision."

The 1915 show must have been a dandy during the writing phase: three of Ziegfeld's authors—Rennold Wolf, Channing Pollock, and J. P. McEvoy—later published amusing tales about the show's evolution. Wolf commented on how chaotic Ziegfeld's creative process was. He acknowledged the dominance of Ziegfeld's contribution ("The *Follies* is 90 percent Ziegfeld"), but then quickly revealed how exasperating the "Ziegfeld" process could be. Ziegfeld believed that the performers were the key to a successful revue and that the author was present to extract as much as possible from the star. With this in mind, Ziegfeld selected his cast. He would not let the authors begin work until he determined who the principals were, so, according to Wolf, Ziegfeld kept "the authors in the air until the final minute."

The 1915 *Follies* was originally tailored to Annette Kellerman's talents. Just one week before the tryout opening, Kellerman concluded that Ziegfeld had not done justice to her talent. When she bolted the show, Ziegfeld moved Ina Claire to the top spot. Wolf's account dripped with sarcasm when he noted that "obviously, none of the scenes designed for Miss Kellerman would do for Miss Claire. The pond scene was elided, the Roman bath became a Turkish harem, and so on. Three days before the Atlantic City opening Mr. Ziegfeld came frantically to the authors . . . and begged them to write a good song for Miss Claire. . . . The song was written that afternoon."

During the week the show was in Atlantic City, it was cut from four hours to two. The following Sunday, the cast rehearsed all night in preparation for the Monday evening New York premiere.

Channing Pollock offered his own horror tales about scene changes. For a skit that featured Bert Williams and Leon Errol, the authors submitted thirteen drafts before Ziegfeld changed the scene from a submarine to a zeppelin. The zeppelin scene was beautiful and extravagant, but after a dozen rehearsals and revisions, Ziegfeld discarded it. Pollock was also surprised that at the first rehearsal, half of the principals had still not been hired. Moreover, although he and Wolf wrote the show and went to every rehearsal, when the *Follies* opened in Atlantic City, neither man had heard or seen three-quarters of the performance!

J. P. McEvoy provides insight into Ziegfeld's feelings about the chorus as well as the humor. He claimed that Ziegfeld would get up during the middle of a comedy scene and say, "That's enough. Bring on the girls." He would walk up the aisle muttering, "'I can't stand these comics.' When he laughed, he

Eddie Cantor was in several editions of the *Midnight Frolic* beginning in 1916 and was in *Kid Boots, Whoopee,* and five editions of the *Follies*. His comic songs interspersed with witty comments were always popular with audiences.

October 25-1916

Irving Berlin

"YOU'VE GOT YOUR MOTHER'S BIG BLUE EYES".

WATERSON, BERLIN and SNYDER CO., Strand Theatre Bldg, Broadway at 47th St, New York

You've got your Mother's big blue eyes - You'll have your Mother's teeth of

Pearl'- I must confess you are the image of your Ma - From your

Toes to your nose to your curls.- The way you love your Daddy shows-You're a just

what your Mother knows - And when you grow to be a great big lady like your

Daddy wants you to - If you're half the lady that your Mother is - - - -

I'll be mighty proud of you - - - .

Left: Irving Berlin composed this song in honor of Patricia Ziegfeld's birth. Right: Marion Davies as she looked in 1916 when she worked for Ziegfeld. Better known for her movies and her liaison with William R. Hearst, she started her career as a dancer.

laughed at the oldest jokes and the most primitive business. . . . In dress rehearsal, the orchestra could play sour, drops could foul, the scenery could fall, the lines could go flat, and Ziggy would never bat an eye, but if fifty girls came on the stage and one girl had her hat on crooked, he would stop the performance."

Ziegfeld did concentrate more overtly on the women, perhaps because he was simply more interested in how he could enhance their glamour. To suggest, however, that he did not consider the comedians important is a mistake. Hyperbole about Ziegfeld's attitude toward comedians distorts one's perspective on what role comedy actually played in the *Follies*. Whatever his reasons for dismissing comedians impatiently during rehearsals, he always gave comedy a place of honor during the actual performance.

Those who contend that he slighted comedians must consider Ziegfeld's public statements about comedy in his shows. In a 1915 newspaper feature, he explained the success of the *Follies* this way: '"It is very simple,' said Ziegfeld. 'I make the production as nearly perfect as possible and I keep it that way. I believe in plenty of comedy and I get the best comedians there are, keeping them as long as I can.'"

Despite the chaos that Wolf and McEvoy described, which apparently was typical of most shows in the series, the *Ziegfeld Follies of 1915* made its debut as scheduled, on June 21. The production showcased Joseph Urban's spectacular settings in twenty-one different scenes. The elaborate sets would once have been considered too good for musical comedy, but they were central to the style of Ziegfeld's shows.

Likewise, Ziegfeld's costumes enhanced the act because he made them integral to the show's content. In addition to Cora McGeachy, Ziegfeld used costume designers Tappe, Charles & Jack, and Lucille (Lady Duff-Gordon). Lucille's beautiful, diaphanous costumes made quite a hit in her debut *Follies,* and she soon became Ziegfeld's principal designer.

The Century Theatre, co-managed for a time by Ziegfeld and Charles Dillingham, was the site of the hit *The Century Girl* (1916).

The comedy had begun to improve as soon as Bert Williams came on the scene. This year, in addition to Williams, Leon Errol, and Fannie Brice, Ziegfeld presented W. C. Fields. George White, who in 1919 would begin producing his own musical revue, the *Scandals,* was a dancer in this year's show.

The 1915 show marked the beginning of what many theater historians refer to as the mastery phase of the *Follies.* There had been previous references to extravagance, but now reviewers called this edition the series's "best show ever," an accolade that was repeated for many years to come.

The *Follies* broke a record at the New Amsterdam Theatre, doing nearly $23,000 worth of business the first week. Including receipts from the *Midnight Frolic,* the theater took in $30,000. *Variety* said ticket agencies were asking $8 for a seat in the first five rows even though they had paid the box office $2.50 or less.

Occasionally Ziegfeld used a motion-picture sequence in a scene. One time thirty cast members had to go to a New Jersey studio to film one. Everyone was to leave on a 7:30 A.M. bus. For theater people, this was the middle of the night. At 7:30 only one chorus girl had arrived. Her early rising was so unusual that the hotel clerk thought she must be ill. Gene Buck was surprised to find the subways running. Dave Stamper thought it would still be dark at 7:30 A.M., and Louis Hirsch said he didn't realize so many people stayed up all night! The troupe finally left for New Jersey—but not until after nine o'clock.

Slightly more than two months after Charles Frohman died, on the very day that her tour ended, Billie signed a lucrative movie deal (July 13, 1915), thereby terminating her relationship with Frohman's theatrical management organization, which had deteriorated rapidly after his death. No one had any doubts about who would manage her—Ziegfeld, of course. Burke agreed to do a movie of *Peggy.* Producer Thomas Ince treated her like visiting royalty when she arrived in California, providing her with access to a 123-foot yacht and a wonderful bungalow on Catalina Island. She was handsomely paid for five weeks—$40,000.

The film industry had been developing slowly, but, as Ince's offer suggests, it began to take off as a business about this time. In fact, Burke's contract for *Peggy* was a landmark in screen history because she was the first big-name, legitimate-stage actress to work in Hollywood and the first to command a star's salary. Another indication of the industry's growth developed within Ziegfeld's own ranks: between January and September 1914, Klaw and Erlanger had produced twenty-five films. Ziegfeld's close association with the two producers makes it certain that he knew what they were doing.

After Burke completed *Peggy,* she was offered a three-year contract worth $540,000, but she decided to return to New York to be with Flo. She signed up instead to do *Gloria's Romance* on location in Florida. For this deal, Ziegfeld got for Billie a fee of from $130,000 to $150,000, the most any actress had been paid for a film to that point. Reports had Flo insisting on a host of "perks" for Billie that set the standard for Hollywood stars to this day: "real mahogany on the sets," twenty costume changes, a Rolls-Royce, Cartier jewels, and the right, when shooting in New York, to live at home and avoid long hours.

The shooting on *Gloria's Romance* was done in late 1915 and early 1916. While on location, Billie and Flo became enamored of Palm Beach. The Ziegfelds began vacationing in Florida, where they soon met the Edward Stotesburys, the Gurnee Munns, Leonard Replogle, John Hayes Hammonds, the Anthony Biddles, and Edward and Marjorie Hutton, among others. Initially, many of their introductions to Palm Beach society came through Ziegfeld's long-standing friendship with fellow producer Charles Dillingham.

Ziegfeld opened 1916 by presenting the third in the *Ziegfeld Midnight Frolic* series (January 24). This show introduced Eddie Cantor, one of the most important actors in Ziegfeld's career and his personal life. Cantor developed an enormous respect for Ziegfeld, whom he described in glowing terms: "Others gave shows, he gave productions. He was everywhere. He hired actors, okayed songs, selected fabrics, created the ideas for costumes and scenery, found the top people to execute those designs, was an expert on lighting. I watched him, but did not know him. His was a reserve that I, with all my audacity, dared not penetrate." Cantor felt that he had been fortunate to have worked with the two giants of taste in New York and Hollywood: Flo Ziegfeld and Samuel Goldwyn. He had not suffered "through little people without taste."

Ziegfeld also thought highly of Cantor's professional talent; over the years, he gave this actor more latitude and more personal credit than any other person ever received in a Ziegfeld show. Ziegfeld would allow Cantor to try out humor even if he did not see its potential. If it worked, he would let him keep it.

Cantor and Ziegfeld's relationship soon became more than a professional association. Ziegfeld took the diminutive younger man under his wing and began treating him like a son. They had a complicated and "peculiar love-hate relationship," said Cantor's daughter Marilyn. They were genuinely devoted to one another but felt compelled to squabble as a competitive father and son might. Although Cantor's politics clashed with Ziegfeld's at times, the actor's intense commitment to his craft matched the producer's.

Late February of 1916 found the Ziegfelds back in Palm Beach, this time registered at the posh Royal Poinciana Hotel. Frequently they went down in private railroad cars loaned by friends and backers, particularly Leonard Replogle of steel fame.

About this time, Ziegfeld and Charles Dillingham became closer—first as friends in Palm Beach and then as colleagues. While competition on Broadway was fierce, Dillingham and Ziegfeld managed to maintain a civil relationship. That spring, the friendship prompted Ziegfeld and Dillingham to form a production partnership. Both sought financial and artistic independence, particularly Ziegfeld. The two men persuaded Otto Kahn and Reginald Vanderbilt to form the Century Theatre Amusement Corporation, and then leased the theater from the corporation and shared profits fifty-fifty. They were to take possession of the theater on July 1 and to present the first show in October. The two men had grand schemes. Ziegfeld, for example, tried to get ballet dancers Waslav Nijinsky and Tamara Karsavina for the opening.

Ziegfeld was also working on a new *Frolic* and attending to *Follies* details. It would be many years before the "Follies" title would become a central professional issue, but as early as 1916 Ziegfeld sued a burlesque group to prevent its use of the copyrighted title. When the producers of a burlesque show called *The Big Revue* changed the name to *The Follies of 1916,* Ziegfeld took action and won an infringement case.

When Ziegfeld produced the *Follies of 1916,* he did not need to resort to any of his legendary publicity stunts; newspaper features materialized without his asking. Production figures indicate that Ziegfeld did not hold back anything, spending almost $16,000 for Urban's scenery and nearly $28,000 on costumes.

Stars such as Fannie Brice, W. C. Fields, and Bert Williams were back, as were Ina Claire and Justine Johnstone. Marion Davies, Frances White, Carl Randall, and Bernard Granville were also featured performers. Bird Millman, who became a regular in the *Midnight Frolic,* made her only *Follies* appearance in 1916. Will Rogers also made his *Follies* debut this year, although he was not in the cast opening night. Rogers was already in the *Midnight Frolic*: he would twirl a lariat, starting with a tiny loop and making it larger and larger, all the while jumping in and out of it; occasionally he roped a friend in the audience.

Ziegfeld had asked Rogers to join the *Follies* in 1916, but Mrs. Rogers talked her husband out of it. Joining the *Follies* meant Will would have to tour with the show, and Mrs. Rogers did not feel the salary was good enough to take him away from his family: she persuaded Will to hold out for $500 per week (he was earning about $400). On opening night Rogers and his wife sat through the long show; he became irritated because he thought that he had missed his big break. His wife was also having second thoughts about passing up the *Follies.* She believed Will's act would have provided a good contrast to all the heavy numbers. They were both miserable as they returned to their Forest Hills home.

A few days later, Ziegfeld phoned Rogers and asked him to appear in the *Follies* that night. Rogers did not hesitate this time, and his act was a hit, but Ziegfeld said nothing about salary. Since Rogers was still in the *Frolic,* he was doing two shows a night and two matinees a week at his old salary. This continued for weeks. But, when it was time for the *Follies* to go on tour, Ziegfeld went to Rogers's dressing room and offered him a two-year contract for $600 a week the first year and $750 a week the second year.

After the 1916 *Follies* opened, Ziegfeld said that the key to his success lay in the fact that he never stopped working: "As soon as one is out of the way I begin making plans for the next, and I never get out of touch with the current edition. About once every two weeks . . . I visit it, and the company never knows when I am coming. That keeps them up to the mark and a performance in San Francisco or Detroit is just as good as one in New York." He also noted that he kept refining the show after the opening: "Can't predict what will draw laughs or what song will be a hit. That's why the show is better after three weeks than it was at opening. We watch audience response and adapt [the] show accordingly."

Another of his comments also helps explain why he had such good luck with keeping high-caliber casts. He noted that everyone wanted to be featured. "It requires the utmost tact and diplomacy to make each feel she is the most talented even if she has to go to the back row for some of the numbers."

Ten days after the 1916 *Follies* opened, the strain of all the activity showed. A news report said that Ziegfeld suffered a nervous breakdown but that ten days' rest would allow him to recover.

During the fall of 1916, Anna Held returned to Broadway with Ziegfeld's rivals the Shuberts in a successful production called *Follow Me!* that played until January 1918, when she became ill. That same year, she starred in a film entitled *Madame La President* (Morosco). The new season also brought another *Ziegfeld Midnight Frolic* (October 2), which was by now well established.

The highlight of the 1916 season occurred on October 23, when Flo's daughter was born in the Hotel Ansonia. The baby was originally named Florenz Patricia Burke Ziegfeld. However, she was christened Patricia Burke Ziegfeld and from that point on the family referred to her as Patty. Ziegfeld may have had trouble limiting his attention to one woman at a time, but he had no such difficulty when it came to little Patty. The worldly, sophisticated Flo Ziegfeld became a man possessed by his devotion to this child. A magazine feature even reported that on her birth he sent her a long telegram.

When Patty was born, Ziegfeld and Irving Berlin were rehearsing a revue called *The Century Girl*. Berlin, the first non-family member to see Patty, wrote a song for her: "You've Got Your Mother's Big Blue Eyes." Charles Dillingham sent the newborn two tickets to the Hippodrome, which he managed for years.

Ziegfeld's personal life had taken a rich but complicated turn when Patty was born. Her arrival prompted the Ziegfelds to leave the Hotel Ansonia for permanent residence at Burkeley Crest.

Ziegfeld lavished time and money on *The Century Girl*. He included music by Irving Berlin and Victor Herbert, hired Max Hoffmann to conduct the orchestra, commissioned costumes from Lucille, and brought in many big-name actors such as Leon Errol, Elsie Janis, Sam Bernard, and Marie Dressler. The show was the last revue in the United States to take its name from the theater in which it played. *The Century Girl* was strictly a musical entertainment and did not have a plot. Its big production numbers and vaudeville acts were enhanced by Joseph Urban's scenery. Despite the theater's location near Columbus Circle, far from the Forty-second Street theater district, the show ran for two hundred performances.

When Flo Ziegfeld and Charles Dillingham assumed the lease of the Century Theatre, they hired Urban to design the sets and redecorate the roof. Ziegfeld wanted lobby drawings to attract crowds to the theater. Urban suggested that fellow Austrian artist Raphael Kirchner be hired to help. Kirchner painted ten 47 x 23" panels for the lobby. Ziegfeld showgirls modeled for the paintings, which were titled "Les Amours de Pierrot." Kirchner also painted an eleventh picture in which Pierrot is central. All eleven drawings were printed in *The Century Girl* program.

In an article that Ziegfeld wrote for *Theatre Magazine,* he said the general public mistakenly thought producers got rich on their shows because they took in nightly receipts and had only the cast's salaries to pay. To document the public's misperception, Ziegfeld detailed his expenses for *The Century Girl,* which included props costing between $12,000 and $15,000 and costumes costing $135,000 (excluding custom-made shoes at $12–$15 per pair). The lowest salary paid a performer was $25 a week, the average showgirls were receiving $40–$50 per week, and the top showgirls, $75 a week. Salaries for cast members with parts ranged from $100 to $2,000 a week. Additionally, Ziegfeld said, there were about 250 employees who never appeared onstage—the orchestra, publicity people, artists, ushers, stagehands, and many others.

Ziegfeld had always kept himself busy, but as the *Follies* and the *Frolic* matured and he created his own theater management company, his work pace became almost frenetic. Though he had succeeded magnificently, he was never able to settle into a steady routine. He was doing well enough financially that he could have said, "I'll do just one production each year," but by now, people were approaching him with opportunities, and he was not willing to say, "Enough. I'll pass." In this respect he embodied the American Dream. He had a vision of what he wanted, and the passion that drove him would not let him rest. At times, he seemed to take on new responsibilities simply because he welcomed the challenges.

Success had not come without setbacks, but the positive experiences solidly outnumbered the negative. Ziegfeld was confident that money and opportunity would always be available. He had no reason to sense the change that was coming in the theatrical world.

Statement

Ziegfeld Follies, Inc.   Aug. 31st, 1917.

1916-1917

Total Net Earnings Follies of 1916 & Dance de Follies
for 1916-1917 as per Statement rendered   160708 34

Cash on a/c to F. Ziegfeld Jr.   41750
    "   "   " " Klaw & Erlanger   41750
                                                            83500

Undivided Balance 1916-1917   77208 24

CHAPTER 8

❖

OVER HERE

❖

Above: Bessie McCoy Davis was a hit in *Miss 1917* when she sang "Man in the Moon" while sitting in a moon sculpture designed by Joseph Urban. When the show flopped, the number was added to the 1918 *Frolic*. Above right: A partial page in the *Ziegfeld Follies* ledger for August 1917 indicates that the revue series was incorporated by this time.

As Ziegfeld turned fifty and achieved maturity as a theatrical producer, he took on more and more professional commitments, so that between 1917 and 1919, he was involved in twelve productions. Several failed; nevertheless, given the quality of every Ziegfeld show and the agony he put himself through, the quantity of offerings suggests that Ziegfeld was driven by more than financial necessity.

He opened the year with a venture patterned after the *Ziegfeld Midnight Frolic*. Along with Charlie Dillingham, Ziegfeld presented the *Midnight Revue* on the roof of the Century Theatre. The show debuted in the Century's Cocoanut Grove on January 18, 1917, and was titled "Dance and Grow Thin." Apparently patrons were supposed to dine and watch the entertainment and then dance off the calories they had consumed. Two dishes on the menu were named after Ziegfeld and one after Dillingham. Unfortunately, since the tables were not terraced, only patrons at the choice tables could see the show. Although the weight of everyone dancing caused the dance floor to vibrate, the orchestra played until 4:00 A.M. The *Midnight Revue* was the only revue/floor show that Ziegfeld and Dillingham presented together.

Comedians Leon Errol and Joe Jackson, singers Van and Schenck, and dancer Gertrude Hoffmann were principal attractions. Instead of Balloon Girls, the Cocoanut Grove had twelve young women disguised as mailboxes who sang a request when patrons dropped letters into them.

In the spate of publicity that now regularly attended a Ziegfeld opening, one of Ziegfeld's reported one-liners about his partner Dillingham illustrates his sense of humor. According to a story in *The New York Telegraph*, Dillingham was so solicitous of his guests at a social gathering that "Mr. Ziegfeld was finally moved to remark: 'Dillingham is the best head waiter I ever had.'"

For several years after Patty's birth, Billie began taking fewer stage roles, but she continued doing films because they required less time. She signed a contract with Famous Players–Lasky for *The Mysterious Miss*

Left: Scene from *The Rescuing Angel* starring Billie Burke (1917).
Right: Billie Burke with daughter, Patricia Burke Ziegfeld

Terry, which was released in 1917. Burke made fourteen films between 1917 and 1921.

Domestic life remained complicated and far more public than any ordinary person would have liked. Ziegfeld was involved not only with Olive Thomas but also with her friend Anna Daly. Yet Ziegfeld steadfastly declined to divorce Billie Burke. This, of course, made Thomas unhappy. Little is known about the private aspect of their relationship, except that Ziegfeld seemed to be attracted by Thomas's volatile temperament. Just when the soap opera appeared to have played itself out, the affair took an interesting twist: Thomas left the *Follies* and married Jack Pickford in May 1917. Ziegfeld was reported to be devastated initially and then, in turn, angry at the news.

The 1917 run of the *Follies* was a critical success. The Chicago review from Percy Hammond demonstrates that Ziegfeld had finally succeeded in his hometown: "They [the *Follies*] sailed into the Illinois last night, Youth at the helm, as usual, and Beauty at the prow, the smartest of the body shows, charming the eye into a wanton posture, and doing something to please and little to affront."

In keeping with past themes of viewing the follies of humankind, a young man bet his future father-in-law that he could show him more in one night in New York than was written in the *Arabian Nights*. The production opened and closed with a lavish Arabian scene; comedy sketches, dances and other specialty acts, as well as the usual beauty parades, provided the material in between. A lesser theme—the war in Europe—surfaced in several patriotic numbers. The 1917 edition of the *Follies* was praised not for its substance but for its sensuous beauty.

A woman representing a tree wears real leaves in the elaborate "Falling Leaves" scene from *Miss 1917*.

While this edition eventually became very healthy financially (estimated net profit was $200,000), the books showed the *Follies* still in a deficit on August 31, 1917, because of an unpaid balance of $65,206.54 from the 1916–17 season. At a time when the average musical was costing $20,000 to $30,000, Ziegfeld invested much more heavily, as the following ledger entries indicate: equipment—$95,336.09; Urban sets—$14,878.08; costumes—$33,389.85 ($17,172.85 to Schneider-Anderson Costume and $16,217 to Lucille). This total on just three staple elements exceeded $140,000.

With the 1917 *Follies*, Ziegfeld made another significant advance, again persuading composer Victor Herbert to work for him. The press noted the achievement with this comment: "A quiet but compelling persuasiveness is a quality that reveals Ziegfeld . . . as a crafty diplomat. Who else could have talked Victor Herbert, a musical producer on his own account, in to composing a soul-stirring finale?"

Unlike Herbert, A. C. Johnston, the official *Follies* photographer, was unknown when Ziegfeld hired him in 1917. Later, he achieved international fame for his photographs of Ziegfeld stars and showgirls.

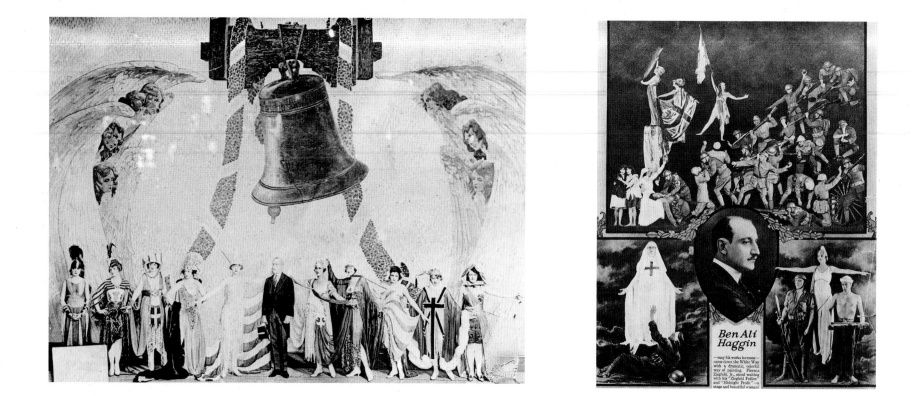

Above: Four comedians from the 1918 *Follies*—W. C. Fields (l), Will Rogers, Eddie Cantor, and Harry Kelly—with Lillian Lorraine. Top left: The patriotic finale to Act One in the *Follies of 1917* included women representing allied countries. Here the women and Walter Catlett (the president) stand before a curtain showing the Liberty Bell.

By October, less than twelve months after Patty's birth, Billie was restless enough to sign on for a production of *Rescuing Angel*. Angela, the main character (Burke's role), was portrayed as maddeningly indecisive about which rich man to marry while pursuing an altruistic goal: restoring her father to financial security after he lost his fortune. The audience probably had difficulty knowing how to react, because the script required that theatergoers identify with a woman who was charmingly cruel to men who were trying to help her. *Rescuing Angel* folded after only three weeks. Although Ziegfeld was listed as co-producer, his role in its creation is not readily evident, except for an indication that he objected to Billie getting involved.

Ziegfeld finished up 1917 with two more revue productions: *Miss 1917* and another *Midnight Frolic*. *Miss 1917* was planned as a successor to *The Century Girl,* but it did not draw the crowds, in spite of a large and well-known cast, beautiful sets, and music by Jerome Kern and Victor Herbert. Reviews of the opening-night performance were generally good, although cuts were suggested. The *New York Evening Post* called *Miss 1917* the "greatest triumph of the Century Theatre," while the *Evening Sun* praised the "gorgeous and elaborate" settings and the "amusing and charming" production. And the *New York Tribune* commented that the show was the best of its kind on Broadway and that all revues should be like *Miss 1917*.

But critical praise could not sustain *Miss 1917*; it lasted only six weeks. A big factor in the poor audience turnout was the Century Theatre's location. Situated between Sixty-second and Sixty-third streets on Central Park West, it was more than fifteen blocks north of the theater district.

Despite their best effort, the Ziegfeld and Dillingham partnership at the Century Theatre failed. Ziegfeld chafed at his relationship with Erlanger, but he still needed an astute financial adviser if he were to succeed. Unfortunately, Dillingham was not his man. By March, the Century Amusement Corporation filed for bankruptcy, showing debts of more than $350,000 and "assets of only $63,871."

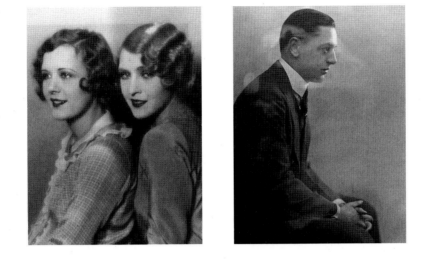

Left: In 1918, Ben Ali Haggin designed the tableau "Forward, Allies!" (upper photo) for the *Follies*. He then used some of the same women for "Patriotic Pictures" in the *Frolic*. Pauline Hall (lower left) was "The Spirit of the Red Cross," and Dolores (lower right) was "America."

From left: Marilyn Miller (left) and close friend Mary Eaton. Ziegfeld groomed Eaton to replace Miller in the *Follies* so Miller could move on to musical comedy roles. Miller was in the *Follies* for two years. Frank Carter was a principal singer in the *Midnight Frolic* (1917 and 1918) and in the *Ziegfeld Follies of 1918*. When he married Marilyn Miller in 1919, he was about thirty-one and she was not quite twenty. Carter's career was really taking off when he died in 1920. This photograph of showgirl Catherine Moylan is typical of Alfred Cheney Johnston's work.

While Ziegfeld was not functioning independently, he was definitely emerging as the dominant partner in the *Follies* portion of the effort. Sometime between May of 1918 and the fall of 1919, the Klaw and Erlanger partnership deteriorated significantly. Little public information surfaced about the reasons for the breakup. Erlanger eventually fired Joseph Klaw, the senior partner's son, possibly because the younger Klaw questioned many of Erlanger's expenses. One report suggests that Erlanger, who was driven by an almost obsessive work ethic, became impatient with the fact that Klaw took time to relax in Europe and elsewhere, without worrying too much about how his absence would affect the organization. Ziegfeld's perfectionist tendencies probably placed additional stress on the arrangement.

On June 18, the *Ziegfeld Follies of 1918* opened at the New Amsterdam Theatre. George Gershwin was the rehearsal pianist and Eddie Cantor appeared without blackface for the first time. Bert Williams was not in this edition, only the second *Follies* since 1910 in which he did not appear. Fannie Brice was also absent. Lillian Lorraine, once *the* star of the *Follies*, made her last appearance (although she appeared in later *Frolics*). Ann Pennington, Dolores, the Fairbanks Twins, Will Rogers, W. C. Fields, Frank Carter, Kay Laurell, and Savoy and Brennan were all present. Rising star Marilyn Miller made her debut with Ziegfeld.

Picking up from the 1917 *Follies* and *Frolic*, this show had a heavy concentration of patriotic numbers. The United States had been in the war for over a year, and military subjects provided a universal and popular topic. While the war was a recurrent theme in the show, there was no plot.

Estimates on the cost of mounting the *Ziegfeld Follies of 1918* ranged from $110,000 to $140,000 with a weekly payroll of $20,000. Cast salaries were just under $12,000 per week and rent was $1,600 weekly.

By 1918, hated theatrical competitors flourished and the film industry had come into its own. After the 1918 *Follies*, Ann Pennington went to work for George White in his *Scandals*; she did not return to the *Follies* until 1923. Ziegfeld was not overjoyed by what he perceived as double treachery: White, who had previously danced in the *Follies*, had not only established a competing revue but then compounded his "sin" by stealing one of Ziegfeld's most popular stars. In September 1918, Ziegfeld received a more severe jolt when Will Rogers signed on with Sam Goldwyn. These two instances of "desertion" evoked much public spleen from the producer; they were, however, just the beginning of what would become a hemorrhage.

Ziegfeld was also feeling beleaguered and more than slightly outraged over the increasingly brazen theater-ticket speculators. Midway through 1918, Ziegfeld announced a "war" on the scoundrels who were profiteering at the expense of poor theatergoers. He allowed *Follies* tickets to be sold only at the box office.

The situation escalated to yet another level when Ziegfeld, Erlanger, Klaw, and Dillingham formed an alliance against the ticket speculators. Few others joined them. Broadway producers became involved in protracted disputes about how to handle the common enemy. This brouhaha, persisting for more than a decade, prompted lawsuits, much publicity, and endless rancor.

Unlike ticket agencies today, which are content to add $2 to $5 to the price of a $30 to $50 ticket, speculators in the 1920s sometimes tripled a ticket's price. The producers' most fundamental fear was that the high costs would inhibit ticket sales, but they also worried that audiences might believe that the producers themselves were to blame for the situation. Ziegfeld and some other producers felt a moral outrage on behalf of theatergoers. Another issue was that since speculators were obtaining prime seats, producers would be unable to provide seats for critics, backers, and celebrities. Of course, they may also have wanted to share in the speculators' profits. A final concern, never mentioned publicly, was that mob loan sharks were involved. This association could have tainted the theater business, which had always struggled with reproaches from conservatives. In sum, the producers were unanimous in their desire to control the problem but, as always, incapable of reaching a consensus about how to accomplish the goal.

Around the same time, Ziegfeld, Klaw, Erlanger, and Dillingham announced a new alliance: to produce plays and manage stars on a large scale, the first of whom was to be Raymond Hitchcock and his *Hitchy-Koo* series beginning on September 2, 1918. Hitchcock had produced *Hitchy-Koo of 1918* independently and had opened the show on June 7, 1918, at the Globe Theatre. The revue was scheduled to close on August 3, after which it would come under the direction of the above-mentioned producers. Ned Wayburn was enlisted to restage the show for its tour, and Dillingham hired dancer Jack Donahue for the cast.

Not long after he signed her as an ingenue for the *Follies,* Ziegfeld fell in love with Marilyn Miller. Still in her teens, she had a Jazz Age version of charisma that transcended her talent and beauty. The nature of their relationship is not clear. It seems that Miller was not emotionally attached to Ziegfeld, since she soon married Frank Carter. She must have walked a fine line to keep Ziegfeld's attention. Miller developed a serious drinking problem following Carter's death a year after they married, and she was rude and cruel to Ziegfeld at times. Yet something elusive held him in the relationship that inflicted so much public humiliation over the years. Despite all these personal problems, Ziegfeld employed Miller in his shows. How much his own feelings for her played into this decision we will never know. He did, however, indicate that at least part of his reason for keeping her was just good business: her enormous talent was a big draw.

During the summer of 1918, Ziegfeld's sorrows over other women worsened. Even though he and

Anna Held had parted on less than amicable terms, Flo did not harbor bad feelings about her. In fact, when the papers announced in late May 1918 that she was dying from myeloma, Ziegfeld was reported to be quite upset. He could not bring himself to visit her, however.

Medical explanations of her illness were bizarre. One physician attributed the myeloma to tight lacing. This doctor had, the accounts said, warned her fifteen years ago that if she did not stop lacing herself so tightly she would pay the penalty. Another report suggested that Held's present illness "was superinduced by her hard work on behalf of American soldiers."

Held died August 12, 1918, at age forty-five. Her funeral at the Campbell Funeral Chapel and the High Mass at Saint Patrick's Cathedral attracted "a cortège of thousands." Held was immensely popular with the American and French people for her unstinting efforts during the war. Ziegfeld seems to have had a hand in arranging her grand exit, but as was his practice, he did not attend the funeral himself.

Held had fared well over the years, despite marrying two men whose gambling had threatened her financial security. Her American estate was valued for probate purposes at $160,220.20; the French appraisal shows substantial property that does not appear in the American accounting. Held would probably have had no financial worries, because the estate, in today's terms, was worth several million dollars.

Late in the year Ziegfeld produced an ill-conceived book show, *By Pigeon Post*, one of his few nonmusical shows that did not feature Billie Burke. Although the production had a capable cast, the story was indistinguishable from all the other war stories on Broadway; it ran for only twenty-four performances.

Meanwhile demand for his rooftop entertainment had grown so significantly that Ziegfeld added the *Ziegfeld Nine O'Clock Frolic*. This show and the new *Midnight Frolic* premiered on December 9.

Ziegfeld was now approaching the apex of his career. By this time, the *Follies* was superbly honed as a theatrical genre, and actors competed keenly for roles in his shows. "To be in a Ziegfeld production," said Dana O'Connell, one of his former dancers, "was to have reached the top. If I said, 'I worked for Ziegfeld,' doors opened and people treated me differently."

Ziegfeld had his foibles, and there certainly were people who hated him, but actors knew him to be a generous employer who treated them fairly, never indulging in the cost cutting measures common when a show folded. Performers who worked for him still talk about the sense of "family" among cast members. Additionally, the excitement then pervading Broadway made entertainers believe anything was possible, particularly if they had been lucky enough to land a job with Ziegfeld. Audiences sensed their optimism.

Little did they know how abruptly that sense of "family" could disappear.

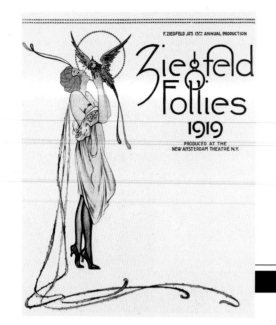

Left: *Follies* program cover. Right: Billie Dove first worked for Ziegfeld in the 1919 *Follies*; she eventually left Broadway and became a leading silent-film actress.

❖

CHAPTER 9

LIGHTNIN' STRIKES

❖

Cast members gave Ziegfeld this loving cup in 1919.

The year 1919 was a watershed for Ziegfeld and other theater people. The end of World War I in November 1918 brought pervasive optimism. Producers thought 1919 would be Broadway's best year ever financially. With the 1919 *Follies*, Ziegfeld's brilliance became fully apparent. He had every right to be proud of the effort, which opened on June 16 and probably came as close as any of his vehicles to being worth its $175,000 production cost. The show took in more than $29,000 each of its first six weeks. Even the matinees sold out, something unheard of in previous seasons. The *Follies* ran twenty-two weeks in New York, with a top ticket price of $3.50 (after the opening-night price of $5); on the road, orchestra seats were $4 a ticket, except in Philadelphia, where they went for $5 on Saturday night.

As with the previous *Follies*, the show had no book. It was a succession of scenes featuring many stars: Eddie Cantor, Bert Williams, Marilyn Miller, Ray and Johnny Dooley, Eddie Dowling, John Steele, Van and Schenck, and George LeMaire. While there were plenty of comedians, their material was not outstanding; neither did the dancing live up to that in past editions. However, the host of lovely women—including newcomers Jessie Reed and Billie Dove—and the gorgeous costumes and sets combined to provide an overall effect of such beauty that this *Follies* became one of the most popular ever.

During the run, Ziegfeld's cast presented him with a fifteen-inch-high silver loving cup. With its dark wood base and its inscription—"a token of love and esteem"—this memento captured the spirit of Ziegfeld's relation with his companies and his staff during the last moments of pristine glory.

Eddie Cantor summed it up when he wrote: "The Ziegfeld actors formed a happy household in those years. A spirit of genuine fellowship and helpfulness prevailed in the *Follies* of '17, '18, and '19 that has rarely been equaled by any other troupe. The older members of the cast took it to be their pleasant duty to give the younger ones the benefit of their stage experience." As an example of the family atmosphere, in the summer, Ziegfeld often served ice cream to the cast. Chorus girls would sit on the balcony to eat it. This

Left: "A Spanish Frolic" in the *Follies of 1919* featured toreador Johnny Dooley (left) and his sister, Ray Dooley, as Carmen; the man on the right looks like Ray's husband, Eddie Dowling, who was also in the scene. By the time the scene ended, Johnny Dooley was in the orchestra pit.

practice continued until one day two of the women got into a fight and threw ice cream at each other, soiling their costumes. Although he had little contact with them, Ziegfeld was good to the chorus girls, sometimes giving them roses. He also sent gardenias to authors of successful scripts and inscribed platinum watches for the stars of long-running shows.

During the run of the *Follies*, twenty portraits of cast members painted by Alberto Vargas on 30 x 40" watercolor boards were displayed in the lobby. Vargas completed the last portrait only hours before the show opened. He continued to paint cast portraits, usually twelve, for every *Follies* between 1919 and 1931 and for *Show Boat*. Several of his paintings also became sheet-music covers for *Follies* songs. This, of course, was decades before he became famous as the creator of magazines' "Vargas girls."

During the rehearsals, Ziegfeld's relationship with Marilyn Miller had hit a new low when he removed Frank Carter, her new husband, from the *Follies*. Ziegfeld's decision sparked violent arguments with his star, but as always, he resisted mightily anyone telling him what to do or thwarting his desires.

The difficulty with Marilyn was that she was not malleable. She was just as fiercely independent as he. She was able for many years to keep him on a string while still doing what she pleased. Though he hated her independence and her violent temper, Ziegfeld did not free himself of her allure easily or quickly.

Theater labor relations were likewise approaching a nadir in 1919. During World War I, organized labor as a whole agreed to a no-strike clause in its contracts in exchange for recognition. When the war ended, labor no longer felt obligated to honor the clause; problems over pay and working conditions led to a nationwide wave of strikes. Owners, reluctant to incur extra costs and fearing an American version of the Bolshevik revolution, responded with vicious strike-breaking tactics. The time was known as the Red Summer of 1919—for both the politics and for the blood spilled.

Above: Ed Wynn and Eddie Cantor picketing during the Actors Equity strike in 1919. Top: Norman Trevor and Billie Burke in a scene from *Caesar's Wife* (1919). The few non-musical shows that Ziegfeld produced nearly always starred his wife.

Many managers escaped financial responsibility for their productions by creating nonstandard contracts or by incorporating their businesses. Abuses included stranding actors on the road when a show closed and unlimited rehearsal periods (six to ten weeks was not extraordinary) during which actors were paid nothing. In one case an actor rehearsed twenty-two weeks and was paid for a total of four nights. Pay was irregular, even when the production was on solid financial footing. Actors were often forced to provide for their own transportation to the opening site and then back from the closing location. They also had to buy their own costumes, even period pieces. The infamous "satisfaction clause" gave a manager autocratic power to dismiss an actor whose performance he deemed inadequate. There was no appeal.

The Actors Equity Association was formed on May 26, 1913, and six months later began a concerted

Sheet-music cover for Irving Berlin's "A Pretty Girl Is Like a Melody," the most famous of the many tunes Berlin wrote for the *Follies*

effort to force reluctant producers to accept a standard contract. Equity demands, all of which seem fairly innocuous today, included paid transportation to the opening and from the closing sites, a limit on unpaid rehearsal time, two weeks' notice on a closing or dismissal, union protection after one week of rehearsals, extra pay for extra performances, full pay for all weeks played, and payment for women's costumes.

The union was negotiating with two management organizations: the National Association of Theatrical Producing Managers (producers) and the United Managers' Protective Association (UMPA), comprising theater owners and bookers. This effort began January 9, 1914, but did not culminate in any tangible victories until October 1917, when the UMPA promised to accept the Equity standard contract. However, because some producers were adamantly opposed to organized labor and partly because of internal squabbling, the UMPA fell apart, so no producers issued standard contracts, despite the October agreement.

On May 2, 1919, a new managers' organization, the Producing Managers' Association (PMA) was formally announced. Between early May and late July, both Equity and the PMA conducted intense internal debates about their positions. The debate within Equity turned on whether they were professional artists who should be above labor disputes. The managers were struggling over how much control they should have over their own destinies. By the end of July, all major managers, including Ziegfeld, had joined the PMA's ranks. For a time, it appeared that some PMA members were willing to negotiate in good faith. On July 22, 1919, though, E. F. Albee took a hard-line stance against the union's requests and persuaded the PMA to adopt a union-busting platform.

Its back to the wall, Equity struck *Chu Chin Chow* as a test case because its actors had been rehearsing for weeks without contracts. The walkout did not succeed completely, but the action enraged PMA members. Over the next week, the feuding members of the PMA were having difficulty reaching a consensus on how to respond. Meanwhile, fifteen hundred Equity members issued a statement after their meeting on August 1, 1919, demanding the PMA recognize their right to make alliances and suggesting that its intransigence was forcing the union into organized labor's camp.

PMA members agreed to meet Equity members on August 6, but when Albee learned of the meeting, he was horrified. He proposed a lockout on all facets of the entertainment industry from burlesque through film and legitimate theater. Once again, Albee's truculence carried the day: the PMA refused to recognize Equity. This obstinacy angered the actors who did not want to strike. The studied resistance from the managers stymied less radical alternatives. At the union's August 6 meeting, the rallying cry was that the time for words had passed; the time for action had arrived. Equity members voted on a strike resolution that very afternoon, and on the evening of August 6, they struck a show named *Lightnin'*.

Because Ziegfeld had, on the whole, been fair to the actors, few of his people had been prominently involved in the union organization effort, with the notable exceptions of Ed Wynn and Eddie Cantor. Initially Cantor, Eddie Dowling, and Phil Dwyer joined the labor action on August 11, but they were persuaded to return when Ziegfeld said that he was not a member of the PMA.

On Monday, August 11, at 5:30 P.M., Ziegfeld announced that he had obtained temporary injunctions prohibiting *Follies* cast members from striking. Cast members were served injunctions as they entered the stage door for that night's performance. The injunction was against principals Eddie Cantor, Gus Van, Joe Schenck, John Steele, Johnny Dooley, Ray Dooley, and Eddie Dowling. There was a blanket injunction for the chorus. The injunctions were effective until a hearing on Friday, August 15. Ziegfeld said he obtained the injunctions because he feared the loss of the $175,000 spent producing the *Follies*. On August 12, after the restraining order was in place, Ziegfeld acknowledged being a PMA member.

That same day, the chorus girls formed a branch union, the Chorus Equity. Two days later (August 14), Edith Hallor, a *Follies* chorus member, was elected to chair this group. Marie Dressler and Ethel Barrymore lent their names to the effort, while Lillian Russell donated $100,000 to help with expenses.

Ziegfeld had been coming to the theater nightly since the strike began, but he was convinced that the actors would wait until after the August 15 hearing before doing anything, so he stayed home that night. When five *Follies* principals (Cantor, Johnny Dooley, Van, Schenck, and Phil Dwyer) and about twenty members of the chorus did not appear at the theater by curtain time on August 13, they caught Ziegfeld by surprise. The actors had obtained a modification in the injunction that afternoon.

The nonstriking members of the company were all made up and ready at the 8:30 P.M. curtain time when the striking principal actors failed to appear. (They had apparently been there much earlier—to allay suspicions about strike activity—and left.) At 8:45 the theater manager announced that "owing to several desertions" the show was canceled, and the two thousand ticket holders would be given refunds.

The next day, Cantor said: "My duty is to stand by the actors and see that justice is done. I am very fond of Mr. Ziegfeld, and enjoyed working for him, but now that he has aligned himself with the Producing Managers' Association, we are going to align ourselves with the actors." Marilyn Miller was the lone *Follies* principal to cross the picket line. On its side, the PMA dug in its heels with the Shuberts suing Equity for $500,000 (August 11). Equity staged highly visible events to rally support, including two benefits (August 18 and 22) and a parade in the rain (August 18). By August 22, all but two theaters on Broadway were dark. Ziegfeld's *Midnight Frolic* and *Nine O'Clock Revue*, which were among the last to close because Equity did not include variety shows in its strike organization effort, ceased production about August 18.

Then the court battle resumed. Initially Justice Hendrick ruled against Equity (August 25), because the union's lawyers had not submitted papers, and ordered the actors to return to work. However, the strike did not end. The actors surprised everyone once again: they simply ignored Hendrick's ruling. On August 26, the Teamsters Union joined the strike, and then Equity was able to shut down the Hippodrome (August 28), forcing Charles Dillingham to resign his position there. This development prompted the PMA to open secret negotiations with Equity. On August 30, Hippodrome management recognized both Equity and Chorus Equity, giving the unions crucial impetus. Equity had momentum but no real victory until the stagehands and musicians shut down the Shubert theaters nationwide on September 5.

The next day, September 6, 1919, the PMA signed an historic general accord. Equity's victory was complete. The PMA gave in on all of the union's major demands.

Both sides were extremely bitter about the labor strife. The managers did not understand the strikers' concerns and were angry because the labor action seriously compromised returns during what they thought would be the most profitable season in history. Equity members were upset with what they perceived as a refusal to bargain in good faith about reasonable requests for humane working conditions.

The *Follies* resumed production on September 10. Although Ziegfeld's shows were closed only four weeks, the strike affected the friendship between Eddie Cantor and Flo for years. Ziegfeld asked him: "How could you do this to *me* when I've been like a father to you? We've never had a dispute about salaries or anything." Cantor replied: "You must understand, Flo, that I have to do it because actors are going to have to make a stand. Why? Because there are producers not like you. . . . You'll have to understand that this is not my doing something to you. . . . We have to have rules; we have to have a standard."

Ziegfeld felt the actors had broken an unspoken pact—if he were fair to them, they owed him, he believed, unquestioning fealty. They had violated his code by being disloyal. According to Cantor, after the strike victory, all the actors "returned to our old posts, but things were no longer the same. Ziegfeld had promised to star me in his next show at a greatly increased salary. Instead, he stalled and avoided the subject. The memory of the strike was still fresh in his mind." Cantor did not work for Ziegfeld again until 1923, except for occasional unplanned, extemporaneous appearances.

In 1919, Ziegfeld did not immediately realize how important the strike and the ruptured friendship with Cantor would become. He certainly was still *the* dominant force on Broadway, but after 1919, history began to overtake him, with a few notable exceptions. The strike marked a turning point in his career.

It was also a turning point for a number of his principals. Ed Wynn was blacklisted for his role in the strike and subsequently encountered difficulties finding work. Since Marilyn Miller was the only *Follies* principal to cross the picket line, it was probably no coincidence that the next year she was given the lead, her first, in *Sally*. Despite his role in the strike, Eddie Cantor was able to find work.

The year 1919 also brought the beginning of serious competition from other revue series. This rivalry already included the Shuberts' *Passing Show* (initiated in 1912), George White's *Scandals* (1919), and the *Greenwich Village Follies* (1919) and would soon include *Earl Carroll's Vanities* (1923). By 1921, Ziegfeld was also competing with radio. The crowding in the field prompted other producers to begin "stealing" many of his stars. Ziegfeld repaid them in kind, by "borrowing" some of his competitors' best performers.

Ziegfeld's *Midnight Frolic* series rolled on successfully, with a new version opening on October 2, 1919. Seven weeks later Ziegfeld also produced *Caesar's Wife*, a new vehicle for Billie, which premiered on November 24. The play marked Billie's return to the stage after having made several silent films in Hollywood. *Caesar's Wife* was a Somerset Maugham script, which was as usual well written and was more serious than anything Ziegfeld had theretofore produced. Critics called it the best serious drama in New York for several years. Unfortunately, like so many of Ziegfeld's theatrical efforts on Billie's behalf, his meticulous plans failed: *Caesar's Wife* did not catch the public's fancy and ran only two months.

By this point, two separate forms of government "intrusion" began affecting business for Ziegfeld and other producers: income tax and Prohibition. The Sixteenth Amendment, which authorized an income tax, had been in effect since 1913, but Ziegfeld was now making enough money to care about its bite.

The Volstead Act, prohibiting the sale of alcoholic beverages, became effective on January 1, 1920. Eventually the law killed the *Frolic*, but since that show was so well established, the full effect did not settle in for nearly two years. However, Ziegfeld's fledgling concert series on Sunday evenings, called *Tonight at 8:10*, had no chance. It opened only two days before the Volstead Act was passed.

Politically Ziegfeld was holding to a middle course. He was friendly with Jimmy Walker and a host of liberal actors, such as Will Rogers. However, his financial backers were generally a pretty conservative lot. His daughter suspects that when Ziegfeld voted, it was for the Republicans.

Billie lobbied for causes such as Liberty bonds and against using animals in scientific research. But, although he may have supported her views, Flo seemed content to lie back and let Billie do the work.

By 1919, film had emerged as a force that would change the entertainment world forever. Ziegfeld loved the movies: the problem was that Hollywood was threatening all live entertainment and, more specifically, his livelihood. Consequently, he made many public statements about film that reflected his professional needs but in no way indicated how he actually felt. Typically he watched three or four movies each weekend: usually one Western and two or three comedies. In fact, he built a $20,000 projection room at Burkeley Crest for screening movies and hired a licensed operator to show the current releases. He admired the work of Dorothy Arzner, the first American woman director, so much that she was one of the few people he wanted to meet when he first went to Los Angeles.

Before long, Ziegfeld started losing his biggest stars to Hollywood. Even a short list of the "defections" reveals how devastating this development was for him: Lillian Lorraine was in *Neal of the Navy* (Pathé) in 1915, Mae Murray entered films in 1916 with *To Have and To Hold*, Olive Thomas signed with Triangle in 1917, and Marion Davies left him to make *Runaway Romany* (Pathé, 1917). Later he lost W. C. Fields, Eddie Cantor, Will Rogers, Mary Hay, Nita Naldi, Lilyan Tashman, Mary Eaton, Gilda Gray, Louise Brooks, Gladys Feldman, Paulette Goddard, Kathryn Perry, Florence Walton, Billie Dove, Imogene Wilson, Dorothy Mackaill, Peggy Hopkins, Justine Johnston, and Ina Claire.

Ziegfeld particularly hated the fact that many women achieved prominence in his *Follies* and then went to Hollywood, leaving him in a continuous "replacement" mode for personnel.

With World War I having just ended, no one, especially not Ziegfeld, was seriously concerned about limits or problems. Optimism and belief in the American Dream abounded. At age fifty-two, Ziegfeld was enjoying the recognition that came with success. When he wanted money for a show, it was available. He had setbacks, but he knew he could always rebound even from incidents as frustrating as the Equity strike. Hard work, talent, the right contacts, and a little bit of luck would carry the day.

The next year, 1920, he got what he perceived as confirmation of that view.

Above, left to right: Mary Eaton made her *Follies* debut in 1920 and appeared in three editions before starring in *Kid Boots*; after appearing in several other musical comedies, she went to Hollywood. Female cast members (said to be from the 1920 *Follies*) gathered around a polished floor that reflects their images. Doris Eaton started as a *Follies* chorus girl in 1918 when she was just fourteen. In 1919 she was a special dancer and Marilyn Miller's understudy. By the next year, Eaton was a principal like her sister Mary.

CHAPTER 10

❖

THE SILVER LINING

❖

The new decade started with a bang as Ziegfeld produced nine shows (two *Follies*, five editions of the *Frolic*, and two book shows) during 1920–21. Despite Prohibition, the *Midnight Frolic* was still very successful, as was the *Ziegfeld Nine O'Clock Revue*, which began March 8, 1920. The next week he also staged a new *Ziegfeld Midnight Frolic* (March 15).

In the early 1920s, the Ziegfelds were staying in Palm Beach for a longer portion of the social season. While there, Ziegfeld ran into writers Guy Bolton and P. G. Wodehouse and composer Jerome Kern. He told them that he was looking for a new vehicle in which to star Marilyn Miller. Ziegfeld proposed a show that had a dancer breaking her ankle in the first act—not a particularly smart ploy in drama. Wodehouse and Bolton then mentioned their unproduced play called "The Little Thing." It was to become *Sally*.

When Ziegfeld returned to New York and approached his partners, neither Erlanger nor Dillingham wanted to produce the project. Their lack of support must have been frustrating, but as it turned out, their reluctance worked to Ziegfeld's advantage, providing him with a crucial opportunity. He was sufficiently confident, in both himself and this show, that he used his own money to mount *Sally*. This was a risky proposition, but he thought this would be the right vehicle for showcasing Marilyn's talent.

Ziegfeld had begun preparations for *Sally* early in 1920 but was forced to set the project aside temporarily. One reason for the postponement was the death of Marilyn Miller's husband in May.

Frank Carter's death devastated Miller. Popular renditions of the story have her being informed just before show time, Ziegfeld persuading her to go onstage that night, and Marilyn stoically performing despite her awful loss and then never missing a performance. The reality, according to her understudy, Doris Eaton, is this: Ziegfeld gave Miller an extended leave. Eaton may even have played Marilyn's role as long as four weeks. Moreover, news accounts indicate that Carter died at 5:30 A.M. Sunday and that Marilyn arrived in Gransville, Maryland, the accident site, that morning.

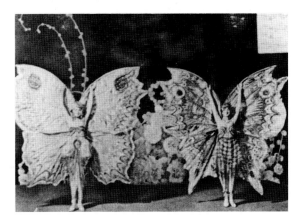

Far left: Marilyn Miller, Walter Catlett, and Mary Hay in a scene from *Sally* (1920). The popular production ran for sixteen months in New York and then went on a long road tour. Left: Two women in the "Land of the Butterflies" scene from *Sally*.

Here Sally (Marilyn Miller) masquerades as Mme. Nookerova, a famous Russian dancer.

In the meantime, Ziegfeld's continuing success in the *Follies* intensified his war with the Shuberts. Correspondence indicates that each party perceived itself as abused by the other. They both also remained adamant that they had not intentionally harmed the other. The gist of the disputes usually focused on whether they knew who had a contract with whom. At one point, an internal Shubert memo alleged that Ziegfeld had stolen not only Marilyn Miller but Pearl Germond, Jessie Reed, Savoy and Brennan, Gilda Gray, the English Pony Ballet, Bert Williams, and Norworth and Bayes as well.

When J. J. Shubert complained that Ziegfeld was once again stealing girls from his Winter Garden show, Ziegfeld replied that he did not know these people were working for Shubert. "I wish to emphatically assure you there is no intention on my part to engage anyone with whom you have a contract, irrespective of [Rufus] LeMaire's offers in your behalf." Ziegfeld's mention of LeMaire was a reference to the fact that this gentleman was wooing Ziegfeld players, claiming that he represented the Shuberts. When confronted with these indiscretions, Shubert argued that he could not control what LeMaire said.

Seventy years after these incidents, it appears that neither organization had clean hands: each was, indeed, raiding the other's shows. The Shuberts recognized Gilda Gray's value to their organization and were willing to go to court to restrain Ziegfeld from hiring her. In the 1920s, citizen recourse to the courts was unusual, but on Broadway, lawsuits were commonplace, as were assumptions that legal expenses constituted a routine cost of doing business. (An internal memo in the Shubert files makes this point, noting that Ziegfeld enticed Marilyn to break a ten-year contract with them by giving her $750 a week and offering to pay her legal fees should the Shuberts sue her for breach of contract.) In this case, the wrangling over Gilda Gray, which began in May, continued until at least November 1920.

Despite the squabbles with the Shuberts, Ziegfeld managed to produce the annual revue, the *Ziegfeld Follies of 1920*, beginning June 22 at the New Amsterdam Theatre. Jack Donahue, Mary Eaton, Charles Winninger, and Moran and Mack made their first *Follies* appearances in this year's edition. Eaton's singing and dancing made her a hit, and Donahue's eccentric dances went over big. This was also the first *Follies* show in which Ziegfeld hired a name band to appear on the stage—Art Hickman from California.

The *Follies* series was not noted for its female comedians, so this year's show was unusual for having two of them—Fannie Brice and Ray Dooley—in addition to W. C. Fields. There were several funny scenes, but increasingly the emphasis was on beautiful women, including those in Ben Ali Haggin's tableaux.

Eddie Cantor refused to appear in the 1920 *Follies* after the disagreement over the actors' strike. He even offered to bet Ziegfeld $10,000 that he would not be in this year's show. Nevertheless, Cantor made a surprise appearance opening night and sang two new songs that were hits. Flo allowed Cantor to drag him

Right: Glenn Hunter and Billie Burke in a scene from *The Intimate Strangers* (1921). Far right: Some of the costumes James Reynolds created for the 1921 *Follies*

onstage but then slipped away before saying anything. Cantor stayed in the show only for the first week, and he was not on the program. He left saying that Ziegfeld would not give him suitable material.

W. C. Fields wrote a pantomime scene entitled "The Family Ford." When Ziegfeld heard about the skit, he did not want it in the *Follies* because he thought pantomime would slow the production's pace. Fields was so convinced of its audience appeal that he rented a rehearsal hall and later sneaked the scene into the dress rehearsal. The cast thought the skit was hilarious, but Ziegfeld did not even smile. However, he finally consented to keep the scene. Fields's instinct proved correct. The audience loved it.

As had become his custom, Ziegfeld labored lovingly over the details until his vision came to life. Doris Eaton recalled that for the "Bells" number in the 1920 show, her sister Mary played a bride preparing for her wedding day. Ziegfeld was not satisfied with the bed, the drapes, or the lights. He even worked on how Mary got out of bed.

Ziegfeld wanted his shows to be superior—to be memorable. In those days, going to the theater was "an event." Audiences in the 1920s dressed with care; men wore tuxedos and women, evening gowns.

Cast member Dana O'Connell noted that some of Broadway's panache in the 1920s derived from the way actors handled themselves away from the theater. When offstage and coming to work, chorus girls and dancers wore dresses, gloves, and stockings. Fancy cars and limousines were lined up, waiting to take the girls to parties. O'Connell thinks that the *Follies* specifically had such allure at least in part because Ziegfeld was a charmer. When he walked into a room, she says, "the Red Sea parted." His personal charm influenced the character of the show. Even though he was not particularly handsome, he was very striking and always commanded attention.

The love-hate relationship with Eddie Cantor was in a hate phase after the first week of the 1920 *Follies*. Ziegfeld sued Cantor and George LeMaire for plagiarizing a scene called "The Osteopath's Office" and using it in a Shubert show. As Ziegfeld noted in a letter to attorney Walter Hirsch, "I am not feeling any too good this morning—disgusted with everything. . . . I was not going to bother about this scene, but they are going up and down Broadway talking so much about it, that now I will." Hirsch warned Flo that he faced difficulties if he sued, because he had not copyrighted the 1919 script and the greater portion of it was action and not dialogue. Still, Ziegfeld eventually won the suit.

Ziegfeld was not as fortunate in his personal life. Little detail of his relationship with Olive Thomas has ever surfaced, but Ziegfeld cared enough about her to be terribly upset when she died in September 1920. Ziegfeld had been unhappy, probably for both selfish and altruistic reasons, when she married Jack Pickford in 1917; he seems to have sensed that Pickford was not the right man for her. Nothing could have been truer, because Thomas died tragically young and under suspicious circumstances.

The Thomas-Pickford relationship had deteriorated quickly after the marriage, but the couple had recently reconciled. In Paris, after a late night out with friends, Olive became critically ill from ingesting bichloride of mercury, then a common treatment for syphilis. She was rendered speechless and blind, suffering what was described as "untold agony" until slipping into a coma hours before she died. The police suspected foul play because Pickford had been involved with drug dealers, was rumored to have syphilis himself, and was the beneficiary of a large insurance policy recently taken on Olive's life.

Suspicions about Pickford's role in the scandal and accounts of Olive's agony left Ziegfeld distraught, but he still refused to attend the funeral, probably because he had such a deep distaste for any reminder of mortality. Gene Buck was an honorary pallbearer and Irving Berlin an usher, and the funeral, which Ziegfeld helped arrange in New York on September 28, 1920, became a public spectacle.

Shortly after Thomas's death, Ziegfeld plunged into creating *Sally*. For this show, he assembled a remarkable support staff. He signed both Guy Bolton and Jerome Kern on September 22, 1920, and

Clifford Grey three weeks later. Bolton wrote the book, Kern the music, and Grey the lyrics. Kern received a 3 percent royalty, while Bolton got 2 percent and Grey, 1 percent. Ziegfeld's reputation for altering productions to suit his own taste had preceded him; Kern's contract stipulated that Ziegfeld had to obtain Kern's permission in writing before he interpolated any music or changed Kern's score.

Ziegfeld also asked Victor Herbert to conduct the orchestra. A Ziegfeld letter to Herbert reveals some of the fervor that Flo brought to the persuasion process:

> My dear Victor: . . . With an artist of your standing it is very hard for me to talk money. Still I am compelled to do so. . . . Nobody in the world appreciates your work more than I do, for my greatest ambition is to do a piece where you have entirely written the music. . . . I really cannot talk money to you, and will leave it entirely to you, and whatever you consider fair will be entirely satisfactory to me. . . . I know the Ballet is very short but to have you there will be electrifying to the audience.

As if autumn of 1920 had not been tumultuous enough, the long-standing business association among Marc Klaw, Abe Erlanger, and Ziegfeld collapsed. Erlanger and Klaw had been together for more than thirty years, and Ziegfeld had been involved for more than thirteen years. According to Ziegfeld, "relations between Klaw and Erlanger had become severely strained," and the problem was readily apparent during the 1919–20 season, because by then "Klaw rendered no services of any kind whatever to Ziegfeld Follies, Inc., the only officers . . . rendering services to the corporation being Mr. Erlanger and myself." The situation came to a head at the board meeting on June 28, 1920, at which time Klaw was not "re-elected as a director." Instead they elected Ziegfeld, Erlanger, and F. S. Golding.

As part of a proposed settlement, Klaw wanted to force Ziegfeld and Erlanger to buy out his share in the *Follies* and *Frolic* corporations for $200,000, and he sued both corporations "to compel an inspection of the books." Ziegfeld testified that Klaw's motive was "to glean competitive data from the books" to help him with his own separate theatrical production company. They became embroiled in a dispute over how much Klaw's share was worth and over who did what to whom.

Ziegfeld's deposition describes the rudimentary structure of the organization. Klaw, Erlanger, and Ziegfeld had incorporated the *Follies* on June 5, 1913, with Ziegfeld as president and director; Joseph Klaw (Marc's son) as secretary; Mortimer Fishel, vice president; and Meyer W. Livingston, treasurer. According to Ziegfeld's sworn testimony, neither Marc Klaw nor Erlanger was an officer at the outset.

When Marc Klaw was named to the board of directors on August 3, 1917, Ziegfeld's salary was $2,050 per month, while Erlanger and Klaw each received $625 a month. In 1918, when Klaw and Erlanger were elected to positions as corporate officers, the salaries changed to reflect their added responsibilities: Klaw became vice-president and Erlanger treasurer. Ziegfeld then received $1,666.66 per month regularly plus $200 per week when the *Follies* played. Klaw and Erlanger each received $833.33 per month. The profit arrangement had Ziegfeld drawing 50 percent and Klaw and Erlanger 25 percent each.

Thus, Ziegfeld had apparently assumed a dominant role in the organization within six years of the revue's inception. Obviously the *Follies* series was a hit, but even so, for Ziegfeld to have gained sufficient power to be elected president of the *Follies* corporation by 1913 is noteworthy. In most organizations, movement through the ranks takes many, many years, particularly with a leader as strong as Erlanger already entrenched at the head. The presidency was a reward for Ziegfeld's good work.

The court action with Klaw could not have come at a more difficult juncture. Ziegfeld was deep in preparations for *Sally*, which premiered on December 21, 1920, at the New Amsterdam Theatre. The show and Marilyn Miller were immediate hits; the show grossed $21,000 during tryouts in Newark, New Jersey, under the name *Sally of the Alley*. It went on to become the fourth longest-running musical of the 1920s, with 570 New York performances plus a long road tour. It ran a total of three years.

In this show, Sally (Miller) went from being a dishwasher to starring in the *Ziegfeld Follies*. She accomplished this feat by masquerading as a socialite and, consequently, risking public shame as well as failure if she were caught. When she was "unmasked," instead of being cast into social exile, she succeeded in making her dream come true. Because of (not in spite of) her deception, she achieved her dream.

Sally marked the first time Ziegfeld offered a star—Marilyn Miller—a percentage of the box-office gross (according to her husband, 10 percent) in lieu of a salary. She drew about $3,000 a week and was the highest paid musical-comedy star to that time. Ziegfeld's personal relationship with Marilyn may have prompted this precedent-setting change, but her cooperation with management during the 1919 strike may also have been a contributing factor.

When he found out that Leon Errol was available, Ziegfeld hired him for the show. As Ziegfeld had already signed Walter Catlett, he had Bolton add a second comic role to his already-finished libretto.

After *Sally* opened, Ziegfeld took Patty to a matinée, her first show. Patty recalled that "Marilyn was so sweet, luscious, and attractive on stage" that she wanted to meet her backstage. What occurred next has been seriously overdramatized in subsequent reports; however, even though it lasted no more than five minutes, almost seventy years later Patty still remembered it vividly and described it as a "socko" moment. She said that Miller was dressed in a magnificent glittering costume and that to a six-year-old, "she looked just like Heaven." The minute that Patty and her father walked into the room, Miller let out a string of swear words that did not mean much to a child. The clear impression, though, was that the gorgeous star did not look very pretty. Patty's only thought was: "I'd never seen anything that beautiful that angry."

The incident backstage with Marilyn mirrored the thematic issues that were raised in *Sally* and many other Ziegfeld productions, particularly those during the 1920s. Ziegfeld became fascinated simultaneously with the American Dream and with the disparity between appearance and reality. While shows such as *Sally* generally approached these themes in a lighthearted manner, using simple mistaken-identity plots and humor to convey their serious concerns, these productions clearly captured the public's imagination.

Between 1917 and 1929, Ziegfeld produced numerous shows with similar themes. Someone who did not have money was pursuing it *(Sally, Kid Boots, Annie Dear, Show Girl)*; someone wealthy had lost or was losing a fortune *(Rescuing Angel, Rose Briar)*; a person from modest circumstances was flirting with a lover from high society who did not know about this person's beginnings *(Sally, Louie the 14th, Betsy)*. Virtually all of these book shows, as well as *Rio Rita* and *Intimate Strangers,* had a principal pretending to be someone other than his or her true self. The title song in *Annie Dear* quipped: "Life's a game that we must play."

With the exception of the Somerset Maugham and Noël Coward pieces that Ziegfeld staged, his book offerings were not outstanding theater, but the themes that recur are clues to the commercial appeal of his work and his personality. His society friends and the general theater public were no more interested in heavy thematic presentations than Ziegfeld was. Many of his friends had made their own fortunes and so were probably as fascinated as he was by the dream.

Ziegfeld was something of a mystery man himself, who assumed roles both literally, at the costume parties he loved, and figuratively, in the distance he maintained between himself and others. In his biography of Irving Berlin, Lawrence Bergreen asserted that the composer was not comfortable in Ziegfeld's presence because Berlin was so shy and Ziegfeld so extroverted and flamboyant. This reflects a common but mistaken perception of Ziegfeld. Though flamboyant in the public presentation of his shows, in private Ziegfeld was quiet, dignified, and reserved to the point of sometimes being ill at ease. In fact, he and Berlin got along rather well, and their common shyness actually seemed to be a point of attraction.

Ziegfeld probably did not analyze these thematic issues closely nor choose his shows on that basis. Nevertheless, the themes recurred so often that he was obviously drawn to them. He also was most likely not aware of the parallels with his own life. In 1920 as *Sally* became a smash hit and made him a millionaire, he was probably conscious only of the silver lining. All he knew then was that he had worked hard to make the most of his considerable talent and that the American Dream had served him well.

The dark underside of the dream was evident in isolated individual occurrences (gambling losses, actor "disloyalty" during the strike), but nothing of sufficient gravity had appeared to cause Ziegfeld or his contemporaries to question the basic integrity of the Dream. However, as F. Scott Fitzgerald noted later in *Tender Is the Night,* the American Dream may have been a wolf in sheep's clothing.

Despite all the hubbub in the theater world and Ziegfeld's mercurial extramarital involvements, his life with Billie and Patty settled into a kind of routine. The annual pattern during these years was to do a show that would open in the summer or the fall. The Ziegfelds spent Christmas at home in Hastings. Then in January Patty and Billie would go to Palm Beach until Easter; Flo spent substantial time there as well, but when he was preparing a show in the spring, he did not always stay the whole season.

Over the summer as it became hot, the Ziegfelds would charter a houseboat and get away to Nantucket, the Hamptons, Sag Harbor, Martha's Vineyard, or Rhode Island. No staff would accompany them except Captain Gray. Away from New York, Ziegfeld got up and retired earlier. While on vacation, he often prepared lunch. Patty remembered that he "cooked fried partridge with a wonderful quince jelly sauce, and he made a dish with tomatoes, beans, and eggs. He'd mix the beans and the tomatoes while they were cooking and then he'd break a dozen eggs on top . . . and fry them. It was rather tasty."

Ziegfeld's taste in food was eclectic. He was not keen on vegetables (the only one he liked was white asparagus), but he ate a whole range of other dishes, including seafood, German cheeses, meat, and potatoes. He also liked preparing a Russian dressing—hard-boiled eggs, vinegar, oil, paprika. He was a dessert eater: chocolate mousse, ice cream, strawberries.

On vacation the family played mah-jongg or bridge or went fishing. They also played a game called "Guggenheim," which was something like "Jeopardy." Flo also relaxed by whittling or paddling a canoe.

At home outside the show preparation season, he arose around 8 A.M. and had breakfast in bed around nine. Jake Hoffman of the Burkeley Crest staff shaved him between 9:30 and 10 A.M., and he left for the office around 11 A.M. Usually he ate lunch in his office. For dinner, he often popped out to Dinty Moore's between 6 and 8 P.M. He went to bed around 10 or 11 P.M. when no show was running. During the season, he stayed in the city until 2–4 A.M. Billie would join him for dinner and then return to Hastings ahead of him.

In Ziegfeld's leisure time he continued with his old nemesis: gambling. He and his friends bet on anything. One year, Colonel Bradley, who owned the Palm Beach gambling establishment that bore his name, was running a horse named Blue Larkspur. Patty told her father not to bet on Blue. Ziegfeld ignored her advice and put $10,000 on Bradley's horse, while Patty placed a $100 bet on another entry. She won.

When it came to money in those days, Flo and Billie were perfectly matched: both were spendthrifts.

"Budget" was not a word that either Flo or Billie recognized—in the professional or the private realm. Fortunately, Billie's mother forced her to set aside a nest egg for the future. As far as Flo and Billie were concerned, money was available to be spent or it was not: it was seen as a means to do what they wanted, not an end in itself. However, even without money, the Ziegfelds did what they pleased.

Ziegfeld exhibited deep emotions for his daughter that had never surfaced for another woman. He loved women deeply but never exclusively. There was always someone else for whom he had what his daughter calls a "sneaker." When it came to Patty, though, the devotion became single-minded, almost a passion. Despite all the media attention and the trappings of luxury, Patty was very much like her parents— shy and exceedingly down-to-earth considering the circumstances in which she grew up. Her easygoing, even-tempered disposition totally captivated Ziegfeld. The single-minded love that Ziegfeld gave to Patty was never available for Billie. A letter that she wrote him around the opening of *Sally* poignantly reveals how well she understood this point and foreshadows tension over his life-style:

> You always love me best when I am far away—and New York is so gay and so interesting—but I am doing my damndest not to do anything you wouldn't want me to—I wish to God I had the same effect on you that others seem to have—and that I seem to have on others—I suppose the fact that I love you is my salvation—and my attraction—men always want something they can't get—Oh well—you do love me I guess—but you love others so much too—It makes me a little desperate at times and I think what's the use and then I remember that I'm somebody's mother too—but Oh God I could do with some loving. . . . I'll be glad when you get back. [Patty] needs a father so—a child misses so much without the man's point of view on life—Girls need their fathers almost more than boys I think—You should give her some of your time. . . . You are always so busy at home with telephone etc. . . .
>
> Dear old Palm Beach. It's broken up many a home. I hope we will survive it—but wish to God you'd got it out of your system before I met you . . . I hope you don't stay away too long—Baby.

Shortly after *Sally* opened, Lillian Lorraine was severely hurt in a fall and was down on her luck. Flo rescued her financially but kept his distance because the newspapers had them resuming their affair. He obviously still felt something for her—but whether love or pity is not clear.

Sally went over so well that Ziegfeld finally attracted the attention of British producers. On January 5, 1921, he signed a contract to prepare a London production for an opening on New Year's Day, 1922.

The *Ziegfeld Nine O'Clock Revue* (February 8, 1921) and *Midnight Frolic* (February 9, 1921) were showing clear signs of difficulty caused by Prohibition. In mid-May 1921, Ziegfeld announced that he would close the *Midnight Frolic* and move it to London. In July, after a six-week hiatus, Ziegfeld reported that he was reopening the *Midnight Frolic* with a soda fountain. He said that the police custom of searching roof patrons for flasks was intolerable. The police relented, but problems for the *Frolic* continued.

That summer, *Sally* was still running successfully at the New Amsterdam, so Ziegfeld was forced to open the 1921 *Follies* at the Globe Theatre. This year's revue cost over $250,000. Ziegfeld no longer attempted to incorporate any plot in his *Follies*. The revue had increasingly become a series of unrelated scenes with beautiful, extravagant "big" numbers that included a host of women.

The *Follies* got off to a wonderful start that summer of 1921, but two less auspicious events intruded on August 7. Newspapers ran an article about Flo and Billie patching up their marriage. The article's thrust was positive, but it reminded the public of the problems involving Marilyn Miller.

That same day, Flo's younger brother, Carl, died of cancer in the Detroit home of their sister. When he died, he had been running the Ziegfeld Musical College, which he opened after leaving the Chicago Musical College.

In the fall, Ziegfeld produced *Intimate Strangers* for his wife. Critics praised the strong cast; Billie's performance, in particular, was judged outstanding. Billie persuaded Flo to give Frances McLaughlin Goldwyn (stage name, Frances Howard) a part as a flapper. Eventually this decision would become important to Ziegfeld's career in Hollywood.

When *Intimate Strangers* went on tour, Billie took Patty with her. One night in the middle of a scene she caught Billie off guard: when Billie looked up she saw a small face, Patty's, staring at her from inside the fireplace on the set. Startled, Billie almost blew her lines. She sternly lectured Patty never to do that again. The Ziegfelds gave their child almost anything she wanted, but there were limits, and one of them was interfering with a performance.

Ziegfeld's *Midnight Frolic* reopened on November 17, 1921, after what had become a six-*month* break. Will Rogers returned to the *Frolic*, he said, because Ziegfeld "gave me my first real opportunity." At the end of the year, Ziegfeld got into at least two donnybrooks with Equity over control of his shows. One involved Equity's right to protect performers whom Ziegfeld considered incompetent, and the other concerned bonuses for extra performances. Ziegfeld lost the dispute over the performer whom he wanted to fire, but he prevailed on the extra-performance issue because he had been paying a bonus, even in New York, which he felt covered extra performances. The union did not yet have a stranglehold on Broadway, but events of this sort clearly indicated that the era of untrammeled power for the producers was waning.

❖

CHAPTER 11

THE GILDED REALM

❖

Above: Polish immigrant Gilda Gray performed in both the *Ziegfeld Follies* and George White's *Scandals*. She also toured Europe and was in six movies. Above right: The 1922 *Follies* chorus was important in creating an atmosphere of beauty. The many women gave the show its impact, often directing the audience's attention in line dances.

It was apparent by late 1921 that the *Ziegfeld Midnight Frolic* was no longer attracting large audiences to the roof, so Ziegfeld assembled a new *Frolic*, a road show, that premiered in January 1922.

On February 7, 1922, while Billie was in Baltimore on tour, her mother died in Hastings. Ziegfeld closed the show for three days so that Billie could come home for the funeral. Billie said later that Flo had maintained a good relationship with her mother. "Flo exerted himself constantly with gifts and jokes and little kindnesses. I am so very grateful to him for making Mother's last days such happy days. He always made her birthday a sparkling thing. Hundreds of colored balloons would arrive for the parties he gave in her honor, and on several occasions he sent out the full orchestra from his roof to play for her."

After things returned to normal following Blanche Burke's death, Ziegfeld once again threw himself into preparing the *Follies*. He opened the *Ziegfeld Follies of 1922* on June 5, at the New Amsterdam, which was now being managed jointly by Erlanger, Dillingham, and Ziegfeld. The 1922 show opened "cold" on Broadway because of the expense and trouble in moving the sets to Atlantic City.

Will Rogers was the principal comedian this year. Besides delivering his usual monologue, he appeared in several skits. Other specialty acts were performed by Nervo and Knox, Lulu McConnell, Gallagher and Shean, Rita Owen, Andrew Tombes, and The Tiller Girls (four numbers). One critic commented that Gilda Gray was the best shimmy dancer that New York had seen. But again, it was the big production numbers—the show had eighty-four chorus girls—that attracted the most attention.

While many critics thought this year's show was the best yet, Robert Benchley of *Life* magazine was critical. He felt that the absence of W. C. Fields and Fannie Brice was a major deficiency and remarked that sitting through the many production numbers waiting for Lardner's sketches or Will Rogers made him realize "there is nothing like canoeing on a summer evening."

The 1922 *Follies* had the longest run of any produced during Ziegfeld's lifetime, playing for sixty-

Left: Vaudeville singer/comedian Lulu McConnell was in the 1922 *Follies;* after appearing in musical comedies, she achieved radio fame on "It Pays to be Ignorant" (1942–49). Right: Nona Otero at the time she was a soloist with the Albertina Rasch Dancers. She danced in two *Follies* and three other Ziegfeld shows.

seven weeks in New York and forty weeks on the road. To celebrate a record one year's run on Broadway, Ziegfeld added Eddie Cantor to the cast on June 4, 1923. Cantor sang six songs and teamed with Andrew Tombes for a parody of the hit "Oh! Mr. Gallagher and Mr. Shean." For the 1922 *Follies,* Ziegfeld introduced his famous slogan, "Glorifying the American Girl."

Shortly after the new show opened, Marc Klaw renewed his suit in the New York Supreme Court asking for access to the accounting books and charging that Erlanger and Ziegfeld were wasting corporate assets. He alleged that the two men had increased the rent on the New Amsterdam from $1,500 per week to $3,000, and he requested that the wasted money be restored to the treasury.

Ziegfeld was on his way to Europe by this time, alone, in the attempt to mount *Follies* in London and Paris. He arrived in France about June 24, 1922. Two telegrams that he dispatched from Europe offer some insight into his domestic life and help explain why Billie put up with the pain that he inflicted. The first one, addressed to Billie, reveals how strongly he felt about his family: "Nothing on Earth interests me but happiness my two beloved ones." The second wire, this one to Patty, demonstrates his devotion to her: "You better bring mummy over. Miss you terribly, love. Did you get a pony wagon?" Patty says that he asked her opinion about a variety of theater matters, such as how she liked a particular actress's voice or what she thought of a costume that he had selected. She thinks that he genuinely cared about her reaction but that he also wanted an evaluation that was free of ulterior motives.

This portrait of a father completely enamored of his child contrasts sharply with the image of a suave New York producer. Both portraits are valid. When he was in his business world, beautiful women were always available. At Burkeley Crest, he lived a quiet, domestic existence that provided respite from the chaotic world of the theater. Ziegfeld was capable of separating those two worlds in his own mind. He was probably not being disingenuous when he told Billie that nothing interested him except his family.

Unfortunately, the women he loved were not always so talented as he at compartmentalization. The picture of domestic bliss with Billie and Patty was soon put to a severe test, thanks to Marilyn Miller. Her fiancé, Jack Pickford, had been dishonorably discharged from the navy after it was discovered that he had acted as a go-between (with access to records) for rich slackers who sought bombproof berths in the navy. While in Europe, Ziegfeld made a statement that Pickford had broken Olive Thomas's heart and had been dishonorably discharged from the navy. With respect to the discharge, Ziegfeld merely repeated public statements in the press, but given Miller's temperament, this was not one of his defter moves.

Angry, Marilyn countered in a manner that would have done the *National Enquirer* proud. She denied the charge about Pickford, called Ziegfeld a liar, alleged that he was making love to chorus girls, and later

A letter from Ziegfeld to his daughter, Patty, written from Washington, D. C., undated claimed that he wanted to leave Billie to marry her. She capped her retort with a professional jab, saying of her contract with Ziegfeld for *Sally*, "It would be a delight for me to get out of it tomorrow."

Marilyn got his attention, no doubt about that. Ziegfeld's cable to Burke about the incident somehow reached the press and was printed in *The New York Times*: "Billie darling, I am nearly insane. For God's sake cable me what it is all about. I am not afraid of the truth, and I swear to God there is nothing to which you can take exception. Wait until I am proven guilty. You and Patricia are all that mean anything to me. Be fair, dearest. Will sail on next boat." The article went on to state that Billie "faltered when asked if she cared to deny she would leave her husband. 'No, I won't deny it. I won't affirm or deny anything. I simply can't talk about it. It's all very, very personal. It's quite true that I sent my husband a cable, but the contents were for him alone.'" When reporters told Billie that Ziegfeld was making love to chorus girls and had offered Miller a huge diamond ring and pearls, Burke threw up her hands.

Billie had put up a reasonable front with the press, but when Flo came home from Europe and tried to make up with her by giving her a $20,000 diamond bracelet from Tiffany's, she threw it at him from across the room. In one of those bizarre moments of black humor, Patty, just five years old, caught the peace offering, kept it, and made it her own. Later, in a gesture of magnanimity, she let her mother wear it.

When Billie and Flo disagreed, as in this case, there were big explosions, but they would quickly make up. Billie usually blew up while Ziegfeld remained quiet and just sat puffing his cigar. She would try to "engage" him over a range of subjects from serious concerns about other women through trivial matters in the kitchen, but Ziegfeld would not "play" in Billie's terms, which infuriated her. When the subject was other women, Ziegfeld would just get a "sheepish grin" on his face.

Even after this disastrous blowup with Miller, Ziegfeld continued his infidelities. Patty has mentioned society woman Mrs. Gurnee Munn (née Louisa Wanamaker), Jessie Reed, and Billie Dove. He liked all different types of women, she said—in the positive sense. The press once quoted him as saying that his favorites were beautiful women with shiny hair, luscious lips, and brown eyes that you can dive into. Billie was quick to react—in private, of course—to his statement. Why? Her eyes were blue.

Having had enough public excitement and exposure to satisfy them for a lifetime, the Ziegfelds vacationed during August 1922 in northern Canada near Riley Brook, New Brunswick.

That fall, Billie's career continued to go well on screen. She was voted the number-one actress in a movie popularity contest for 1922. Between 1916 and 1922, Billie had appeared in seventeen films. In New York,

Ziegfeld also produced *Rose Briar* for her on December 25, 1922. The show, which had many elements of a revue, ran for nearly six months.

After years of living a vagabond existence in the theater, Flo embraced life at the Burkeley Crest estate, probably because it reminded him of his childhood environment and because he was almost fifty years old when Patty was born, old enough to appreciate a family. Ziegfeld traveled to Chicago fairly often alone to visit his own parents; Billie and Patty usually went with him only twice a year.

Rosalie Ziegfeld was sweet, gentle, and solicitous of her guests' well-being, and Ziegfeld clearly adored her, picking her up and carrying her to the dining-room table at mealtime. Ziegfeld was more like his mother than his father, particularly in his gentle manner with women and in his thoughtfulness.

Dr. Ziegfeld presented a study in contrast to his wife. Patty relates that "when he hugged you, you knew you'd been hugged." Despite his public reputation as a stern "Prussian," he was very jolly beneath that German strictness, and when the Ziegfeld men got together after lunch at family gatherings, Patty would hear gales of laughter. Patty recalls, "He had a very loud voice, and when he spoke you listened. My God, when he played the piano, he almost shook it off the legs. He played with great force."

Ziegfeld also cared a great deal for his sister, Louise, with whom he was on good terms. When Lou was sick once and a dog was howling, Patty remarked that a dog howling meant that a person was dying. Ziegfeld got very upset and finally called long-distance to check on his sister. Louise had married Willis Buhl, who was from a well-to-do, old-line Detroit family. She was a vivacious, fun-loving woman who led a gay life after Willis died in 1916. When the *Follies* tour came to Detroit, she entertained the cast, and when Flo's big book shows went on the road, he sometimes came out to Detroit.

Just as they maintained a small nucleus of family contacts, Billie and Flo socialized primarily with a limited circle of friends. As for larger social gatherings, they hosted only the number required to satisfy professional obligations. Among Hastings residents, Ziegfeld's only pal was a wealthy miner and gem collector named Colonel William Thompson. While Ziegfeld often worked hard, very hard, he would come home and relax—except during the few weeks of show rehearsals. Though he loved publicity for his cast members, he shunned coverage that focused on him personally.

Burkeley Crest was the perfect place to relax away from the theater. A solidly built structure, erected between 1855 and 1868, it was set in the middle of Hastings-on-Hudson. The house stood on a large estate that was approximately fourteen acres when Billie bought it. Later it was closer to twenty-four acres, enough land to make it feel like open country. The house sat up on a very broad hill in the middle of the estate. The

Above: Billie Burke at the time she appeared in *Rose Briar* (1922). Above right: Louise Ziegfeld (sister) and Flo, Jr.'s parents ride atop camels in Egypt. Louise met her future husband during this trip.

land toward the street sloped down, away from the back of the house, while the grounds on the opposite side, the front of the house, kept climbing gently.

Burkeley Crest was not an enormous house by the standards of the Florida mansions that their friends owned, but it was substantial: approximately eight to ten thousand square feet. It had twenty-two rooms on three floors, with the main living quarters on the first, the Ziegfeld family suites on the second, and servants quarters on the third. The dining room seated up to twenty people, but the pantry and kitchen were small by modern standards: in fact, when the Ziegfelds bought their first Frigidaire, the workmen had a difficult time getting it into the kitchen because the approach halls were so narrow. Billie and Flo had individual bedrooms and baths, and there was a shoe closet in Billie's quarters where she and the dog hid during thunderstorms.

The good taste that Ziegfeld brought to the stage carried over to Burkeley Crest: the house reflected a quiet "old money" ambience. Flo enjoyed a comfortable life in an informal home. Billie collected furniture and decorative items while traveling, buying only those articles that meant something to her. The Ziegfelds hired decorators only to coordinate the decor with the objects that they had purchased.

The financial resources and the staff required to run an estate of this size were substantial. It cost Ziegfeld $10,000 per month to maintain Burkeley Crest. At one time the Ziegfelds had fifteen people working for them. The staff included a butler; a chambermaid; a cook; a parlor maid; a waitress; a laundress; Flo's valet, Sidney Boggis; a governess for Patty; and Billie's personal maid. Outside there were two gardeners, a kennelman, several chauffeurs, and a man in charge of the garage.

Patty had two playhouses. One, which they called the doll house, was a small structure much like those that little girls typically have in their backyards. The other—a replica of George Washington's home, Mount Vernon, about two-thirds scale, with a doorframe about five feet high—was quite another affair. William Randolph Hearst had originally used it on the set for a Marion Davies movie. Inside, it had a living room, dining room, library, two upstairs bedrooms, porch, and covered passageway to the kitchen.

Flo and Billie loved plants and flowers, so they had a vegetable garden and grew raspberries. Flowers were everywhere: tulips, narcissus, flowering bushes such as mock orange and weigela, and thousands of tube roses. At one time the tulip beds contained 17,000 blooms.

The Burkeley Crest grounds also had a zoo that was home to an array of animals. Ziegfeld was shy with people but was comfortable with and genuinely loved animals. His friend circus owner John Ringling would invite Ziegfeld to come to the dock and check the animals when boats arrived from Europe. Over the years, the stock at Ziegfeld's estate included an elephant; an exotic cat; lion cubs; a pair of blue macaws; deer; Billie's pet monkey, Charley; a black Pekingese dog; and two Canadian bears, Tunney and Dempsey.

Above: A formal portrait of Flo and Billie, c. 1927. Left: Burkeley Crest, the Ziegfelds' twenty-two-room mansion in Hastings-on-Hudson, New York

Father and daughter wandered the estate and visited the animals together. Sometimes the visits went the other way around. While still a calf, Ziggy the elephant was given free rein inside the house. One morning, he tried to climb a narrow staircase off the pantry, only to discover that he was exactly as wide as the staircase. He became wedged between the walls and started bellowing, and Flo had to come downstairs to extricate the poor fellow. After Ziggy's miscalculation, he was banished from the house.

For a while, they also kept goldfish in the house, until Billie had a bad experience with them. Billie was always worried about people and animals and birds being cold. She came home one night in the dead of winter—zero degrees outside. She just knew her goldfish were freezing, so she heated a large kettle of water and poured it into the aquarium. Needless to say, the next morning, for reasons that Billie couldn't explain, her poor darlings were belly-up. After that, Patty was not allowed to have goldfish—they were bad luck!

Delia Leonard, the family cook, said that the staff liked working for the Ziegfelds because they were so generous. At the holidays, Billie distributed more than seventy baskets containing a whole turkey and fixings plus candy. Ziegfeld reserved the entire first row of the mezzanine for the household employees on opening nights and invited them to film screenings on Sundays. When Delia was too busy to see the picture with the rest of the household, Ziegfeld paid the operators to rescreen the film for her.

The family's auto collection usually included at least four vehicles ranging from two Rolls-Royces to a

Above: Burkeley Crest from the rear (west side). Above right: The gates leading to the Burkeley Crest estate

Dodge station wagon. Billie's Belgian-made Minerva had a plush interior that costume designer John Harkrider said had solid-gold appointments. By the early 1920s Flo and Billie relied entirely on chauffeurs, because he wanted to work while traveling to and from Hastings.

It would probably have been easier for Ziegfeld to live in the city, but he enjoyed Burkeley Crest and the "country" enormously. Despite the inconvenience for their professional acquaintances from the city, the Ziegfelds regularly entertained on Sundays at Burkeley Crest. This was a continuation of the German custom from Ziegfeld's Chicago years. Sunday was the day on which to relax with friends, family, and business associates. Ziegfeld always wanted his daughter to attend the Sunday meals, even though she often preferred to play with friends. He "produced those Sunday dinners the way he produced his *Follies,* and he could not bear a false note in either the dinners or the shows," according to Patty. Joseph Urban's daughter Gretl corroborates some of Patty's perceptions about the Burkeley Crest dinners, referring to them as "quite an affair." Patty recalls a relaxed atmosphere during Sunday dinner, with people joking amidst animated conversation. The general tone was reminiscent of the Ziegfeld Club gatherings in Chicago.

There were usually fourteen to sixteen people at the table, including the Ziegfelds, the Jerome Wagners, and the Urbans, leaving room for four or five other couples from outside the core circle of friends. Sometimes, during tea, the total size of the gathering might reach twenty. From the theater world, key authors, composers, and designers were invited. Jerome Kern, Irving Berlin, Rudolf Friml, Ned Wayburn, and John Harkrider often visited. Mary Urban raised English sheepdogs to show and always brought her dog along. Inevitably Billie tried to pull back the dog's bangs, and Mary would patiently explain that the breed had weak eyes and couldn't stand the sun. In general, Ziegfeld invited few cast members—perhaps to maintain a proper distance as their employer. Even Eddie Cantor, with whom Flo had a close professional relationship, seldom if ever received an invitation to Sunday dinner.

Ziegfeld believed in God and an afterlife. Billie experimented with Christian Science, but Ziegfeld simply was not interested in organized religion—period. Neither he nor Billie was a member of any church, but Ziegfeld was spiritual; he had a serene inner belief that good would prevail. When Billie got upset, he calmed her down. He could be volatile when provoked, but it took a serious problem to make him lose control. His weak spot was that he had no tolerance for stupidity.

When it came to women's fashion, Ziegfeld liked women to be chic but natural and not overdressed. He believed that a woman's hair was an important element in her overall fashion statement and always fussed about his actresses' hair as he prepared shows, insisting that the women brush it until shiny, but he disliked dyed hair. He had allowed women in his shows to bob their hair for several years, but in 1924, he came out

Far left: Patty Ziegfeld's Mount Vernon playhouse. Left: The living room at Burkeley Crest as it looked in 1921. The walls were painted a pale Adam green, and the heavy taffeta drapes were the same color. The carpet was sand colored, and the chintz slip covers had pink water lilies with bright green leaves and storks.

publicly against bobbing, saying that the mob psychology that had so many women bobbing their hair "made them all alike as two peas in a pod. It has destroyed that elusive and priceless quality which women of charm must have—personality." Ironically, one year after Ziegfeld denounced bobbing as a mutilation of a woman's hair, his own wife arrived at the dinner table one evening wearing a hat. When Flo inquired about whether some unusual occasion prompted her to retain her bonnet, she replied: "No. I just like my new hat." Ziegfeld pushed her a bit more, only to have her remove her hat, revealing a 1925 bob, at which point she burst into tears, admitting that she did not much care for it. Ziegfeld liked it, though.

Ziegfeld's reading during these years focused on magazines that covered theater, such as *Variety, The New Yorker,* and *Judge.* He rarely read fiction, but he did like mysteries. He stayed abreast of current events and gleaned ideas for his shows by reading six daily newspapers: *The Times, Daily News, Daily Mirror, Tribune, Journal,* and *Post.* He did not read plays other than those he was interested in producing. In part at least, he kept up with what others were doing because Billie often alerted him about theater developments.

Some bills that have survived from the spring of 1925 provide a peek at details in the Ziegfeld lifestyle. Flo's telegram bill from Western Union for March 1925 was $601.40. He wrote between three and seventeen telegrams each day at a cost ranging from forty cents to $3.68 each. A bill dated April 9, 1925, indicates that a Maryland merchant sold him eight pounds of caviar for $44 and shipped it to Palm Beach.

By 1923, Patty was old enough for school. Initially Flo and Billie sent her to the Lincoln School in Manhattan. However, the Ziegfelds' approach to education did not appeal to the principal's notion that there was some correlation between regular attendance and academic performance. Cultural enrichment field trips, such as accompanying Billie on the road with a play, had not yet caught on with exclusive New York schools. The result was that, by the end of the spring term in 1924, the principal informed Flo that Patty "might be happier at another school." That fall Patty went to Halsted School in Yonkers. Generally Ziegfeld allowed Billie to discipline Patty, but his daughter vividly recalls that when her father did get involved, it was an event to remember. He could, she said, "make you just want to shrivel up."

The beginning of 1923 also saw some significant change among Ziegfeld's office staff. He had gathered about him a cast of characters who at their respective levels within the organization were as quirky as he was. Emily England had been Ziegfeld's secretary since 1912, but in February 1923, Matilda Golden joined the staff. Eventually "Goldie" became Ziegfeld's personal secretary and developed a fearsome reputation as the "keeper of the key," because she jealously controlled access to Ziegfeld.

Goldie seldom elicited moderate reactions. If she liked someone, she treated that person magnificently. If she did not, Goldie could and often did make life very difficult. Jack Harkrider noted that Ziegfeld's

Above: John Ringling and Flo Ziegfeld at Madison Square Garden sometime during the run of *Sally*. Ziegfeld obtained many of his animals from Ringling. Above right: Patty, Flo, and Billie in the sun parlor at Burkeley Crest, c. 1924

money problems caused her to develop an incredible officiousness that was fine for the bill collectors but perhaps not so appropriate for Ziegfeld's staff. Fiercely loyal to Ziegfeld, Goldie also protected him from temperamental actors and nasty rumors about what did or did not take place with the steady stream of women who came to his office. Once Goldie even handled a deranged woman who, according to her report, "carried an umbrella in one hand and a revolver in the other, when she came in, gunning for Ziggie. I told the woman that she was perfectly right, that Ziegfeld ought to be killed, and if she would sit down I'd bring him in and help her do it. Then I rounded up some of the boys who were upstairs. They got her out."

For ten years, Goldie put up with a man whose work habits were profoundly erratic. Frequently he could not sleep after 6:00 A.M. and so would begin working in bed. At other points, he would sit up all night writing to associates. Now and then he would call Goldie at 3:00 A.M. to ask a spelling question. He would dictate letters, pages long, that were rendered as one long sentence, and Goldie regularly struggled with hastily scrawled notes (always in pencil) that were only occasionally legible.

Other staff members were similarly devoted to Ziegfeld. Kathryn Dix, who worked for him from 1916 to 1923 and from 1927 to 1932 as telephone operator and as Billie's private secretary, was so protective that even two years after Ziegfeld died, when creditors were dunning the estate, she persistently claimed in a sworn court deposition that she had no idea what had happened to his financial records. The plaintiff's attorney clearly did not believe her; his interrogation implied that she herself hid or destroyed the books or that she knew who had disposed of them. She never gave the creditors a useful shard.

Other regular employees included Sam Kingston (business manager), Bernie McDonald (set construction), Alice Poole (switchboard), Ed "Pop" Rosenbaum, Sr. (road tour manager), O. O. McIntyre and Will Page (publicity), and Alfred Cheney Johnston (house photographer). In the turbulent world of theater, where frequent staff turnover was a fact of life, many of Ziegfeld's employees stayed with him for long stretches. Kingston was with him on and off over three decades.

Loyal though they may have been, Ziegfeld's staff was not one big happy family. In fact, they squabbled constantly, a situation that Ziegfeld exacerbated through his own habits. Sometimes he would get upset over the staff's inability to bring order from chaos and would scream, "Jesus, what kind of place am I running here?" He was never on time for appointments, so Goldie routinely had to cover for him. He also hated answering mail and would let it sit for months untouched, allowing no one to answer it, remove it, or even straighten the piles. Goldie thinks that he actually liked the clutter on his desk.

These surviving anecdotes simultaneously complicate and help unravel the mystery of Ziegfeld's many accomplishments. Genius alone does not allow one man to achieve as much as Florenz Ziegfeld did,

Far left: Ziegfeld greeting his newly purchased chimpanzee, Sally, on its arrival from Germany, August 16, 1922. Left: Patty Ziegfeld feeding Dempsey or Tunney, one of the family's two bears, c. 1926

Apparently animals and birds liked Flo Ziegfeld as much as he liked them; here a falcon perches on his head.

nor does brilliance necessarily elicit loyalty of this measure from this number of individuals.

Ziegfeld had a gift for making people feel special. The little touches were not the sum of his gift, but they contributed substantially. By this point, too, an aura of greatness surrounded Ziegfeld. The combination made performers and staff eager to work for him and willing to put up with his work style in the belief that they were serving a higher cause: Ziegfeld's vision. At the same time, his inchoate approach to realizing his visions took its toll on the people who worked with him. He expected them to be as willing to strive for those standards as he was. The very trait that had raised him to spectacular heights began contributing to serious problems with the people whose help he needed.

Ziegfeld's compulsive, almost hyperbolic, desire to communicate with people in his shows was often lampooned or recalled in anecdotes that smack of the apocryphal. There are stories about him sending a thousand-word telegram from the back of the theater to the actors' dressing room—inside the same building—and of his discussing an issue extensively on the phone only to wire virtually the same content in a lengthy, corroborative telegram. He would also pepper his staff with numerous "missiles" in one day.

Naturally, this eccentric, not to speak of expensive, behavior was fodder for Eddie Cantor and other comedians. Nevertheless, it is a mistake to focus only on the quirkiness of the behavior. The morsel to glean from these grand gestures: whether the telegram was positive or negative, the person receiving it knew the urgency of Ziegfeld's message. No one working for this man could ever be complacent. The telegrams were for staff and performers palpable reminders of Ziegfeld's high standard and key elements of his success.

Relatively few of the Ziegfelds' telegrams have survived. However, a recently discovered packet of 125 wires between Flo and Billie, covering a six-week period in early 1923, provides a revealing window into the Ziegfelds' world. Billie's telegram on February 3, 1923, indicates how important professional camaraderie was to her relationship with Flo: "How I should love to see you. You couldn't make me fight. . . . Business so bad. Let's do a musical comedy with lots of comedy. If have a funny face we might just as well use it. I think your authors could fit me. Am tired and homesick for you tonight. Devotedly, Baby."

As these telegrams show, Billie also expressed her concern about beautiful women, which she often phrased in amusing ways: "I can't bear to think of you all beautiful and sunburned. You are so much dearer and more attractive than all the other men in the world that it's a joke. Only I hate to tell you, but all those other old cats do, so please don't forget that I am here and besides all that you are married to me."

Several weeks later, Billie's fears intensified; she actually named one of the women:

Hope you are happy with the fish—but dearest try not to love any one—you don't know how I suffer

Left: Matilda Golden was Ziegfeld's personal secretary for more than a decade until his death. Right: Ziggy, a former circus elephant, was a birthday gift from Ziegfeld to his daughter.

with your being so crazy about Louisa [Louisa Wannamaker Munn] and different people. You think I don't know she knows what a wonderful lover you are—she's not hanging around for something to eat—I know that—I try not to think of it but I suffer inside just the same—I don't have any lovers but I do want my husband and I want all of him and when you don't want me let's call it all off—no double crossing. My devoted love always. Bill.

Somehow Billie survived repeated public allegations about Ziegfeld's love affairs and even joked with him about his extramarital love life: "Can't imagine your feeling blue down there. That don't go, dear, altho I hear you have been left rather flat for another heavy swain. Cheer up, darling. Love, Billie."

Early February brought a crisis over Patty's health. There was a physiological basis to the problem; the "upsets have come from nervous tension she lives under," Billie wrote. Flo wanted Billie and Patty to join him in Florida, but Billie had been so worried about Patty's health, the unpaid bills, and Ziegfeld's infidelities that the doctor became concerned about her health as well and advised them not to travel.

A clear portrait of Billie's mental state comes from this note:

I saw my doctor today and he frightened me rather. . . . I am down to one hundred and eighteen and can't put on any flesh, but the bills for five thousand came in Saturday. That upset. They must be paid my darling. If you really mean I can have my six week's pay, it would take away all my anxiety, but I would want it now for I know you would forget, but if I can have it and get cleaned up maybe my poor nerves would calm down. . . . I am glad you want us. I am more miserable than I have dared tell you.

Even though Flo did well later in 1923 with *Kid Boots,* the money problems were coming from every which way. The Ziegfelds were so far in arrears on the electric bill that their standing with the city was in jeopardy. Problems were also appearing in the professional realm. One production supplier, Elsie Farley, wrote that she held off contacting Ziegfeld about his account with her interior decorating firm because she knew that he had been ill. She had decided to halt work for Billie until Flo made at least a partial payment on his account. The account included exterior and interior painting at Hastings and labor for the *Follies.*

Despite money problems and Billie's nervous disorder caused by worrying about the bills, the Ziegfelds were at this moment nonchalantly working out details to rent a houseboat, *The Chieftain,* for seventeen days at a cost of $3,000 (March 15–31, 1923). The rental arrangement called for a crew of ten—captain, engineer, assistant engineer, cook, assistant cook, steward, messboy, and three sailors. Ziegfeld also had to pay extra for running expenses such as the crew's wages and food and the deck/engine room consumables.

Left: Florenz Ziegfeld, Sr., late in life. Right: In his office, Ziegfeld looks at photos of aspiring showgirls.

One week later something renewed Billie's faith in Ziegfeld's love for her (what, precisely, remains a mystery), but her reinvigorated belief that he really cared also reflected just how desperate she was:

> My dearest, for the first time in the nine years that I have loved you I feel you really care enough to have made me very, very happy. I feel such a load off my poor skinny shoulders and my faith in you has been justified. . . . I do love you so and when I think you don't care what I am going through I just don't want to live. I am very happy and very, very grateful and terribly anxious to see you. Devotedly, Billie.

By this time, in 1923, Ziegfeld's parents were elderly: his father was eighty-one years old and his mother in her mid-seventies. Dr. Ziegfeld was well enough to be sending telegrams several times a month, but Rosalie had become quite frail. Nevertheless, it was Dr. Ziegfeld who died first, on May 20, 1923, after a four-day illness with pneumonia. Rosalie, William, Louise, and Flo were present when he died.

The *Follies* traditionally had a summer run in New York followed by a fall tour that extended into the following spring. But the 1922 edition ran in New York through much of 1923. Will Rogers had promised to stay with the 1922 show until its New York run ended. He was, of course, by now one of Ziegfeld's biggest stars, but he was also one of the producer's best friends within the acting community.

The genuine warmth in Ziegfeld's note to Rogers when the star left the show provided a solid transition for Rogers's later return: "My dear Will: It is with sincere regret that the time has come where you are leaving the *Ziegfeld Follies*. . . . I have never had anyone appear in any of my attractions that was a greater joy to be associated with than you. . . . Give my love to your family, and it is with regret that I must say 'au revoir' to my friend. A REAL MAN [written in hand]. Very sincerely yours, Ziegfeld."

Ziegfeld did not open the *Follies of 1923* until October 20. *Variety* reported that the show grossed $42,000 during the first week, a very strong start. One reviewer said the 1923 edition represented a decline because it lacked snap and comedy. W. C. Fields and Will Rogers were missing, and Eddie Cantor did not join the show until November. The show had no book. Paul Whiteman, who played the violin in knickers, and his orchestra were a popular attraction, but this year's sets were not as elaborate as those in the past, and the costumes did not attract much attention. Ziegfeld kept the 1923 edition in New York through May 10, 1924, because rising costs discouraged a tour. Touring had always been lucrative, but the popular 1922 *Follies,* with its large cast and elaborate scenery and costumes, was still on the road in early 1924. The cost of sending out a second large troupe was prohibitive.

This year's show opened on a Saturday night for a public dress rehearsal. Victor Herbert had waited

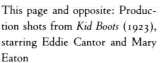
This page and opposite: Production shots from *Kid Boots* (1923), starring Eddie Cantor and Mary Eaton

until 2:00 A.M. to conduct his music for "Legend of the Drums." Somehow, shortly after he started his number, the wrong music cue was given, and the orchestra began the finale prematurely. The finale triggered the lowering of the curtains, but Herbert stood there ready to resume where he had left off. After the house lights came on, the puzzled audience waited a minute and then left.

Even though two numbers that were to follow "Legend of the Drums" were omitted, the opening-night show lasted five hours and ten minutes. By Monday night, the show had been cut to two hours and fifty-seven minutes. One of the numbers Ziegfeld cut was a gold mesh bag illusion that had cost $27,000.

It was reported that Ziegfeld looked at more than 17,000 women to get 100 for the *Follies*. By the time rehearsals were imminent, he had whittled the number to 1,100 women. Of these, Ziegfeld then selected 150 to begin rehearsals. On the Saturday before the show opened, the day for final costume fittings, Ziegfeld selected the 100 women who would be in the show.

Ziegfeld's feud with Marilyn Miller continued; on December 18, 1923, Flo claimed that he dropped her from the cast of *Sally* because she had been absent so much. There was also friction over the fact that he had reduced the number of dances she performed. She said that her dancing was hindered by a knee injury and contended that she quit the show; Flo countered that he had decided not to renew her contract.

The next day, ignoring the fact that he had been quoted as saying that he fired her, Ziegfeld alleged that Miller quit *Sally* because she was jealous of Mary Eaton in *Kid Boots*. Some people associated with Ziegfeld's shows in those days say that the real issue was missed performances: they claim that on many occasions Marilyn was unable to dance because she was drunk. Prior to the death of her husband, Miller had missed few performances, according to Doris Eaton, her understudy from 1918 to 1920.

While Ziegfeld was preparing the 1923 *Follies*, late in the year, he was also mounting *Kid Boots*, which on several accounts was to prove a pivotal show for both Ziegfeld and Eddie Cantor. It verified that Ziegfeld could sustain his success with book shows, and it gave Cantor his first star vehicle. Just as important, the show provided the two men an opportunity to reconcile their differences.

Cantor claims that when he and William Anthony McGuire contacted Ziegfeld about doing *Kid Boots*, Ziegfeld never mentioned their bitter parting. He just invited Cantor back into the fold, acting as though nothing had happened. He may have been motivated, in part, by Cantor's success in Shubert shows.

Cantor and McGuire, along with composer Harry Tierney and lyricists Otto Harbach and Joseph McCarthy, dreamed up the plot for *Kid Boots* after Cantor showed up for a social occasion dressed in a flamboyant getup that included checked knickerbockers and a golf cap.

Kid Boots opened December 31, 1923, at the Earl Carroll Theatre. After opening night, Ziegfeld cut a few dance numbers to shorten the show but, amazingly for him, made few other changes. He did change the costumes and scenery in Act One—at a cost of $20,000—even though the show was a hit. Apparently, he just did not like them.

Ziegfeld was pleased with Cantor's performance but worried constantly about Cantor slipping in double entendres, which Ziegfeld thought were funny but out of place. Patty says that Ziegfeld "was always working on him [Cantor] to cool it. And then he'd come in one night to listen and would catch him at it."

After the *Kid Boots* opening (New Year's Eve), according to Cantor, Flo "put his arm around my shoulders. 'I won't see you at midnight, Eddie, Happy New Year.' There were tears in my eyes. All my life I'd longed for a father and now, of all the men in the world, Ziegfeld was treating me like a son."

Kid Boots was a critical and financial success. It ran just short of fourteen months in New York. The tour grossed $35,000 in Boston the first week. Ziegfeld took $5,500, while Cantor's 10 percent cut earned him approximately $3,000 for the week. After the show ran for one thousand performances, Ziegfeld honored Cantor at the *Follies,* giving him an inscribed platinum pocket watch that his daughter Marilyn has kept running for nearly seventy years.

Despite his surface-level success, the early 1920s had been very troublesome for Ziegfeld. The *Follies* were having long runs, but it was increasingly difficult to sign, let alone retain, good headliners, because of growing competition from both film and other Broadway revues. His relationship with Marilyn Miller had deteriorated into a sordid mess that severely strained Ziegfeld's relationship with Billie. His brother Carl and his father had died. He was in debt despite earning substantial profits from *Sally* and the *Follies.*

What sustained him during these trying years was Patty's adoration and Billie's conviction that she had married one of the century's great men. A note that Billie wrote Flo—after David Belasco praised Ziegfeld's contribution to the theater—captures the spirit of what Billie and Flo shared: "Belasco was so dear. . . . He thinks you are a genius—and that you are doing such wonderful work (when not at Palm Beach). Thank God you havent [sic] enough money to loaf all the time with these numbsculls [sic]—or you would never achieve any of these glorious things you have given the world and as a result put yourself in the foremost rank of the great men of the day."

Although Ziegfeld could not have been pleased with Billie for repeatedly needling him about his affairs, he had to know that her jealousy was borne of a passionate love. Part of the sustaining force in the marriage may well have been the fact that Flo never quite knew what Billie would do next.

Right: The Ziegfelds vacationing in Riley Brook, New Brunswick, in 1923. Far right: Flo, Patty, and Billie at Lake Louise in Canada, c. 1929. Below: Ziegfeld in front of the boathouse at Camp Patricia, c. 1929.

❖

CHAPTER 12

CAMP PATRICIA

❖

Many of Ziegfeld's difficulties in the 1920s concerned legal problems resulting from his debts. Early in 1924 Ziegfeld still owed $10,000 in rent (from 1921) on the New Amsterdam Roof Theatre; Ziegfeld's Midnight Frolics, Inc., also owed the NewAm Theatre Corporation $10,000. Both were threatening to take legal action to recover the debt. Ironically, Ziegfeld was a co-owner and partner in both companies. Many of Ziegfeld's creditors were finding him as elusive as his landlords. A cartoonist named Bert Green became upset when Ziegfeld refused to pay him for artwork that he had submitted. After trying unsuccessfully for weeks to serve Ziegfeld the legal papers for a suit, Green's lawyers finally devised a plot that got them past "Goldie's gate": an associate pretended to be delivering a gift—six bottles of whiskey (during Prohibition). When queried about the suit, Ziegfeld said that the cartoons Green submitted were not what the artist had promised and they were late.

Other people were suing Ziegfeld, including Olive Cornell, whom he had said was incompetent; Gallagher and Shean, who challenged his right to enforce a nonstandard contract that controlled their careers; and violinist-composer Mischa Elman, who sued Ziegfeld for peremptorily canceling a project. Some suits Ziegfeld won; many he lost. Occasionally suits arose because he simply did not have the money to pay his bills. In most other cases, as was true earlier in his career, a difference had arisen over a professional issue and the nub of the legal action was Ziegfeld's right to control his or the litigant's destiny.

To make matters worse, labor disputes continued, becoming more nettlesome as time passed. Because of a conflict over an Equity closed-shop rule, Ziegfeld canceled tours for the *Follies* and *Sally*. He said that many prominent members of Equity did not believe in a closed shop. Then, in a characteristically independent move, Billie complicated his interaction with labor by joining Equity in mid-May 1924.

One happy note regarding his relations with his actors was the reappearance of Will Rogers in the 1924 *Follies*. Less than three months after Rogers's "defection," on August 29, 1923, Ziegfeld had written

Will a note in the attempt to persuade him to return: "It's time you were back. . . . Please wire me immediately after talking to your boss, Mrs. Rogers, [of] your decision. . . . I would endeavor to get two great scenes for you . . . practically making you the star of the organization in the *Follies*. . . . There is no time to lose and I hope you realize that your pictures should come second to your public appearance. . . . I want you to come without fail, Bill. Answer quick."

Ziegfeld was not successful in luring Rogers back for the 1923 *Follies* but, thinking ahead to the 1924 show, he struck where Rogers, the family man, was vulnerable. Ziegfeld bought his children wonderful gifts at Christmas: an exquisite mah-jongg set for Mary, a motorized scooter for Will, Jr., and a sailboat "the size of a swimming pool" for Jimmy. Apparently his ploy worked: Rogers agreed to return in 1924, and the kids were impressed enough that Jimmy mentioned the gesture nearly seventy years later.

The 1924 edition of the *Follies* opened on June 24. Despite Will's presence in the show, there was little emphasis on the comic element. The objective was still visual beauty but without the opulence of earlier editions. Ludwig Kainer was the primary set designer this year, although Urban still participated, and Julian Mitchell returned after a nine-year absence. Ann Pennington was back, although fewer outstanding individual dancers appeared. There was, however, dancing from the Tiller Girls and the London Empire Girls.

On October 30, 1924, Ziegfeld opened his fall edition of the *Follies* (still the nineteenth), featuring several new cast members, such as Mitti and Tillio. The popular shadowgraph illusion from 1923 was added to this version, but two-thirds of the scenes were retained from the June show.

The camp in New Brunswick where the family had vacationed in 1923 did not meet Billie's standards: there was no indoor plumbing, and they all stayed in one room that had the sleeping quarters at one end and the dining quarters at the other. Billie went on a tear, cleaning, organizing, and putting up partitions made of blankets. After that experience, in 1924 Ziegfeld took a ninety-nine-year lease on an island in the Canadian Laurentians, 125 miles northwest of Quebec—which he renamed Billie Burke Island.

Camp Patricia on Billie Burke Island had six cabins built of peeled logs, with electricity and modern plumbing: a main house, guest lodge, dining room and kitchen, a storehouse, a dorm for the guides, and a house for Billie. Inside there was "plenty of luxury." The staff of eighteen included a trained nurse; Patty's companion, Blackie; the family chauffeur, Jim, to run the Chris-Craft boat; Armand, to run the Lake Edward boat; eight guides; Captain Gray; Dr. Wagner; and Ziegfeld's valet, Sidney. The boat operator traveled twelve miles each day to gather supplies for the assembled masses.

After arriving at camp, Ziegfeld usually took four to five days to "simmer down and relax enough to

Above, left to right: Flo Ziegfeld, standing at left; a guide; daughter, Patty, with Captain Gray's arm around her; and Billie Burke. The group had to use a horse-drawn wagon to reach the camp at Riley Brook, New Brunswick. Norma Terris and second husband, Dr. Jerome Wagner, were close friends of the Ziegfeld family. The main cabin at Camp Patricia. Below: Florenz Ziegfeld, his wife and daughter, and his mother

Right: Billie Burke and a feline friend in *Annie Dear* (1924). Below: Child prodigy Lina Basquette was sixteen when she became a featured dancer and choreographed her own numbers in the *Follies*. In 1925, at age eighteen, she left Ziegfeld to marry forty-year-old Sam Warner. Bottom:

Ziegfeld dismissed Imogene Wilson from the *Follies* after her scandalous affair with comedian Frank Tinney. She eventually ended up in Hollywood and became a leading lady, making about twenty films under the name of Mary Nolan.

cook. Then, suddenly, he would turn into a prototypical French-Canadian woodsman, talking in monosyllables, stalking through the woods silent as a cat, and growing a beard."

At camp, Billie insisted that everyone bathe in the lake each morning, despite the fact that "the water was 'oomph' degrees." The woods surrounding Camp Patricia were so primitive that deer would come up to the cabin door. Billie, who was not amused by their curiosity, would shoo them away.

Remote as the camp was, Billie and Flo were never ones to let the isolation spoil their fun. They regularly invited a select group of visitors whom they considered part of the extended family. Over the years this group included Irving Berlin, John Harkrider, Leonard Replogle, and Paul Block, among others.

One year, Ziegfeld's friend Jerome Wagner came up to camp disguised as the Duke of Athol. Being British, Sidney got all dressed up to meet him. Said Patty: "We turned the place upside down. We met the Duke, and my father shook hands with him, and when he turned around to shake hands with someone else, my father kicked him in the butt. Everybody absolutely fell apart. It turned out that Daddy had recognized Wagner as an impostor. Sidney, of course, was dashed to think that he wasn't going to socialize with this wonderful Englishman he had been preparing for weeks to meet."

Wagner, who was twenty years younger than Ziegfeld, was an Ivy League man, short, balding, and portly. About 1914 he started going to the New Amsterdam Roof, where he met theater people and soon became a regular in theater circles. Wagner later became the house doctor for the Ziegfeld Theatre. What nobody knew for years was that he was a proctologist—an odd choice, certainly, to serve one hundred or more female cast members. Doc was always around—out at Hastings, on trips, and at camp. He and his wife, Norma Terris, were like family. Ziegfeld needed an ear away from theater, and Wagner fit the bill. Doc gladly acted as court jester, allowing Ziegfeld to play practical jokes on him and make him the butt of rough humor. In addition, Wagner played "very bad bridge," which most likely delighted Ziegfeld, who needed an easy mark when he and his cronies played.

That fall of 1924, Ziegfeld signed a contract for the film version of *Sally*. He also announced plans to spend $1 million constructing a two-thousand-seat theater in Chicago.

Not yet sufficiently busy with these other two projects, Ziegfeld opened *Annie Dear* on November 4, 1924. Critics praised the cast and the dancing. The costumes were gorgeous, and the stage settings were stunning. One review said Ziegfeld had reached an artistic peak with this show.

While one critic said *Annie Dear* was Clare Kummer's best work, another complained that her music was weak. Ziegfeld hired Sigmund Romberg and Cliff Grey to bolster Kummer's original score. After the opening, Ziegfeld cut some of Kummer's numbers and wanted other changes; however, Kummer insisted

Left: W. C. Fields being sketched by comic strip artist Harry Hershfield in 1925, while Fields was starring in *The Comic Supplement*. Between 1915 and 1925, Fields was in seven editions of the *Ziegfeld Follies*. Right: Helen Shea in *The Comic Supplement*

that the cut material be restored. When the producer and Kummer could not reach an agreement, Ziegfeld closed the show, making this the first in a string of unsuccessful productions over the next two years.

When the *Follies* stopped in Chicago this year, Ziegfeld as usual arranged for his mother to attend the show. Ziegfeld was devoted to Rosalie. Victor Kiraly, one of Ziegfeld's stage managers, narrated a touching story about how Flo "did" Christmas for his mother:

Louise Brooks, Leon Errol, and Anastasia Reilly in *Louie the 14th* (1925)

> On Christmas Day, for every year attained by her, Flo sent her by his manager a ten dollar gold piece; the bag became weightier each season. In addition, the stage hands of the *Follies* . . . secured the largest tree available, to be set up in the spacious parlor of her residence. Hundreds of miniature electric lamps and a mass of decorations adorned the tree, in readiness for the big event, to honor and bring joy to Mrs. Florenz Ziegfeld, Sr., who, already feeble, seldom left her own rooms upstairs. It was in 1924, the last time that . . . Ziegfeld's sister led the old lady downstairs to view the tree with its multitude of lights. But Flo's mother stood still, showing no sign of perception; she was stone blind and sobbing, knowing full well that the annual surprise was no longer to be enjoyed by her.

At the end of 1924, despite advice not to attempt this production, Ziegfeld began work on *The Comic Supplement,* which was written by J. P. McEvoy and starred W. C. Fields. *The Comic Supplement* opened at the Shubert Theatre in Newark, New Jersey, on January 9, 1925. The show was a series of scenes in the life of the Jones family, with Fields in the role of Pa Jones. *Life* magazine said that the costumes by John Held, Jr., were advanced for a revue, and Norman Bel Geddes's sets were masterpieces.

While the actors were rehearsing a pantomime called "A Back Porch," Ziegfeld stopped them and told McEvoy that the sketch was terrible. McEvoy persuaded Ziegfeld to let the audience decide. When *The Comic Supplement* played in Washington, D.C., the sketch had the audience shaking with laughter. Ziegfeld, standing next to McEvoy, turned to him and said, "See? I told you." McEvoy responded: "But the people are laughing their heads off." Ziegfeld added sadly, "They don't mean it." Nevertheless, after the show closed, Ziegfeld used the sketch in the spring edition of the *Follies* and kept it for the summer 1925 edition. Fields also used the material in his silent movie *It's the Old Army Game* (1926).

After the tryouts in Newark, *The Comic Supplement* moved to Washington. One paper said Ziegfeld was "not half-way along the road toward reaching a hit. He has merely made a commendable start." It did not reach New York. The show cost only $81,678.13, but even so it lost money. Though Ziegfeld and Erlanger were no longer working together on production details, Erlanger was backing Ziegfeld in his book

Above left: Dorothy Knapp debuted on Broadway in 1923 and was in the 1924 and 1925 *Follies*. By 1929, she was earning $1,000 per week as the lead in *Fioretta*. However, she lacked sufficient talent for a lead role and was dismissed. She then filed—and lost—a $500,000 lawsuit over her dismissal. In 1933 she married a Montreal radio announcer. Above right: The beautiful and talented Louise Brooks aspired to be a great dancer but gave up dancing for films. She probably could have been a major film star, but she did not get along well in Hollywood.

shows, generally in a seventy-five–twenty-five split. In this case they lost around $40,000.

The outstanding producers in Ziegfeld's day—Frohman, Shubert, and Erlanger—had their own theaters in New York (sometimes several) as well as numerous houses across the country, so that they controlled their fates even when their shows left New York. Ziegfeld's press agent said that Ziegfeld had always railed against the fact that Erlanger had become a very wealthy man just because he owned "walls and a roof," while Ziegfeld worked desperately hard producing smash hits and was not making nearly as much money. He recalled Ziegfeld saying: "If I only had a theater of my own . . . things would be different."

For some time Ziegfeld had been trying to acquire such a theater. He had a variety of motives. He wanted the control it would afford him over his own productions. More than that, Ziegfeld craved the prestige associated with having his own theater. He knew, too, that he could save significant money if no rent drained off a substantial portion of the income—sometimes as much as 40 percent of the profit.

For all of these reasons—control, prestige, and profit—Ziegfeld wanted his own theater. His first attempt, when he teamed with Dillingham at the Century, having failed, he had recently begun leasing the Cosmopolitan Theatre at Columbus Circle (that white elephant location) from W. R. Hearst. Ziegfeld had Urban redecorate it. Urban painted sixteen panels on canvas that were then set into the theater's walls and ceiling. Flemish tapestries were hung on the balcony-level wall; below them were solid bronze torches. His lease gave Ziegfeld complete control of the theater and its productions.

Then Ziegfeld and Hearst realized that they had a mutual interest in building a theater near Hearst's Warwick Hotel, at Fifty-fourth Street and Sixth Avenue. The theater district was still concentrated around Forty-second Street, so the Warwick was a bit far north. Hearst wanted a cultural attraction nearby to draw hotel patrons. When Ziegfeld mentioned his desire for a theater, Hearst and his right-hand man, Arthur Brisbane, agreed to finance a theater across the street from the Warwick.

On January 8, 1925, Ziegfeld announced their plans, saying that the theater would be completed by November 1926. Work began immediately to erect what was to be the finest theater in New York City. Ziegfeld and Hearst selected Joseph Urban as architect. (He was assisted by Thomas Lamb.) Ziegfeld retained his interest in the New Amsterdam Theatre and continued to lease the Cosmopolitan.

Louie the 14th opened in the Cosmopolitan Theatre on March 5, 1925. Ziegfeld had always liked Leon Errol's humor, so he was optimistic about the show. The production's gorgeous costumes, lovely stage settings, and large choruses (eighty-eight chorus girls; forty singers) helped overcome the weak book. For the banquet scene, Ziegfeld acquired the gold service of the Russian Imperial family (at a cost of thousands of dollars) and engaged a real chef to cook the meal.

Bernard Sobel, Ziegfeld's press agent, had the chorus girls parade in bathing suits to City Hall to aid the military recruiting drive. This publicity stunt prolonged the show's run and launched its tour. The tour was cut short, however, when Leon Errol injured his ankle.

On March 10, 1925, Ziegfeld opened the spring edition of the *Follies*. Many scenes from the June and October editions of the 1924 show were carried over into this one (still called the nineteenth edition—the same as the 1924 shows); Ziegfeld also took the best scenes from *The Comic Supplement* for his *Follies*. Later, on July 6, Ziegfeld opened the *Follies of 1925* but carried over scenes from the 1924 and the spring 1925 editions. The 1924 and 1925 shows are, therefore, closely aligned, and many theater historians combine discussions of the two. Together, the 1924 and 1925 editions ran 510 performances.

Ziegfeld worked closely with Ben Ali Haggin on his tableaux for this edition. Each scene lasted less than a minute, during which the women, who were nude under chiffon coverings, had to remain absolutely still. The scenes were artistic and not vulgar, yet, during rehearsal for the 1925 show, Will Rogers complained to Ziegfeld about the nudity. He told Ziegfeld, "Fix the nudity or I quit." Ziegfeld covered the women enough to suit Rogers, and Rogers appeared in the spring and summer editions.

The culmination of a very busy year came when the summer *Follies* opened. Even though this was Ziegfeld's twentieth edition of the show, its production involved difficulties. Cast members were reluctant to accept Dorothy Knapp, whom they dubbed the "Sultana" because she had a handsome salary and a dressing

Billie, Flo, and Patty Ziegfeld sailing to Europe aboard the *Majestic* in 1925

room to herself. Gossip among the cast suggested that she "had a connection to Ziegfeld's office."

One day while the actors were rehearsing a skit by J. P. McEvoy, they complained of too much noise. Someone in the back of the theater was laughing so loudly that the actors had to stop rehearsing. Ziegfeld sent his stage manager to eject the nuisance. When the manager returned after throwing the man out, Ziegfeld asked who it was. The manager replied, "That was McEvoy laughing at his own stuff."

Salary sheets from around 1925 are revealing. Will Rogers was pulling in $3,100 per week during the spring before he left, while principals such as Ray Dooley, Ann Pennington, and W. C. Fields earned between $700 and $1,750 per week. Dorothy Knapp, not even a principal, received $200 a week. Staff salaries were far lower, but they were very solid for the times: Sam Kingston—$250, Bernard Sobel—$175, telephone operator Alice Poole—$45, and Julian Mitchell for dance direction—$150.

Financially, the *Follies* were still doing well, but reviewers complained that the shows were repetitive. Just as it appeared that the revue had become irrevocably stale, John Harkrider arrived. In his unpublished autobiography, Harkrider claims to have made a splashy debut, staging a spectacular dance with Louise Brooks at a society affair attended by Ziegfeld. (He concedes at the outset of this highly entertaining account that he has not bothered himself seriously with facts, but he insists that his narrative accurately captures the spirit of the times.) Harkrider says that when Ziegfeld challenged him about what he had to offer the producer, he replied that he had talent. Ziegfeld scornfully noted: "I *make* talent." Harkrider responded: "Buck? He can't write his way out of a bag. Weyburn [*sic*] could turn the Russian ballet into an amateur dance troupe. Urban's sets haven't changed in ten years. Or haven't you read your reviews since then?"

This scathing critique and Harkrider's initial costume design apparently caught Ziegfeld's attention. Harkrider's imaginative, flamboyant designs made even Ziegfeld look like a piker, and the two men struggled constantly over costs. Nevertheless, the chemistry worked: Harkrider would have a significant role in Ziegfeld's shows for the rest of Ziegfeld's career.

Just three weeks after the spring edition of the *Follies* opened, First National Pictures released the silent-film version of *Sally*. Ziegfeld had agreed to work on the film, but there is no indication that he significantly affected its production. The release provided the first telling indication that Ziegfeld had to concede ground to film, by selling rights on his theatrical productions. Less than three months later, he made public his plans to join Jesse Lasky in a series of film projects. The first of these films was *Glorifying the American Girl* (1929), an overt attempt to cash in on the success of the *Follies*.

Originally Ziegfeld was to be the director, so he was concerned with cast selection, lobbying for Constance Bennett and Greta Nissen to be included and pressuring Lasky to arrange shooting to accommodate Flo's busy schedule. Despite this flurry of activity, the project was delayed for years.

On July 23, 1925, the indefatigable Ziegfeld said that he was planning to produce *Louie the 14th* and *Kid Boots* in London. Two days later, the Ziegfeld family embarked on a grand five-week tour of Europe, arriving in Paris on July 31. Naturally they went first class, sailing on the RMS *Majestic*, staying at the Ritz, shopping, and visiting the *Folies Bergère*. On August 5, they went to Deauville, playground of the rich, where Ziegfeld got his gambling "fix." By August 13 they had journeyed to England, where one of Ziegfeld's friends announced that the producer needed chorus girls. The heart of London became so clogged with crowds of girls seeking auditions that the police finally gave up on unsnarling the mess.

Most news about Hollywood was bad news for Ziegfeld, but one development in 1925 caught his attention: Samuel Goldwyn released a very successful rendition of *Ben Hur*. Back in 1899, Klaw and Erlanger had bought the stage rights to Lew Wallace's novel *Ben-Hur*, which they produced successfully for the next twenty years. By 1907, the film industry was advancing well enough for competition to develop over movie rights to the property, prompting the Kalem Company to produce an illegal short version of the title. Somehow, Klaw and Erlanger slipped in to nab the rights—beating out the likes of D. W. Griffith, Samuel Goldwyn, and Adolph Zukor—and immediately sold them to Goldwyn. They cut Ziegfeld into the deal, which turned out to be one of the sweetest ever made. Goldwyn agreed to give them 50 percent of the profit, which ultimately totaled more than $3 million.

On October 27, Ziegfeld announced that he would open the Club de Montmartre in Palm Beach. It was to be a restaurant-theater backed by George and Paris Singer and A. J. Drexel Biddle, Jr.

Between 1922 and 1925, the *Follies* were on a strange trajectory. Most critics felt that the revue was losing its cutting edge. Nevertheless, during this period Ziegfeld introduced some of his most original numbers, such as the Tiller Girls' precision dancing and W. C. Fields's brilliant "A Back Porch." In addition, he was still devising innovative staging techniques, including the "Lace-Land" scene with its radium lighting effect, and he introduced classical dance that had not been seen in popular Broadway shows.

Late in 1925, with Marc Klaw and Abe Erlanger still battling over how to divide the booty from the *Follies* empire, they began wrangling over rights to the revue's name. The dispute left Ziegfeld unable to use the title in his own production. As 1926 approached, he decided to escape the internecine feuding by taking the show to Palm Beach for that city's first and only New York–caliber production.

Above, left to right: "Amado" was the Palm Beach home of Charles Munn. Flo and Billie at the Breaker's Hotel in Palm Beach. Gurnee Munn's Palm Beach home, "Louwana"

❖

CHAPTER 13

ALL THAT GLITTERS

❖

On 1915, the winter after Billie and Flo married, they began vacationing in Palm Beach, Florida, called by *Fortune* magazine the "only international resort in the United States." According to James Kilpatrick, "Palm Beach in the twenties was rich, rich, rich." Palm Beach had to be seen to be believed, but a brief anecdote captures its essence. Colonel E. R. Bradley, owner of Bradley's Beach Club, once dubbed "the world's sportiest and classiest gambling house," was chatting with a widow whose husband had left her $62 million. According to Kilpatrick, she "couldn't resist talking about her good fortune. The colonel quietly shushed her. 'Don't mention it,' he advised. 'They might not think that was very much down here.'"

For the first eight years or so, Billie and Flo stayed in the Royal Poinciana Hotel. This 1,150-room hotel, set on thirty-two acres, was fabled for its service. The dining room seated 1,600 and had 400 white-gloved waiters in attendance. Gradually the Ziegfelds worked their way into Palm Beach's most exclusive society, through the contacts provided by Marjorie Meriweather Hutton. She and Billie became close friends, while her husband, E. F. Hutton, of investment fame, became one of Flo's closest companions.

People who go to Palm Beach for the season (not just for a vacation) know that those who are accepted in society do not stay at a hotel. They either own a residence or rent one for the season, which runs from just after Christmas until Easter. It is "unchic" to stay past Easter. In 1924, the Ziegfelds rented Zilla Villa on South Ocean Boulevard, the oceanfront street that is *the* address in Palm Beach, for two seasons. The following two seasons they rented Concha Marina, and another year they stayed at Louwana. Later they were at Trailside, also on Ocean Boulevard. These were splendid mansions, on a scale that explains why Patty Ziegfeld recalls Burkeley Crest as being a fairly modest place by comparison.

When the Ziegfelds went to Florida, all bets for work and school were off. Patty met with tutors, but, she said, "school never interfered with anything. I'm surprised that I learned to read and write." Life there revolved around sports, food, and parties. Three times a week Ziegfeld and Patty went out on the ocean for

Left: J. Leonard Replogle and Flo Ziegfeld (right) in costume. Right: Flo Ziegfeld wearing an Oriental costume for a Palm Beach party

Edward F. Hutton (left) and Flo Ziegfeld were prize winners in the cowboy and Indian costume group at a 1929 "Whoopee Party" hosted by the Ziegfelds.

Ziegfeld's true sports love: deep-sea fishing, which sometimes included fishing for tarpon at night.

Flo and Patty became quite good fishermen. *The New York Times* reported in 1922 that Flo landed the largest sailfish of the season (almost eight feet long and 77½ pounds), the second largest ever caught off Palm Beach to that time. Probably the most sensational fishing story from Ziegfeld's Palm Beach days occurred in March 1921, when he hooked a whale that dragged him seventeen miles out to sea. Ziegfeld and six other fishermen battled with the beast until almost midnight, when a search party was sent out after them (Billie was holding dinner and was concerned about the hungry, irritable guests who had not yet eaten).

Ziegfeld also liked several sports for which Palm Beach was ideal. He played golf for exercise and enjoyment. He got out on the tennis court, but Patty does not recall this being his forte. When he swam, he refused to get his head wet, so he always did the breaststroke, with his head high out of the water.

Food, at least Billie Burke style, was an event unto itself, as she became known for her epicurean taste. Once Billie set up a very formal dinner to introduce sixty members of Palm Beach society to a couple that was being feted in both Europe and America. Billie had planned traditional fare: iced cucumber soup, stone crab, baby trout, roast beef, chocolate mousse, and angel food cake with fresh coconut icing. Unbeknownst to Billie, Flo decided to give the affair a twist, so he arranged that Dinty Moore, his favorite chef from New York, send in fifty pounds of corned beef, with an abundance of cabbage, yellow turnips, and "quantities of Irish potatoes." When the butler and his assistant arrived with the "plebeian" corned beef, the surprise created a sensation. Delia Leonard said that the event was "unanimously declared to be the best dinner ever given in the colony. . . . Some of the ladies present ate so much, that they had to be assisted to their cars."

Social life in Palm Beach was dominated by leisure pursuits. The men visited the stock exchange in the morning. At lunch everyone dined at an exclusive establishment such as the Bath and Tennis Club or the Everglades Club. Then, "dressed to the nines," they went to the beach; a few of them swam, but mostly they just sat there, with men wearing coats and ties and women in dresses. Another popular activity was tea dancing at the Cocoanut Grove, where they enjoyed Ford Dabney's music and Mrs. Roach's cakes. Later in the day they went to the movie theater for charity events, hunted crawfish and stone crabs with glass-bottom buckets, or went on treasure hunts where the prizes were furs, diamonds, stock, and gold pieces. In the late afternoon, they often napped before dining out. Some evenings they played bridge (but without Billie, who said, "I don't like cards, and I don't like to be yelled at").

The other major evening activity was attending elaborate costume parties. During the Palm Beach years, the Ziegfelds gave two parties whose coverage shows how well the Ziegfelds had succeeded in penetrating Palm Beach social circles. On March 21, 1928, they celebrated Flo's sixty-first birthday with a

Left to right: The famous Palm Beach Bath and Tennis Club. Flo the sportsman enjoyed fishing off the Florida coast, c. 1929. The Everglades Club ballroom in Palm Beach

Ziegfeld poses with the large sailfish that he caught in Palm Beach in 1922.

large, festive gathering with music from Ziegfeld's shows played by the Morton Downey Band and Rudolf Friml. Billie decorated three large tables with roses and orchids and lighted the patio with multicolored bulbs. The second event, reported in *Palm Beach Life* in March 1929, was a *Whoopee* theme party. *Palm Beach Life* was a slick, chatty gossip sheet on what was doing in the city and who was who in society, with an abundance of photos. The Ziegfeld's *Whoopee* party was such a hit that *Palm Beach Life* gave it *two* full pages of coverage, with a detailed description of costumes and guest list that included the cream of Palm Beach society. According to the report, Ziegfeld, E. F. Hutton, and a number of other men opened festivities by emerging from tepees "in the full regalia of Indian chiefs on the warpath." Billie won an award for her costume, a pink and white cowboy outfit that included fluffy fur, a gold-beaded jacket, and a magnificent ten-gallon hat.

Many of Palm Beach's best-known wags were real characters who would have appealed to the Ziegfelds (and vice versa). Paris Singer was a member of the Singer sewing machine family. His father, Isaac, had twenty-five children, eight of whom were legitimate: Paris was not among that select group. His long-term relationship with Isadora Duncan did little to endear him to the more conservative members of his social circle. Singer arrived in Palm Beach in 1917 and opened the Everglades Club shortly thereafter. His shenanigans at that establishment prompted one of Ziegfeld's good friends, Tony Biddle, to open the rival Bath and Tennis Club with a $10,000 founder membership fee. Ziegfeld was one of its earliest members.

The Huttons were not as colorful personally as Singer, but they were far more significant to Ziegfeld. Marjorie Hutton was then, and remained for many decades after the 1920s, the grande dame of Palm Beach Society. When she and her husband befriended the Ziegfelds and made gestures such as inviting them to cruise with them on their yacht, the *Hussar*, they ensured that the Ziegfelds would be accepted.

When the Huttons built Mar-a-Lago, with more than 110 rooms, they provided Palm Beach with one of its enduring symbols of 1920s wealth that decades later still dominates the city. Patty remembers the mansion, which Joseph Urban partially redesigned, as one of her childhood haunts.

About the same time that Urban worked on Mar-a-Lago, he and Ziegfeld became involved in a real-estate deal to build the famous Paramount Theater in Palm Beach. The Paramount, which opened on January 9, 1927, was visionary because it mixed functions in a manner that many decades later became common in America. Replete with one of Urban's famous murals (this one in emerald green), the Paramount combined cinema, live theater, residences, restaurants, commercial shops, and offices.

Leonard Replogle, another Palm Beach regular, was one of Ziegfeld's best friends. He was a rosy-

Far left: J. Leonard Replogle, who made his fortune in steel, became one of Ziegfeld's closest friends. Left: Ziegfeld knew Anthony J. Drexel Biddle, Jr., from his Palm Beach days. Below: The Joseph Urban-designed Paramount Theatre in Palm Beach

cheeked fellow who always had a cigarette in his hand. By the time he was forty years old, he had made a fortune in the steel business. At age forty-three, he owned his own steel company and controlled numerous other enterprises. Replogle became prominent in the Republican party and ran for political office.

Replogle was so tight with his money that he would never admit to backing Ziegfeld, but based on conversations she overheard, Patty Ziegfeld suspects that he supported several shows. Away from the business environment, he was a jolly companion who loved deep-sea fishing as much as Ziegfeld.

The Ziegfelds had become an integral element of the Palm Beach social set, but their position was not solid. Though doing well financially, Ziegfeld did not have the kind of wealth that the Palm Beach elite did. Moreover, he lost much of what he did have on gambling and his theatrical enterprises.

Ector Munn, one of the scions of that well-established Palm Beach family, provides a useful perspective on the Ziegfelds' place in Palm Beach society: he liked Billie a great deal but was somewhat uncomfortable with Flo because he sensed that the producer was always most interested in people who would back his

Top: Bradley's Beach Club, where the elite of Palm Beach society went to gamble; at one time it was more exclusive than Monte Carlo; most of its patrons were millionaires. Middle: Club de Montmartre, where the *Ziegfeld Palm Beach Nights* opened in January 1926. Bottom: Flo Ziegfeld in Palm Beach

Bee Jackson, world champion Charleston dancer, was not an original cast member in 1926 but became a principal dancer when the show toured.

shows. Several of Munn's friends invested in Ziegfeld's theatrical enterprises, but Munn wryly noted that so far as he knew none of them *ever* made any money off those opportunities.

Ziegfeld sometimes vacationed alone in Palm Beach for extended periods. When writing him there (January 15, 1923), Billie complained: "I guess you are happier than you have been since Paris. It's too bad we never talk things over except with the Western Union." Three days later, still upset over his time away, she became more strident: "I do not approve of these separations. Only hope you are benefited." Billie feared, as earlier telegrams revealed, that he would fall in love with someone in Palm Beach while she was in New York. Even more worrisome to Billie than the women was Ziegfeld's gambling. In Palm Beach gambling facilities were readily available, and the surroundings were all too comfortable.

The irresistible lure of gambling came from Bradley's Beach Club. Colonel Edward R. Bradley opened the club in 1898, shortly after Henry Flagler and his Royal Poinciana Hotel had established Palm Beach as a resort playground for the wealthy. Bradley's was so much a part of Palm Beach social life that Joseph P. Kennedy once quipped: "When Bradley's went, Palm Beach lost its zipperoo."

The key to Bradley's success was that he provided a posh but secure retreat. He was scrupulous beyond reproach and was so strict with patrons and employees alike that he was able to run an illegal establishment for nearly fifty years without being closed down once. Male employees were not allowed to bring their wives with them to Florida, and they had to live on the premises. Bradley would not admit anyone who was not wealthy enough to sustain big losses, and to avoid being accused of corrupting local citizens, he excluded Florida residents. Patrons had to be and *look* at least twenty-five years old, and after 7:00 P.M. everyone had to be dressed in evening clothes. Bradley also kept no books, to protect his patrons and himself.

Bradley's had no identifying sign except the initials "B.C.," signifying "Beach Club." The entrance was dimly lit to protect the identity of patrons who might not wish to be recognized. The doorman was dressed in evening clothes, like the patrons. The atmosphere inside the small, octagonal game room at the back of the building was richly understated. Roulette, faro, hazard, or *chemin de fer* tables were set in the octagon's angles. It was "quiet as a church except for the muted sound of the slap of cards, the rolling of dice, the jumping of roulette balls, or the click of the croupiers' sticks."

Billie captured the spirit of Ziegfeld's attitude toward gambling when she wrote: "His were the most spectacular stakes, naturally. He would win or lose fifty thousand dollars in an evening, sitting dour-faced and silent at the roulette wheel hours after everyone else had gone home, determined to break the bank, determined to be the best." She often pedaled home alone on her bicycle from Bradley's, crying over

A group of happy campers on vacation in the late 1920s: (seated left to right) Blackie, Patty Ziegfeld's companion; the camp nurse; Patty; Mary Carewe; Billie Burke; and Flo Ziegfeld. Standing is costume designer John Harkrider, who started working for Ziegfeld in 1926 and whose first costumes were a hit in Palm Beach.

Ziegfeld's gambling. His habit was so compelling that Irving Berlin even wrote a song about Billie's plight, "Gambler's Bride," when she left Flo temporarily after a particularly disastrous run of losses.

Ziegfeld's risk-taking created a double-edged sword: it empowered him to accomplish things that other men only thought about, but it came back to haunt him both professionally and personally.

The 1926 edition of the *Follies*, called *Palm Beach Nights*, was the quintessential example of Ziegfeld's risk-taking and of why the revue series had such appeal for society people. He acquired the Palm Beach Supper Club, which offered nothing distinctive in its design. John Harkrider thought that several women, including Mrs. Paris Singer and Mrs. Anthony Biddle, persuaded their husbands to finance the club renovation, believing, correctly, that if Palm Beach offered Ziegfeld the right setting, he would stage a theater premiere there.

Ziegfeld opened the Club de Montmartre in January 1926. Local reception to his creation was enthusiastic. Critics commented on Joseph Urban's "wonderful achievement in transforming the barnlike structure . . . into such a beautiful place. . . . The blue dome of the ceiling is like a midnight sky." The backdrop depicted a moonlit Palm Beach night. The ceilings were done in "arabesques in three different blacks. . . . Entire sidewalls, the ceiling and all of the decorations employed were painted in New York" and then moved to Palm Beach.

The Club de Montmartre membership list included the notable names in 1920s Palm Beach society: E. F. Hutton, Edward Stotesbury, J. Leonard Replogle, Paris Singer, Jules Bache, Frederick Glidden, and Otto F. Kahn, as well as theater personalities Rudolf Friml and Ned Wayburn.

Preparation for this show may have been even more chaotic than that for previous shows, partly because Ziegfeld staged it in Florida, far from his New York production facilities, but mostly because John Harkrider was involved. Ziegfeld was accustomed to spending lavishly on his shows, but even he was shocked when Harkrider ran costume costs to $90,440.27 and the scenery bill to $47,408.25. Despite the show's popularity in Palm Beach, it ran only three months in New York and lost around $30,000.

Harkrider was extremely young, only twenty-five, but his designs made a brilliant impression immediately. Ziegfeld brought him out to Burkeley Crest for a presentation to potential backers. As Harkrider describes, Ziegfeld would develop preliminary ideas, including costume and scene sketches and occasionally sample costumes. Then he would present his plan to potential backers. In this case, Harkrider concentrated on his idea for bird costumes, including the egret-feather number that established his reputation on Broadway.

In order to raise money for more than eighty shows over a thirty-six-year period, Ziegfeld was always searching for "angels." Hosting Sunday dinners at Burkeley Crest and spending at least a portion of the season in Palm Beach gave Ziegfeld personal pleasure, to be sure, but these activities also afforded him crucial opportunities to meet and relax in comfortable surroundings with the people who could help him.

The psychology of fundraising justifies Ziegfeld's lavish life-style in Palm Beach and at Burkeley Crest. Ziegfeld said that if he were to court backers with adequate resources for his kind of show, he had to live that way. He succeeded in large measure because he was their social peer and sometimes their friend. Then and only then could he invite them to participate vicariously in the celebrity and the glitter that surrounded Broadway in the first third of the twentieth century.

Harkrider claims that he insisted on and eventually obtained Ziegfeld's permission to control the scenery for the Palm Beach show completely—lighting, setting, and choreography—to the exclusion of Ziegfeld organization veterans. Initially Harkrider usurped the stage for his number, leaving Wayburn out in the cold. Ziegfeld suggested a compromise that gave Harkrider the space at night. Harkrider refused to give Bernie McDonald a peek until just before the opening, claiming that too much rehearsal would damage the delicate feathers he had selected for the spectacular costumes. He says that Ziegfeld capitulated but "stopped and turned to me. 'You know something?' he said. 'You're the biggest gamble I've ever taken. You damned well better pay off.'"

When Harkrider finally revealed the costumes, the stunning headdresses and arches, topped by "28-foot long plumes" that caught "some of the lavender and blue light," spoke for themselves. Harkrider had been vindicated in technical terms, but he had created bitter enemies among the senior production staff. He himself was infuriated when Ziegfeld proudly said of the scene: "It's the best I have ever done."

One description of the scene said that "out of the ocean came these marvelous girls. They looked as though they were dripping wet, in one-piece backless coveralls and enormous white headdresses of feathers all the way to the ground, so that they looked like the foam on the ocean coming in." The Palm Beach press hailed the show's opening as "the most brilliant affair of the season to date."

Shortly after the opening, Paris Singer hosted a party at the club for showgirls from the *Palm Beach Nights* so "they might meet some of Palm Beach society . . . and enjoy a little social contact after their hard work at rehearsals and during their performances." The social contact caused a lot of "chitchat" among society folk, particularly as the group of chorus girls included Paulette Goddard and Susan Fleming, then only fourteen and fifteen years old, who were jokingly referred to as "San Quentin Quail."

Although the revue opened as *Ziegfeld Palm Beach Nights*—tickets were $200 opening night and $12 thereafter—its name was soon changed to *Ziegfeld's Palm Beach Girl*. By the time the show (considerably revised) opened in New York (June 24, 1926; Globe Theatre), Ziegfeld had changed its name to *No Foolin'*, after one of the show's songs. Then, in early July, he started advertising the show as the *Ziegfeld American Revue of 1926*; that same title appears on a theater program dated July 12, 1926. Ziegfeld probably changed the name to impress upon the public that the show was a musical revue like the *Follies*. In an August newspaper advertisement, the show is billed as the "*Ziegfeld Revue*, another *Ziegfeld Follies*."

Over the summer, on July 16, 1926, Marc Klaw and Abe Erlanger had finally decided how to divide their business and dropped litigation after six years of bitter wrangling. The new arrangement had Ziegfeld and Erlanger dividing Klaw's 25 percent; thereafter, Ziegfeld drew $62\frac{1}{2}$ percent and Erlanger $37\frac{1}{2}$ percent on any show in which they invested as partners. The other important outcome of the event was that Ziegfeld regained the right to use the *Ziegfeld Follies* title. Thus, *No Foolin'* finished its tour as the *Ziegfeld Follies*.

Because the "Follies" name was not used until after the show's New York run, the 1926 revue was not officially a *Follies*. However, Ziegfeld always considered it part of the *Follies* series. A theater program from November 1926 at Cleveland's Ohio Theatre renders the title as the *Ziegfeld Follies of 1926* and says it is the twentieth in the series—actually, 1926 was the twentieth *year* of the series.

While the Broadway revue retained many numbers that were presented in Palm Beach, the two shows were substantially different. The Palm Beach show consisted almost totally of singing and dancing. Many of the songs that had a Florida theme were dropped before the Broadway engagement commenced, necessitating several cast changes. Prior to the show's Broadway debut, Ziegfeld hired J. P. McEvoy to write several comedy sketches and engaged James Barton to star in them. Ben Ali Haggin created a tableau for the New York crowd. Dabney's Band, conducted by Will Vodery, had provided the music for the Florida show, but it was absent in New York. (Additionally, in Palm Beach, Art Hickman's orchestra had played dance music, and supper was served after the show.)

Palm Beach was the epitome of the Jazz Age in general and of Ziegfeld's social set specifically, with its easy luxury; its elitism; its studied, carefree attitude toward money; and its glitter. Ziegfeld already had a sense of grace, poise, and elegance, but life in Palm Beach certainly deepened his understanding of what appealed to the social set in New York and Florida. For that reason, when he presented shows, he was not imitating something he had read. He was reflecting life as he knew it.

Unfortunately, despite the serene surface waters that Palm Beach suggests, a dangerous eddy lay beneath. In 1926, though, despite problems with declining interest in the *Follies* and with a series of flops, genuine professional catastrophe was the furthest thing from Ziegfeld's mind.

Top left: Will Rogers, Billie Burke Ziegfeld, Patty Ziegfeld, and Florenz Ziegfeld prepare to lay the cornerstone for the Ziegfeld Theatre in December 1926. On the step to Rogers's right is Bernie Sobel (in dark coat and light hat), Ziegfeld's press agent. Top right: Entrance to the Ziegfeld Theatre. Above: A star's dressing room at the Ziegfeld Theatre

❖

CHAPTER 14

HIS VERY OWN THEATER

❖

The twelve months between summer 1926 and summer 1927 proved to be one of the most significant years in Ziegfeld's career. He launched *Palm Beach Nights* to great fanfare in Florida and brought it to New York, only to receive confirmation that the *Follies* was struggling. Just when the revue series appeared to have played itself out, a new novel by Edna Ferber, *Show Boat*, appeared in serial form in *Woman's Home Companion*, between April and September 1926. A number of people mentioned it to Ziegfeld, including Billie, who became aware of it very shortly after publication.

Despite the serious difficulties Ziegfeld had in mounting a successful show over the last two years, the press elevated Ziegfeld and his family to the level of household name, where personal and not just professional matters became fair game for coverage. A tale circulated in a Berlin newspaper that Ziegfeld had lost a fortune to an uncle named Sigfried Ziegfeld from Germany. Florenz Ziegfeld denied that he had an uncle by that name who was supposed to have made a fortune in the United States.

In another family event, this one sad, Flo's brother William died on June 6, 1927.

A few weeks later, on June 23, 1926, some of Patty Ziegfeld's jewelry, worth $10,000, was stolen from Flo's office. He offered a $500 reward because the items were irreplaceable keepsakes. The kind of press coverage that this event received was indicative of Ziegfeld's place in 1920s culture.

As the consummate Broadway public relations man, he capitalized on this celebrity to mount a campaign about a topic that was increasingly on his mind: nudity on Broadway. For several years, he had faulted his competitors for parading nude women onstage. Many critics have written Ziegfeld off as a brazen hypocrite, because he was not above baring a little female flesh in his shows, too.

If Ziegfeld had been completely candid, he would probably have admitted that at times he was trying to play both sides of the issue at once—attract male ticket buyers with a bit of nudity and still protest the vulgarity of his competitors' shows. But Ziegfeld had a genuine, deep-seated aversion to vulgarity in any

Left: The Ziegfeld Theatre as it looked shortly after its 1927 opening night. Right: This interior shot of the Ziegfeld Theatre shows the elaborate ceiling and wall mural designed by Joseph Urban.

The Ziegfeld Theatre's stage and orchestra pit

realm: he felt the same way about off-color jokes in shows and about shoddy costumes and scenery. The real issue in his campaign about nudity in his competitors' shows was that their presentations offended his artistic sensibility.

Ziegfeld allowed just enough time to stun the audience with a beautiful scene, then he brought down the curtain. Almost everyone associated with a Ziegfeld show has commented on the artistic integrity of his scenes featuring undraped women. Ziegfeld provided a concise summary of his view: "Against the unredeemed vulgarity of uninspired revues, mine is rhythm, pattern of grace and nuance, charm of color and atmosphere, and the graciously glorified beauty of girls, and when it becomes necessary for me to bare the breasts of America for the purpose of drawing money . . . I am through."

In pursuing his campaign against vulgarity, Ziegfeld suggested establishing an inspection committee composed of representatives from the District Attorney's Office, Actors Equity, the clergy, the drama critics, the merchant community, and civic leadership. He submitted the plan to the Society for the Suppression of Vice.

In terms of publicity, the summer of 1926 kept getting stranger and stranger. Ziegfeld angered some members of his cast when he was quoted in the *New York Times* as saying that gentlemen do not prefer blondes: "Blondes are useful for purpose of contrast, but dark and Titian-haired types are more beautiful and more popular." The blondes in Ziegfeld's chorus threatened to strike unless he retracted his statement. If anyone thought this was a joke, he was in error, said Paulette Goddard, leader of the committee. Ziegfeld's remark threatened their earning power and hurt their feelings.

Ziegfeld tried to placate them by saying that there were more beautiful blondes around than brunettes. He added, though, that if they wanted to strike, so be it. Eventually the blonde chorus girls decided not to walk out. Though Ziegfeld had elicited badly needed publicity, this kind of labor contretemps, which appeared to be a trivial matter, was symptomatic of things to come.

In August 1926, when Doubleday published *Show Boat* in book form, it became an immediate success; eventually it sold 320,000 copies. Jerome Kern moved very quickly in pursuing the rights to the dramatic version of *Show Boat*. In October, he asked Alexander Woollcott to introduce him to Edna Ferber. Within one month, by November 17, 1926, Ferber signed a contract giving Kern and Oscar Hammerstein II the dramatic rights. Nine days after the signing, on November 26, the two men performed part of the score for Ziegfeld. The next day Ziegfeld offered the part of Ravenal to Harry Fender, who had been in other Ziegfeld shows. And, on December 11, 1926, Ziegfeld signed contracts with both Kern and Hammerstein

A caricature of the cast from *Betsy* (1926)

to produce what theater historian Miles Kreuger called "the musical that was to become the crowning achievement of the manager's long career." Paul Robeson was Kern's first choice for Joe. Ziegfeld signed him, but the long delay in opening the production forced Ziegfeld to let him seek work elsewhere.

While working on *Show Boat* contract issues, Ziegfeld also busied himself with Jesse Lasky on their film deal. Ziegfeld signed the contract for *Glorifying the American Girl* assuming that he would work in New York and continue doing live theater. However, when Lasky wrote on November 4, 1926, he contended: "The script presents a lot of technical difficulties which make it apparent to all of us that this picture really should be made in Hollywood." By allowing the shooting location to be switched to Hollywood, Ziegfeld effectively cut himself out of the action. This seemingly trivial decision eventually had an enormous effect on Ziegfeld's career. It kept him in New York where he produced several of his most memorable shows, but it also caused him to miss his chance to switch media smoothly.

The truly momentous event of 1926 was the completion of the Ziegfeld Theatre, which the press covered thoroughly, including a feature article in the *New York Times* and a radio broadcast. Dedication took place on December 9. Eight hundred people attended the ceremonies.

For Ziegfeld the theater was the culmination of a dream. This $2.5 million theater, seating 1,666 patrons, reflected his personality. It was opulent and well appointed, its equipment provided cutting-edge technology, and the dressing-room design evidenced a genuine concern for the actors' comfort. The theater was reputed to be the most comfortable ever built.

The egg-shaped auditorium contained a $500,000 stage (40 feet deep and 90½ feet across) and was capped by a magnificent Urban-designed mural that depicted romances and myths from all epochs. It was the only theater mural in New York that covered the whole ceiling. Ziegfeld was generous in the space he allocated for the staff and himself. Reports on the size and luxury of Ziegfeld's seventh-floor office vary, but floor plans reveal that it was of relatively modest size: 29 feet by 21 feet. Ziegfeld had a private balcony off his office that seated six to eight people, but he rarely used it. The office had neutral-colored walls broken up by doors to a bathroom and the balcony box. It was furnished with a large desk, an audition piano, and easy

Left: Joseph Urban designed Jim's mansion, the setting for a triple moonlight wedding in *Rio Rita* (1927). The bride and groom shown on the mansion's steps are Captain Jim (J. Harold Murray) and Rio Rita (Ethelind Terry). Below: Three scenes from *Rio Rita* (1927). Top to bottom: The Lady Pirates; Mexican señoritas; The Texas Rangers

chairs. Ziegfeld had many of the same photos on the walls that he had at the New Amsterdam.

The seventh floor also had two dressing rooms and a good-sized tryout room. The sixth floor had nine dressing rooms and sizable separate facilities for the men's and women's chorus. This floor also housed the tailor, laundry, and sewing rooms, as well as the director's office. The basement contained the usual mechanical facilities, but it also had a smoking lounge, a musician's room, and a music library.

Hearst stayed in the background about his role in the Ziegfeld Theatre. He and Ziegfeld, rough contemporaries in age, were uncannily similar. Hearst was a very large man, tall and heavyset, with a high voice. Like Ziegfeld, he was somewhat shy. His fortune in the newspaper business made him one of the wealthiest men in America, but he spent so lavishly and gambled so heavily that he repeatedly stretched his vast resources to the limits, spending as much as $15 million a year. Nevertheless, he seldom worried about money. He loved theater and had a knack for public relations that rivaled Ziegfeld's.

Hearst had married Millicent Willson in 1903, but about 1916 he met Marion Davies, who was working for Ziegfeld, and began a lifelong affair with her. Millicent would not divorce him, so he lived on the West Coast with Davies. Mrs. Hearst and the five children stayed in New York and Palm Beach. Her twins, David and Randolph, played with Patty Ziegfeld.

While Ziegfeld became one of Hearst's best friends, he was guarded around Hearst for fear of irritating him; the newspaper mogul was not a pleasant man if crossed. They did have several disagreements over the theatre—particularly when Urban was designing the expensive equipment for the stage.

In late 1926, Ziegfeld took a suite across the street from the theater at Hearst's Warwick Hotel. He stayed at the apartment after long days of rehearsals or when he and Billie went into town.

While still completing the last details on the theater project, Ziegfeld turned his attention to *Show Boat*. Miles Kreuger, author of the definitive book about this production, says that Ziegfeld was not so reluctant to produce this script as legend has it. In fact, just twenty-two days after Kern and Hammerstein became officially involved in the project, a news item referred to the upcoming show as a Ziegfeld produc-

Below: Paulette Goddard and Susan Fleming were just teenagers when they appeared in *Rio Rita;* their elaborate costumes were typical of the show. Bottom: Showgirl Grace Moore was in the 1927 *Follies.*

Right: Flo Ziegfeld and Eddie Cantor in Ziegfeld's office; the men are examining a copy of Cantor's book (published in 1930). Far right: Sam Kingston, Ziegfeld's general manager; Ziegfeld; and Walter Kingsley, Ziegfeld's general press agent, inspect one of the first commercial televisions, c. 1927. Ziegfeld planned to use the television, which was hooked to a radio, for selecting chorus girls from around the country.

tion (November 28, 1926). Ziegfeld wrote Harry Fender on November 27 that "this show is the opportunity of my life, and is an opportunity that comes once in a lifetime for the man and woman who play the two parts I mentioned above [Ravenal and Magnolia]." Kreuger notes that "either the authors were particularly persuasive, or the stories of Ziegfeld's doubts were startlingly exaggerated."

Earlier in 1926, before he became involved with *Show Boat,* Ziegfeld had asked Richard Rodgers to work with Lorenz Hart on *Betsy.* Ziegfeld assumed his usual low-key approach, telling them he didn't want the music for at least two weeks, knowing full well that they were already working on *Peggy-Ann.*

Rodgers and Hart were supposed to collaborate with Irving Caesar and David Freedman, authors of *Betsy*'s book, but Ziegfeld did virtually nothing to coordinate the project. Rodgers's account of the situation, if a bit jaundiced, is revealing. He notes that at one point, Ziegfeld wanted a meeting about *Betsy* and sent the chauffeured Rolls-Royce to bring Rodgers and Hart to Burkeley Crest. Ziegfeld and Billie were very gracious during and after a wonderful meal, but Ziegfeld never let them begin discussions of *Betsy.* This puzzled the two men until they "repaired to the drawing room, where at last Larry and I discovered the reason why we had been so grandly entertained. . . . Ziegfeld simply instructed us to go to the piano and perform all the songs from *Betsy* for the amusement of his nine-year-old daughter."

According to Rodgers, the show was too complex for the limited time it received in tryouts: for example, it got only one week at the National Theatre in Washington. He described that week with biting humor: "Freedman and Caesar fought with each other, Larry and I fought with Freedman and Caesar, and Ziegfeld went charging around the theater, screaming like a wounded water buffalo."

Rodgers was particularly hurt when Ziegfeld interpolated an Irving Berlin song, "Blue Skies," and neglected to tell anyone. Then, when it received repeated ovations, Ziegfeld ordered the lighting crew to place a spotlight on Berlin, making Rodgers feel even worse. Rodgers observed: "A few words in advance might have eased our wounded pride, but Ziegfeld could never be accused of having the human touch—at least not where men were concerned. He did show consideration for girls, but even there his overriding ego, or insecurity, would occasionally take over." Rodgers did not think that Ziegfeld really believed in the show.

When *Betsy* opened on December 28, 1926, it flopped, with the exception of Borrah Minnevitch's Harmonica Orchestra and Belle Baker's rendition of "Blue Skies." *Betsy* ran only thirty-nine performances and lost about $107,000.

Many of Ziegfeld's employees loved him and claim that he was always gentle in delivering criticism. However, production people and behind-the-scene artists—composers, authors, choreographers, and costume designers—as a whole received treatment that bordered on the cavalier. They were not, for whatever

Left: In this 1927 *Follies* scene, set in a taxi cab, Eddie Cantor defends his honor against Frances Upton's amorous advances. Right: An ad written by Ziegfeld to promote the 1927 *Ziegfeld Follies*

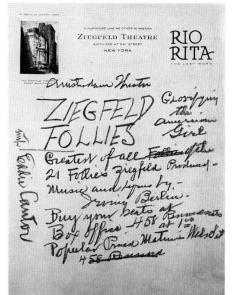

Sheet-music cover for the title song from *Rio Rita*

reasons, Ziegfeld's favorite people. He seems to have created a hierarchy in his mind that had the actors at the apex, the creative suppliers (composers, set designers, authors, choreographers, and costume designers) on the next level, stage production people near the bottom, and office staff at the lowest level. The further removed a person was from the performers' group, the more callous Ziegfeld was toward him or her. Perhaps this was because as business people focused on money, they forced limitations on Ziegfeld and reminded him of what he could not accomplish. This issue is crucial because it offers another clue to Ziegfeld's tragic flaw—spending without thought for a budget, which made the inspired visions achievable but which eventually landed him in a nasty thicket financially.

Some apparent exceptions to this schema were those whom Ziegfeld perceived to be artists—Urban, for example, and Harkrider. Once, when Harkrider demanded to be paid, Ziegfeld said: "I thought you were an artist, not a banker. Bankers need money—you and I have more important business." There were also notable exceptions among the actors. Ziegfeld was not very close to either Ed Wynn or W. C. Fields. In these instances, personal feelings seem to have come into play. It is not clear why he reacted to Wynn as he did, aside from the fact that he may have resented Wynn's role in the 1919 Equity strike. Some writers have alleged that Ziegfeld disliked Fields intensely, but Ziegfeld's daughter believes that he had no particular animosity toward the comedian; he just did not approve of the comedian's drinking because he thought it impaired his work. The lack of warmth toward Fields may also have been a holdover from the fact that Fields was the Equity shop steward for the *Follies* during the 1919 strike. In Ziegfeld's response to Fields's drinking, we see yet another twist in his personality. Ziegfeld was deeply involved with Lillian Lorraine and Marilyn Miller, despite the fact that both of them had problems with alcohol.

This distinction between his treatment of men and women may derive from Flo's relation to his parents. Dr. Ziegfeld was hard on Flo, Jr., and initially disapproved of his decision to pursue popular entertainment. This may have caused Flo, Jr., to approach all men with a measure of competitiveness. His mother, Rosalie, on the other hand, was so gentle and, in some regards, vulnerable that she evoked a tender reaction. In this respect, Rosalie, about whom we know very little because she was so retiring, may have been a more important influence on his career. When he treated women with such respect and adoration, lavishing special attention on them, he was perhaps acting out his feelings for his mother.

His relationship with Stanley Sharpe fills in some detail about interaction with staff. Sharpe joined Ziegfeld as business manager about 1926. Once with Ziegfeld, Sharpe stayed through thick and thin, believing so deeply in Ziegfeld that he passed up an opportunity to go to Paramount Studios. His daughter claimed that when things got tough for Ziegfeld during the Depression, Sharpe went three years without a paycheck, out of respect for the man's artistry. (Since Sharpe was a family man, he must have received some money or he would not have survived.) Finally, Sharpe sued Ziegfeld for back pay. Ziegfeld became very angry with Sharpe for "disloyalty." To make matters worse, Ziegfeld suspected that Sharpe was embezzling theater funds and so fired him. Sharpe's family emphatically denied this allegation. Based on comments Billie made, Patty Ziegfeld suspects that the Sharpe family was probably correct—the culprit may have been another man in the business office.

In a related point, Bernard Sobel asserted that Ziegfeld would put two people on the same job, for example Sharpe and his cohort Dan Curry, "deliberately setting up a rivalry which would operate to his advantage." Ziegfeld's relationship with business people was at best complicated, at worst antagonistic.

Ziegfeld was feeling the pressure from having launched a string of financially unsuccessful ventures, including *Annie Dear,* his 1925 and 1926 revues, and *Betsy.* In addition to the flops that reached Broadway, he had also started several projects that never materialized, including one about Joan of Arc around 1926. Ziegfeld's detractors began asserting that he was finished and that he would never produce another hit. Even his supporters were beginning to have questions about whether he had peaked.

About this time, Ziegfeld called on his friend David Sarnoff, who showed him an early version of television. Always interested in technological advances, Ziegfeld considered using television for interviewing showgirls—to reduce casting costs. Ziegfeld also told his daughter that color television was going to be the wave of the future in the entertainment industry.

Ziegfeld's relationship with John Harkrider during these years was complicated. Talented as Harkrider was, he was so temperamental that most producers refused to work with him. Ziegfeld was one of the few people who was able to "corral" Harkrider well enough to make him an asset. Harkrider would have it that Ziegfeld was ready to toss Joe Urban and Gene Buck off to the side to let Harkrider do his brilliant stuff but that the producer had difficulty mustering the courage to act on his conviction. Buck left in 1926 anyway to produce his own shows, such as *Yours Truly* (1927) with Leon Errol. Urban did not leave until after Ziegfeld's death, so the tension between Harkrider and Urban must have been constant.

After the fiasco with *Betsy,* Ziegfeld once again concentrated on *Show Boat.* The origins of this production comprise an interesting study in the elusiveness of history. Miles Kreuger presents persuasive evidence that Hammerstein and Kern pursued the project from the outset and were the power brokers who persuaded others to join them. Kreuger's documentation, particularly contractual materials, makes it difficult to contravene his version of the story. However, there are at least two other versions to weigh before concluding that Kreuger's makes the most sense. These come from Patty Ziegfeld and Harkrider.

Patty Ziegfeld distinctly recalls that when Irving Berlin visited Camp Patricia in 1926, her father asked him to do *Show Boat*. Berlin was not interested, however, because he did not think the project had much merit. Hence, Ziegfeld decided to work with Kern and Hammerstein. Patty concurs with Kreuger that her father was not nearly so reluctant about *Show Boat* as legend would have it. She differs, though, in suggesting that Ziegfeld rather than Kern provided the impetus for converting the novel to dramatic form.

Since Kern and Hammerstein signed several weeks before Ziegfeld they probably exerted more influence than Patty realized. It is possible, though, that Ziegfeld was pursuing the same project simultaneously on his own. Kern and Hammerstein may simply have gotten to Ferber earlier. In her autobiography, Edna Ferber shed some light on the story when she noted that Alexander Woollcott introduced Kern to her and that Kern was thoroughly involved with her before Ziegfeld's name ever came up.

Harkrider's rendition claims that he saw the potential in *Show Boat* first and went to Ferber with sketches. He says that young Oscar Hammerstein went to Ferber behind his back and persuaded her to let Hammerstein and Kern have the project. Harkrider also suggested later that when Ziegfeld and Kern insisted on allowing Harkrider to design the costumes, Hammerstein opposed the idea vigorously. When Ziegfeld overrode Hammerstein's objections, Hammerstein made Harkrider's life on the set miserable.

While Ziegfeld was struggling with *Show Boat* in late 1926, he was also preparing another of the biggest shows in his career—*Rio Rita*. Gretl Urban worked on this show with her father. Her perspective on *Rio Rita* and the Ziegfeld Theatre's opening captured the spirit of the event. She reported that the stage crew had been delighted with the theater's modern equipment. Then everyone left for lunch:

> I was fussing with some . . . flowers . . . when Flo made an unexpected appearance. He came up on the stage and we both looked out into the auditorium. Even in the faint working light we were aware of its beguiling beauty. Flo put his arm around me and said: "Your father sure hit the jackpot this time."
>
> In a sudden feeling of elation, we hugged each other and kissed warmly. Within a moment there was Bernie telling me that I was needed backstage. . . . When I came back on the stage, there was Flo with his legs straddled over the seats in the front of him, looking around with a beatific smile on his face. That's the way I like to remember him—sitting in his very own theater, built by his very own Joe Urban.

After all those years of frustration, Ziegfeld returned with a vengeance. No Broadway producer ever had a run of luck like the one that Ziegfeld began in February 1927.

Ziegfeld opened *Rio Rita* on February 2, 1927, at his new Ziegfeld Theatre. While the show was not innovative, for extravagance it had no rival. The story followed Captain Jim (J. Harold Murray) and his Texas Rangers as they searched for a bandit in Mexico. This plot offered many opportunities for colorful costumes and settings—especially when Jim got sidetracked by falling in love with Rio Rita (Ethelind Terry), a Mexican señorita.

Joseph Urban created five magnificent settings costing nearly $50,000. The first was done in the reds, browns, and yellows of the Mexican mesa. For the second scene, Urban presented dark, rough rock over an underground chamber. Scene Three was set in a gray and blue walled courtyard of a mansion. The deck of a brown and green barge decorated as a cabaret provided the next setting; as the barge floated in the Rio Grande, the audience could see a Mexican village and snowcapped mountains. For the final scene, Urban constructed a mansion with a square portico and gray pillars.

The settings were enhanced by John Harkrider's beautiful Mexican costumes. Several other designers were engaged for specific numbers. The luxuriousness and variety of the costumes were unprecedented. No two straw hats were alike; jewels and metal braid glittered on the Mexican clothing. Pirates in the cabaret scene wore red and gold; Aztec goddesses appeared in metal headdresses and feathers; courtyard dancers wore scarlet, black, and gold; and the ladies of the ensemble stood out in bright shawls and velvet dresses.

Ziegfeld had also assembled a talented cast. The outstanding performance of the Albertina Rasch Dancers, the comedy of Bert Wheeler and Robert Woolsey, and the strong singing of the principals more than made up for the undistinguished plot and music. All the good aspects of the show combined to overshadow the weak ones, and Ziegfeld had a smash hit. *Rio Rita* sold more than $1 million worth of tickets in twenty-two weeks. An August 1927 newspaper report said it had been earning $45,000 a week since its February opening.

When *Show Boat* was ready to open, in December 1927, *Rio Rita* moved from the Ziegfeld to the Lyric Theatre; after two-and-a-half months at the Lyric, it moved again, to the Majestic Theatre, to accommodate *The Three Musketeers*. According to the advertisement Ziegfeld ran in *The New York Times* on March 12, 1928, *Rio Rita* played sixty weeks (including tryouts) and took in the highest receipts of any show to date. But, only a month into its tour (May 1928), Ziegfeld closed the show in Boston because it was not earning $37,000 per week—the amount needed to break even. The show's net profit was $243,069.31.

Rio Rita proved a financial and critical boon, and apparently Ziegfeld was outdoing himself in getting along with cast members. They surprised him with a bronze plaque to commemorate the opening of the Ziegfeld Theatre. All 140 performers had contributed to pay for the $1,400 memento.

So successful was *Rio Rita* that by May 5, 1927, Ziegfeld announced that he had concluded negotiations with Sir Alfred Butt to mount an English production. The show's financial success also prompted Sam Kingston and Billie to concoct a savings plan. Ziegfeld had intended to direct the income into his next production, but Sam and Billie persuaded him to channel some of the profits into a savings account in Billie's name. In March she began receiving "royalties" that averaged about $450 a week.

Just days after Ziegfeld opened *Rio Rita* and the new theater, he contracted a serious case of bronchitis and was ordered to rest at home. The doctor reported that Ziegfeld was overworked. The next day the papers announced that because Ziegfeld was still quite ill, he would postpone the opening of *Show Boat* from April 1927 until September 15. However, the real reason for the delay was that Kern and Hammerstein, who were as much perfectionists as Ziegfeld, were unable to complete the script for the April premiere.

Ziegfeld located the nub of the problem and was very frank with Kern about what needed to be done.

I feel Hammerstein not keen on my doing *Show Boat*. I am very keen on doing it on account of your music, but Hammerstein book in present shape has not got a chance except with critics. But the public no, and I have stopped producing for critics and empty houses. I don't want Bolton or anyone else if Hammerstein can . . . I want to do it. If he refuses to change it or allow anyone else to be called in if necessary, you and he return the advance as you yourself suggested. . . . Answer. Flo.

Shortly after Ziegfeld delayed the *Show Boat* opening, he and Marilyn Miller reconciled and signed a five-year contract. She said Ziegfeld was the greatest musical-comedy producer in the world. He said he was looking forward to producing *Rosalie* for her in October. This is a good example of Ziegfeld's loyalty. When he believed in someone, he stuck by that person even when things were tough.

Ziegfeld barely had time to adjust to his renewed success when he was beset by a series of legal snafus that must have nearly overwhelmed him. Within three months, five different suits were initiated and a sixth one reached its conclusion—an average of one legal action every three weeks. On March 31, 1927, Eaves Costume sued him over a $17,819 costume bill; Arthur Hammerstein challenged Ziegfeld's claim to production rights for *Show Boat* (April 1); Irving Caesar and David Freedman sued him over royalties (April 2); Ziegfeld won the case involving cartoonist Bert Green (May 4); Edward Royce's breach-of-contract suit over *Rio Rita* royalties reached court on May 27; and Elizabeth Hines, who was to star as Magnolia before Ziegfeld was forced to postpone *Show Boat*, sued him for breach of contract.

During the summer of 1927, Ziegfeld's attorney persuaded him to try to take advantage of the impressive bull run in the stock market. Making one of the more momentous decisions of his life, Ziegfeld invested in excess of $2 million in Chrysler, Eaton Axle, and Mexican Seaboard Oil stock.

Ziegfeld produced the *Ziegfeld Follies of 1927* at the New Amsterdam, as *Rio Rita* was still going great guns at his own theater. *Vogue* magazine noted that this *Follies* lacked the originality and talent of previous editions but that it could not be outdone for splendor and colorful effects. The show was, in fact, largely an appeal to the senses. Once again Urban's scenery and Harkrider's costumes accounted for most of the splendor. Irving Berlin wrote the entire score. During the show's run, however, Eddie Cantor inserted Walter Donaldson's song "My Blue Heaven."

Critic Robert Benchley felt Ziegfeld's great feat in this *Follies* was in making ballet tolerable. Nicknamed "Anti-ballet Bob," he said his anti-ballet stance began to change when he saw the Albertina Rasch Dancers in *Rio Rita*. After seeing them again in the 1927 *Follies*, he was completely won over.

The *Follies* closed abruptly, after only 167 performances, because Eddie Cantor became ill. Ziegfeld, who doubted the seriousness of Cantor's illness, took a complaint before an Actors Equity hearing board, alleging that although Cantor said he was too ill to work, he was seen around town. Ziegfeld claimed that it cost $35,000 to end the tour early and that Cantor still had two years left on his present contract.

Ziegfeld tried to persuade Cantor to return: "I have always treated you like a father who dearly loves his child, but you have always been a naughty, expensive child trying to ruin your dear, loving father, and you need a good spanking. Now, Eddie, before it's too late, be a good boy. Love, your heartbroken father." Cantor responded vehemently that he would not throw away $4,500 a week if not seriously ill. He offered to return to the *Follies* if Ziegfeld's doctor said he was well enough. He also said that if he was seen around town it was because he was visiting a Park Avenue physician each day.

When Jerome Wagner examined Cantor he said that the actor had pleurisy and needed rest. After a two-hour hearing, Equity dismissed Ziegfeld's complaint. In a show of good faith, Cantor offered to reimburse the entire production cost if he failed to work for Ziegfeld when he was well.

Cantor recalled the incident, saying: "When [Ziegfeld] discovered that I really had pleurisy and that even though my chest was strapped and I was scarcely able to breathe, I had decided the show would go on, he realized his mistake. Three days later he wired me from his camp: 'Caught a little bear at six this morning. Shall I bring him for your kids? Love and kisses, your father, Flo.'"

Later, in 1929, Ziegfeld told Eddie that he was very lucky because he had a wonderful family, money, and a hit in New York, and he was working "for the biggest producer in the world. You've got everything."

"Not everything," Cantor replied. "I haven't a Rolls-Royce." Four days later, Ziegfeld casually invited Cantor to dinner at Dinty Moore's. When they reached the restaurant, Ziegfeld took Cantor over to a gray Rolls-Royce convertible. The card attached to the car read: "Eddie, now you have everything. Flo."

The opportunity to do *Show Boat,* the opening of his theater, and his preparation for *Rio Rita* dramatically improved Ziegfeld's circumstances. He was set for two of the greatest years in American theater, but his marriage remained troubled, as this letter from Billie indicates:

> I am feeling rotten—I hate your going away always—to find your happiness—all I ever seem to give you is worry. . . . Your real happiness you find with friends. . . . It makes me very unhappy—it robbs [sic] marriage of the only thing worth while [sic]—dependency on each other. When that isn't there marriage isn't anything—but it's just one of the things I will carry in my head to my grave I suppose— the fact that you do not really love me or need me—It's not your fault—just my misfortune and maybe yours that you did not find the qualities in me that go to bring you happiness—but I don't think you mind like I do. . . . God has certainly been good to you—There are few men with as much in their lives as you have—do be a little grateful. My devoted love—Baby.

This passage reveals a good deal about the Burke-Ziegfeld interaction. She had reached an accommodation that let her tolerate his infidelity and independent life-style, but she would never be happy with it. Another potent consideration was that she understood what drove Ziegfeld as an artist. Burke was still active on the stage, but in her memoir she disparages her own professionalism by noting that she devoted only part of her time to her art and that an "artist is a person who devotes himself ruthlessly, even selfishly, to his craft or his skill, forgetting every other consideration, and the measure of his integrity as an artist is, I think, not whether the critics find his works well done but whether he has given his art his full devotion." Billie may have perceived herself as a burden and not a true professional, but a woman capable of making this statement is an astute, self-aware ally of a sort that most artists never have. Her self-disparaging remarks in these two preceding passages belie the power of her contribution to Ziegfeld's accomplishments.

Midway through 1927, Ziegfeld had two strong shows on the boards and two more in the works. The comeback was under way and was beginning to spawn apocryphal stories. One had him sitting in a barber chair, his face obscured by a towel. Several gents around him were gossiping about the fact that Ziegfeld was washed up and would never produce another hit. As the legend goes, Ziegfeld then revealed who he was and vowed to prove them wrong by staging four hits on Broadway at once.

Right: The principals dressed for their roles in *The Three Musketeers* (1928). In the center (wearing crown) is Yvonne D'Arle (Queen Anne), and on either side of her are Dennis King (D'Artagnan) and Clarence Derwent (Louis XIII). Below: Caricature of Flo Ziegfeld by Al Frueh, date unknown

CHAPTER 15

❖

AN ARTIST STANDING ALONE

❖

Everyone involved in *Show Boat* was more than a little nervous about this new type of musical theater. Ziegfeld was fortunate in gathering a magnificent stage crew and cast, but in doing so he had to handle some healthy egos.

As always, one of the healthiest belonged to John Harkrider. If his account of the preparation for *Show Boat* has any validity, it is a wonder that the production ever appeared. Harkrider, as usual, antagonized Hammerstein, Urban, Urban's artists, and Bernie McDonald's set builders. Urban's response to the problem went something like this: "Ze same old story, Flo. He demands that my painters paint as he directs. He tells them which brush to use. Which colors to use. Which areas to paint first. It iss un insult. They threaten to quit. I, too. After all these years, Flo. It iss like we are droppings from a cow."

An argument over the wedding scene got so heated that Hammerstein, Urban, and McDonald decided to quit unless Ziegfeld fired Harkrider. Ziegfeld achieved a compromise that kept Harkrider out of everybody's hair. In return, Hammerstein agreed not to interfere in staging concerns.

When Ziegfeld read the original *Show Boat* dramatic script, he declared: "That's the gloomiest story I've ever read. That will die on Broadway. It has to have humor in it." As a remedy, he asked for a change in the Captain Andy character. Billie Burke bolstered him when he occasionally had doubts about the show's prospects; Flo had not done plays with deep character, but she had. However apprehensive he was about the weighty themes, Flo loved the story and the music from the outset.

The music program changed a good bit even during the tryouts. There were two interpolations, "Bill" and "After the Ball." Norma Terris said that she suggested the latter song and that in Pittsburgh, she told Jerome Kern that one song was not right for a particular love scene. When she arrived the next day, Kern said he had something for Norma and handed her the song "Why Do I Love You?"

Far left: One of the few photographs to show Ziegfeld smiling. Left: First page of cast list from *Show Boat* (1927) program. Right: Second page of cast list from *Show Boat* program

Charles Winninger as the original Captain Andy in *Show Boat*

Terris also claimed credit for having Kim do imitations. She said that "during rehearsals Jerry Kern wrote a completely new song for me to do when I came back—as Kim, my own daughter. . . . Somehow, it just did not seem right, so I went to Mr. Kern and said . . . 'let me do my impersonations—pretend I'm a young Elsie Janis.' . . . True to my vaudeville training, I went into my act—doing Ted Lewis, Ethel Barrymore, Bea Lillie and Garbo. . . . We worked it out and my impersonations went into the show opening night in Philadelphia—and I modestly report 'they stopped the show at eleven o'clock.'"

The long evolutionary development of the script worked in its favor. Much of the progress involved Hammerstein gaining the confidence to leave Ferber's novel behind so that he could create an independent dramatic product with a life of its own. Finally, after nearly a year of work, the show started rehearsals. Ferber depicts Ziegfeld entering the theater when the company was ready to collapse:

Florenz Ziegfeld would choose this moment to . . . come quietly down the aisle, an imposing figure, handsome, erect, broad-shouldered. . . . You sensed that an electric personality had entered the house. . . . Ziegfeld's curiously flat plangent voice would come across the footlights:

"What the hell's this? You're dragging around like a lot of corpses. . . You're supposed to play as if you were giving a performance. If you let down in rehearsal you'll do the same thing a week after we've opened. Any of you boys and girls too tired to go on please get out. Go home!"

The show began its tryout on November 15, 1927, at Washington's National Theatre. Running time on the original version was around three hours, forty minutes. The show required heavy cutting.

Three days after the Washington premiere, Edna Ferber gave Ziegfeld a perceptive critique. She noted that Howard Marsh's performance was wooden. Ironically, she drew a contrast between Marsh's lackluster characterization and the excitement that Dennis King engendered whenever he performed (King later played Marsh's role in the 1932 revival). She cited the "constipated quality" of Marsh's tenor voice and complained that his costume had none of the flair a riverboat gambler would exhibit—that, in fact, it made him look like a businessman on his way to the office at the Equitable Building in Manhattan.

Ferber also criticized the tall red hat that Norma Terris was supposed to wear. "That red hat of Magnolia's (World's Fair scene) would have made Lillian Russell at sixteen look like a hag. . . . No wonder Ravenal deserted a woman who'd wear a hat like that. Can't she have a soft little close-fitting curled-brim one, with a plume coming over the shoulder."

Terris's recollection of the incident indicates that Ziegfeld listened to Ferber: "I had a magnificent red dress in the World's Fair scene, topped with a beautiful (*I* thought) hat, with a high crown and a white

Right: Helen Morgan in one of her *Show Boat* gowns. Far right: *Show Boat* cast members signed a salary list after receiving their weekly paycheck. Charles Winninger, at $1,500 per week, was the highest paid because of his major role and his reputation; Norma Terris followed at $1,250 per week.

SALARY LIST		

Received from FLORENZ ZIEGFELD SHOW BOAT COMPANY
Salary in full for week ending Sat. January 26, 1929 and in full of all Claims and Demands to Date

NORMA TERRIS		1250
HOWARD MARSH		1000
HELEN MORGAN		700
SAMMY WHITE		700
AUNT JEMIMA		450
CHARLES WINNINGER		1500
EDNA MAY OLIVER (3) perfs.		262 50
MAUD REAM STOVER		
JULES BLEDSOE		400
JACK DALEY		140
ALLAN CAMPBELL		100
THOMAS GUNN		100
CHARLES ELLIS		200
ELEANOR SHAW		50
ROBERT FARICY		125
LAURA CLAIRON		60
BERT CHAPMAN		125
ANNIE HART		85
FRANCIS X. MAHONEY		65
SIDELL SISTERS		350
DOROTHY DENESE		100
WILLIAM VODERY		100
BARBARA NEWBERRY		300
		8387 50

B. Newberry replacing E. Puck at rate of $400 weekly. (3) perfs. paid her this week.

bird in the middle of it. . . . Ziegfeld took one look at that hat and literally rolled down the aisle laughing at me. 'Her chin's too long—get rid of that hat!' I was heartbroken, because I thought I looked gorgeous."

Throughout the rest of her three-page critique, Ferber counseled Ziegfeld to energize the production by including blacks in the background and by making the scenes as gay and natural as possible. She concluded: "I hope all this doesn't sound too offensive. You see, I love that show so much I sort of forget I didn't write it." Even though she suggested improvements, Ferber thought Ziegfeld had a hit.

As the Broadway opening drew near, Ziegfeld began bombarding Bernard Sobel with telegrams. To make his points, he loved to draw pictures for Sobel of what he wanted done with publicity, often sketching the layout. Sobel bore the full burden of what happened in the newspapers, as the following telegram demonstrates: "Why did papers all fail to announce opening of *Show Boat* sale. Not even *Telegraph*. Am giving Sunday *Telegraph* big ad. You should own it. . . . Send out notice 21 thousand applications for opening night seats received. The 16 hundred seats have been allotted in order of their receipt. I regret other checks had to be returned. No standing room opening night. Don't neglect evening papers."

The tone in this telegram reflects a change in Ziegfeld's approach to public relations over the years. When he was young, he resorted to publicity hoaxes and stunts. By 1927, those tactics were no longer necessary. As he was counseling Sobel, eternal vigilance was necessary, but Ziegfeld had the reputation and the contacts to get by with simply asserting that he wanted this item or that printed. He also had the drawing power by this point to create an event just by announcing that he was planning a project.

Rehearsals in New York, said Edna Ferber, were chaotic beyond anything she could have imagined. "Costumes were wrong or missing; lights refused to work; Norma Terris and Howard Marsh . . . struggled with the duet, Only Make Believe, while a vast vital figure hurled itself, shirt-sleeved, down the theater aisle. It was Joseph Urban. . . . 'Wo ist mein himmelblau!' he bawled to the electricians. 'Gott verdammt!' . . . The famous Urban heaven-blue having been found the duet emerged more clearly."

On December 27, 1927, Ziegfeld opened *Show Boat* at the Ziegfeld Theatre. There was high drama that night because even though advance sales had overwhelmed the box office, no one knew how the New York critics and audiences would react. The audience reaction was anything but typical. People seemed stunned into a silence that was agonizing for Ziegfeld—he was not sure whether they disliked it or were so profoundly moved that they did not want to speak.

Of course, the response was stupendous. Brooks Atkinson reported in *The New York Times* on January 8, 1928, that other members of the press had already declared it "the best musical show ever written." Atkinson could find no reason to disagree and labeled it "one of those epochal works about which garrulous old men gabble for twenty-five years after the scenery has rattled off to the storehouse."

Show Boat was not a typical musical comedy. In the 1920s, musicals were generally about the upper class, but *Show Boat* was a story about ordinary people. It realistically portrayed life on the Mississippi and was based on American history, something new for a musical. Moreover, it spanned forty years instead of just a few days. Also new to a musical was the attention to serious topics such as interracial marriage, desertion of one's family, and alcoholism (portrayed sympathetically for the first time).

Show Boat had drama, character development, and a strong plot, characteristics lacking in most musicals. While the typical musical included songs and dances designed to showcase a performer's talents or grab the audience's attention, *Show Boat*'s numbers grew out of the plot. Songs flowed from the dialogue, and—highly unusual for the times—the authors included idiomatic speech in songs to capture the flavor of the South. Even the dances retained the essence of the characters. Also, instead of the one-dimensional characters that were common in most musicals, those in *Show Boat* were well developed.

In Ziegfeld's original production, black performers had major roles and there was even an all-black chorus (Jubilee singers) in a show mostly about white people. And in an era when blacks and whites on stage together was still not common, Jules Bledsoe had an important role as Joe, while his wife, Queenie, was played by a white woman in blackface, Tess Gardella (Aunt Jemima).

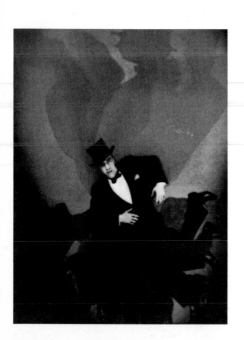

Left: The chorus accompanies Marilyn Miller as she dances in the palace square in *Rosalie* (1928). Far left, above: Jack Donahue, a principal actor in *Rosalie*, was one of the best dancers of his day. His career as a comic was just beginning when he died at age thirty-eight. Far left, below: Marilyn Miller dressed as a West Point cadet for her role in *Rosalie*

Show Boat had a lasting influence on the theater. Kern and Hammerstein had invented a new format—the musical play—because neither the operetta nor the traditional musical comedy was sufficient. Their new kind of musical started a trend toward shows that integrated plot and musical numbers. Composers who followed Kern were forced to consider the production in its entirety, instead of just writing popular songs. *Show Boat*'s success also legitimized serious, even controversial, topics as subjects for musicals.

After *Show Boat* had made him a millionaire again, Ziegfeld's friend Leonard Replogle quietly began lobbying him to protect his financial assets by incorporating. Ziegfeld resisted because it would make him beholden to stockholders and would rein him in. Records suggest that he did eventually follow Replogle's advice; there are signed incorporation papers and references to Ziegfeld, Inc. But this information must be weighed against Patty Ziegfeld's insistence that although he may have come close to incorporating, he never did so because it would have meant that he could not freely get his hands on the money. Unfortunately, there is no evidence with which to settle this question conclusively.

While Ziegfeld was preparing *Show Boat*, he was also working on *Rosalie*. A year earlier William Anthony McGuire had sent him an outline for the show in a forty-two-page telegram (besting Ziegfeld at his own foible). Ziegfeld liked the idea, but because McGuire was so unreliable when drinking, he hired Guy Bolton and P. G. Wodehouse to help write the book. Ziegfeld named the show after his mother.

Rosalie opened on January 10, 1928, at the New Amsterdam after frantic rehearsals. It cost $146,308.83 to mount the show, which ran through October 27, 1928; Ziegfeld's net profit was only $9,151.61.

Marilyn Miller gave a strong performance as a princess who falls in love with a West Point cadet but cannot marry a commoner, displaying the magnetism and personality that made her a star. Jack Donahue, who was originally a dancer in vaudeville, was praised for his brilliant comedy. He played a fellow cadet and friend of Miller's love interest. A strong supporting cast with Bobbe Arnst, Oliver McLennan, Frank Morgan, Margaret Dale, and Clarence Oliver contributed to the show's good reception.

Joseph Urban again designed the scenery: a public place in Romanza, the deck of the S.S. *Ile de France*, West Point (Lover's Lane and the ballroom), the Parisian Club for Ex-Kings, and an outdoor ballroom. Costumes, created by John Harkrider, included Balkan dress and Hapsburg uniforms, royal garments, cadet uniforms, and ball gowns. Ziegfeld had been so extravagant with the sets and costumes that one spectator was overheard to comment that all that was needed was "costumes for the audience."

In February, Ziegfeld announced that due to high salaries he could not make money on the *Follies*, so he was sticking with musical comedies, adding that he did not want to be identified with the current vulgar revues. A month later, he unveiled plans for one more edition of the *Follies*, but that idea quickly fell by the wayside under the onslaught of details connected with having three shows on the boards simultaneously.

Ziegfeld raised the term "frantically busy" to new heights by opening *The Three Musketeers* on March 13, 1928. This show continued the Ziegfeld tradition of grand style. John Harkrider's costumes included numerous plumes and embroidered gowns, and Joseph Urban provided elaborate settings.

Preparation for the third show in less than three months was more chaotic than usual because Ziegfeld committed a terrible blunder: he left all of the writing to William Anthony McGuire. Rehearsals opened with only one half of the first act available. After that McGuire stayed only hours ahead of rehearsals; he was even rewriting on the opening night of the tryout, forcing actors to read from cue cards in their hands.

Harkrider said that Dennis King and Vivienne Segal entered the production as enemies and did nothing to alter that situation. The feud escalated until Segal put a "tack into the seat of King's pants, which caused him to jump with a start when he sat down. . . . It pained him so much that an understudy had to finish the play. Flo threatened to go to Actors Equity about the feud—which was sufficient to halt it."

Rudolf Friml's romantic compositions were well received, while McGuire was commended for carrying out the difficult task of adapting Dumas's novel for the stage. With *The Three Musketeers*, Ziegfeld solidified his position as a great producer. The production captured the romance and swashbuckling spirit of Dumas's novel while faithfully portraying the characters.

With the opening of *The Three Musketeers*, Ziegfeld had four shows playing on Broadway concurrently. As *The New York Times* critic commented: "To [Ziegfeld's] competitors his success is disheartening. The versatility of showmanship that has gone into four comparatively individual productions, the command of dramatic as well as musical direction, the sense of fitness in casting and that final lustre of style which transmutes plain songs and dances into bright visions of unreality reveal Mr. Ziegfeld as something more than a ballyhooer of legs and knees."

The stress of opening three shows in less than eleven weeks and four shows in seven months finally broke Ziegfeld's health. Dr. Wagner sent him to camp with an order not "to do any work of any sort, nor to receive telephone calls, cables or telegrams."

In March 1928, Flo sustained a nearly perfect record for nonpayment of author royalties, forcing P. G. Wodehouse and George Grossmith to sue him. This dispute arose because Ziegfeld delayed significantly on starting rehearsals for *The Three Musketeers* while he worked on *Show Boat*. When Grossmith

Ziegfeld engaged Harriet Hoctor as premiere danseuse for three of his book shows.

Left, above: Vivienne Segal as Constance in *The Three Musketeers*. Left, below: Dennis King as D'Artagnan in *The Three Musketeers*. In 1932 he played Gaylord Ravenal in Ziegfeld's revival of *Show Boat*.

would not return from England for rehearsals, Ziegfeld brought in McGuire and gave him book credit.

A few months later, Ziegfeld announced that he planned to do eight productions between August of 1928 and the spring of 1929. This included six musicals (*Whoopee, Nell Gwyn, East Is West, Joan of Arc, Follies, Six-Cylinder Love*) and two nonmusicals: *The Stay* and a production for Billie Burke. Only *Whoopee* came to fruition.

Just to make sure that Ziegfeld had not become convinced he was omnipotent, Canadian customs authorities spoiled a party in Leonard Replogle's railroad car by arresting Replogle, Ziegfeld, and Wagner for a liquor violation in September 1928, as they returned from Camp Patricia. They were "held up by customs authorities . . . after they had come across the border with 148 bottles of rare Canadian liquors in the private car of J. Leonard Replogle, noted steel and railroad magnate."

Ziegfeld and Wagner paid fines, but Replogle slipped the noose, even though it was "Uncle Rep's" Napoleon brandy that was confiscated. Ziegfeld and Wagner took the fall because a conviction would ruin Replogle's chances for political office. The officials made a significant haul, but they missed the two cases that Billie had on board. On Replogle's next birthday, Ziegfeld got his revenge when he ordered a cake and placed empty half-pint brandy bottles with candles in their necks around the whole delicacy. He also had John Harkrider make a jacket festooned with Ivory soap labels that said "99.44% pure."

Success with *The Three Musketeers* did nothing to lure McGuire into mending his ways. Preparation for *Whoopee* in late 1928 was once again a race to the wire, with final script revisions still in progress when tryouts began. Harkrider went all out on *Whoopee* costumes. "I had placed the topper, a nude Indian princess, astride a white horse with a Chief's headdress of white feathers draping from eight carved poles carried by eight warriors. She was saved from total nudity only by a sprinkling of diamonds around her nipples and a scant covering around her hips. Behind were a coterie of her tribe (also in headdresses)." The costumes won rave reviews. However, the Indian headdresses were so heavy that in the awful summer heat—with no air-conditioning—at nearly every performance, one of the chorus girls fainted onstage.

Eddie Cantor, the show's star, could not give Ziegfeld the satisfaction of a smooth opening either, succumbing to severe laryngitis just before the Pittsburgh tryout. The prominent throat doctor recommended by Joe Urban had been in a terrible accident, but Ziegfeld, desperate for a solution to his problem, approached the poor man on his sickbed. Giving him $1,000, Ziegfeld sent the ailing physician on a stretcher to Cantor's hotel, where he treated the actor—successfully. Cantor's voice returned just in time.

The *Whoopee* premiere took place on December 4, 1928, at the New Amsterdam Theatre. Seymour

Felix's choreography was described as brilliant, and the chorus performed his intricate and technically difficult routines with remarkable precision. Eddie Cantor was a hit in one of his funniest roles, ad-libbing freely and causing Flo to worry no end what he would do next.

Whoopee was an immediate success for Ziegfeld in critical, financial, and personal terms. The source of the personal satisfaction? Twelve-year-old Patty was just delighted when she was named an honorary member of Chief Caupolican's Indian tribe.

The production cost $149,962.78; but since Ziegfeld got $15,000 for Australian rights, his total cost was $135,000. Net profit was $34,000.

Ziegfeld had established a remarkable record over two years: he had launched six consecutive hit shows. Small wonder that he was indulging in grand gestures. On November 7, 1928, at 8:15 P.M., he sent a telegram to Billie: "Darling, first act over. Took two-and-a-half hours. Everything went great. Don't know what to cut. Everything marvelous. Will phone you. Love, Flo." Three minutes later, at 8:18, he wired Patty her own telegram. On November 18, 1928, Ziegfeld announced that he would give one chorus girl from each of his five shows a month's trip to Europe with all expenses paid. They would appear for one night in the London production of *Show Boat* at the Drury Lane Theatre.

Ziegfeld tried for a seventh hit in a row when he revived the *Midnight Frolic* on December 29, 1928. Despite having good talent in the show, he lost $23,289.55, and his incredible streak of hits came to an end.

By the end of 1928, Ziegfeld had achieved a stunning recovery from his problems of the mid-1920s, and he was riding high. Perhaps his desire to provide well for his daughter was a motivating force during these years, but this alone does not appear to be a sufficient cause for such an obsessive workaholic pattern. Ziegfeld might have simply begun thinking about his mortality. Or, buoyed by his successes, he may have felt driven to accomplish what he could while his luck persisted.

His life with Billie seems to have been reasonably stable, as the passionate love affairs that began around 1908 were no longer occurring, or at least were not becoming public knowledge. Some observers believe that the awful humiliation with Marilyn Miller in 1922 taught him a lesson about getting involved with principals. More likely, his change of heart was prompted by a desire to avoid hurting Patty, who was by now old enough to be seriously affected had any of these indiscretions become public.

Whatever the cause, during the two-year period between the *Rio Rita* opening on February 2, 1927, and the *Whoopee* premiere on December 4, 1928, Ziegfeld exhibited a display of theatrical genius that may never again be equaled.

Above: Ziegfeld arrives in Chicago January 24, 1929, to open one of his shows. Above right: Ziegfeld's daughter believes this photograph of Flo Ziegfeld and a Great Dane was taken for an automobile ad.

❖

CHAPTER 16

GOING DOWN WITH THE AVALANCHE

❖

A s 1929 began, Ziegfeld still had two hit shows running in New York: *Show Boat* and *Whoopee*. *Rosalie* and *The Three Musketeers* had closed in late 1928 after very healthy runs. And, significantly, the year 1928 had come and gone without a new *Follies*—breaking a tradition begun in 1907.

Clearly, the times had changed. Costs were higher, competition from film and radio increased, and profits were down sharply. Previously the road tour was the money-maker because costs were lower and initial production expenses had been recouped in New York, but by the late 1920s, the road had collapsed. These problems made it difficult to sustain the talented casts that marked the halcyon days of the *Follies,* a factor that was evoking increasingly negative comments from the reviewers. Finally, it appears that Ziegfeld's imagination and the big revues had simply run their course.

What was striking was not that the series ended but that it had lasted as long as it did. For any vehicle to survive under the same person's management for two decades is a rare feat—regardless of quality. Ziegfeld produced one more *Follies* (1931), but the hiatus in the series marked the end of an era.

Exhausted by the pace that he had kept for two years, Ziegfeld did not open another stage production until midway through 1929. He kept busy, however, with numerous other projects. Before the year was out, Ziegfeld agreed to three film deals. Along with Kern, Ferber, Hammerstein, and music publisher T. B. Harms, Ziegfeld signed a contract with Universal for a sound film of *Show Boat*. The group split $100,000 and took a 15 percent cut of net profits over $125,000. Ziegfeld also signed a contract for sound versions of *Sally* and *Whoopee* and announced a plan to create a *Follies* film.

In 1929, *Sally* was produced as a sound film by Warner Brothers. Marilyn Miller's detractors accused her of being long on charm and connections but short on raw talent; however, the film demonstrates that she

was more talented, as both a dancer and an actress, than her critics have acknowledged.

This film and the talkie version of *Show Boat,* both produced during 1929, are of interest because they employed sound within two years after the first feature-length talkie, *The Jazz Singer* (1927), indicating once again how enthusiastically Ziegfeld pursued new technology. The film version of *Show Boat* opened in Palm Beach on March 16, 1929, to much press hoopla. Ultimately it was not very successful.

Late in 1929, *Glorifying the American Girl* reached the screen, where, due to inept Paramount handling, it did not fare well. Saddled as it was with a weak script and some poor acting, this production was no landmark in film history, but it was innovative technically because it interspersed a limited quantity of two-color footage. The cast included Mary Eaton, Eddie Cantor, Helen Morgan, Rudy Vallee, Ring Lardner, and Johnny Weissmuller. Ziegfeld, Billie Burke, and Otto Kahn played themselves in cameo roles.

On June 13, 1929, Ziegfeld and Samuel Goldwyn became equal partners in a new company to produce musical shows for talking films. The arrangement came about when they agreed to do a film version of *Whoopee,* using color and a wider screen. Under the terms of their contract, Ziegfeld was to serve as consultant and would allow Eddie Cantor to star in the movie, his very first.

Meanwhile, he was working on a deal to present his shows in England. The huge success of *Show Boat* at the Drury Lane Theatre (it had already amassed a $500,000 profit) enabled Ziegfeld to surmount the traditional English reluctance to do American shows. Ziegfeld's deal, completed early in 1929, involved a theatrical syndicate, headed by Edward Laurillard, which leased a theater for seven years to do British versions of Ziegfeld's shows. They planned to open with *Rio Rita.*

On July 2, 1929, *Show Girl* opened at the Ziegfeld Theatre, starring Ruby Keeler in a vehicle created specially for her. Ziegfeld wired Louis Wiley at *The New York Times* to thank him for a nice notice on *Show Girl* and added: "I personally thought that Ruby Keeler gave one of the greatest performances of a character such as 'Dixie Dugan' that I have ever seen in my thirty-five years experience. . . . I also think that Jimmy Durante is the greatest comedian I have ever had. I may be wrong."

Despite Ziegfeld's support, Keeler was very anxious about her performance. She was only twenty years old, and this was the first show in which she had lines; previously, she just danced. During tryouts she once froze at the top of a celestial staircase. Her husband, Al Jolson, rescued her by standing up and singing her next number, "Liza," to get her started. When this extemporaneous "bit" worked, Ziegfeld asked Jolson to continue bolstering Keeler until she settled into the routine. The audiences loved it.

Reviews were mixed. Some critics felt that Keeler brought a quiet charm to her role, while others

Far left: Nell Brinkley's sketch of 1931 *Follies* cast members. Middle left: "Ol Schnozzola," Jimmy Durante (shown here in 1932), was a big hit in *Show Girl* (1929) with partners Clayton and Jackson. *Show Girl* marked the trio's Broadway debut; previously they had played in nightclubs and vaudeville. The team split up in 1931, and Durante went to Hollywood where he made more than twenty-five movies. Later he had a hit radio show and was on television. Left: Ruby Keeler was a nightclub dancer at age fourteen before she debuted on Broadway in 1927. She originated the role of Dixie Duggan in *Show Girl* but left the show abruptly after a month. Between 1933 and 1941 she starred in many Warner Brothers musicals, often with Dick Powell. Keeler was married to Al Jolson from 1928 to 1940.

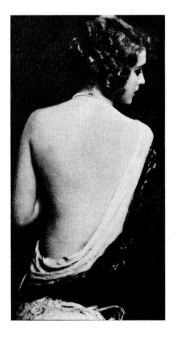

Gladys Glad started working for Ziegfeld in 1926 and was the "Follies Girl of 1931." This photograph, from a 1938 magazine article, shows how she looked about 1927. Ziegfeld considered Glad to be his most beautiful (and, reportedly, highest paid) showgirl.

thought she lacked the fire of a showgirl who makes it on Broadway. Keeler left after only five weeks, apparently due to ill health. Dorothy Stone flew in from Hollywood to take over the role beginning August 8.

Most reviewers thought Clayton, Jackson, and particularly Durante dominated the production with their comic routines brought straight from their nightclub act. The consensus was that the book and music were mediocre. The plot was loose even for a musical, and one critic said he had the feeling that nothing happened. The surviving script for this show confirms the opinion of the reviewers: the idea, drawn from J. P. McEvoy's novel, had potential, but William Anthony McGuire's script was not very good.

While working on *Show Girl,* Ziegfeld began interaction with Vincent Youmans that represented his relationships with composers. Youmans's writing for *Show Girl* was peripheral, but he and Ziegfeld became thoroughly involved on *Smiles.* Their initial correspondence was very warm, with Youmans writing: "It is a mighty great pleasure to run into a real fellow as you do once in a while in business nowadays and I want to say that I found one in you this afternoon."

That summer, in 1929, Ziegfeld began to get nervous about the signs of trouble on Wall Street and decided to sell his stocks. However, his friend Paul Block persuaded him to keep his holdings. Block, too, was uneasy about the market, but his financial adviser encouraged him to stay in. Ziegfeld had actually sent a boat from Camp Patricia with a telegram to E. F. Hutton telling him to sell his holdings, but Block talked him out of it, causing him to send a speedier Chris-Craft to overtake the slower boat and countermand the order to sell. Ziegfeld lived to rue the day that he had access to the faster boat.

On October 29, 1929, Ed Hutton tried all day to reach him about the crash, but Ziegfeld was testifying in court. The subject of the dispute, with the Strauss Sign Company, was trivial. Ziegfeld was dissatisfied with a sign that Strauss had designed for *Show Girl*; as a result, he refused to pay the $1,600 bill and countersued. To ensure an airtight case, he summoned his entire staff to testify. When the telephone operator called in sick, the office was left completely unattended. Had Hutton reached Ziegfeld, he could have reduced the damage to Ziegfeld's portfolio.

Billie Burke described how swift and terrible the blow was. She says that when he came home, Ziegfeld

sat down heavily on the edge of my bed looking utterly wretched and weary. I had never seen Flo Ziegfeld like this before. I pulled his head down and took him into my arms.

"Well, poor old darling, what is it?"

Flo sobbed. They were great, struggling sobs.

"I'm through," he said. "Nothing can save me."

The next afternoon I watched him walking in the lovely garden he had planted with such care and taste. His shoulders sagged and his step was uncertain.

He did not know it then, but his moment of insight was accurate. With the exception of Burkeley Crest, Flo and Billie lost everything they had. Estimates on their losses range between $1 million and $3 million. Ziegfeld had mounted nearly eighty shows and for fifteen years had ruled Broadway. He was laid low by a combination of external circumstances and his own flawed greatness.

Several years would pass before the cycle completed its inexorable course, but hereafter fate, in the form of the American Depression, rather than Ziegfeld's overweening drive for perfection, ruled the showman's existence. He was to be as much a victim of events that took place on October 29, 1929, as the men who committed suicide, such as his friend James Donahue, who poisoned himself.

Ziegfeld had spent a professional lifetime being consumed by visions of splendor. A fire that burns this brightly consumes its source and anyone in its vicinity (family, production people, cast members, office staff). He risked millions of dollars by sticking with Wall Street, despite numerous well-publicized signs all during 1929 that the market was shaky. He rendered himself even more vulnerable to the crash by gambling away millions. Finally, he sealed his fate by testifying in the trivial lawsuit on October 29. Ziegfeld was in part the victim of a national plight, but he contributed directly to his predicament, driving home the verity of Greek tragedy: men of stature who fail to perceive and correct their tragic flaws inevitably fall.

Flo had grown up, reached maturity, and achieved enormous success believing that the American Dream was a reality. Until October 29, 1929, he could survey his circle of intimates—Ed Hutton, Leonard Replogle, Irving Berlin, Eddie Cantor, Will Rogers—and find proof that the Dream was true. Some of these men had risen from poverty. Others, like Ziegfeld, were first-generation Americans whose fathers had made something of themselves but had not accomplished anything like what their sons achieved.

The Depression caused Ziegfeld to question the Dream. He commented that "all I've worked for is crumbling before my eyes." His spirit was nearly crushed when he could not recover his former glory. He occasionally said, "I can't do this anymore." Before, Flo had always known instinctively what to do next. He never had difficulty locating money for his next project. Now he had to struggle to mount a show at all.

With the coming of the Depression another reality set in: the Ziegfelds had to cut back to bare-bones staff at Burkeley Crest, letting everyone go except Sidney and Delia. The trappings of success disappeared.

California began to look attractive to him—it offered a broader vista than Broadway. The film industry was still nascent and in some respects as inchoate as Broadway had been when he first arrived, and it

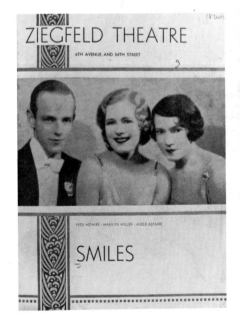

The program cover from *Smiles* shows Marilyn Miller with Fred and Adele Astaire. The Astaires had been dancing together professionally since Fred was seven and Adele eight-and-a-half. They remained a team for over twenty-five years.

desperately needed men of Ziegfeld's caliber. The difficulty was that Hollywood's scale of economics and the technical challenges meant that Ziegfeld would have to work with someone else, a point made even more frustrating by the fact that he was a virtual novice in making films.

One week after the stock market crashed, Ziegfeld's *Bitter Sweet* debuted in New York. It had been in Boston for tryouts on October 29. *Bitter Sweet* had beautiful costumes and outstanding music, and star Evelyn Laye was marvelous. According to theater historian Gerald Bordman, the show was well received, but the onset of the Depression shortened its run.

Noël Coward, who brought the hit show from England, directed the actors and insisted that they speak his lines precisely as he wrote them. He stayed in New York for about a week, during which time he came out to Hastings, where he played and sang naughty songs in an exaggerated British accent.

Apparently Coward and Ziegfeld were a bit too much alike in wanting to control the production, so there was more than a little tension over whose approach would prevail. When Coward refused to allow the producer to incorporate beautiful chorus girls, Ziegfeld allegedly threatened not to promote the production. When the show was a hit in Boston and on opening night in New York, all the enmity was forgotten, and they celebrated lavishly.

Rodgers and Hart, who were reluctant to join forces again with Ziegfeld, decided to work on *Simple Simon* because Ed Wynn assured them that he could handle Ziegfeld. As Rodgers's vivid insider autobiography indicates, Wynn was not up to the job.

Simple Simon had an insipid script with juvenile humor. One of the few bright moments was the song "Ten Cents a Dance," which became a roaring hit. Ziegfeld almost cut the number, though, when Lee Morse, the principal female singer, who had consumed a bit more alcohol than she could handle, forgot the lyrics. Ziegfeld, appropriately disgusted with Morse's amateurism, fired her and brought in Ruth Etting, who had already proven herself in the 1927 *Follies* and in *Whoopee*. Etting's rendition was so popular, it became her signature tune. *Simple Simon* reached Broadway on February 18, 1930. Ed Wynn wrote for and starred in the production, which ran just short of four months. Small doses of Wynn could be very amusing, but he could not carry a long show, especially one with such a poor script.

The effort to bring *Simple Simon* into existence left Ziegfeld drained. Even newspapers outside New York carried an article about his attempts to avoid a "complete nervous breakdown." Breakdown or no, Ziegfeld announced, while heading for vacation, that he was going to work on the film version of *Whoopee* with Sam Goldwyn. In his own description of the venture, Ziegfeld wrote that he

was offered one million dollars a year to devote himself to pictures and try and bring to the screen what he does to the stage: an indefinable unexplainable something that all producers lack. All have strived for but failed. Ziegfeld refused all offers until he concluded his partnership alliance with Samuel Goldwyn to film one picture only. See if his stage triumphs can be transferred to screen in their entirety. *Whoopee* and Cantor were selected for Ziegfeld.

Abe Erlanger, Ziegfeld's longtime mentor and business partner, died on March 7, 1930. While the two men were no longer close, the relationship had survived twenty-three years. Erlanger's death shook

Ziegfeld badly. Many people detested Erlanger and almost everyone feared him, but he had been very loyal to Ziegfeld through the bitter failures as well as the glorious successes. Ziegfeld even attended his partner's funeral.

When he went to Hollywood for *Whoopee!*, Ziegfeld predictably located the fellows who enjoyed high-stakes bridge. In this case, his cronies included Irving Thalberg, Joe Schenck, and Sam Goldwyn; they played in a little cottage at the back of Goldwyn's estate. The Ziegfelds entered the social whirl, throwing parties for Norma Shearer, Irving Thalberg, Paulette Goddard, Clara Bow, Louis B. Mayer, Lilyan Tashman, Nita Naldi, and others. Even though the Depression was having its effect, they managed to find a decent little place to stay: a beach house in Santa Monica that belonged to Marion Davies's sister.

Beginning April 12, 1930, Ziegfeld and Sam Goldwyn worked on *Whoopee!* Goldwyn's confidence in the project convinced Cantor to sign on, for $100,000 and a 10 percent cut of the action. Ziegfeld finagled the title of co-producer and 20 percent of the profit. Although Ziegfeld participated in the movie's production, the essence of the deal was that Goldwyn and Ziegfeld made a trade: "cash for cachet." The two producers argued from the beginning. Flo was in New York producing his next stage show, so they exchanged telegrams. Ziegfeld wanted Lillian Roth, Adele Astaire, and Ruby Keeler in the movie. Goldwyn hired other stars, ignoring Ziegfeld's advice.

Goldwyn had Ziegfeld meet with the film scriptwriters. Ziegfeld said afterward: "When . . . they read me their conception of *Whoopee* for a picture eliminating everything in it that was any good and convincing me without any question of a doubt that they knew nothing about a musical show I knew then that it would be humanly impossible for me to get my conception of *Whoopee* on the screen and put in a can the sensation that I had produced for the stage." The Broadway version had sixteen songs. Goldwyn used only the title song, "Makin' Whoopee," probably because he wanted to avoid paying royalties.

According to Cantor, the other studios avoided Ziegfeld because they feared his extravagance. Even Goldwyn, who was more interested in artistic concerns than most, disagreed on the topic of money versus art, as Patty Ziegfeld's memoir indicates: "Daddy and Mr. Goldwyn would talk for hours about show business . . . but they were worlds apart in their outlooks. Mr. Goldwyn had his eye on the penny, Daddy on the effect."

Goldwyn eventually adopted many of Ziegfeld's notions about how the show should be staged. He also imitated Ziegfeld by creating a chorus that he called the Goldwyn Girls. Finally, Ziegfeld gave Goldwyn the idea of using two-strip Technicolor. Because Ziegfeld came to Hollywood so late and worked seriously on only one film, his direct influence there was limited. What he did convey was his standards for excellence.

Whoopee! made a big splash critically and financially, earning $2.3 million. Ziegfeld wanted more work with Goldwyn, but Sam was not interested. Ziegfeld also kept after Goldwyn about hiring Billie.

True to form, when Ziegfeld decided that film was the medium of the Depression, he announced in mid-April that he was creating a billion-dollar concern, with Ed Hutton as one of his backers, to produce motion pictures. Ziegfeld said that he was impressed by the profits in movies. He noted that *Ben Hur*, made at a cost of $5 million, had returned $8 million and was still going strong.

His interest in film piqued, Ziegfeld announced in late August that he planned to spend six months in California and six in New York. He was said to be negotiating for a studio on the West Coast and a distribution deal. He asserted that film people needed to surround themselves with showmen from legitimate theater. He never followed through on the film production, but it is one more indication that his attitude toward film was shifting, even if he was not happy about having to acknowledge the new medium's potential.

By July 1930, Ziegfeld was pulling the script together for his new show, *Smiles*. Again, he found himself struggling with William Anthony McGuire over delivery of the script. He made an impassioned plea on July 4 for McGuire to finish. One week later, he pitched his tone even higher, writing: "You promised to call me. Tomorrow is your last day. I am frantic. I depended on your absolute promise to have Miller book in time thirty days before rehearsals. . . . Can't you realize I must have it now?" He finally became so exasperated that he fired the errant McGuire.

In the fall of 1930, Ziegfeld signed Vincent Youmans to compose the music for *Smiles*. Ziegfeld gave Youmans, who was known for zealously guarding his artistic integrity, control over the orchestrator, musical director, and lyricist. This concession, though unusual, seemed innocuous enough. Ziegfeld also called in Ring Lardner to write lyrics for the comedy songs. Lardner could not rescue the show, but critics praised his "If I Were You, Love." Recruiting Lardner delayed the October opening in Boston by one week.

The real problems began when Marilyn Miller developed an antipathy for the orchestrator, John Lannin, and one song she was to sing. She told Ziegfeld to get rid of both. When he did, Youmans threatened to withdraw his songs and/or the orchestrations. In Ziegfeld's terms, Youmans had made a fatal mistake: he challenged the producer's artistic control. Ziegfeld got an injunction on November 9, 1930, barring Youmans from the theater and from withdrawing his materials and services.

Ziegfeld's letter to Ring Lardner, dated November 9, 1930, just nine days before opening night, clarified his view of the issue: "This is a tough bunch to handle. . . . I was finally compelled to get a court restraining order to prevent Youmans from running the show. He was under the impression he was the producer and owner of the show. The only thing he forgot to give me a cheque for 200,000 dollars."

Youmans countered on November 17 by suing Ziegfeld to keep the producer from firing John Lannin. He said that Ziegfeld replaced Lannin without "giving the plaintiff an opportunity to express his desire or wishes in the matter." In a seven-page statement to the New York Supreme Court, Ziegfeld noted that his $200,000 investment in *Smiles* was providing work for one hundred people. He said that he had accepted Lannin as music director at Youmans's insistence, only to learn that Lannin was incompetent and that Youmans may have been motivated by the fact that he owed Lannin several hundred thousand dollars. Ziegfeld also alleged that Lannin and Youmans "went out on drinking parties constantly."

Ziegfeld had brought in Victor Baravalle and then Frank Tours to replace Lannin. He accused Youmans of accepting the new staffing arrangement, only to change his mind and try to undo the agreements and submitted affidavits from Stanley Sharpe and Dan Curry testifying to this fact. Ziegfeld also denied that Youmans was the only one competent to judge a musical director's capabilities.

While the two men were still bickering over who did what to whom, the show had its premiere, with Ziegfeld demanding that Youmans write additional songs. The wrangling then deteriorated into an intricate exchange over specific songs, with Ziegfeld alleging that Youmans had delivered only ten of the sixteen required numbers and Youmans asserting that he had delivered the required number. On November 28, 1930, Ziegfeld wrote in his most unctuous prose: "I demand the delivery of the above numbers forthwith." Youmans responded with a registered letter that nailed Ziegfeld for his indecisiveness. He noted testily that he had delivered the sixteen songs required by the contract as well as eleven additional numbers. External evidence from actors and production staff suggests that Youmans probably had a point about Ziegfeld not being able to make up his mind. This prolonged, rancorous incident shows how difficult it could be to work with Ziegfeld. In the end, on December 12, 1930, Judge Isidor Wasservogel denied Youmans's injunction, thereby sustaining Ziegfeld's decision to fire Lannin.

The row is illuminating because it offers concrete evidence about how Ziegfeld fought on matters of artistic integrity: doing battle with Ziegfeld was not a trifling matter. A fascinating consideration about Ziegfeld's record given these lawsuits: would his shows have been even better had he not driven off some of his best authors and composers?

Smiles debuted at the Ziegfeld Theatre on November 18, 1930. Ziegfeld said this was his most lavish show yet. (Each production tended to be more lavish than the last.) Critics were especially impressed by the Chinese costumes in the garden scene, which allegedly required more than a year of design and handwork. The Joseph Urban garden consisted of green hedges and terraces with two large glass lanterns hanging in rose-colored frames. Centered in the garden toward the back of the stage was a tall, ornately designed Japanese screen. The screen's panels folded, and Marilyn Miller emerged, dancing.

Fred and Adele Astaire were an unequivocal success; in fact, the cast as a whole was considered a good one. The problem was that the story moved too slowly. Reviewers critical of the book said it was heavy-handed and lacked humor. The situation with Marilyn Miller compounded the difficulties. Her dancing was not up to snuff because she was sick (from a persistent sinus condition) and was drinking heavily. Her problems contributed to the demise of an already troubled show.

The original draft had Smiles (Miller) choosing the wealthy Bob (Astaire) as her husband. The finale called for the betrothed couple to walk down a long stairway, ahead of Adele Astaire and Paul Gregory. Ring Lardner told Ziegfeld that no one would believe that Miller would prefer Astaire to the dashing Paul Gregory. Ziegfeld replied that if Miller and Gregory appeared first, the Astaires would steal the show. The quick-witted Lardner shot back, "Well, that would only be petty larceny." But Ziegfeld recognized a good suggestion and altered the ending.

By the beginning of 1931, with a string of losing shows that dated back to 1929, Ziegfeld was on the verge of bankruptcy. Bernard Sobel described how serious Ziegfeld's financial problems were:

> Up to then, his millionaire friends had come to his aid, but this time they also went down with the avalanche. . . . Business fell off at the box office. . . . Creditors began to demand an accounting. . . .
>
> One solemn day, the famous Ziegfeld Theatre was without a show. Snow covered the roof, and the windows were white with frost. The glorifier walked into his office wearing his handsome beaver-lined coat, still an impressive picture of prosperity. Yet, oddly enough, instead of removing the heavy coat, he kept it on all day long. He had to do so, as a matter of fact, to keep warm, for there was no fire in the furnace and he didn't have enough money to buy coal.

In the midst of this painful confrontation with fiscal reality, Ziegfeld's eccentricity increased markedly. Goldie said that he became even more superstitious about ensuring that the trunks of the elephants in his vast figurine collection be raised, that the brim of his hat be down during rehearsals, and that Joe Urban design the scenery. Blowups were occurring more frequently over trivial issues such as a spot on a cast member's costume. And he was spending inordinate amounts of time writing letters to everyone involved with a show, in a handwriting that Goldie found increasingly illegible. In sum, he was an unhappy, frustrated man, a bit disoriented in a world that was dictating a set of restrictions that he never learned to accept. At sixty-four years of age he was not finding this an easy or pleasant adjustment.

After a four-year interval since the last *Follies*, Ziegfeld located a backer, Mitchell L. Erlanger (Abe's brother), to help him produce a new edition. In April 1931, he announced that he would revive the series.

In preparing for the next show, Ziegfeld knew all too well how important publicity would be. A telegram on June 13 captures the feel of his relationship with Bernard Sobel. The didactic tone must have grated on the nerves of the highly educated press agent: "Last nite we photographed the worst looking girls in the show. Never use a bad picture and only allow the most beautiful to be photographed." In another instance he wrote: "Don't overlook the terrific sensational and greatest thing ever happened to a show. Right on same page with our criticism in Washington Herald in big box was story about Senate being adjourned so Vice President could come to our opening. Make every paper in New York print it."

Tough critiques were typical, but another side of Ziegfeld's character emerged if he realized he had offended someone he respected. Once, when he had hurt Sobel's feelings, Ziegfeld followed with an apology that contains a touch of humor involving his valet. "My dear Bernie, I would not hurt your feelings intentionally for the world. You ought to know that. Regards. Ziegfeld. I know that he means this. Sidney."

In the summer of 1931, Ziegfeld was separated from Billie and Patty while Billie was filming movies. Despite the Depression and recent flops, a note to Billie shows that he could still rally some of the old optimism: "Well here we stay another week. Must make many changes so show suits me. I miss my two babies. It's been such a hard pull but I guess the result will be worth it. I feel like phoning every hour."

Flo opened the 1931 *Follies* on July 1. This was the only *Ziegfeld Follies* to play in the Ziegfeld Theatre and was the last edition produced by Ziegfeld himself. Gene Buck and Dave Stamper, who first had a song in the 1912 *Follies,* also worked on this edition. Dancing was the strong suit in this year's show. Hal Leroy and Mitzi Mayfair made quite a team: Mayfair could kick backward and touch not only the back of her head but also her chin. The Rasch Dancers were in the show, as were the vaudeville tap dancers Buck and Bubbles. According to John Bubbles, their act was so popular that no one could follow them. After being tried in various spots, they were put on next to last, the one reserved in vaudeville for the top-billed act. Theirs was one of the few black acts in the *Follies,* and according to Bubbles, he and Buck would have worked for Ziegfeld for free.

According to *The New York Times,* Ziegfeld hired the Brittons, a comedy act, after Eddie Cantor saw them at the Palace and called the producer. Ziegfeld went to see the Brittons and allegedly laughed aloud. When the act moved to another theater, Ziegfeld saw it again—and allegedly laughed again. The *Times* also noted that "when Mr. Ziegfeld laughs, even once, it's news. If he does it again, it's a contract."

Before the show opened, Ziegfeld met Muriel Harrison on the street and told her that if she was not working she should join the show. Harrison had been in Ziegfeld's *Miss 1917, Simple Simon,* and three other *Follies* (1918–20). Now, at nearly thirty-five years of age, she was back in the chorus of the *Follies.* When Harrison's mother died in 1931, Ziegfeld paid Muriel's round-trip train fare so she could go home.

Ziegfeld had his detractors, but as this note from Joseph Urban after opening night indicates, Ziegfeld's commitment to quality aroused real devotion among his best people: "Dear Billie, Many thanks for your sweet wire. Your enormous success gave us the necessary spirit for the last twelve hours work and a pink and silver curtain opened on Flo's big night and brought us all good luck. The show is tremendous and even Pat can see it so lean it is. We all worked hard on it because we love you and Flo. Your devoted Joe."

Initial reaction to the 1931 show was positive. Ziegfeld found the warm response from the audience very gratifying, as he wired home on July 16: "Darling, I would like to call you up every minute. . . . You never heard such applause in a theater. Nine different things in the show stop the show cold, so the next person can't go on without repeated bows."

Clearly the Dream was still alive, though battered.

Just after the new show got under way, State Supreme Court Justice Frederick P. Close decided that Flo was not above the law: he announced that no matter how busy Ziegfeld was, he had to comply with a subpoena to appear as a witness in a suit by Charles H. Totty over a bill for $721 worth of flower bulbs. The imagination could run amok conjuring the exchange that prompted such a public statement from a judge who had to know that the newspapers would record his words.

As Ziegfeld's fortunes spiraled downward, he must have realized that he was close to the bottom when he found himself in a salary dispute with the principals from *Smiles*. Fred and Adele Astaire sued him over three week's salary they believed he owed them from the year before (1930). Ultimately an arbitrator persuaded Ziegfeld and the Astaires to accept a compromise that paid the actors $4,000—one week's salary.

The 1931 *Follies* was not so successful as many of its predecessors, but it was a comeback worthy of some attention, as Gene Buck told Billie: "I have sufficient imagination and knowledge of Flo and his personality to realize what you've been through lately and I can imagine how overjoyed you were to learn of the great success of the *Follies*. The situation of his again producing the *Follies* . . . in the depths of the depression . . . was loaded with DRAMA and meant more than any venture Flo ever embarked upon."

In late September 1931, Flo went to Los Angeles to stay with Patty while Billie toured with *The Vinegar Tree*. Billie was on the road for several months to earn income for bills that continued to mount.

By November 1931, Ziegfeld returned to New York. Fifteen-year-old Patty was temporarily on her own. Flo's longing for his family was becoming even more obvious: "I hope your cold is better and only wish I had my little family together either out on the coast or here. Let's hope things will straighten out very soon. Patty called up last night. Seems strange to leave her alone in Hollywood of all places."

Hindsight makes it evident how crucial the 1919 Equity strike was. In historical terms, this was the turning point. In personal terms, the reversal in Ziegfeld's fate came when the strike prompted the bitter dispute with his protégé Eddie Cantor—a man who had the virtues that Ziegfeld prized but who was just enough younger to be drawn to the values of the nascent labor movement.

By late 1931, Florenz Ziegfeld was in deep trouble. It was an open question whether he could survive, let alone make a successful transition to the new entertainment media, film and radio.

The dance team of Velez and Yolanda in *Hot-Cha!* (1932)

❖

CHAPTER 17

ALL THAT BEAUTY

❖

iegfeld had been separated from his family since the summer of 1931. By the winter of 1932, he found the situation disconcerting. In a letter to Patty, he was candid about his feelings:

> Well here I am alone and it's lonesome. I hope you had a nice trip and everything was allright upon your arrival—you can't realize how hard it was to let you go alone. Everything was so different last year. You know daddy is getting old and needs rest but our expenses are always so big and show business has changed so. Daddy must try pictures. . . . Don't neglect your golf and tennis and first thing I want you to do is learn really to dance. . . . You must write daddy. Only takes a few minutes when you take your daily lessons—love and kisses. Daddy. Take care of Mother.

Ziegfeld assuaged his loneliness by concentrating on preparations for *Hot-Cha!* The financial situation was so tough that Eddie Cantor had to lend Ziegfeld $100,000 to produce the show; Ziegfeld repaid the loan in $5,000 installments over a twenty-week period. Cantor's loan was insufficient to cover costs, so Ziegfeld had to ask Dutch Schultz and Waxey Gordon, notorious gangsters, to back the show. Having to accept mob money irritated and humiliated Ziegfeld no end, but there was nothing to be done about it.

The *Hot-Cha!* setting was reminiscent of *Rio Rita*, but it had little of that show's appeal. Recognizing that the new show was not up to snuff, Ziegfeld worked harder than usual trying to create a success. The odds were against him, as a letter to his family notes just before *Hot-Cha!* opened: "My two darlings, Well 3 weeks on the road are over with an expense of over $90,000. How I ever got things this far and how I am alive handling this mob and temperamental authors I don't know. I realize what is wrong and I only hope I have the strength to fix it by Tuesday night. I only wish you and Pattie were to be at the opening."

During the road tour Ziegfeld contracted a serious case of the flu. Billie, who was acting in *Mad Hopes*, became so concerned that she wrote Flo's valet asking whether she should come to Ziegfeld's side. In

Left: Paul Robeson, shown here in the 1940 Broadway show *John Henry*, was Ziegfeld's original choice for Joe in *Show Boat*. When that show's opening was delayed, Robeson was released from his contract. He later played the role in the 1932 Broadway revival and the 1936 movie.

Above left: Obituary for Florenz Ziegfeld, Jr.; contrary to the newspaper headline, Ziegfeld was age 65 when he died. Above: Dancer Eleanor Powell as she appeared in *Hot-Cha!* Three years later she went to Hollywood, where she starred in M-G-M musicals for fifteen years.

Pittsburgh for *Hot-Cha!*, his condition worsened. John Harkrider described a dramatic scene there; he sensed that the producer was dying and so was reviewing his life. The conversation ended with Ziegfeld muttering: "All that beauty, Jack. All that beauty."

Charles LeMaire recounted a similar incident, this one in New York at the Warwick Hotel. LeMaire knew that Ziegfeld was ill, but he stopped by, hoping Flo might repay part of a $2,000 loan.

> Mr. Z. was propped up . . . his smile was wan and his voice weak as he complimented me on my "healthy looking suntan." . . . "I just thought back, Charlie, you've come a long way since I introduced you as my protégé after the 'Lights' number you did for my *Midnight Frolic*." . . . He looked at me with a stern eye, "You must be just about the most successful designer on Broadway and I hope you are taking care of your money," he said authoritatively. . . . I said goodbye without asking for my money and as I was going down in the elevator, I came to realize how much this man's acceptance of my talent had ment [*sic*] to me. Ziegfeld really didn't owe me anything, I was the debtor.

Hot-Cha! arrived on Broadway on March 8, 1932. Most critics agreed that the book was weak. Bert Lahr played a speakeasy waiter from New York who went to Mexico City and became a bullfighter. Reviewers found the singing poor, but they consistently praised the dancing, sets, and costumes. The first-act finale, a brilliant fiesta scene, was full of voluptuous and fiery colors. Mantillas, streamers, and laces were set off against a blue sky and picturesque architecture. Charles LeMaire was the primary costume designer. However, John Harkrider designed Eleanor Powell's gold pajama costume, which had long, loose sleeves and pants with large accordion pleats. Powell danced in front of the curtain between scenes.

During the run of *Hot-Cha!*, Flo revealed that despite the consideration he showed toward most cast members, he could also be cruel to his stars, as this telegram to Lahr indicates: "Dear Bert, Can't understand why you let show down in second act bull fight scene which cost me fifty thousand. You ruined completely. . . . Call entire company for rehearsal. Let's get proper pacing."

Unfortunately, no matter how hard Ziegfeld pressed his company and staff, *Hot-Cha!* never caught on, which cost him dearly, because production expenses ran $500,000. He lost more than $115,000.

In late March, Ziegfeld was still not well. He nevertheless charged forward with plans for his first foray into radio, with a show called "The Follies of the Air." Eddie Dowling was the master of ceremonies, but Ziegfeld's influence and even his presence were abundantly evident. Dowling, Ziegfeld, and Al Goodman, the orchestra leader, met two weeks before the show debuted to outline and cast it. They wrote until Sunday, the day of the performance, and then rehearsed from noon to 8:00 P.M., just before show time.

Rose Mariella was a waitress before joining the chorus of the original *Show Boat* about October 1928. She appeared in six Ziegfeld shows in New York, including the *Show Boat* revival, but refused to go on the road.

The show's premiere broadcast took place on April 3, 1932. The thirty-minute show ran thirteen weeks—through June 26. Ziegfeld pulled out all the stops on his guest list, which included, among others, Billie and Patty, Will Rogers, John Steele, Lupe Velez, Helen Morgan, Jack Pearl, Leon Errol, Paul Robeson, Ray Dooley, Fannie Brice, Ruth Etting, and Frances White. During the May 1 and June 12 programs, he aired *Show Boat* music. Ziegfeld was not excited about appearing before audiences, but he seemed relaxed enough during his radio debut.

Ziegfeld's voice has been described as high-pitched and even as irritating. Tapes of his radio show and footage from newsreel features do not entirely bear out those impressions. His voice was in the tenor range and had that flat, nasal twang one often hears in both Chicago and New York. When he said, "I wish to thank you for what I trust is your gracious acceptance of the first of the Ziegfeld radio shows," the word "first" came out as "foist." Billie shed some light on this issue when she said that he sometimes used a high, nasal pitch for effect, but that normally he had a "large resonant voice, as anyone who ever talked to him on the telephone ought to remember. Or anyone at whom he was ever angry."

During that inaugural show, Will Rogers expressed a widespread sentiment when he noted that "every man that flies the ocean from now on will always be just an imitation of Lindbergh, and every musical show that is produced is just an imitation of Ziegfeld." (Rogers always called him "Ziegfield.")

The show contained a nostalgic blend of music, humor, and patter that evoked the splendor of another era, from "the scrapbook of Ziegfeld memories." One event that Ziegfeld restaged was the glittering evening when the Prince of Wales visited the *Follies of 1919*.

Ziegfeld was seriously ill in the late spring of 1932, but doctors could not restrain him from directing Billie as she negotiated a contract with David Belasco. He instructed her in detail, declaring that "you're to receive fifteen percent straight and guarantee of fifteen hundred weekly. If you're not worth these terms, I'll not permit you to do it." He went on at length—for four pages. He also advised her about staging details for a radio appearance: "Good morning, Darling. I mailed you the music 'The Little Canoe' but as you and Rogers together will only be on six or seven minutes, maybe eight, and as you have no orchestra I deem it advisable not to sing a song."

Ziegfeld's health continued to be precarious. He suffered a relapse severe enough to cause him to summon his heart doctor one night at 3 A.M. These problems precluded any trips to California, prompting him to write a chatty note to his daughter: "My darling Patty, you don't know how much I wish I could see you and Mother. Today [it has] been over seven weeks now since I've been in bed. . . . I hope Mother gets Harpo Marx in her show if only for a few weeks. The two together would be a scream. . . . Next Sunday we're going to broadcast *Show Boat* with original cast. All my love, Daddy."

That spring, Ziegfeld leased the Earl Carroll (renaming it the Casino) to revive *Show Boat*. He desperately needed a hit. The *Show Boat* reprise proved not to be a simple revival, as this note indicates: "Hello my darlings, This certainly has been blue Monday. That G.D.S.O.B. Urban with the unions tied me in a knot. Curry in hospital but I have not jumped out of the window yet."

Ziegfeld restaged *Show Boat* on May 19, 1932. Since *Show Boat* had run for two years in New York and its revival occurred during the depths of the Depression, it would be easy to imagine the new version bombing or leaving jaded New Yorkers flat. Nothing of the sort happened on opening night, commented Edna Ferber, who described the New York reaction to the revival: "When Show Boat was revived . . . I saw a New York first-night audience, after Paul Robeson's singing of Ol' Man River, shout and cheer and behave generally as I've never seen an audience behave in any theater."

The art-deco Casino Theatre had a much bigger stage than the Ziegfeld did, but it was not as elegant. The 1927 production was the more important historically, yet some people who saw both versions thought that the cast in 1932 was stronger. Robeson as Joe was more relaxed, and he imbued the role with a warmth that Bledsoe did not project. Dennis King offered a charisma that Marsh simply could not muster.

Norma Terris again performed as Magnolia and Kim, this time at a salary of $1,000 per week. Terris said that she knew Ziegfeld had never recovered from the crash, so she returned half of her weekly salary on the condition that Ziegfeld not know where the money had come from.

In late June, papers on both coasts reported that Ziegfeld had developed a lung ailment. Dr. Boynton Wilbur expressed concern that Ziegfeld might never recover fully. He was confined to his home in Hastings, where a nurse was in attendance day and night.

Money concerns meanwhile were so severe that they consumed Ziegfeld's thoughts. He wrote his business manager, Dan Curry, on July 5, 1932, outlining a plan for recouping:

> Well they carried me out. I hated to go and leave so many problems in your hands. Doctor claims it's life or death with me. . . . I suggest that you immediately lay off everybody possible. . . . Convince everybody that I am very sick, Dan. I am no good to anyone dead. . . . Alive and well I am an asset to all and they have had all I've made for years. Now they must give me the chance.

Ziegfeld's health problems and his anxiety over the debts became so serious that Billie could hear evidence of the strain in his voice during his radio show. She canceled her contract for a play with Homer Curran, signing on instead for a movie (A Bill of Divorcement) so that she would have time to bring Flo to California. There was some discussion of having him recover in a New Mexico sanatorium, but Billie decided that he would be better off with her in California. Flo's sister, Louise, who had helped him out financially during recent difficulties, paid for a private railroad car to make the trip more comfortable.

Billie and Patty went East in an entourage that included Howard Hughes and two of Will Rogers's children, Mary and Jimmy. (Hughes was seeing Mary at the time.) It was an extremely hot trip during July. Ziegfeld was up and about, but he was not well enough to leave the train. Patty's recollection is that he was coherent and his spirits were fine. However, Billie described him as being only half-conscious. Ziegfeld would not admit to himself or his family how ill he was.

Billie had rented a house in Santa Monica, at 2407 La Mesa Drive, where Ziegfeld could recuperate. She tried to make Flo rest; nevertheless, unbeknownst to her, Sidney helped Flo send telegrams and make phone calls. As Flo would tell Billie, "I do love to telephone." She could not refuse him under the circumstances, so, cost notwithstanding, she let him "communicate" to his heart's content. That month Billie paid a $6,000 telegraph bill (equivalent to about $65,000 today). Most of the time, however, Flo was in bed with a severe, painful case of pleurisy. Dr. Radwin came to the house every other day.

In the midst of all of Ziegfeld's problems, Dan Curry, his business manager for seven years, died. In response to a request from Billie, A. C. Blumenthal shouldered some of the financial burden by guaranteeing an additional $12,000 per week in salaries that was needed to keep Show Boat in business. Blumenthal was a family friend who had married Peggy Fears, one of Ziegfeld's most gorgeous showgirls.

On July 17, Ziegfeld's health took a turn for the worse. Finally Billie brought him to the Cedars of Lebanon Hospital in serious condition. His lung infection had spread, and he developed pneumonia. Nevertheless, his heart, which was once weak, had improved.

While he was still in great pain, he received a little relief from Jimmy Durante: "According to my secret operatives you're not sick. You're just in there writing a new *Follies*. Now, listen, if I go in it I want top billing and my dressing room must be perfumed daily. That's my ultimatum. If you need any help writing it just move over. Here's to a speedy recovery. Best, Schnozzle."

Just as Ziegfeld's health reached its nadir, so did his financial situation. On July 21, the courts rendered a judgment against him for unpaid taxes. That same day, an unidentified person from Ziegfeld's business office wrote Billie with grim news. Ziegfeld's habit of pushing people, especially stagehands, so hard over the years had caught up with him:

Dear Mrs. Ziegfeld: Mr. Ziegfeld's personal affairs are in such shape [that] bankruptcy is not only important, but urgent. . . .

Our Western Union credit has been cut off. . . . Our telephones in the Ziegfeld Theatre will be cut off in a day or two. . . . The State Tax Department has a judgment out against us and I am expecting them in any minute to attach things, but there isn't anything here that Mr. Ziegfeld owns. . . . Nothing could be done with the Stage Hands Union. They brought forth all the threatening telegrams Mr. Ziegfeld sent them some time ago, and now no power on earth can move them to change their rules.

On July 22, Ziegfeld seemed to improve a bit. He spent the afternoon having Patty read telegrams, which he then answered. He had dinner with Patty and Billie in the nondescript, antiseptic hospital room. They celebrated some small victory with rare roast beef, asparagus, and champagne. The discussion that evening ranged widely. Ziegfeld talked about television, radio, and film musicals and contemplated leaving New York permanently. He knew it was going to be difficult to recover from his financial problems, but he expressed a desire to get back into the fray. It was a pleasant evening, which left them all sensing that Ziegfeld was on the mend.

Filming of *A Bill of Divorcement* was under way, so Billie sometimes worked twelve-hour days. She returned to the studio after dinner, around 7:00 P.M., for a screen test with young Walter Pidgeon. Patty went to a movie with a companion because Ziegfeld seemed fine.

Just before 10:00 P.M., according to one account, "he was stricken suddenly by abdominal pains." His nurse, Helen Kennedy, rushed out for Dr. Radwin and placed an urgent call for Billie. "He knew that death was coming," Dr. Radwin said. At 10:31 P.M. on July 22, 1932, Ziegfeld "gasped sharply twice and fell back upon his pillow" as Billie raced to reach his side. She arrived shortly after he died. About twenty minutes later Patty arrived. Cause of death was enlargement of the heart and other complications.

Years later, the doctor said that the press knew Ziegfeld had died before his widow learned about it. One of the nurses had been on a newspaper's payroll and had called in a report before Billie could get to the hospital. Even after all his financial setbacks, in death, Ziegfeld was page-one news.

Billie had been very strong during Flo's illness, but after her husband died, she cried for days. Patty found it hard to believe that her father was dead. She recalls walking out of the hospital as if in a dream.

That evening, Will Rogers spirited Patty and Billie away to his ranch. He also planned the funeral.

Early the next morning, Will Rogers went over to Eddie Cantor's to tell him. On hearing the news, Cantor sat down and wept openly in front of his startled children. Marilyn Cantor Baker recalled that "it was the first time that I'd ever seen him cry. Perhaps it was because Daddy never had a father . . . Ziegfeld was the closest thing he had." Cantor knew that he had been close to a giant with no peer on Broadway.

Ziegfeld's mother had been ill for years. Doctors believed that the news of Flo's death would be too much for her. Her other two sons were already gone. She faded away quietly three months later, unaware that her last son had preceded her in death. Only her daughter, Louise, survived her.

Newspapers all across the country ran front-page headlines bearing the news of Ziegfeld's passing. Expressions of condolence to Billie such as this one from William Randolph Hearst poured in by the thousands: "I am inexpressibly grieved to hear of the death of your dear husband. . . . His death is a staggering blow. . . . Mr. Ziegfeld was a marvelous man, a unique and towering figure in the life of the stage. A man of extraordinary appreciation and taste and refinement. . . . Such a man will be greatly missed. . . . I extend to you my heartfelt condolence and I mourn the loss of a dear friend."

Billie rallied for the funeral. It was a short service, handled by the Rev. Franklin L. Gibson, rector of Saint Athjanasius Episcopal Church. Approximately one hundred close friends attended private services at Pierce Brothers mortuary on July 24, including Ethel and John Barrymore, Eddie Cantor, Marion Davies, Leon Errol, Mr. and Mrs. Sam Goldwyn, W. R. Hearst, Katharine Hepburn, Harold Lloyd, Louella Parsons, Will Rogers, Norma Shearer, Irving Thalberg, and Walter Wanger.

According to the *Los Angeles Times*, Billie and Patty "fought back tears as they entered the chapel with Will Rogers. They all were weeping as they left, however, and the widow seemed on the verge of a collapse."

Will Rogers delivered a eulogy that later appeared in *The New York Times:*

Our world of "make believe" is sad. Scores of comedians are not funny, hundreds of "America's most beautiful girls" are not gay. Our benefactor has passed away. He picked us from all walks of life, he led us into what little fame we achieved. He remained our friend regardless of our usefulness to him as an entertainer. He brought beauty into the entertainment world. The profession of acting must be necessary, for it exists in every race, and every language. And to have been the master amusement provider of your generation, surely a life's work was accomplished. And he left something on earth that hundreds of us will treasure till our curtains fall and that was a "badge," a badge which we were proud, and never ashamed of, and wanted the world to read the lettering on it "I worked for Ziegfeld."

So good-by Flo, save a spot for me, for you will put on a show up there some day that will knock their eyes out. Yours, Will Rogers.

Will's son Jimmy said that "no two men lived who had greater, deeper respect for one another. My dad didn't have that feeling with any of the other people he worked for." When Ziegfeld was sick and on the verge of bankruptcy, his father helped pay the producer's medical bills. Typically, Rogers insisted on keeping his generosity low-key to avoid embarrassing the great producer during his turbulent last days.

In a culminating irony, the man of theater, a New Yorker through and through, died on the West Coast and was then buried at Forest Lawn in Los Angeles. Four decades later, in June 1974, Patty Ziegfeld transferred her father's remains to Kensico Cemetery in Valhalla, New York, near Burkeley Crest, to be with Billie and Blanche Burke in the family plot, as well as closer to the theater world he cherished. Billie and Flo's dignified but simple plots are distinguished by twin nameplates in the ground. Nearby, over Blanche Burke's grave, is a bronze statue of a beautiful woman in ancient garb and a classic Greek pose. At long last, Ziegfeld came home to New York, where he rests in a peaceful, wooded setting.

In a telegram to Billie after Ziegfeld's death, Gene Buck summed up Ziegfeld the man:

It's hard to realize he's gone. You were the finest influence in his colorful and hectic life. His passing as sudden and sad as it seems to us now, I think is for the best. Flo was never made to retire behind the scenes in the drama of life. . . . So very few understood the perplexities of his nature. There could only be really . . . one Flo. And now his extraordinary, unusual, and fascinating spirit has gone to rest. To many he will ever be a legend. To us and a privileged few, [he was] a real dreamer and an artist, with all the idiosyncrasies that go with a person that chooses to live by his imagination.

Right: Milton Berle on stage with chorus girls in the 1943 *Ziegfeld Follies*. Berle was a child actor in silent movies and performed on Broadway and in six other films. However, he is probably best known as "Mr. Television" because of his popularity in that medium's early days. Far right: Airline hostess Beatrice Lillie with passengers Bette Graham and John Philip in a scene from the 1957 *Ziegfeld Follies*. Lillie, an English actress and comedian, started her career as a singer at age sixteen before accepting comedy roles. For many years she divided her time between New York and London before moving to New York in the 1950s. She made seven American films (including *Thoroughly Modern Millie* in 1961), but the stage was her first love.

CHAPTER 18

❖

AND BEAUTY DEAD, BLACK CHAOS COMES AGAIN

❖

Billie Burke closed her memoir by noting that she associated her life after Flo's death with these lines from Shakespeare's "Venus and Adonis":

For him being dead, with him is Beauty slain;
And Beauty dead, black chaos Comes again.

Immediately after Ziegfeld died, black chaos came and with a vengeance in business affairs. A. C. Blumenthal had assumed control of financial problems. Newspaper estimates of Ziegfeld's debts ranged from $1 million to $2 million. The district attorney's office seized the files in the Ziegfeld Theatre. Bills poured in, process servers were everywhere, and courts rendered judgments against the estate.

Billie's financial plight was so desperate that within one month of Ziegfeld's death, she and Blumenthal felt compelled to join Ziegfeld's bitter enemies, the Shuberts, in continuing the *Follies*, so that she could pay off some of Ziegfeld's numerous debts.

Ziegfeld's will divided the estate equally between Billie and Patty, but after having earned millions of dollars, Flo left no tangible assets for the creditors. A 1934 probate inventory done by estate executor William S. Coffey showed $2,773.05 cash at the Citizens Bank in White Plains, New York. No other property was in Ziegfeld's name: no real estate, stocks, bonds, jewelry, clothing, or even household goods.

It took quite some time for the full impact of his problems to become clear. Half a dozen debts were for amounts between $20,000 and $50,000, but the majority involved less than $10,000. A court record from March 21, 1934, estimated claims at more than $500,000. On December 21, 1934, more than two years after Ziegfeld died, nearly fifty creditors were owed $280,996.48.

The financial quagmire best representing Billie's plight was a suit initiated by the Bank of the United States over $37,787.84 outstanding on a loan. Bank officials believed that substantial assets remained in the estate, partly from film properties and partly from the cachet of the name "Ziegfeld." To prove this point, they needed access to the financial records, and to obtain these, they needed the cooperation of Louis Levy, Ziegfeld's attorney.

In its petition, the bank complained that Levy had "refused and continues to refuse to offer said Will for probate and to qualify as executor thereunder." Depositions from a hearing in March and April of 1933 reveal that Levy had begun an elaborate and obstinate game of cat-and-mouse, refusing to provide a Santa Monica street address for Billie and Patty. The bank had served citations at a variety of locations, sought information through Blumenthal, even run ads in Hastings and Westchester papers to announce the citation—all to no avail. In May the court ordered that Ziegfeld's will be admitted to probate.

Billie had a difficult time of it for several years. Sam Goldwyn gave her a $300-per-week personal contract to help her through the travails caused by Ziegfeld's debts. He used her in only one movie for his own studio, but he loaned her out, giving her the money he made from the loan-outs.

One of Billie's first sacrifices in making good on the financial obligations was the lodge at Camp Patricia, which must have been in her name. She sold that structure, built for $80,000, at a Sheriff's sale for $2,500. Then the Loew Theatre circuit picked up the lease on the Ziegfeld Theatre.

In mid-April 1933, there was a brief respite from the onslaught of creditors when the Ziegfeld Theatre reopened—as a movie house instead of a stage for live theater. The following week, a Broadway tribute to Ziegfeld was broadcast nationally. Billie was working in Hollywood, but she listened to it. Many Broadway luminaries and former Ziegfeld stars turned out for the spectacle, including Eddie Cantor, Gene Buck, Charles Winninger, Lillian Lorraine, and Eddie Dowling. One of the most difficult moments came when Lillian Lorraine began singing "By the Light of the Silvery Moon." Overwhelmed by emotion, she collapsed and was unable to complete the number.

Meanwhile, Shubert and Ziegfeld representatives worked out a license arrangement for the title "Ziegfeld Follies of 1933." The contract imposed conditions, including one that the production "be of the same character and quality as were the *Follies* produced by the late Florenz Ziegfeld." The license, good for only one edition, paid Billie and the Erlanger estate 3 percent of the gross.

Once it became clear that Billie and the Shuberts were making money from the new edition of the *Follies* and after the Ziegfeld estate went into probate, creditors began arriving at the courthouse steps. They were asking for a slice of the profits on the current show, which was now grossing about $60,000 a

Hugh O'Connell, Bob Hope, and Eve Arden act out a scene from the *Ziegfeld Follies of 1936*. Hope had been a chorus boy in *Smiles* before making film shorts in New York. After a radio appearance, he went to Hollywood and became a star. Arden was in the 1934 *Ziegfeld Follies* as well as the 1936 show. She made more than fifty movies before achieving her greatest success, on radio, as star of "Our Miss Brooks." She later played the same role on television.

week. The name was estimated to be worth approximately one-third of that total.

This situation prompted a long wrangle over rights to the name of the show. The court in White Plains ordered Billie to show cause why she should not pay $5,000 to the Ziegfeld estate for her share in the title of *Ziegfeld Follies*. This action was brought by Coffey on behalf of creditors. She was holding out on paying until the courts gave her the right to the *Ziegfeld Follies* name.

During 1934, two other events made the scene even more depressing. Charles Dillingham, Ziegfeld's partner and friend for more than thirty years, died on August 30, completely insolvent. Despite having made millions from theatrical enterprises, he had filed for bankruptcy in 1933 owing more than $7 million on assets of only $108,000. Late in 1934, two years after Rosalie Ziegfeld's death, the Ziegfeld home on Adams Street in Chicago was auctioned off for a pittance.

Meanwhile, the bank case wended its way through the courts. In 1935, the Surrogate Court ruled that after legal expenses the balance of the estate belonged to the Internal Revenue Service. There is no record of the family receiving anything.

Moderate success with the 1933–34 *Follies* lured the Shuberts and Billie Burke into producing another edition, the *Ziegfeld Follies of 1936*, beginning January 30 (Winter Garden Theatre). In this *Follies*, Fannie Brice made her last Broadway appearance. Besides Brice, other noteworthy personalities in this year's edition were comedian Bob Hope, Josephine Baker, dancer Harriet Hoctor (who had been in three Ziegfeld musicals but no *Follies)*, and singers/actresses Gertrude Niesen and Eve Arden.

On May 8, 1936, Fannie Brice became ill with neuritis and was confined to bed. Milton Berle appeared in the show on Friday and Saturday; on Sunday, May 10, it was suspended. Initially Brice was expected to return in three or four weeks. However, the *Follies* did not reopen until September 14, 1936. When it resumed, it was billed as the 1936–37 edition. Hope, Baker, Hoctor, and Niesen had left the cast, but Bobby Clark and Gypsy Rose Lee were added. Billie Burke Ziegfeld was listed as the producer.

According to *The New York Times*, the production did not contain enough fresh material to be called a new show but was merely a revised version.

By the mid-1930s, sufficient time had elapsed for people to begin getting a handle on Ziegfeld's contribution to the theater. The result was a movie extravaganza in the form of *The Great Ziegfeld*, which cost M-G-M Studios $2 million to produce. The movie opened in April 1936, to great fanfare in both the newspapers and the film newsreels of the day. The Hearst newsreel even did a feature on the New York opening that showed thousands of spectators and theatergoers milling around outside the theater.

The movie was Ziegfeldian only in its cost and the public relations hype. Even though it was very successful in its day, receiving four Academy Award nominations and winning two Oscars (including one for best picture), it did not exhibit the Ziegfeld touch in its pace—which was plodding—or in its handling of visual effects. The enthusiastic response from the audience and the critics gave significant testimony, though, to the power of the Ziegfeld name four years after his death.

When it became apparent that the movie was financially successful, Coffey sued for a portion of the profits because the movie company had used the Ziegfeld name. M-G-M claimed that its movie was fictionalized biography, while Coffey argued that it was a musical revue and that the Ziegfeld corporation controlled the name "Ziegfeld." The estate requested and received a $17,500 settlement.

In May 1936, Universal Pictures released its classic version of *Show Boat*, starring Allan Jones, Irene Dunne, and Paul Robeson, as well as several actors from the original Broadway production, including Charles Winninger, Helen Morgan, and Sammy White. The 1936 film version of *Show Boat* holds up very well.

The next year, on October 15, 1937, the court ordered an auction on the rights to and interest in seventy-two Ziegfeld shows. The auction earned only $28,000, just under $400 for each property. The buyers were mostly writers and composers interested in regaining rights to their own material, among them Jerome Kern, Irving Berlin, Oscar Hammerstein II, and Sigmund Romberg. In the ultimate, ignominious irony, the buyers were warned by an attorney that "the Shuberts owned the Ziegfeld name and that any use of the copyrighted materials must not be under the names Ziegfeld or Ziegfeld Follies."

The final step in the painful saga after Ziegfeld's death occurred in April 1940, almost eight years after it began. Billie was forced to sell Burkeley Crest. The sizable estate with its twenty-two-room house, acres of land, stables, swimming pool, tennis court, and greenhouses sold for $36,000; household objects earned another $6,000, making a grand total of $42,000.

Ziegfeld's legacy did not die with him, as producers from New York to Hollywood sought to use his name. On April 1, 1943, a new edition of the *Ziegfeld Follies* opened at the Winter Garden Theatre, produced by the Shubert brothers in association with Alfred Bloomingdale and Lou Walters, by special arrangement with Billie Burke. Milton Berle was the star of this production; other principals included Ilona Massey and Arthur Treacher, both from the movies, and dancer Jack Cole. There were eleven showgirls and seventeen "Follies Dancing Girls." The show, a typical fast-paced revue with sketches, songs, and beautiful girls, had the longest run of any *Follies*: 553 performances.

The first of many *Show Boat* stage revivals after Ziegfeld's death was produced by Oscar Hammerstein in 1946. M-G-M remade the film of *Show Boat*, but the 1951 movie was not as good as the 1936 Universal rendition.

There was also a perfectly soporific movie entitled *The Ziegfeld Follies* that starred Fred Astaire, Judy Garland, Lena Horne, Lucille Ball, Esther Williams, Fannie Brice, and William Powell. The big names could not breathe life into a production paced so poorly that Ziegfeld must have turned over in his grave.

An attempt was made in 1956 to launch yet another edition of the *Follies*, starring Tallulah Bankhead, but it lost $400,000 and folded before it got to New York.

In 1957, the Shuberts managed a fiftieth-anniversary edition of the *Ziegfeld Follies*, but it was decidedly disappointing. The show had only eleven chorus girls—fewer than in the first *Follies* in 1907. Much of the production's material was taken from the failed 1956 show. Charles Conway and Mark Kroll bought the show and costumes at bargain prices. They signed comedian Beatrice Lillie, comic Billie de Wolfe, and singer Jane Morgan. After much revision and $300,000 in production expenses, the show made its Broadway debut to less than enthusiastic reviews and played only 123 performances.

Approximately forty years after it was built, the magnificent Ziegfeld Theatre was torn down in 1967 to make way for the Hilton Hotel. Material from the Ziegfeld Theatre cornerstone was donated to the Smithsonian Institution.

After Flo's death, Billie Burke continued her successful stage and film career, acting in ten more stage productions and sixty-eight more films. Perhaps her most memorable screen role was as Glinda, the good witch, in *The Wizard of Oz* (1939); she was also in the *Topper* movie series and in films such as *Dinner at Eight* (1933). She also worked in radio (doing her own show after World War II) and television. On February 1 and February 8, 1950, Billie was featured on Ralph Edwards's "This Is Your Life" radio show, which included a good deal of material about Ziegfeld.

Billie lived comfortably in the Los Angeles suburb of Brentwood next door to Patty until she died on May 14, 1970, at the age of eighty-five.

A production scene from the *Follies*, year unknown

❖

THE ZIEGFELD TOUCH

❖

Unquestionably, Ziegfeld's contribution to the theater world directly and to the entertainment industry indirectly was significant. As biographer Deidre Bair has observed, the key to writing biographies is to discern how "the individuals shape the time in which we live, how their lives have been played out against the major events of our times, and how they influenced those events." By this measure, Ziegfeld stands up well. Broadway impresario Anna Sosenko put Ziegfeld's contribution in perspective by asking: "Who ever says anymore that she was a 'Shubert Girl' or a 'Dillingham Girl'? Nobody—the public doesn't remember anymore who Lee Shubert, Charlie Dillingham, . . . or Charles Frohman were."

In short, Ziegfeld's name became a metaphor for panache on Broadway, a metaphor that worked its way into the language as shorthand for the best of New York theater.

Sosenko contended that the key to Ziegfeld's achievements was his hubris—the "gall of the gods" was her phrase. He spent money he did not have and became involved with female stars, a sure formula for trouble, but he simply rose above such concerns. Sosenko believed that without the vices and the failures, the monumental strengths would have been absent. The crucial point, she said, was that he learned from his mistakes. Something would go wrong, but he would "fiddle" until he found the right combination.

Ziegfeld's genius lay in his grasp of what appealed to the American public. He had an uncanny ability to combine the exotic with the familiar, "high" culture aesthetics with "low" culture entertainment. He brought Paris and New York fashion to his costumes by attracting world-class designers such as Lucille, Erté, Charles LeMaire, and John Harkrider. He hired accomplished composers who were creating the outstanding music of the era, some classical writers such as Victor Herbert and outstanding composers of ragtime and modern music, including Irving Berlin, Richard Rodgers, Vincent Youmans, Jerome Kern, Rudolf Friml, and Sigmund Romberg. He introduced precision dancing and ballet elements into musical-comedy numbers and had a knack for popularizing songs. Over the years, says scholar Rosaline Stone, Ziegfeld shows featured an impressive range of dances: marches, acrobatic numbers, novelties, the shimmy, fandangos, classical ballet, tap, modern dance, Spanish dances, minstrel numbers, tangos, the fox-trot, cakewalks, rags, and the turkey trot.

He had no qualms about devising a circus scene that had Marilyn Miller riding in on a live horse and then following that scene with a Ben Ali Haggin tableau. He mixed foreign and American elements. He would blend an exotic "Spanish Frolic" or "Arabian Nights" scene with "Prohibition" and "American Eagle" scenes that reflected local concerns.

The clash between classical and popular, in Ziegfeld's life and in his art, paralleled a similar trend in American culture between 1900 and 1930. The rural frontier culture was giving way to an urban sophistication that was heavily influenced by European art. As American culture assimilated European values, the ensuing healthy tension prompted a unique blend of cultures, culminating in theater with the best editions of the *Follies* (1917–22) and with the spectacular run of book shows from 1927 to 1928 that included *Show Boat*.

The music Ziegfeld liked also provided this combination as he commissioned songs that reflected American values. Even a short list of the songs that he used indicates how well he understood popular taste in music: "A Bicycle Built for Two," "Shine on, Harvest Moon," "A Pretty Girl Is Like a Melody," "My Man," "Second Hand Rose," "Old Man River," "Makin' Whoopee," and "Ten Cents a Dance."

Only a few of the hundreds of original songs from Ziegfeld shows have endured over the years. While the majority are outdated, they were pleasing to the audiences of their day. On the other hand, many of the best-remembered songs from Ziegfeld's productions were ones that he borrowed from other Broadway shows or vaudeville—with the notable exceptions of *Show Boat* and Irving Berlin's tunes. But, had Ziegfeld not interpolated these songs, many would not have become hits or achieved lasting popularity.

Ziegfeld transformed scenery from hack work into art by giving free rein to Joseph Urban, a genuine artist, whose scene designs are still being exhibited at galleries. The wonderfully crafted productions drew the high society people who made it fashionable for local New Yorkers, not just tourists, to frequent Broadway. With those elements, he mixed popular entertainment features. He loved to shock theater audiences by bringing live animals on stage—elephants, horses, cows, ostriches, cats, dogs.

His *Follies* consistently reflected topical concerns: he staged airplane numbers by 1909, had patriotic scenes in 1917, and commissioned songs about Prohibition. Likewise his authors and comedians used topical material, Will Rogers being the quintessential example, reading the daily newspapers to generate

Composers gathered in Washington, D.C.; many of them worked for Ziegfeld at one time or another.

ideas for his monologue each evening. These characteristic elements of the *Follies* were the forerunners of contemporary popular entertainment such as *The Tonight Show* and *Saturday Night Live*.

His comedy had that freewheeling, wacky, somewhat unsophisticated quality that the American film industry preserved so well in the 1920s and 1930s. This brand of humor is exemplified by scenes such as "At the Osteopath's," in which Eddie Cantor found himself being twisted into odd pretzel shapes by the loony Dr. Cheeseboro Simpson. It was also evident in Will Rogers's monologues when he poked fun at government, society, and any person or institution that smelled of pretense or aristocracy.

The crown jewel in his popular entertainment, of course, was always beautiful women in stunning costumes or in enticing degrees of dishabille. He presented women with an elegance and a genuine respect that the other producers missed. Ziegfeld was not above titillating his audience, but he would not brook vulgarity, which violated his sense of artistry. Presenting attractive women, some of whom were nearly nude, was not then and still is not unique. Ziegfeld's consummate accomplishment was to glorify women in ways that appealed to both sexes. He showed enough flesh to lure male customers while still presenting the showgirls with class and dignity, so that women were just as eager to see Ziegfeld's shows as men.

Ziegfeld's staging innovations were also striking. He exhibited an American attitude toward technology—always searching for the innovation that would delight the audience. He introduced the telescopic stage and experimented with phosphorescent paint on costumes. He stretched the limits on what could be done with props as he brought scale-model airplanes and real cars onstage. He created the animated song sheet by having human faces appear through holes in a musical-score backdrop. Audience interaction became part of the Ziegfeld repertoire in 1915 when he introduced the *Midnight Frolic.*

Ziegfeld brought a precision and an elegance to lighting that set standards for years to come. He always knew not only what effect he wanted but also exactly how to achieve that effect. He could spotlight a showgirl so she looked her absolute best while still maintaining the integrity of the scenic design. Joseph Urban helped in this regard because of his exacting color work and light rehearsals that resulted in brilliant colors and a consistency of presentation, even on the road.

Not the least of Ziegfeld's accomplishments was that he helped change the status of the chorus girl. He was one of the first American impresarios to make the chorus line integral to production numbers. Early chorus girls acted as mere decorations; even the sixteen chorus girls who accompanied Anna Held in 1906 did little more than wear beautiful clothes. By the next year, the Anna Held Girls were more noticeable—in part because there were more of them—but their role was still relatively unimportant. Over the years, however, Ziegfeld placed greater emphasis on the chorus girls. Instead of keeping them stationary, Ziegfeld had them moving about—in the aisles, on the stage, and in the *Midnight Frolic,* among the tables. By the early 1920s chorus girls "made" the show. Their beauty, their gorgeous costumes, and their deportment contributed to the show's aesthetic, sensual appeal. The chorus was necessary to achieve the spectacular effect Ziegfeld required for individual scenes. The women drew the audience's attention to a specific place onstage or framed a scene for added effect.

As the role of the chorus girl changed, so did her appearance. The early chorus women in burlesque wore tights and were quite hefty; they were also hardened, mature women who were considered "wicked." Ziegfeld's chorus girls, in contrast, were young, attractive, wholesome-looking girls. Although they were usually sixteen to twenty-three years old, many were fourteen or fifteen years old. Ziegfeld glamorized the chorus girl and made her a symbol of the modern, independent woman. Her status, as well as her salary, increased, and she even became a suitable mate for the wealthy.

Today, Ziegfeld's glorification of women provokes ambivalent reactions. In his day, though, the attention he lavished upon women was one step in the process of bringing women into the center of society.

While Ziegfeld's transformation of the chorus girl was a significant accomplishment, the heart of his contribution to theater in the first third of the twentieth century was a blend of the powerful imagination that conjured the "world" of the *Follies,* total devotion to his art, an unfailing sense of elegance, and unparalleled standards for theatrical production. These personal traits were manifested on the stage, giving a Ziegfeld show class that set it apart. The standards that made him demand tasteful presentations of partially clad women also prompted him to stress clean humor. In the process, he raised the revue form progressively from burlesque to vaudeville to art. Other producers contributed to this change, but Ziegfeld led the way.

An account of Ziegfeld's contribution must also include his treatment of minorities. He broke the color barrier on Broadway by hiring Bert Williams for a featured role. The friendship between the two was genuine and mutual, which caused no small measure of consternation in some circles, as did Ziegfeld's decision to use large numbers of blacks in *Show Boat.* Ziegfeld also hired black musicians and purchased songs from black composers. Nevertheless, daring as he was, he never hired a black woman as a chorus member or a showgirl for the *Follies,* and he helped perpetuate blackface routines. And, except for Bert Williams and the team of Buck and Bubbles, blacks did not appear as principals in the *Follies.*

Additionally, Ziegfeld treated his actors with a respect and an integrity that was unusual for the time. He did not strand them on the road, he provided decent dressing rooms, he paid them well, and most importantly he seemed genuinely interested in them as people who wanted to develop professionally.

In the larger sense, Ziegfeld embodied (and controlled) his times. When theater was the dominant form of entertainment, he was king of that realm. However, beginning in 1919 with the Equity strike, the labor environment changed radically for everyone, but especially for Ziegfeld. As the labor movement became stronger, just at the time the road-tour industry collapsed, costs rose sharply for everyone, but with Ziegfeld's damn-the-expense approach, he was affected more dramatically than his colleagues. More telling, though, was labor's ability to dictate what the producer did. He was no longer able to drive his employees the way he had in an earlier time. The unions would not cooperate with Ziegfeld because they resented the way he had interacted with them over the past decade. Now they had the power to make life difficult for him.

The burgeoning film industry caught Ziegfeld in a historically anomalous position. He loved the medium and had been involved with it early on—with Edison's film of Sandow, with his investment in the movie version of *Ben-Hur,* and with a wife who was one of the era's most beloved film stars. He could have gone into film but chose not to do so because at that time it was weak technologically in his strongest suits— lighting, color, and sound. Nevertheless, because he chose theater as his artistic métier, he found himself on the horns of a dilemma. On the one hand, he rode the Broadway crest to the theater's grandest era; on the other hand, over a short span, Broadway slid into a steep descent from which it has still not emerged. Since the plot curves for film and theater (numbers of ticket buyers, profits, and critical reputation) crossed in the 1920s, film has been creating an ever-widening gap.

In the 1920s Ziegfeld began paying the price for his decision as he watched star after star succumb to the lure of the screen's big money and mass appeal. Dispersion of live theater depended on the railroad, whereas film could be reproduced in volume and then, with its simple and cheap technology, sent to virtually millions of people in every city and even village. Sound and color were available before Ziegfeld died, and he eagerly experimented with those technologies, but they came a bit late for him to take full advantage.

The last of the crucial historical developments was the Depression, which, like the labor movement, hit Ziegfeld harder than other producers. Had Ziegfeld been younger when the Depression struck, perhaps he would have had more energy with which to counteract its devastating effect. He was old enough that even though it did not kill him immediately and directly, it certainly was a major contributor.

He and Billie as a husband-wife theatrical team were quintessential representatives of the Jazz Age, with all of its glamour, energy, and profligacy. Billie was eighteen years younger and made a successful switch from theater to film as an actress because her career did not depend so heavily on color, lighting, and sound. Ziegfeld, like his Broadway contemporaries Abe Erlanger, Charles Dillingham, and Marc Klaw, did not survive the transition.

Not only was Ziegfeld a man of his times, but he significantly influenced his times and those that followed. He led the way in making musical comedy the dominant Broadway form. As Miles Kreuger has said, the history of musical comedy may be divided into two eras: before and after *Show Boat*. By blending music and action with theme, Ziegfeld permanently transformed what people did in musical theater.

Numerous stars, particularly the comedians, learned their trade and got their starts with Ziegfeld: Eddie Cantor, W. C. Fields, Will Rogers, Fannie Brice, Ed Wynn, Jimmy Durante, and Leon Errol, to name just a few. Though Ziegfeld supposedly detested comedians, he had an acerbic wit and loved practical jokes. More important, he consistently gave comedy a significant place in his shows and managed somehow, despite this alleged aversion to humor, to attract the best comedians in the business, men and women who have become legendary in their field.

Ziegfeld also had an impact on film. When song and dance director Busby Berkeley choreographed the movie *Whoopee!*, he transcribed Ziegfeld's effects from stage to film; Berkeley, of course, became the leading choreographer of film musicals in the 1930s. Ziegfeld's influence also extended to Samuel Goldwyn. As A. Scott Berg (Goldwyn's biographer) comments, although Goldwyn may not have admitted it, he assimilated many of Ziegfeld's theatrical values.

Ziegfeld's influence on radio and television was indirect because these media matured after his death. Nevertheless, many of his performers became radio personalities. While television did not emerge fully until twenty years after his death, variety and talk shows, particularly those with daily monologues, owe a lot to Ziegfeld's models in the *Follies* and especially the *Midnight Frolic*.

The underpinnings for Ziegfeld's accomplishments derive from a complex, seemingly inscrutable personality. Several characteristics are pivotal to understanding the man behind the shows. He was, first and foremost, absolutely driven by his goal of demolishing "all the current methods of staging shows." He had an American version of tragic hubris that made him press for his vision (and accompanying standards) long past a time that others could handle the pressure. In doing so, he spent excessive sums of money, he used sweet persuasion to get the maximum effort from employees, and, when that failed to elicit all their potential, he cajoled them into seeking yet another level of excellence.

His contentiousness makes some sense within the context of his whole personality. The raging desire to achieve high standards left him perpetually disappointed with himself and those around him. When Ziegfeld initiated a lawsuit, it was usually in response to workmanship he considered unacceptable.

His flair for publicity, for advancing his people and theatrical causes, is ironic. The man who created new standards in promoting shows was shy enough to be accused of being cold and aloof. Those who knew him well found him approachable, but he could be very reserved with those he had not yet learned to trust.

The women in his life were yet another key to Ziegfeld's personality. The man whom some writers have described as a heartless womanizer provided Lillian Lorraine with a stipend long after she was washed up. In spite of horribly acrimonious, public exchanges with Marilyn Miller in the early 1920s, he rehired her years later even after her career started to falter. Eventually, Miller realized how much Ziegfeld cared about her career and how valuable his loyalty was to her, and she spoke fondly of him in later years.

This was also the same man who doted on his mother, his wife, and his daughter. Certainly he hurt Billie with his philandering and gave her ample cause to be angry with him, but just as obvious is the fact that he loved her deeply in his own peculiar fashion. His affection for Patty was so unabashed that even in his own lifetime it became the subject of much commentary and of many jokes among the actors and professional staff. He was, according to those who knew the family, like putty in her hands.

The apparent contradiction in his relationship with women—being both cruel and solicitous—is crucial. Ziegfeld simply loved beautiful women. He took great pleasure in their company and delighted in making them happy by lavishing time, praise, and gifts on them. There was obviously a sexual aspect to this pleasure. Simultaneously, though, he respected women and was deeply concerned with the individual woman's welfare. Thus, many women considered him one of the outstanding men they had known. One writer mentioned that Ziegfeld seemed more comfortable with women than with men. Somehow he trans-

A collage showing some of the women who appeared in the *Follies* between 1907 and 1931 (not every year is represented)

ferred these attitudes to his productions, so that members of the audience, both male and female, sensed his relationship and took vicarious pleasure in it.

Finally, there was Ziegfeld's attitude toward money. Here again, he was a man of his time. Money in Ziegfeld's case was simply the means to the end: making artistic visions become realities. The paradox was that he was a producer who thought like an artist. When he was gambling, money was also simply a tool for achieving the excitement that he needed so badly to make his life seem worthwhile. Most of his friends gambled freely the way he did, but as Billie noted, they would go home when they were beaten. Flo would stay, grimly determined to beat the odds because he had to be the best at everything he did, even when it cost him his financial well-being and, at the end of his career, his ability to mount the kind of shows he envisioned. In short, the blind ambition that made him great also destroyed him.

The probate records at the Westchester County Surrogate Court offer a harsh, almost cruel, symbol of Ziegfeld's fate that is depressing even in the 1990s, sixty years later. In the framework of Greek tragedy, these records are signs of Ziegfeld's punishment for his "splendid failure to do the impossible," William Faulkner's phrase about his generation of Jazz-Age fiction writers who conjured potent artistic visions but failed, ultimately, to "match the work to the . . . dream."

So, too, with Ziegfeld in the theatrical realm. His artistic quest was magnificent. His gift was instinctive. True, he had learned the mechanics of his craft, but the great gift that emerged has to be called genius. It has been suggested that for Ziegfeld an imaginary curtain rose and he could see in his mind what he wanted to produce down to the smallest detail. And if he could see it, he could make it happen.

No man in his generation on Broadway achieved what he did and few among the generations to come will rival him. In his own terms, he failed to accomplish all that he imagined, and he compromised his visions to make them real in a flawed world. Most distressing to his cultural heirs is the fact that he was unable to leave a complete record of his splendid visions. The extant photos, represented in part by those in this book, are mostly black-and-white relics despite the fact that Ziegfeld's genius, by general accord, lay in generating spectacle with color—in costumes, sets, backdrops, and lighting—and with movement on the stage— flashing lights, live animals, moving props, dramatic pacing—all ephemeral. While we have a record of certain aspects of Ziegfeld's accomplishment, it is but a faint reflection of former grandeur. Theatrical entrepreneurs in the intervening years have discovered it is not easy to re-create the Ziegfeld touch.

Tragedy, whether it occurs in ancient Greece or during the American Jazz Age, simultaneously uplifts and chastens those reading about the great ones who, like Ziegfeld, rise brilliantly but fall from Olympian heights. In bestowing his gift, the Ziegfeld touch, this artist exacted a terrible penalty on himself and those who loved him, but these sacrifices led to the most singular moment in American theatrical history—the Great White Way during the Jazz Age, when Florenz Ziegfeld was master of his world.

INTERMISSION

International Temple of Music

MICHIGAN AVE. & SIXTEENTH ST.

"TROCADERO"

Dr. F. Ziegfeld
PRESIDENT

Washington Hesing
VICE PRESIDENT

W. D. Preston
TREASURER

Alfred M. Snydacker
SECRETARY

OFFICE ROOM 20
CENTRAL MUSIC HALL

Chicago Novbr 3d 1892

Dr Ziegfeldt
Ans'd Nov 5/92.

Dear Madam:

Permit me to communicate to you that I am in receipt of a letter from Herr Fritz Scheel, conductor of the Hamburg Bülow Orchestra, wherein he asks me to obtain, if possible, permission for him to dedicate a musical composition to you. Herr Scheel is one of the greatest conductors in Germany and a composer well worthy of your kind consideration.

Hoping for a favorable reply

I am Very Respectfully

F. Ziegfeld.

To Mrs Potter Palmer
Lake Shore Drive
City

Central Music Hall.

Right: A letter from Florenz Ziegfeld, Sr., to Chicago socialite Mrs. Potter Palmer on colorful Trocadero stationery. Opposite: A poster promoting Sandow and the Trocadero Vaudevilles while they were under Ziegfeld's management in the early 1890s

186

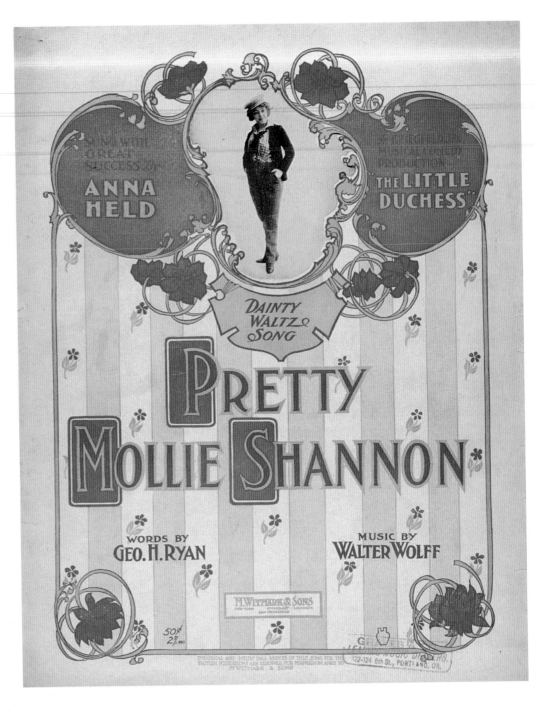

Above: Program cover from *The Turtle* (1898). The farce was daring by American standards, but it drew audiences for almost five months. Right: Sheet-music cover for "Pretty Molly Shannon" from *The Little Duchess* (1901)

Anna Held sang her trademark song, "I Just Can't Make My Eyes Behave," in *The Parisian Model* (1906).

Right: Mae Murray made the first of four *Follies* appearances in 1908. By 1921, the year of this sketch, she was a leading film actress. Opposite, above left: Mlle. Genée had danced with the Berlin Opera and had been in twenty ballets with the Empire Theatre in London before Ziegfeld engaged her to dance in *The Soul Kiss* (1908). Opposite, below left: Anna Held on the sheet-music cover for the title song from *Miss Innocence* (1908). Opposite, right: The popular Anna Held appeared on the cover of *The Theatre* magazine in January 1909.

MAE MURRAY

THIS CERTIFIES THAT

Florence Ziegfeld
of New York City, N.Y.
and Ethelbert Appleton Burke
of Hastings, N.Y.

were united in

MARRIAGE

according to

the Ordinance of GOD and the Laws of

New Jersey

on the 11th day of April

in the year of OUR LORD

One Thousand Nine Hundred 14

Witnesses Herman L. Roth.
William M. Fonda
Conrad Engelden
Luth. Pastor
234 Garden Str.
Hoboken N.J.

Behold, I stand at the door, and knock: if any man hear my voice, and open the door, I will come in to him. Rev. 3:20.

Left: The 1914 marriage certificate of Billie Burke and Florenz Ziegfeld, Jr. Below: This painting of Billie Burke hung on the wall in Ziegfeld's office. It also appeared inside the program for *Rio Rita*. Opposite, clockwise from top left: One of the large bottles of cologne that Ziegfeld had imported from Paris. Hazel Dawn dressed for her title role in *The Pink Lady* (1911); her pink satin gown was overlaid by a thin net embroidered with rhinestones and bugle beads. The number "At the Ball That's All" was added to the *Ziegfeld Follies of 1914* after Ziegfeld saw it performed in an all-black revue in Harlem. Program cover from the Moulin Rouge, c. 1912

This *Midnight Frolic* program cover, by Raphael Kirchner, was one of the few done in color. The early *Frolic* program covers (1915–17) were black-and-white line drawings, while covers from 1919 and 1920 featured photographs (head shots) of women. The artist painted this in 1916 or 1917, when he worked for Ziegfeld. (Kirchner died at age forty-one in 1917.) While this program cover would have been daring in 1916 or 1917, by the 1920s, the idea of women smoking was becoming acceptable.

ZIEGFELD ROOF
Atop New Amsterdam Theatre

A Ziegfeld Beauty
DRAWN BY
- RAPHAËL-
- KIRCHNER -

Ziegfeld Midnight Frolic

ZIEGFELD MIDNIGHT FROLIC

ZIEGFELD
ROOF,
ATOP NEW
AMSTERDAM
THEATRE

A L'ECREVISSE

MENU

ZIEGFELD ROOF, ATOP NEW AMSTERDAM THEATRE
"THE MEETING PLACE OF THE WORLD"

SPECIALTIES DE LA MAISON

Tortue verte Claire en Tasse	.80
Supreme of Sole, Fin-de-Siecle	1.90
Half Lobster, Armenonville	2.75
Sea Bass Saute, Grenobloise	1.25
Crab Flakes, Ziegfeld	1.75
Escaloppine of Veal au Marsala	1.75
Breast of Milk Fed Chicken, Tosca	2.75
Filet Mignon Cocotte, Grisette	2.75
Boneless Royal Squab, Follies	3.00

SUPPER

Crab Flake Cocktail 1.50	Lobster Cocktail 1.60	Hors d'Œuvres 1.50	Grape Fruit Supreme 1.00
Celery 60	Stuffed Celery 90	Olives, Green 30	Olives, Ripe 30
Tomate Surprise 1.00	Terrine de Foie-Gras, p. p. 2.50		Canape d'Anchois 1.00
Smoked Salmon 1.50			Canape of Caviar 2.50

Soupe a l'Onion, passe gratine 80		Tortue verte, Claire 60
Consomme Double 60	Cream of Tomato aux Croutons Souffle 60	Essence de Volaille 60
Broiled Lobster	Lobster Newburg	Crab Meat, Mornay 1.75
	Crab Meat, Maryland 1.75	

Breast of Guinea Hen, Eugenie 3.00	Chicken a la King 2.25	Champignons sous Cloche 2.00
Chicken Leg, Americaine 1.50		Chicken Liver en Brochette, Colbert 1.75

Steak Minute, O'Brien 2.00	Spaghetti Ziegfeld 1.50
Spanish Omelet 1.50	Shirred Eggs a la Turque 1.75	Scrambled Eggs, with Irish Bacon 1.50
	Poached Eggs, Grand-Duc 1.50	

COLD

Crab Meat Ravigotte 1.50	Cold Lobster, Mayonnaise

Assorted Cold Meat 2.00	Virginia Ham 1.50	Beech-Nut Ham 1.00	Beef Tongue 1.25
Chicken Salad 2.00	Lobster Salad 2.25		Crab Meat Salad 1.75
Salade Nicoise 75	Coeur de Laitue 75	Coeur de Laitue and Tomato 90	
Russian Dressing 30	Fruit Salad 1.25	Combination Salad 80	Roquefort Dressing 40
	Romaine 75		

Club Sandwich 1.00	Chicken Sandwich 90	Ham Sandwich 75	Tongue Sandwich 75
Roquefort Cheese 80	Swiss Cheese 75	Camembert 75	Cream Cheese 60	Bar-le-Duc 75

Vanilla—Chocolate Ice Cream 85	Peche Melba 1.00	Coupe St. Jacques 1.00
Souffle Vanilla or Chocolate (2) 3.00	Souffle Surprise 1.50	Crepes Bar-le-Duc 1.25	Coupe Dame Blanche 1.00
	"Sherry" Petits Fours 50	

Demi-Tasse 25	Coffee with Cream 50	Tea 50	Chocolate 60

Above left: The outside of a *Midnight Frolic* menu (date unknown). Above right: The inside of the *Frolic* menu. Right: Joseph Urban sketch of the mountain terrace scenery for the second edition (August 1915) of the *Midnight Frolic*

Below: Joseph Urban's sketch of the zeppelin scene from the 1915 *Follies;* Ziegfeld eventually cut the scene after requesting numerous rewrites. Right: Raphael Kirchner painted the "Les Amours de Pierrot" series, including this one entitled *Expiation,* in 1916 for the Century Theatre lobby.

THE THEATRE

35 Cents
$3.50 a Year

TITLE REG. U. S. PAT. OFF.

SEPTEMBER 1915
VOL XXII NO. 175

E MAGAZINE
R PLAYGOERS

Miss Ina Claire
Gown by Lucile, Ltd., New York and Paris

Ina Claire dressed in a Lucille gown for the song "Hello, Frisco" in the 1915 *Follies*. Claire was a talented singer, dancer, and mimic. After two years with Ziegfeld, she appeared in a nonmusical production and became the foremost female comedian on Broadway. In the 1930s and 1940s she appeared in many screen comedies.

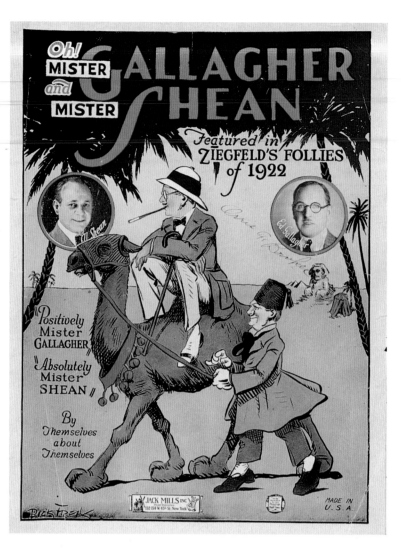

Jerome Kern and B. G. DeSil-
va's song "Look for the Silver
Lining" became a hit after
Miller sang it in *Sally* (1920).

Al Shean and Ed Gallagher
were a hit in the 1922 *Follies*
with their song "Oh! Mr. Gallagher and Mr. Shean." They
performed the number in
vaudeville for several years.

This original costume sketch is dated 1922, but it is similar to an outfit worn in the *Follies of 1923*.

TheatreMagazine

35 cents

JANUARY 1925

ZIEGFELD FOLLIES GIRL

ALBERT VARGAS

The Magazine for Playgoers—

Alberto Vargas's rendition of the "Follies Girl"; similar sketches were used on the covers of sheet music for the 1924 and 1925 editions.

Sheet-music cover for "Homeland" from *Louie the 14th* (1925)

Left: Joseph Urban sketch of a Spanish shawl backdrop used in *Rio Rita* (1927). Opposite: Part of the ceiling mural designed by Joseph Urban for the Ziegfeld Theatre

·SHOW·BOAT·   ·ACT·I·Scene 1 + 8·

Above: Joseph Urban's sketch of the Mississippi levee set for *Show Boat* (1927). Right: Norma Terris wearing her costume from the "World's Fair" scene in *Show Boat*. Opposite: Walter Donaldson composed "Makin' Whoopee," and Eddie Cantor sang the song. Donaldson started his own music-publishing house in 1928; he went to Hollywood when films began to use sound.

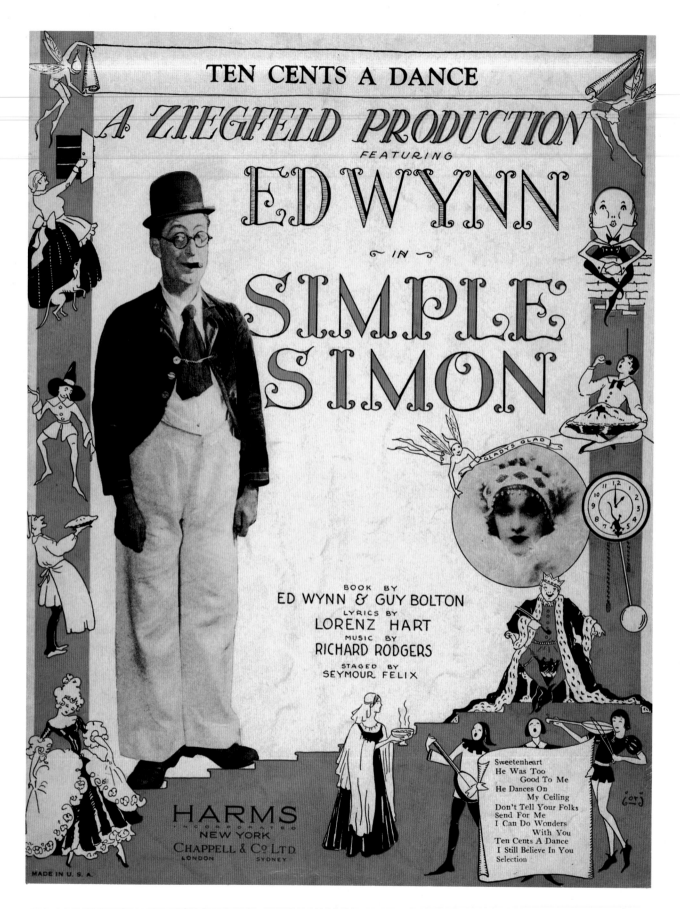

Sheet-music cover for "Ten Cents a Dance" from Simple Simon.

Above: Ziegfeld owned quite a collection of elephant statues; this glass and bronze elephant that belonged to him is a decanter. Left: A Vargas drawing of "The Last Follies" in 1931.

Norma Terris wearing one of her *Show Boat* costumes. The artist painted the picture from a black-and-white photograph, with Terris advising him as to the colors. The original costumes and scenery were used again in the 1932 revival.

This bronze statue of a woman marks the site of Blanche Burke's grave. The graves of Billie Burke and Florenz Ziegfeld are nearby.

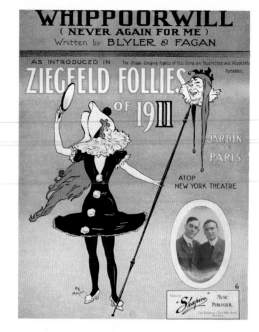

A selection of *Follies* sheet-music covers.

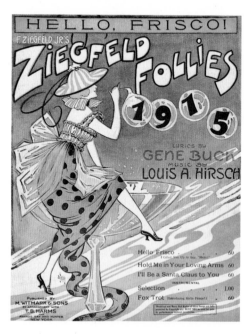

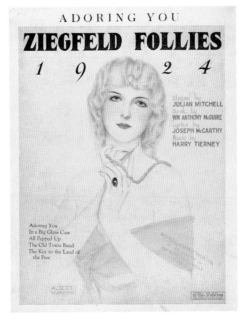

Right, above: For the 1931
Follies, Joseph Urban designed
a scale model of the jungle
scene. The lightweight wood
and metal miniature set was
easy to assemble and disas-
semble. The showgirls and
elephants were made of card-
board. Right, below: The
Oriental scene from *No Foolin'*
(1926) that Joseph Urban
designed for Greta Nissen's
pantomime. Opposite, left:
Charles LeMaire's sketch of
the parasol costume for the
"Lace-Land" scene, 1922. Opposite, above right: A costume
sketch from *The Century Girl*
(1916). Opposite, below right:
Leon Errol dressed for the title
role in *Louie the 14th* (1925)

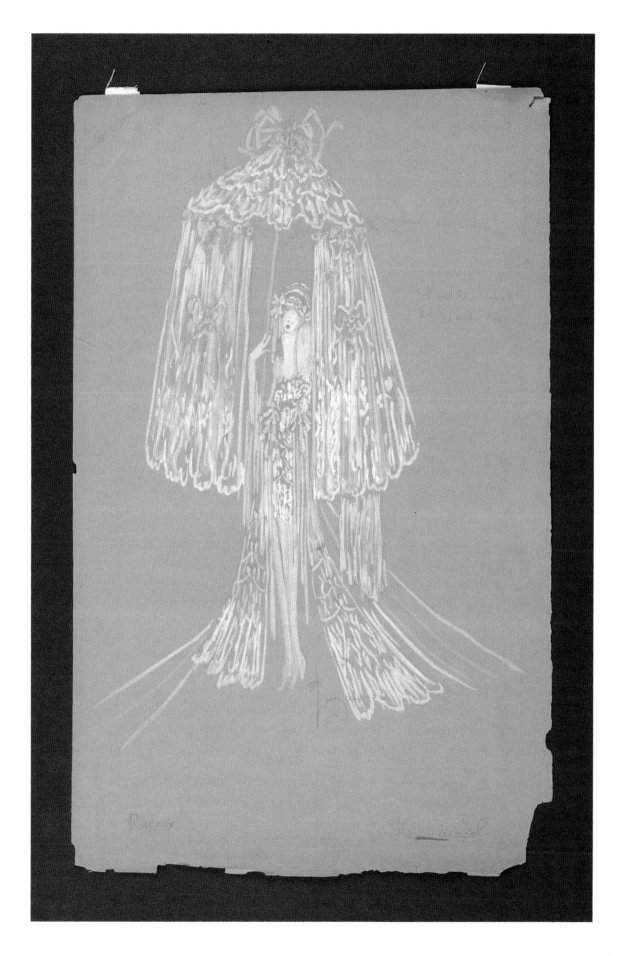

Clockwise from top left: The 1907 *Follies* had a reproduction of Charles Dana Gibson's bathing girls; Annabelle Whitford, shown on this sheet-music cover, was the featured bathing beauty. The sheet-music cover for "Swing Me High, Swing Me Low" shows Lillian Lorraine (center) and chorus in a *Follies* scene. Sheet-music cover for "My Man (Mon Homme)" sung by Fannie Brice in the *Follies*. Nora Bayes and Jack Norworth sang their hit song "Shine on, Harvest Moon" in the *Follies of 1908*.

"My Arabian Maid" was written for the Arabian night scene in the 1917 *Ziegfeld Follies*.

"The Broadway Glide" closed Act One of the 1912 *Follies*. In this number, every man and woman on Broadway did the turkey trot as they crossed Herald Square.

❖

ZIEGFELD SHOWS

❖

Women wearing miniature battle-ships for headdresses, 1909

ANNIE DEAR

NEW YORK RUN: November 4, 1924–January 31, 1925; Times Square Theatre
AUTHORS: Book, music, and lyrics by Clare Kummer; dance music and additional music by Sigmund Romberg with lyrics by Clifford Grey
STAGING: Edward Royce
PRINCIPALS: Billie Burke (star billing), Ernest Truex, Marion Green, May Vokes, Bobby Watson
PLOT: On her wedding day Annie Leigh (Burke) runs away from her groom (Green), who seems a bit rough (he wears a beard and is from out West). Annie becomes a servant on the Long Island estate of George Wimbledon (Truex). When Annie's groom, a wealthy mine owner, appears at Wimbledon's estate without his beard, Annie doesn't recognize him. She falls in love with him, and they reconcile.

BETSY

NEW YORK RUN: December 28, 1926–January 29, 1927; New Amsterdam Theatre
AUTHORS: Words by Irving Caesar and David Freedman; book staged and revised by Anthony Maguire; lyrics by Lorenz Hart; music by Richard Rodgers
STAGING: Sammy Lee

PRINCIPALS: Belle Baker (featured), Al Shean, Pauline Hoffman, Jimmy Hussey, Ralph Whitehead, Dan Healy, Bobby Perkins, Allen Kearns, Evelyn Law, Madeline Cameron, Barbara Newberry, Vanita La Nier

PLOT: A Jewish mother (Hoffman) won't let her other children marry until her oldest child Betsy (Baker) finds a husband. Betsy's brothers try to fix her up so they can marry.

BITTER SWEET

NEW YORK RUN: November 5, 1929–February 15, 1930; Ziegfeld Theatre. February 17–March 22, 1930; Shubert Theatre

CO-PRODUCER: Arch Selwyn

AUTHOR: Noel Coward

DIRECTOR: Charles B. Cochran

PRINCIPALS: Evelyn Laye, Gerald Nodin, Sylvia Leslie, Mireille, Zoe Gordan, Dorothy Debenham, Nancy Barnett

PLOT: The elderly Marchioness of Shayne (Laye) finds one of her party guests embracing the pianist. Via flashbacks, she tells the story of her own life and career. On the eve of her wedding (in 1875) to an important gentleman, she ran away with her music teacher (Nodin). She danced in a Viennese café where her lover was bandmaster. When an officer kissed her, her lover challenged him to a duel and was killed. Lady Shayne then returned to society and became a famous singer. She married the Marquis of Shayne, although the music teacher remained her one true love.

HIT SONG: "I'll See You Again" (Noel Coward)

Three production shots from *The Century Girl* (1916): Above: Two live soldiers before an army of fake ones. Right, above: Women dressed as cards. Right: A well-dressed Roman couple

BY PIGEON POST

NEW YORK RUN: November 25–December 14, 1918; George M. Cohan Theatre

AUTHOR: Austin Page

PRINCIPALS: Frank Kemble Cooper, Phoebe Foster, Peggy O'Neil, Jerome Patrick, John Sainpolis, Vincent Serrano

PLOT: Carrier pigeons help France during World War I. They are assisted by a French Army captain (Patrick), a Red Cross nurse (Foster), a female chauffeur (O'Neil), a general (Cooper), and a colonel (Sainpolis).

CAESAR'S WIFE

NEW YORK RUN: November 24, 1919–January 31, 1920; Liberty Theatre

AUTHOR: W. Somerset Maugham

STAGING: Iden Payne

PRINCIPALS: Billie Burke (star billing), Norman Trevor, Ernest Glendenning, Harry Green, T. Wigney Percyval, Frederic DeBelleville, Margaret Dale, Hilda Spong, Mrs. Tom Wise

PLOT: Sir Arthur Little (Trevor), a British viceroy in Egypt, has married a woman twenty years his junior (Burke). His wife, Violet, falls passionately in love with her husband's secretary, Roland Parry (Glendenning). She confides to her husband that

she loves Roland and asks his advice. Sir Arthur tells his wife she must do her duty to the state; Roland Parry cannot be reassigned because he is needed in Egypt. So Violet tells Roland she was just flirting with him and sends him away.

THE CENTURY GIRL
NEW YORK RUN: November 6, 1916–April 28, 1917; Century Theatre
CO-PRODUCER: Charles Dillingham
AUTHORS: No book; music by Victor Herbert and Irving Berlin
STAGING: Ed Royce, Leon Errol, and Julian Mitchell
PRINCIPALS: Leon Errol, Elsie Janis, Hazel Dawn, Sam Bernard, Marie Dressler, Frank Tinney, Adelaide Bell, Arthur Cunningham, Harland Dixon, Irving Fisher, John Slavin, James Doyle, Vera Maxwell, Maurice and Walton, Gertrude Rutland, Doyle and Dixon, the Barr Twins, Billie Allen, Harry Kelly

THE COMIC SUPPLEMENT
NEW YORK RUN: None; the show opened on January 9, 1925, at the Shubert Theatre in Newark, New Jersey, and closed there in February.
AUTHORS: Book and lyrics by J. P. McEvoy; music by Con Conrad and Henry Souvaine
STAGING: Dances by Julian Mitchell; book by Augustin Duncan; technical director, T. B. McDonald
PRINCIPALS: W. C. Fields (featured), Brooke Johns, Ray Dooley, Clarence Nordstrom, Martha-Bryan Allen, Pauline Mason, Alice Hegeman, the Kelo Brothers, Hansford Wilson
PLOT: Scenes in the life of the Jones family—Pa (Fields), Gertie (Dooley), Ma (Hegeman), George (Nordstrom), and Myrtle Jones (Allen).

Dance and Grow Thin—*see* **Midnight Revue**

FOLLIES OF 1907
NEW YORK RUN: July 8–August 24, 1907; August 26–September 14, 1907; Jardin de Paris (New York Theatre Roof)
AUTHORS: Words by Harry B. Smith; music and lyrics by "everybody"
STAGING: Principals directed by Herbert Gresham; chorus directed by Julian Mitchell; music directed by Charles Zimmerman
PRINCIPALS: Nora Bayes, George Bickel, Emma Carus, Mlle. Dazie, Grace LaRue, Grace Leigh, May Leslie, Dave Lewis, Frank Mayne, William Powers, Charles J. Ross, Florence Tempest, Prince Toki, Harry Watson, Jr.
NOTABLE NUMBERS: Emma Carus sang a travesty of the operatic version of Oscar Wilde's "Salome" while lady peacocks stood in the background. When it was time for Salome to dance before Herod for John the Baptist's head, the overweight Carus

MISS EMMA CARUS

Above: Emma Carus was a principal singer in the *Follies of 1907*. A few years later she introduced Irving Berlin's hit tune "Alexander's Ragtime Band." Left, above: Vonnie Hoyt, wearing her costume from the *Follies of 1909*, was also in *Miss Innocence*. Left: Elise Hamilton was a chorus girl in several early *Follies*.

Above: Chorus girls in a rather
daring bathing scene for 1910.
Right: Eva Tanguay doing her
popular interpretation of Salome
in the *Follies of 1909*

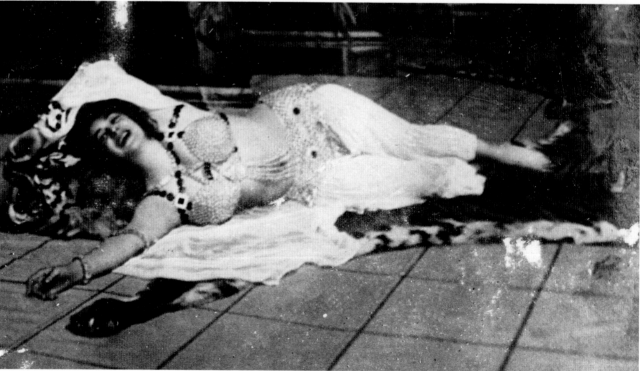

disappeared and the slender Mlle. Dazie appeared. Wearing makeup to look like Carus and dressed in a costume identical to hers, Dazie performed the dance.

Dazie had two other numbers that attracted the press: her eccentric Jiu-jitsu dance and the "Dance of Seven Veils." According to one review, the latter dance made the thermometer on the roof rise "to 94 degrees." The reviewer noted that after Dazie took off the seventh veil, there was not enough material left for an eighth one. At this point, an agitated man came to the footlights and said the police were raiding the place. The audience watched as Dazie cowered timidly before the police. Before long, however, the pseudo-policemen joined the finale in a can-can.

FOLLIES OF 1908

NEW YORK RUN: June 15–September 5, 1908; Jardin de Paris (New York Theatre Roof). September 7–October 3, 1908; New York Theatre
AUTHORS: Book by Harry B. Smith; music by Maurice Levi
STAGING: Principals, Herbert Gresham; ensemble numbers, Julian Mitchell
PRINCIPALS: Nora Bayes, Barney Bernard, George Bickel, Seymour Brown, Mlle. Dazie, Arthur Deagon, Grace LaRue, Grace Lay, Mae Murray, Jack Norworth, William Powers, Billie Reeves, William C. Schrode, Gertrude Vanderbilt, Harry Watson, Jr., Lucy Weston, Annabelle Whitford
HIT SONG: "Shine on, Harvest Moon," composed and sung by Nora Bayes and Jack Norworth
NOTABLE NUMBERS: In Scene Two, the chorus girls appeared as a swarm of giant mosquitoes that had just come from New Jersey via subway. They buzzed around the subway entrance looking for victims, singing: "We travel in bunches; We carry no lunches, For we find lots of food over here. We are the lighthearted mosquitos."

In the taxicab number, twelve young women were dressed as taxis, complete with "For Hire" signs and meters. When the theater lights were turned down, the women turned on their headlights (attached to their shoulders) and moved around the stage.

FOLLIES OF 1909

NEW YORK RUN: June 14–September 11, 1909; Jardin de Paris (New York Theatre Roof)
AUTHORS: Words and lyrics by Harry B. Smith; music by Maurice Levi
STAGING: Principals, Herbert Gresham; ensemble numbers, Julian Mitchell
PRINCIPALS: Nora Bayes, William Bonelli, Evelyn Carlton, Marion Carson, Bessie Clayton, Arthur Deagon, Rosie Green, Harry C. Kelly, Lillian Lorraine, Mae Murray, Jack Norworth, Harry Pilcer, Billie Reeves, Sophie Tucker, Gertrude Vanderbilt, Annabelle Whitford
HIT SONG: "By the Light of the Silvery Moon" (Irving Ber-

lin), introduced by Gus Edwards in vaudeville and added to the *Follies* during the show's run
NOTABLE NUMBERS: In "The Greatest Navy in the World," the chorus girls (one for every state) wore headdresses that looked like miniature battleships. The headpieces were wired for lights in the portholes and were lit up when the stage lights were turned down. The chorus lined up in front of a harbor-scene backdrop to simulate a naval display.

In an elaborate jungle scene, Sophie Tucker wore a leopard costume and sang "Moving Day in Jungle Town." Cast members dressed as wild animals scurried up trees when the actor portraying hunter Teddy Roosevelt appeared.

Lillian Lorraine was prominent in this year's show. Besides singing "By the Light of the Silvery Moon," she appeared in a tub full of soap bubbles singing "Nothing but a Bubble." In Act Two, while the chorus sang, an airplane on a monorail carrying her appeared at one end of the theater and gradually circled around the ceiling. Lorraine sang "Up, Up in My Aeroplane," as the airship circled above the audience.

FOLLIES OF 1910

NEW YORK RUN: June 20–September 3, 1910; Jardin de Paris (New York Theatre Roof)
AUTHORS: Words by Harry B. Smith; music by Gus Edwards et al.
STAGING: Julian Mitchell; musical director, Frank Darling
PRINCIPALS: George Bickel, Aline Boley, Fannie Brice, Evelyn Carlton, Rosie Green, Shirley Kellogg, Mindel Kingston, Lillian Lorraine, Vera Maxwell, Betty Neil, Bobby North, Harry Pilcer, Billie Reeves, William C. Schrode, Lillian St. Clair, Peter Swift, Grace Tyson, Harry Watson, Jr., Bert Williams
HIT SONG: "Lovey Joe" (Will Marion Cook/Joe Jordan), an interpolation
NOTABLE NUMBERS: The show started with chorus girls marching through the audience from the back of the theater to the stage. A Dutch band headed by Bickel and Watson then marched around the audience twice; they were half way through their act before they got to the stage.

In another number, Lillian Lorraine and eight young women appeared on swings that moved back and forth over the audience. Lillian sang "Swing Me High, Swing Me Low" as the women accompanied her on silver bells that they manipulated with cords.

The show included what the critics described as an excellent illusion. A large blackboard appeared at center stage with two actors nearby. The first actor boasted that he could draw a picture and the picture would become real. He took the chalk and drew a picture of a chair; a minute later he was sitting up on the face of the blackboard several feet above the stage. The second actor declared that he, too, could do it; soon he was sitting on a chalk-drawn chair. Next they drew a table and then a glass that became real. Soon they had a ticking clock and a lighted lamp. All

Above: These four showgirls—Phyliss, Mauricette, Dinarzade, and Dolores—were originally Lucille models; here they are wearing Lucille-designed gowns from *Miss 1917*. Right: Anna Held in the title role of *Papa's Wife*. Held starred in many Ziegfeld shows between 1896 and 1909 but was never in the *Follies*.

objects were drawn in full view of the audience with the stage lights on.

There was also a moving-picture illusion of a comet crossing the earth with Anna Held's face as the comet's steering gear. Eleanor St. Clair sang in accompaniment to the moving picture.

Billie Reeves and Harry Watson enlivened the show with their cockfight in a travesty of "Chanticleer." Bert Williams appeared in the scene dressed as a blackbird.

For information on other Follies, *see* Ziegfeld Follies and the desired year.

THE FRENCH MAID

NEW YORK RUN: September 26–October 1, 1898; Herald Square Theatre
AUTHORS: Libretto by Captain Basil Hood; music by Walter Slaughter
PRINCIPALS: Anna Held, Charles Bigelow, Eva Davenport, William Armstrong, Edward J. Heron
PLOT: Admiral Hawser (Heron) and Lieutenant Fife (Armstrong), British naval officers, arrive in Boulogne and stay at the same hotel where the admiral's wife (Davenport) and her niece—Lt. Fife's sweetheart—have come for a surprise visit. The hotel manager is afraid that one of the men is his wife's former husband. The officers meet the charming French maid Suzette (Held), and Fife and an Eastern prince (also an admiral) agree to escort Suzette to a masquerade ball. Suzette already has two lovers: the hotel's headwaiter and a gendarme. The waiter has his brother take Suzette to the ball where they meet the gendarme. The gendarme suspects the admiral's wife and her niece of being spies and follows them. Mrs. Hawser thinks she has an admirer and tells the landlord. The landlord doesn't know her husband and so throws him out of the hotel.

A GAY DECEIVER

NEW YORK RUN: February 21–26, 1898; Harlem Opera House (tour)
CO-PRODUCER: William A. Brady
AUTHORS: Paul Wilstach and Joseph Grismer
PRINCIPALS: M. A. Kennedy, W. G. Beach, Edwin Holland, Carrie Mills, Lizzie Evans, Marie Valleauz, Charlotte Dean, Dolores Lettani
PLOT: A man (Kennedy) admires a prima donna; because he is married, he pretends to be his twin brother. Still masquerading as his brother, he visits his own home and finds his wife flirting with another man. For obvious reasons, he cannot reveal his identity.

HIGGLEDY-PIGGLEDY

NEW YORK RUN: October 20, 1904–March 25, 1905; Weber Music Hall
CO-PRODUCER: Joseph Weber

AUTHORS: Dialogue and lyrics by Edgar Smith; music by Maurice Levi

STAGING: George Marion; dances by Sam Marion

PRINCIPALS: Anna Held, Joseph M. Weber, Harry Morris, Marie Dressler, Charles A. Bigelow, Aubrey Boucicault, Frank Mayne, May McKenzie

PLOT: Two wealthy Americans tour Europe on vacation. Adolf Schnitz (Weber) is a mustard merchant who brings along his daughter (Dressler). Gottlieb Gesler (Morris) is president of the American-Swiss Cheese Sandwich Trust and escorts his friend Mimi De Chartreuse (Held).

HOT-CHA!

NEW YORK RUN: March 8–June 18, 1932; Ziegfeld Theatre

AUTHORS: Book by Lew Brown, Ray Henderson, Mark Hellinger, and H. B. Kraft; music and lyrics by Lew Brown and Ray Henderson

STAGING: Dances by Bobby Connolly; dialogue staged by Edgar MacGregor

PRINCIPALS: Bert Lahr (featured), Lupe Velez (featured), Marjorie White, Lynne Overman, Buddy Rogers, Eleanor Powell

PLOT: A speakeasy waiter (Lahr) from New York goes to Mexico City and becomes a bullfighter.

THE INTIMATE STRANGERS

NEW YORK RUN: November 7, 1921–January 21, 1922; Henry Miller Theatre

CO-PRODUCERS: Abe Erlanger and Charles Dillingham

AUTHOR: Booth Tarkington

PRINCIPALS: Billie Burke, Glenn Hunter, Charles Abbe, Alfred Lunt, Frances Howard, Elizabeth Patterson, Frank Kirk, Clare Weldon

PLOT: Isabel (Burke), a woman at the upper limits of what is considered marriageable age, meets a man (Hunter) in a railroad station where both are marooned by a storm and must spend the night. The man falls in love with Isabel and courts her. Isabel can see her new love is wondering about her age, so she pretends to be older than she is.

Just Girls—*see* **Ziegfeld Midnight Frolic (1915)**

KID BOOTS

NEW YORK RUN: December 31, 1923–August 30, 1924; Earl Carroll Theater. September 1, 1924–February 21, 1925; Selwyn Theatre

AUTHORS: Book by William Anthony McGuire and Otto Harbach; music by Harry Tierney; lyrics by Joseph McCarthy

STAGING: Edward Royce

PRINCIPALS: Eddie Cantor (star billing), Mary Eaton (featured), Harry Fender, Beth Beri, Ethelind Terry, Harland Dixon, Marie Callahan, Jobyna Howland, John Rutherford, Horton Spurr, Harry Short, Paul Everton, Robert Barrat, George Olsen and his Orchestra

PLOT: A caddie master (Cantor) at the Everglades Golf Club in Palm Beach uses crooked balls when he gives golf lessons and bootlegs liquor as a sidelight. Because he knows so much about club members, he can't be fired. He does have a well-intentioned side and manages to straighten out the love life of Polly (Eaton) and Tom (Fender) but costs Tom the club championship with his crooked ball.

LA POUPÉE

NEW YORK RUN: October 21–29, 1897; Lyric Theatre

CO-PRODUCER: Oscar Hammerstein

AUTHORS: Comic opera by Maurice Ordonneau and Arthur Sturgess; music by Edmund Audran

PRINCIPALS: Anna Held, Frank Rushwood, G. W. Anson, Rose Leighton, Arthur Cunningham, Ferris Hartman, W. Steiger, Trixie Fraganza, G. S. Fredericks

PLOT: A young novice (Rushwood) in a poor monastery is promised 100,000 francs from his uncle if he marries. The novice, Lancelot, wants to be a monk, but he also wants the money for his monastery. He decides to marry a lifelike doll to gain the fortune. Lancelot goes to a puppet-maker, Hilarius (Anson), to buy the doll. When the doll breaks, Hilarius's daughter, Alesia (Held), who has fallen in love with Lancelot, takes its place. Hilarius (unknowingly) and his wife (who is aware of the substitution) take Alesia to Lancelot's uncle's house. Lancelot and Alesia are married, and Lancelot finds out he has a real wife.

THE LITTLE DUCHESS

NEW YORK RUN: October 14, 1901–February 8, 1902; Casino Theatre. From February 10 to February 15, 1902, the show ran at the Harlem Opera House, the first stop on its tour. After touring outside New York, the show returned to the Grand Opera House a year later.

AUTHORS: Book by Harry B. Smith; music by Reginald de Koven

STAGING: Stage director, George Marion; musical director, Herman Perlet

PRINCIPALS: Anna Held (star billing), Sydney Barraclough, Charles A. Bigelow, Joseph W. Herbert, George Marion, Charles Swain

PLOT: An actress (Held) masquerades as a duchess to avoid her creditors.

LOUIE THE 14TH

NEW YORK RUN: March 3–December 5, 1925; Cosmopolitan Theatre

AUTHORS: American adaptation and lyrics by Arthur Wimperis from the German book by Frank and Julius Wilhelm; music by Sigmund Romberg

STAGING: Edward Royce
PRINCIPALS: Leon Errol (star billing), John T. Doyle, Harry Fender, Doris Patston, Hugh Wakefield, Ethel Shutta, Pauline Mason, Evelyn Law, Judith Vosselli, Edouard Durand, Simone de Bouvier
PLOT: Louie Ketchup (Errol) is an army cook who has stayed in France after the war. He becomes an Alpine guide who leaves his group stranded in the mountains. He meets wealthy Paul Trapmann (Doyle) who is giving a dinner party. When Trapmann realizes there will be thirteen people at dinner, he invites Louie so there will be fourteen. Louie comes to dinner posing as a Rajah; his crude manners are a source of amusement.

MAM'SELLE NAPOLEON
NEW YORK RUN: December 8, 1903–January 16, 1904, Knickerbocker Theatre
AUTHORS: Adapted by Joseph W. Herbert; music by Gustav Luders
STAGING: Joseph W. Herbert
PRINCIPALS: Anna Held (star billing), Arthur Laurence, Frank Rushworth
PLOT: Mlle. Mars (Held) is in love with a member of Napoleon's Imperial Guard. Her lover (Rushworth) is involved in a plot to betray Napoleon, but Napoleon (Laurence) does not believe the man is guilty and lets him remain free. A grateful Mlle. Mars recites (in French) the fable about the lion and the mouse, implying that she hopes to repay Napoleon one day. The play ends with Napoleon returning from Elba and Mlle. Mars performing a service (undefined) for him.

THE MANICURE
NEW YORK RUN: April 24, 1899; Manhattan Theatre
CO-PRODUCER: William A. Brady
AUTHORS: Adapted by Joseph Grismer from Sylvain and Artus's French original
PRINCIPALS: Louise Thorndyke Boucicault, James Colville, James Barrow, F. Newton-Lindo
PLOT: A manicurist (Boucicault) has a foundering business that is taken over by a deputy sheriff (Colville) and his assistant. The manicurist doesn't want anyone to know the sheriff has control of her business, so she is nice to him. The sheriff becomes infatuated with her—while remaining faithful to his wife. However, the manicurist's fiancé and the sheriff's wife become jealous. The sheriff's wife watches him closely, thereby forcing him into some sticky situations.

Midnight Frolic—*see* **Ziegfeld Midnight Frolic**

MIDNIGHT REVUE
OPENING: January 18, 1917; titled "Dance and Grow Thin"; Cocoanut Grove (Century Theatre Roof)

CO-PRODUCER: Charles Dillingham
AUTHORS: Songs by Irving Berlin and Blanche Merrill
STAGING: Leon Errol (except for Gertrude Hoffmann's numbers, which she staged)
PRINCIPALS: Will Archie, Rita Boland, Hattie Burks, Leon Errol, Irving Fisher, Dolly Hackett, Edith Hallor, Gertrude Hoffmann, Joe Jackson, Janetta Methven, Van and Schenck

MISS INNOCENCE
NEW YORK RUN: November 30, 1908–May 1, 1909; New York Theatre
AUTHORS: Book and lyrics by Harry B. Smith; music by Ludwig Englander
STAGING: Julian Mitchell
PRINCIPALS: Anna Held (star billing), Lawrance D'Orsay, Emma Janvier, Vida Whitmore, Charles Bigelow, Lillian Lorraine, Maurice Hegeman, F. Stanton Heck
PLOT: For many years Anna (Held) had been a model pupil at the School for Innocence run by Miss Sniffin (Janvier). Now grown up, Anna goes off to Paris with a detective (Bigelow) in search of her parents. She sees the sights of the city and falls in love with Captain Mountjoy (D'Orsay).

MISS 1917
NEW YORK RUN: November 5, 1917–January 12, 1918; Century Theatre
CO-PRODUCER: Charles Dillingham
AUTHORS: Book and lyrics by Guy Bolton and P. G. Wodehouse; music by Victor Herbert and Jerome Kern
STAGING: Ned Wayburn
PRINCIPALS: Lew Fields, Bessie McCoy Davis, Elizabeth Brice, Charles King, Van and Schenck, Irene Castle, Bert Savoy, Vivienne Segal, Andrew Tombes. Vera Maxwell and Marion Davies had lesser roles in the show.

MLLE. FIFI
NEW YORK RUN: February 1–April 22, 1899; Manhattan Theatre. April 24–29, 1899; Harlem Opera House (tour)
CO-PRODUCER: William A. Brady
AUTHORS: Adapted by Leo Ditrichstein from Dumanoir and Carre's French original; Joseph Grismer apparently adapted it for the road tour, as his name appears on the program.
PRINCIPALS: Rose Coghlan, Aubrey Boucicault, Grace George, Louise Beaudet, John T. Sullivan
PLOT: A young married couple, Florence and Vicomte de Pussiac (George and Boucicault), cannot use the principal of the wife's dowry while she remains married. To avoid their many creditors, the couple decide to divorce just long enough for the wife to gain use of her money and pay their debts. The husband writes a compromising letter addressed to a former girlfriend, Mlle. Fifi (Beaudet), so his wife will have grounds for divorce.

Opposite: Claire Luce stands inside her luminous ball for a number from *No Foolin'* (1926).

Then an admirer of the wife brings Mlle. Fifi to de Pussiac's apartment where Mlle. Fifi tries to win back her old love. At this point, Florence walks in on them. Upset over her husband's apparent infidelity, Florence divorces her husband, but the two later reconcile.

NO FOOLIN' (ZIEGFELD AMERICAN REVUE OF 1926)

NEW YORK RUN: June 24–September 25, 1926; Globe Theater

AUTHORS: Jokes, jingles, and rhymes by Gene Buck, Irving Caesar, and James Hanley; comedy scenes by J. P. McEvoy; music by Rudolf Friml

STAGING: Edward Royce; comedy scenes staged by Walter Wilson

PRINCIPALS: James Barton (featured), Yvonne Accent and Jenesko, George Baxter, Beth Berri, Louise Brown, Lew Christy, the Conner Twins, Edna Covey, Ray Dooley, Peggy Fears, Irving Fisher, Mlle. Edmonde Guy, Mary Jane, Charles King, Edna Leedom, Claire Luce, Moran and Mack, Barbara Newberry, Greta Nissen, Helen O'Shea, William Powers, Andrew Tombes, Polly Walker, the Yacht Club Boys

HIT SONGS: "No Foolin'" (Gene Buck/James Hanley) and "Florida, the Moon and You" (Gene Buck/Rudolf Friml)

NOTABLE NUMBERS: A luminous ball consisting of tiny mirrors that sparkled in the spotlight was suspended at the rear of the stage. The ball was lowered to the floor where it opened in half. Out of the ball stepped Claire Luce wearing a feathered outfit and ready to dance. The ball from which Luce stepped was just large enough for her to stand up in (and was probably very warm). During one performance, the ball stuck shut; everyone waited to see what would happen as the orchestra kept repeating the music, while Luce tried to free herself. Finally, after what seemed an eternity to the cast, the ball opened, and Luce emerged.

Following Luce's dance, eleven women dressed in white feathers paraded on stage. The women represented various birds: Goddess of the White Cobra Bird, Goddess of the White Pheasant, Goddess of the White Nightingale, and so forth.

Two funny skits featured James Barton and Ray Dooley. In "Day Coach" the stage was set up as a railroad car; Barton was the conductor trying to coax the obnoxious Gertie (Dooley) to hand over her ticket. Barton chased Dooley over seats, passengers, and luggage from one end of the stage to the other.

In the "Whip Dance" skit, Barton played a Latin lover and Dooley his mistress. Barton sang and cracked his whip while his adoring lover meekly followed him in a fast-paced Spanish dance.

Greta Nissen performed an oriental pantomime in the role of "Mlle. Bluebeard." Miss Nissen did a beautiful dance, but it was the setting (Joseph Urban's) and the costumes (Greta and Agnes Nissen's) that made the number special. The sabre dance

was arranged by Michael Fokine with music adapted from "Themes of Famous Russian Composers."

OVER THE RIVER

NEW YORK RUN: January 8–April 20, 1912; Globe Theatre

CO-PRODUCER: Charles Dillingham

AUTHORS: Book by George V. Hobart and H. A. DuSouchet, based on *The Man from Mexico*; music by John Golden

PRINCIPALS: Eddie Foy (star billing), Maud Lambert, Lillian Lorraine, Melville Stewart

PLOT: A man (Foy) disturbs the peace while out on the town and is sentenced to thirty days in jail on Blackwell's Island. Instead of telling his wife the truth, he says he is going to Mexico.

PAPA'S WIFE

NEW YORK RUN: November 13, 1899–March 31, 1900; Manhattan Theatre

AUTHORS: Lyrics and book by Harry B. Smith; music by Reginald de Koven and A. B. Sloane

PRINCIPALS: Anna Held (star billing), Charles Bigelow (featured), Henry Bergman, Henry Woodruff, George Marion, Eva Davenport, Dan Collyer, Agnes Findlay, Olive Wallace

PLOT: An innocent young woman (Held) straight from a convent becomes the bride of an older man (Henry Bergman). Soon after her marriage she learns that her husband cannot be faithful and attempts to reform him.

THE PARISIAN MODEL

NEW YORK RUN: November 27, 1906–June 29, 1907; Broadway Theatre

AUTHORS: Book and lyrics by Harry B. Smith; music by Max Hoffmann

STAGING: Julian Mitchell

PRINCIPALS: Anna Held (star billing), Henry Leoni, F. Stanton Heck, Charles Bigelow, Ashley Miller, Edouard Durand, Gertrude Hoffmann, Mabella Baker, Ethel Gilmore, Adele Carson, Eleanor Kent

PLOT: Anna (Held), a model in a Paris dressmaking shop, is in love with Lucien (Leoni), a struggling artist. Anna inherits a fortune from a former customer on the condition that she not mention her wealth until after she is married. When she leases an expensive home and begins wearing stunning clothes, Lucien suspects she has a wealthy lover. Anna cannot offer a plausible explanation for her sudden wealth, so Lucien courts another woman. Anna attempts to win him back.

A PARLOR MATCH

NEW YORK RUN: September 21–October 31, 1896; Herald Square Theatre

AUTHORS: Charles Evans and William Hoey

PRINCIPALS: Anna Held (featured), Charles Evans, William Hoey, Jason T. Galloway, M. J. Sullivan, William M. Armstrong, Hugh Mack, William Keough, Stuart Connover, Harriet Sheldon, Allene Crater, Aimee Van Dyne, Virginia Aragon, Minnie French

PLOT: A tramp (William Hoey), who collects items for an auction room, is stealing possessions from a well-to-do family. The family members are too busy with their affairs to notice him. When he is about to be discovered, the tramp hides in a closet. A drunken member of the family sees the tramp but thinks he is experiencing delirium tremens. A spiritualist (Stuart Connover) is finally called in. Charles Evans plays the book agent who visits the family.

THE PINK LADY

NEW YORK RUN: March 13–December 9, 1911; New Amsterdam Theatre

NOTE: Marc Klaw and Abe Erlanger were the official producers of this show, but Ziegfeld had significant artistic input.

AUTHORS: Adapted from Georges Berr and Marcel Guillemaud's *Le Satyre* (French); book and lyrics by C. M. S. McLellan; music by Ivan Caryll

STAGING: Herbert Gresham; musical numbers by Julian Mitchell

PRINCIPALS: Hazel Dawn, William Elliott, Alice Dovey, Alice Hegeman, Frank Lalor, Maurice Hegeman, May Hennessey

PLOT: On the eve of his wedding, a young man, Lucien (Elliott), takes his former sweetheart, Claudine (Dawn), to a restaurant where they unexpectedly meet the man's fiancée (Dovey). Lucien introduces Claudine as Mme. Dondidier, the wife of an antique dealer, and then hurries to M. Dondidier's shop and persuades him to go along with the deception in return for a rare snuffbox. Since Dondidier (Lalor) already has a wife (Hegeman), complications arise. Everything is straightened out at the Ball of the Nymphs and Satyrs.

THE RED FEATHER

NEW YORK RUN: November 9, 1903–January 2, 1904; Lyric Theatre

AUTHORS: Book by Charles Klein; music by Reginald de Koven; lyrics by Charles Emerson Cook

PRINCIPALS: Grace Van Studdiford, George L. Tallman, Thomas Q. Seabrooke, Elise de Vere, Olive C. Moore, Louis Casavant, Stanley Hawkins

PLOT: Countess Hilda von Draga (Van Studdiford) is also the bandit known as "The Red Feather." Captain Travers (Tallman) of the army has been assigned to capture the bandit. He is unaware that "The Red Feather" is also the woman he is courting.

RESCUING ANGEL

NEW YORK RUN: October 8–November 3, 1917; Hudson Theatre

Opposite: Greta Nissen is Mlle. Bluebeard, and Joseph Marievesky is her husband in an Oriental pantomime from *No Foolin'* (1926). Nissen was originally a ballerina, but after a brief stage career she went to Hollywood and made twenty-four films.

CO-PRODUCER: Arthur Hopkins
AUTHOR: Clare Kummer
STAGING: Arthur Hopkins
PRINCIPALS: Billie Burke (star billing), Claude Gillingwater, Walter Schellin, Marie Wainwright, Frederick Perry, Dana Desboro, Richard Barbee, Robert McWade, Elmer Brown, Rhoda Beresford, Roland Young
PLOT: Angela (Burke), the daughter of an aristocrat (Gillingwater) whose fortune has declined, decides to save the family from poverty by breaking off her engagement to the boy next door and marrying one of two millionaires she met in Hawaii. Angela chooses the millionaire son (Perry) of a prizefighter/saloonkeeper over the millionaire statistician (Young). Immediately after the wedding, Angela's old boyfriend tells the groom that Angela married him for his money. The groom is understandably upset, and Angela runs home and proposes to the statistician. Then she realizes she loves her husband and goes back to him.

RIO RITA

NEW YORK RUN: February 2–December 24, 1927; Ziegfeld Theatre. December 26, 1927–March 10, 1928; Lyric Theatre. March 12–April 7, 1928; Majestic Theatre
AUTHORS: Book by Guy Bolton and Fred Thompson; music and lyrics by Harry Tierney and Joseph McCarthy
STAGING: Book by John Harwood; dances by Sammy Lee; dances of the Albertina Rasch Girls by Albertina Rasch; musical director, Oscar Bradley
PRINCIPALS: Ethelind Terry, J. Harold Murray, Vincent Serrano, Ada May, George Baxter, Bert Wheeler, Robert Woolsey, Gladys Glad, Noel Francis, Helen Clive, Katherine Burke, Avis Adaire
PLOT: Captain Jim (Murray) of the Texas Rangers tracks a bank robber known as Kinkajou. The search for the bandit takes the Rangers into Mexico, where Jim falls in love with Rio Rita (Terry). General Esteban (Serrano) also loves Rita and convinces her that Jim thinks the robber is her brother, Roberto (Baxter). After Jim discovers the identity of the real crook, he wins Rita's love. Woven into the plot are the love stories of Dolly (Ada May) and Chick Bean (Wheeler) and of lawyer Ed Lovett (Woolsey) and Bean's first wife, Katie (Adaire).
NOTABLE NUMBER: The Albertina Rasch Dancers were the outstanding feature of the show. Their "Moonlight" ballet attracted particular attention. In this number the sixteen dancers wore "soft, billowing blue gowns and floated about the stage." Charles Le Maire designed the dresses for this scene.
NOTES: *Rio Rita* marked the first time that Bert Wheeler and Robert Woolsey appeared as a comedy team. (Walter Catlett eventually replaced Woolsey in this show.) Wheeler and Woolsey were also in the movie version of *Rio Rita* (1929) and later appeared together in several screen comedies. Besides the 1929 RKO movie of *Rio Rita*, M-G-M produced a remake with Abbott and Costello in 1942.

ROSALIE

NEW YORK RUN: January 10–October 27, 1928; New Amsterdam Theatre

AUTHORS: Book by William Anthony McGuire and Guy Bolton; lyrics by P. G. Wodehouse and Ira Gershwin; music by Sigmund Romberg and George Gershwin

STAGING: Dialogue, William Anthony McGuire; ensembles and dances, Seymour Felix

PRINCIPALS: Marilyn Miller (star billing), Jack Donahue (featured), Bobbe Arnst, Oliver McLennen, Frank Morgan, Margaret Dale, Clay Slement, Clarence Oliver

PLOT: While in Paris, Lt. Richard Fay (McLennen), a West Point cadet, falls in love with Rosalie (Miller), a girl from Romanza. Fay visits Romanza and discovers that Rosalie is a princess and cannot marry a commoner. He meets Rosalie again when she and her family visit America, including West Point. Meanwhile, a revolution in Romanza dethrones Rosalie's father (Morgan) and clears the way for Rosalie to marry Fay. Jack Donahue plays Fay's fellow cadet—an aviator who is afraid to fly.

ROSE BRIAR

NEW YORK RUN: December 25, 1922–March 10, 1923; Empire Theatre

AUTHOR: Booth Tarkington

PRINCIPALS: Billie Burke (star billing), Frank Conroy, Julia Hoyt, Allen Dinehart, Ethel Remey, Richie Ling, Paul Doucet, Florence O'Denishawn

PLOT: An upper-class young woman, Rose Briar (Burke), becomes a cabaret performer when her fortunes decline. One of the cabaret's frequent visitors (Conroy) comes in complaining about his pampered heiress bride (Hoyt). Rose learns that the couple plans to divorce and that the wife now wants to marry Mr. Paradee (Dinehart), the restaurant owner. Rose wants Paradee for herself and goes about trying to win his affection.

SALLY

NEW YORK RUN: December 21, 1920–April 22, 1922; New Amsterdam Theatre

AUTHORS: Book by Guy Bolton; lyrics by Clifford Grey; music by Jerome Kern; butterfly ballet music by Victor Herbert

STAGING: Edward Royce

PRINCIPALS: Marilyn Miller (star billing), Leon Errol (star billing), Walter Catlett, Dolores, Irving Fisher, Mary Hay

PLOT: Sally (Miller), a dishwasher at Alley Inn, dreams of becoming a famous dancer. A former Grand Duke named Constantine, now the waiter "Connie" (Errol), takes Sally to an elegant party given by a wealthy friend. When the Russian ballerina who is scheduled to dance for the guests does not appear, Sally takes her place. Sally is a hit and gets a part in the *Ziegfeld Follies*. After becoming a star, Sally marries the wealthy Blair Farquar (Fisher) whom she met at the party. Connie marries a beautiful

Opposite: Ada May and J. Harold Murray in a scene from *Rio Rita* (1927). Left, above: Marilyn Miller, in the title role of *Rosalie* (1928), wears a folk costume of her character's native Romanza. Left, below: Marilyn Miller wears an elaborate costume in *Sally* (1920), the show that made her a star. Miller had the lead role in several other musicals on Broadway and in three movies before she died at about age thirty-five.

Right: Husband and wife Sammy White and Eva Puck in a scene from *Show Boat*. Far right: Ziegfeld handwrote the original contract he gave Norma Terris in July 1927. It reads: "July 23, 1927. Miss Norma Terris, I hereby engage you to open on or about October 25, 1927 - You to appear either in Showboat, Ziegfeld Follies or some other of my productions which would offer suitable part for your line of work. You to receive nine hundred dollars per week for the run of the play to which you are assigned - unless I am compelled to change my mind it is my intention to have you play Magnolia in Showboat - Equity contract to govern this contract with usual conditions a principal performer enjoys. Regular contract form of Equity to be signed. We to agree what __ year salary will be. Monday—Ziegfeld accepted; Norma Terris signed; Leo Fitzgerald witnessed." Opposite, above: This photograph from *Show Boat* indicates how elaborate Joseph Urban's scenery was. Standing in front of the crowd and the "Cotton Blossom" are (left to right) Charles Winninger (holding hat), Howard Marsh with Norma Terris, Frank White, Eva Puck, and Edna May Oliver (pointing). Opposite, below: Flo Ziegfeld in 1927 with the original cast from *Show Boat*. Left to right they are Annie Hart, Charles Ellis, Aunt Jemima (Tess Gardella), Thomas Gunn, Laura Clarion, Eva Puck, Sammy White, Howard Marsh, Helen Morgan, Ziegfeld, Eleanor Shaw (child), Norma Terris, Charles Winninger, Edna May Oliver, Jules Bledsoe, and musical director Victor Baravalle.

society woman (Dolores). Walter Catlett plays a press agent who helps Sally.

HIT SONGS: "Look for the Silver Lining" (B. G. DeSylva/Jerome Kern) and "Little Church Around the Corner" (P. G. Wodehouse/Jerome Kern), both interpolations

SHOW BOAT

NEW YORK RUN: December 27, 1927–May 4, 1929; Ziegfeld Theatre

AUTHORS: Book and lyrics by Oscar Hammerstein II, adapted from the novel by Edna Ferber; music by Jerome Kern

STAGING: Dialogue, Zeke Colvan; dances and ensembles, Sammy Lee; musical director, Victor Baravalle

PRINCIPALS: Norma Terris, Howard Marsh, Charles Winninger, Helen Morgan, Eva Puck, Sammy White, Jules Bledsoe, Edna May Oliver, Aunt Jemima (Tess Gardella), Charles Ellis

PLOT: The show follows the lives of Magnolia Hawks (Terris), the daughter of showboat owner Captain Andy (Winninger), and Gaylord Ravenal (Marsh), a riverboat gambler. The story begins in the late 1880s when the couple first meets on a Natchez levee. After the mulatto Julie (Morgan) and her white husband, Steve (Ellis), leave the boat, Magnolia and Ravenal become the principal actors aboard the *Cotton Blossom*. Magnolia and Ravenal marry and move to Chicago where Ravenal has mixed success as a

gambler. The couple sees the 1893 Chicago World's Fair and has a daughter, Kim (as a child, Eleanor Shaw). After Ravenal gambles away all their money, he leaves his family. Unknowingly Magnolia replaces her friend Julie as a nightclub singer and is a hit. Later Kim (as a woman, Norma Terris) becomes a Broadway star. Magnolia and Kim return to the *Cotton Blossom* in 1927 and are reunited with everyone except Julie and Steve.

HIT SONGS: "Old Man River," "Can't Help Lovin' That Man," "Make Believe," "Why Do I Love You?" (Hammerstein/Kern), and "Bill" (Wodehouse/Kern), an interpolation

NOTES: Joseph Urban provided fourteen different settings for the show, and John Harkrider's costumes spanned four decades. With prodding from Ferber and Hammerstein, Urban and Harkrider paid close attention to period details to make sure the costumes and sets were authentic.

There were thirty featured players, the Jubilee Singers, the Dahomey dancers, and a large chorus (nearly one hundred).

The hit song "Bill" was not written for *Show Boat*; Kern had written it years earlier for the 1918 show *Oh Lady, Lady!*, but it was not used. P. G. Wodehouse wrote the song's lyrics.

During the 1922–23 season, Elizabeth Hines had starred as *Little Nellie Kelly*, a role that Norma Terris assumed during that show's tour. In 1927 Terris won the role of Magnolia, a part for which Hines had originally been signed.

Universal Pictures purchased movie rights to *Show Boat* in

October 1926, intending to make a silent film. The studio completed the silent film in 1928, but never released it because, in the intervening years, sound had been added to pictures. Universal added dialogue and songs to its silent version and reshot many scenes. In March 1929, the sound version premiered. In 1936 Universal Pictures released a totally new version of *Show Boat* starring Irene Dunne as Magnolia, as well as Charles Winninger, Helen Morgan, Sammy White, and Francis X. Mahoney, from the original Broadway production. Allan Jones played Ravenal, while Paul Robeson appeared as Joe.

The London production of *Show Boat* opened May 3, 1928, at the Drury Lane Theatre with Americans Edith Day (Magnolia) and Paul Robeson (Joe). Jerome Kern telephoned Ziegfeld from London and told him that judging from the opening-night reception, the London run would be a long one. The production, in fact, ran for 350 performances. Later London revivals ran for 264 performances (1943) and 910 performances (1971).

Terris (Magnolia) said that Ziegfeld watched every rehearsal of *Show Boat*. Terris noted that he knew all the lines and every gesture. She said he always insisted that women on stage wear silk stockings that he kept in a refrigerator. Terris would get a knock on her dressing room door, and there would be someone with cold stockings for her.

Terris also tells a story about a shrunken costume. One night her theater maid, Margaret, discovered that the wardrobe mistress had sent Norma's nightgown out to be cleaned and it returned *shrunk* almost to her knees. Margaret paid a taxi driver $10.00 to break all speed rules and to drive like "a son of a gun." She dashed to Norma's apartment where there was a nightie almost like it—Norma really slept in it. The maid arrived just in time for Norma to perform the scene. After that Ziegfeld saw to it that Terris always had at least *two* nightgowns.

The show took in over $2.5 million during its first year (422 performances) on Broadway. During its six-week tryout, the production grossed $226,780. Yet, Ziegfeld said that *Show Boat* still had not paid back its production costs. Eight percent of the income went for royalty payments. Payments of $200,000 went to Ferber, Kern, Hammerstein, and Sammy Lee (dance director).

Dancer Harriet Hoctor in a costume from *Simple Simon* (1930)

SHOW BOAT REVIVAL

NEW YORK RUN: May 19–October 22, 1932; Casino Theatre
AUTHORS: Book and lyrics by Oscar Hammerstein II, adapted from the novel by Edna Ferber; music by Jerome Kern
MUSICAL DIRECTOR: Oscar Bradley
PRINCIPALS: Norma Terris, Dennis King, Charles Winninger, Helen Morgan, Edna May Oliver, Tess Gardella, Paul Robeson, Eva Puck, Sammy White, Charles Ellis, Robert Raines, Eleanor Eaton
PLOT: See *Show Boat* (above); some characters are played by different actors.

SHOW GIRL

NEW YORK RUN: July 2–October 5, 1929; Ziegfeld Theatre
AUTHORS: Written by William Anthony McGuire, based on the novel by J. P. McEvoy; music by George Gershwin with special numbers by Vincent Youmans; lyrics by Gus Kahn and Ira Gershwin
STAGING: Dialogue by William Anthony McGuire; dances by Bobby Connolly; ballets by Albertina Rasch; general stage director, Zeke Colvan; technical director, T. B. McDonald
PRINCIPALS: Ruby Keeler (featured); Clayton, Jackson, and Durante (featured); Ed Wynn; Eddie Foy, Jr.; Harriet Hoctor. (Dorothy Stone also received featured billing when she replaced Keeler.)
PLOT: The loose plot is woven around Dixie Dugan (Keeler), a girl from Brooklyn who becomes a showgirl and appears in the *Ziegfeld Follies*. Much of the show is about theatrical life. The trio of Clayton, Jackson, and Durante appeared as stagehands at the Ziegfeld Theatre. Eddie Foy, Jr., played Denny, a greeting-card salesman and friend of Dixie's from Brooklyn.
NOTABLE NUMBER: The high point of the production was the ballet number from the scene "An American in Paris." After wandering around Paris, an American tourist dreamed of home. The dream was danced by Harriet Hoctor and the Albertina Rasch Dancers. George Gershwin's music and Joseph Urban's panoramic view of nighttime Paris contributed to the success of the scene.

SIMPLE SIMON

NEW YORK RUN: February 18–June 14, 1930; Ziegfeld Theatre
AUTHORS: Book by Ed Wynn and Guy Bolton; music by Richard Rodgers; lyrics by Lorenz Hart
STAGING: Dialogue by Zeke Colvan; ensembles and dances by Seymour Felix
PRINCIPALS: Ed Wynn (star billing), Ruth Etting, Paul Stanton, Will Ahearn, Bobbe Arnst, Alfred P. James, Hughie Cameron, Alan Edwards, Harriet Hoctor, Doree Leslie
PLOT: Simon (Wynn) is a Coney Island shopkeeper who sells books and newspapers but reads only fairy tales because he does not like bad news. He falls asleep in front of his shop and dreams that his fellow merchants from Ferrymen Alley are fairy-tale characters (Cinderella, King Cole, Jack and Jill, Snow White, etc.) and that he is the hero.
HIT SONG: "Ten Cents a Dance" (Rodgers/Hart)

SMILES

NEW YORK RUN: November 18, 1930–January 10, 1931; Ziegfeld Theatre
AUTHORS: Dialogue by William Anthony McGuire; music by Vincent Youmans; lyrics by Clifford Grey and Harold Adam-

Harriet Hoctor (right) and the
Albertina Rasch Dancers perform
the ballet for "An American in
Paris" from *Show Girl* (1929).

VIVIENNE OSBORNE

VIVIENNE SEGAL

LESTER ALLEN

HARRIET HOCTOR

LEWIS HECTOR

JOSEPH MACAULAY   DOUGLASS DUMBRILLE   DENNIS KING   DETMAR POPPEN

CLARENCE DERWENT

Dennis King in The Three Musketeers

REGINALD OWEN

YVONNE D'ARLE

JOHN CLARKE

A sketch of cast members from *The Three Musketeers* (1928) theater program

son; additional lyrics by Ring Lardner

STAGING: Ned Wayburn; dialogue, William Anthony McGuire

PRINCIPALS: Marilyn Miller (star billing); Fred and Adele Astaire (star billing); Tom Howard (featured); Eddie Foy, Jr. (featured); Paul Gregory (featured), Edward Raquello, Adrian Rosley, the Aber Twins, Kathryn Hereford

PLOT: At the end of World War I, four soldiers (French, American, English, and Italian) find an orphaned French girl (Miller) whom they nickname Smiles. They send her to live in the United States. A decade later all the ex-soldiers are living in New York, and Smiles is working for the Salvation Army. Two bored members of high society, brother and sister Bob and Dot (the Astaires), wander into the Bowery mission where Smiles works. Bob invites Smiles to a costume party at his Southampton home and falls in love with her. One of the ex-soldiers, Dick (Gregory), also loves Smiles. After her suitors follow her to Paris, Smiles decides to wed Dick.

THE SOUL KISS

NEW YORK RUN: January 28–May 23, 1908; New York Theatre

AUTHORS: Book by Harry B. Smith; music by Maurice Levi

STAGING: Herbert Gresham and Julian Mitchell

PRINCIPALS: Adeline Genée (featured), Cecil Lean, Florence Holbrook, Amelia Rose, Vera Michelena, Dot Quinette, Ralph C. Herz

PLOT: A model named Suzette (Holbrook) refuses to kiss a sculptor (Lean) who says he loves her. J. Lucifer Mephisto (Herz) bets a million dollars that the sculptor cannot stay faithful to Suzette for one year. Mephisto tempts the sculptor with a series of famous and beautiful women. The sculptor falls in love with "The Dancer" (Adeline Genée) and asks her to marry him. Suzette marries a millionaire, and Mephisto goes off with a chorus girl.

THE THREE MUSKETEERS

NEW YORK RUN: March 13–December 22, 1928; Lyric Theatre

AUTHORS: Book by William Anthony McGuire, based on Alexandre Dumas's novel; lyrics by P. G. Wodehouse and Clifford Grey; music by Rudolf Friml

STAGING: Book by William Anthony McGuire; ballets and dances by Albertina Rasch; ensembles by Richard Boleslavsky

PRINCIPALS: Dennis King (star billing), Vivienne Segal, Lester Allen, Vivienne Osborne, Yvonne D'Arle, John Clarke, Reginald Owen, Joseph Macaulay, Detmar Poppen, Douglass Dumbrille, Louis Hector, Clarence Derwent, Naomi Johnson, Harriet Hoctor (featured dancer)

PLOT: D'Artagnan (King) meets the three musketeers (Dumbrille, Poppen, and Macaulay) and is befriended by them. He has

Above: Chief Caupolican during an engagement of *Whoopee* (1928) at Cleveland's Ohio Theatre; he played the role of Chief Black Eagle. Left: Katherine Burke appeared in *Whoopee* as well as in *Rio Rita*; here she wears a feathered headdress most likely designed by John Harkrider.

RUTH ETTING

PAUL GREGORY

TAMARA GEVA

JACK RUTHERFORD

FRANCES UPTON

WILL PHILBRICK

PAUL WHITEMAN

MARY JANE

Some of the busy people on the stage of the New Amsterdam Theatre who make WHOOPEE in the successful musical comedy which bears that modernistic title and which is earning an average of $45,000 a week for impresario Ziegfeld.

A caricature of *Whoopee* (1928) cast members

a romance with Constance (Segal), a confidant of the Queen of France (D'Arle). When the queen gives the Duke of Buckingham (Clarke) some jewels, D'Artagnan and the three musketeers go to England to retrieve the gems and to protect the Queen's honor. Lady De Winter (Osborne) is an ally of Cardinal Richelieu (Owen) and an enemy of the Queen.

THE TURTLE

NEW YORK RUN: September 3, 1898–January 28, 1899; Manhattan Theatre. April 23–29, 1898; Grand Opera House (tour)

AUTHORS: Adapted by Joseph W. Herbert from the French comedy by Leon Gandillot

PRINCIPALS: W. J. Ferguson, Sadie Martinot, McKee Rankin, M. A. Kennedy, Leo Ditrichstein, Henry Bergman, Ulric B. Collins, Alfred C. Hollingsworth, Harry Allen, Agnes Findlay, Grace George

PLOT: A retired grocer (Ferguson) nicknamed "The Turtle" and his wife (Martinot) quarrel and decide to divorce. The wife then decides she wants to reconcile with her husband. Complications of plot and mistakes by the characters provide the humor.

WHOOPEE

NEW YORK RUN: December 4, 1928–November 23, 1929; New Amsterdam Theatre

AUTHORS: Book by William Anthony McGuire, based upon the comedy *The Nervous Wreck* by Owen Davis; music by Walter Donaldson; lyrics by Gus Kahn

STAGING: William Anthony McGuire, dialogue; dances and ensembles by Seymour Felix; musical director, Gus Salzer

PRINCIPALS: Eddie Cantor (star billing), Ruth Etting, Ethel Shutta, Paul Gregory, Frances Upton, John Rutherford, Tamara Geva, Jack Gifford, Mary Jane, George Olsen and his Orchestra (featured)

PLOT: Henry Williams (Cantor) is a hypochondriac who goes to a dude ranch in Mission Rest, California, to improve his health; he is romantically pursued by his nurse (Shutta). While at the ranch, Henry meets Sally (Upton). Sally and Henry run away to an Indian camp so Sally can escape the advances of Sheriff Bob (Rutherford). Sally really loves a half-breed named Wanenis (Gregory). At the Indian camp, Sally and Henry discover that Wanenis is not really an Indian.

HIT SONGS: "Love Me, or Leave Me" and "Makin' Whoopee" (Donaldson/Kahn)

NOTABLE NUMBERS: In one scene, balloons were dropped from the ceiling into the laps of the audience. (It took ten tanks of gas—at $30 per tank—to fill four thousand balloons, and five hundred balloons were released at every performance.)

For the ballroom scene, the entire ensemble dressed in orange, and the ballroom was decorated with orange canopies. Critics praised the scene for its beauty and artistry, and the patrons were awestruck.

In the dance with Black Eagle, two sections of chorus girls alternated steps simultaneously, displaying impressive footwork never before seen on Broadway. According to *The New York Times*, the dance was "full of fire" and "electrifying."

NOTES: Buddy Ebsen was a chorus boy in this show; after Ziegfeld died, Ebsen and his sister were featured dancers in the 1934 Shubert-produced *Ziegfeld Follies*.

Dancer Ruby Keeler was in the *Whoopee* cast during tryouts; however, she left before the New York opening so she could be with her new husband, Al Jolson. (Mary Jane took her place.)

Ziegfeld said he paid Eddie Cantor $750,000 in salary for the two years he was in *Whoopee*.

A WINSOME WIDOW

NEW YORK RUN: April 11–September 7, 1912; Moulin Rouge (New York Theatre)
AUTHORS: Based on the long-running satirical comedy by Charles Hoyt, *A Trip to Chinatown* (1891); music by Raymond Hubbell
STAGING: Julian Mitchell
PRINCIPALS: Harry Connor, Emmy Wehlen, Leon Errol, Elizabeth Brice, Charles King, Ida Adams, Frank Tinney, the Dolly Sisters, Mae West
PLOT: The president of the Purity League, Ben Gay (Errol), has promised to stop the entertainment at the "Poodle Dog" restaurant. Although he has forbidden his wards (King and Adams) from going there, they accompany their friend Welland Strong (Connor) to the restaurant. Gay also ends up at the "Poodle Dog" after mistakenly receiving a letter from a widow (Wehlen) inviting him to meet her there. When Gay ruins his suit and puts on a chef's outfit, Strong takes the suit, along with Gay's credentials in the pocket. After the police raid the place, Strong uses Gay's credentials to get everyone except Ben Gay released.

Ziegfeld American Revue of 1926—*see* No Foolin'

Ziegfeld Follies 1907–1910—*see* Follies of 1907, 1908, etc.

ZIEGFELD FOLLIES OF 1911

NEW YORK RUN: June 26–September 2, 1911; Jardin de Paris (New York Theatre Roof)
AUTHORS: Words by George V. Hobart; music by George V. Hobart, Maurice Levi, and Raymond Hubbell
STAGING: Julian Mitchell; musical numbers arranged by Gus Sohlke and Jack Mason
PRINCIPALS: Fannie Brice, Brown and Blyer, Stella Chatelaine, Tom Dingle, the Dolly Sisters, Leon Errol, Lillian Lorraine, Vera Maxwell, Bessie McCoy, Clara Palmer, Walter Percival, Peter Swift, Harry Watson, Jr., Bert Williams
NOTABLE NUMBERS: The funniest comedy skit of this

Bessie McCoy was a child when she started her vaudeville career; she was about twenty-three when she made her *Follies* debut in 1911.

edition of the *Follies* featured Bert Williams as a construction worker and Leon Errol as a nervous tourist at Grand Central Station. The station was undergoing construction, so Williams acted as Errol's guide. Williams tied a rope to Errol and himself and then led the way over the girders. As they climbed higher and higher, the wobbly Errol fell off several times, but Williams saved him. Finally, after receiving a measly five-cent tip, Williams let Errol fall for good and even threw his luggage after him. As Errol neared the ground, there was an explosion from the construction site below. Williams informed the audience that Errol had been caught in the blast and was now being hurled toward the Metropolitan Tower. He said there was hope if Errol could grab the tower's little gold ball. Unfortunately, in Williams's words, Errol "muffed it."

Another well-liked number was the skit "Tad's Daffydils." Bessie McCoy, dressed in a clown suit and cone-shaped hat, led eight young women in a dance. The skit originally featured Tom Dingle as a Sailor Man and Bessie as Chief Daffy doing eccentric dances. However, later programs reveal that Dingle was dropped from this scene.

ZIEGFELD FOLLIES OF 1912

NEW YORK RUN: October 21, 1912–January 4, 1913; Moulin Rouge (New York Theatre)
AUTHORS: Words by Harry B. Smith; music by Raymond Hubbell
STAGING: Julian Mitchell
PRINCIPALS: Ida Adams, Grace DuBoise, Leon Errol, Bernard Granville, Charles Judels, May Leslie, Lillian Lorraine, Vera Maxwell, Jose Sadler, Rae Samuels, Harry Watson, Jr., Bert Williams
HIT SONG: "Row, Row, Row" (William Jerome/Jimmy Monaco), an interpolation sung by Lillian Lorraine
NOTABLE NUMBERS: Bert Williams and Leon Errol were reported to be hilarious in a taxicab number featuring Williams as a forlorn driver with a broken-down hansom. Errol appeared as a smartly dressed drunk in need of a cab to Seventh Avenue. When asked whether he knew where it was, Williams said: "Oh yes, I know where 'tis. . . . It's fur!" (The prominent street sign with "Seventh Avenue" painted on it let the audience know that Williams intended to take his drunken fare for a long ride before bringing him back to his original location.) His tired old horse, overhearing Williams say that the trip would be long, refused to set out, but Williams solved this problem handily by telling the horse: "Oats, Nicodemus, OATS."

"A Palace of Beauty," featuring young women as famous beauties, was the outstanding spectacle number. This scene marked the first time the showgirls paraded across the stage one by one in a spotlight. The first to appear was a Harlequin dressed in thin black lace. As each girl walked to her place, the orchestra played "Beautiful, Beautiful Girl."

The usual self-referential scenes about the theater and the

Top: Vera Maxwell and Walter Percival in a production scene from the 1911 *Follies*. Above: Leon Errol as the customer and Bert Williams as the taxi driver in a 1912 skit; the two men worked together frequently, often writing their own material.

ongoing tension between high and low culture appeared in the manuscript for the show. First nighters complained about a rotten, long-hair problem play. One asked the other: "And what was the problem?" The other responded: "I dunno. But to-morrow night the problem will be to find the audience."

There was also a reference to *The Pink Lady* and a topical scene about Teddy Roosevelt and William Taft that mentioned income tax, trusts, the Philippines, tariff reform, and Cuba.

ZIEGFELD FOLLIES OF 1913

NEW YORK RUN: June 16–September 6, 1913; New Amsterdam Theatre

AUTHORS: Words by George V. Hobart; music by Raymond Hubbell; additional numbers by Gene Buck and Dave Stamper

STAGING: Julian Mitchell

PRINCIPALS: Elizabeth Brice, Martin Brown, Evelyn Carlton, Stella Chatelaine, Jose Collins, Rose Dolly, Leon Errol, Florence Nugent Jerome, Ethel Amorita Kelly, May Leslie, Ann Pennington, Peter Swift, Frank Tinney, Nat Wills

HIT SONG: "If a Table at Rector's Could Talk"

NOTABLE NUMBERS: In the first of two big numbers arranged by Julian Mitchell, Chief Hawkeye delivered a prologue from the roof of the Hotel McAlpin as his Indian friends looked down upon night life in New York City. In the other number, the first-act finale titled "Opening of the Panama Canal," a warship was raised in the canal locks.

Leon Errol and Stella Chatelaine brought down the house with their satirical dance "Turkish Trottishness." During the dance Errol kept losing his pants.

In a funny drunk scene in a subway, Errol and the subway porter, Frank Tinney, made several bumbling attempts to rob the ticket window, only to find that someone else beat them to it. The disgusted would-be thieves then took a roll of tickets and draped them over a dummy. When the police arrived, they arrested the dummy.

In another memorable scene, Elizabeth Brice was a telephone switchboard operator who sang the number "Hello, Honey." Callers appeared as the switchboard lights went on and then disappeared as the lights went off.

Nat Wills, who nearly always portrayed a tramp, made his initial appearance in evening clothes. He sang the well-received "New York, What's the Matter With You?" Later, as a tramp, he sang the hit "If a Table at Rector's Could Talk."

Versatile Martin Brown and Rose Dolly provided some entertaining moments when they imitated famous ballet dancers in the "Palais d'Danse" scene.

Comedian Frank Tinney amused the audience with a blackface monologue that satirized the preceding acts. Tinney, who had been appearing in blackface since he was a child, also appeared in a powdered wig and knee breeches minus the blackface. He said, "I've waited four years to play a real part like this." His classic operatic bagpipe solo was also well received.

Above: Jose Collins (far right) and the Tangomaniacs as they appeared in the *Follies of 1913*. From 1911 to 1916, Collins was in vaudeville and on Broadway; she then went to London and became a musical comedy star. Left: Leon Errol and his wife, Stella Chatelaine, danced together in the *Follies* from 1911 through 1914. Below: Nat Wills had the best songs in the 1913 *Follies*. He toured vaudeville for eight years, usually playing the part of a tramp, until his accidental death from carbon monoxide poisoning in 1917.

ZIEGFELD FOLLIES OF 1914

NEW YORK RUN: June 1–September 5, 1914; New Amsterdam Theatre

AUTHORS: Book and lyrics by George V. Hobart; additional lyrics by Gene Buck; music by Raymond Hubbell; special numbers by Dave Stamper

STAGING: Leon Errol

PRINCIPALS: Herbert Clifton, Arthur Deagon, Kitty Doner, Leon Errol, Rita Gould, Kay Laurell, May Leslie, George McKay, Louise Meyers, Vera Michelena, Ann Pennington, Gertrude Vanderbilt, Bert Williams, Ed Wynn

NOTABLE NUMBERS: Bert Williams sang "Darktown Poker Club," which he followed with a pantomime of a poker game. In the scene, Williams appeared alone on the darkened stage with a small spotlight shining on his head and shoulders. He held his cards close to his face and pantomimed the entire game: the draw, the study of the hand, the bets, the suspicious looks, the raise, the call, and the disgust of the loser. Williams also appeared as a caddie trying to teach golf to Leon Errol.

In the "Tango-Palace" scene, Ann Pennington was a hit wearing a striking costume while dancing a buck and wing (a fast, intricate tap dance). In another scene, Errol the iron worker and Williams the plasterer conversed on the 1313th floor of a skyscraper under construction. They discussed the dangers of their work as Errol tried to convince Williams that they were as safe as they would be at home in bed. After some funny dialogue ensued, Errol fell off the building during an electrical storm.

Leon Errol stood out as a drunk who entered a dance studio and was mistaken for the instructor (Ed Wynn) who had just left. Eight young women in the class eagerly copied Errol's every move (including staggering and rolling on the floor), thinking they were learning a new dance.

The most striking scenery provided a backdrop for two musical numbers. Rita Gould sang "I Love That Man"—in front of a beautiful curtain depicting Broadway and Forty-second Street. And Bert Williams sang before a set showing Broadway and Fifth Avenue after a severe snowstorm.

ZIEGFELD FOLLIES OF 1915

NEW YORK RUN: June 21–September 18, 1915; New Amsterdam Theatre

AUTHORS: Lines and lyrics by Channing Pollock, Rennold Wolf, and Gene Buck; music by Louis A. Hirsch and Dave Stamper

STAGING: Julian Mitchell and Leon Errol

PRINCIPALS: Lucille Cavanaugh, Ina Claire, Phil Dwyer, Leon Errol, W. C. Fields, Bernard Granville, Justine Johnstone, Kay Laurell, Mae Murray, the Oakland Sisters, Ann Pennington, Charles Purcell, Carl Randall, Helen Rook, Melville Stewart, Olive Thomas, Will West, Bert Williams, George White, Ed Wynn

HIT SONGS: "Hello, Frisco" and "Hold Me in Your Loving Arms"

Above: Four years after dancer George White was in the 1915 *Follies,* he inaugurated its main competition, the *Scandals.* He produced thirteen editions of his revue between 1919 and 1939. Left, above: Louise Meyers appeared as Prunella in the *Follies of 1914* and sang a song of the same name. Left, below: Leon Errol and Bert Williams at the Bukem Court Apartments in the 1915 *Follies.* Opposite: Ann Pennington was one of Ziegfeld's biggest dancing sensations. Between 1913 and the spring of 1925, she was in eight editions of the *Follies.* She left Ziegfeld to dance with George White in his first *Scandals* (1919) but returned to the *Follies* in 1923.

BERT SAVOY and JAY BRENNAN

Above: Female impersonator Bert Savoy and partner, Jay Brennan, were popular vaudevillians who appeared in two *Follies*. Right: After working in four Ziegfeld shows between 1916 and 1918, Lilyan Tashman turned to the dramatic stage and then films. She had made more than forty movies by the time she died at age thirty-four following cancer surgery. Opposite: Fannie Brice strikes a comic pose, most likely for the 1916 *Follies*, in which she had two ballet-related numbers. In addition to singing Blanche Merrill's comic songs that year, Brice was part of the big "Nijinski" scene, in which she and the male chorus sang together.

NOTABLE NUMBERS: One of the show's best production numbers was "Radiumland" with Bernard Granville leading the chorus in the song "My Radium Girls." The young women wore white dresses in contrast to the black background.

In the "Apartment House" scene, Bert Williams played a hall boy asleep on the couch at 1:00 A.M. When the switchboard got busy, Williams was occupied as the tenants (mostly women) talked on the phone or went in and out with their callers. Williams knew every tenant and made amusing comments about each one.

Ed Wynn was involved in a big scene that depicted the filming of the *Follies*. Wynn stood in the left-hand aisle next to the orchestra pit. The actors in the film walked over to that area and took their cues from him. The film began with the setting up of the stage and progressed through the film's plot, with the live Wynn directing all the film action.

Ina Claire sang the satirical "Marie Odile." Dressed as a nun, she told how David Belasco put her over as "Marie Odile" and how she got away with it. When Claire tried out this satirical number in Atlantic City, it flopped. When Ziegfeld asked Irving Berlin why the number had died, Berlin told him that it was too highbrow and that half the audience did not understand half the lyrics. But Ziegfeld liked the number and decided to keep it. The song was a hit in New York, where virtually every critic mentioned it in his newspaper review.

Wynn also did a comedy monologue in which he told the audience he did not have time to play a whole role so he was just going to tell them what he would have done so they would not miss anything.

The billiard scene, where W. C. Fields played against himself, quickly established Fields's comic identity.

Joseph Urban designed a pool of water surrounded by green shrubbery with golden elephants sitting on either side of the pool. As water poured forth from the elephants' uplifted trunks, Aphrodite (Kay Laurell) rose up from the pool to signal the commencement of the mermaids' water sports.

One of the most popular of the many dances in this year's show was a pantomime number, "Flirtation Medley Dance," performed by George White and the ever-popular Ann Pennington.

Bernard Granville and Ina Claire sang the hit "Hello, Frisco" in front of a display showing the area between the Atlantic and Pacific Oceans. As they sang about the recently inaugurated transcontinental telephone service, female faces appeared at the sites of American cities.

ZIEGFELD FOLLIES OF 1916
NEW YORK RUN: June 12–September 16, 1916; New Amsterdam Theatre
AUTHORS: Book and lyrics by George V. Hobart and Gene Buck; music by Louis A. Hirsch, Jerome Kern, and Dave Stamper
STAGING: Ned Wayburn
PRINCIPALS: Don Barclay, Helen Barnes, Fannie Brice, Ina

Claire, Marion Davies, W. C. Fields, Bernard Granville, Emma Haig, Sam Hardy, Justine Johnstone, Gladys Loftus, Bird Millman, Ann Pennington, Tot Qualters, Carl Randall, William Rock, Will Rogers, Frances White, Bert Williams

NOTABLE NUMBERS: Joseph Urban continued to astonish both audience and critics with his sophisticated sets. According to the reviews, Urban's best setting was for the scene "On the Banks of the Nile." The scenery gave the impression of a flat desert extending for miles with a huge Sphinx in the background.

Special effects were used in the *Follies*. Frances White led twenty chorus girls (The Sparkling Girls) in a dance number called "Somnambulistic Melody." A mat that was electrically charged in places was laid on the stage. The women, who were dressed in white, danced on the mat in semi-darkness. When their feet hit the charged sections of the mats, sparks flew from their shoes. In a cinema-like illusion created by Frank C. Thomas, a war vessel appeared to be moving along in the ocean. A zeppelin and airplanes flew over the ship and beyond it. The ship sank, but a submarine emerged to take its place.

Bernard Granville sang "Good-bye, Dear Bachelor Days." As he performed, the furniture and pastels in his library were stripped away, leaving "paintings" in white relief. Girls' heads appeared through these in simulated pastels.

Fannie Brice sang two comic songs she had recently performed in vaudeville: "The Hat" and "The Dying Swan." In the latter number, she wore a pink ballet skirt and was so funny that vaudeville star Elsie Janis (sitting in the audience) was almost hysterical with laughter. Both of Brice's songs were written by Blanche Merrill, although the program did not carry a credit until after Merrill took out an advertisement in *Variety* complaining about Ziegfeld's failure to credit her work.

Ina Claire's imitations of Jane Cowl, Geraldine Farrar, and Billie Burke in the "Pictorial Palace" scene were also outstanding. In the same scene the audience applauded Fannie Brice's imitation of Theda Bara.

Ann Pennington made her entrance in a moving picture. In the movie she ran down a path to greet the audience. She continued running right onto the stage—in person. Her dancing was the biggest hit of the show. Later, on the banks of the Hawaiian river, she and Bernard Granville led the entire company in a hula dance.

In the 1916 show, the cast of 118 included thirty-two step dancers; twelve show girls, who did what Wayburn called "picture dancing"; and ten specialty girls, young women who were featured in gowns or dance numbers.

ZIEGFELD FOLLIES OF 1917

NEW YORK RUN: June 12–September 16, 1917; New Amsterdam Theatre

AUTHORS: Book and lyrics by Gene Buck and George V. Hobart; music by Raymond Hubbell and Dave Stamper; patriotic finale by Victor Herbert

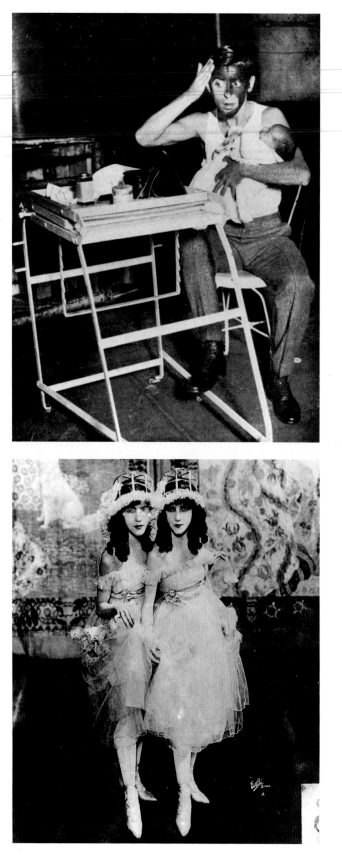

Right, above: A 1917 photograph shows Eddie Cantor holding his daughter while applying blackface makeup. Right, below: Over the years, Ziegfeld employed many sisters in his shows, but the Fairbanks Twins were two of the most popular.

STAGING: Ned Wayburn

PRINCIPALS: Don Barclay, Fannie Brice, Eddie Cantor, Walter Catlett, Dorothy Dixon, Dolores, the Fairbanks Twins, W. C. Fields, Irving Fisher, Edith Hallor, Peggy Hopkins, Carl Hyson, Allyn King, Gus Minton, Tom Richards, Will Rogers, Lilyan Tashman, Russell Vokes, Bert Williams

HIT SONG: "That's the Kind of a Baby for Me" (Alfred Harriman/J. C. Eagan), an interpolation

NOTABLE NUMBERS: The show had several beautiful numbers. Right after the "Garden of the Girls" song, Edith Hallor sprinkled flower seeds on the stage. Then one by one, beautiful women representing different kinds of flowers sprang up through a trap door. When the backdrop of glowing beads (horse pills dipped in silver paint) was lifted, two Venuses (Allyn King and Eleanor Lang) appeared in what seemed to be giant bubbles.

The Chinese lacquer scene, described by *The New York Times* as "unbelievably lovely," depicted a rooftop parapet adorned with fruit. The moonlight revealed lower Manhattan in the background. The scene then shifted to three sets of red and gold ladders with lighted rungs. On the semi-dark stage, approximately fifty young women in Chinese dress climbed up and down the ladders in unison.

The patriotic finale to Act One required two scenes. The finale began with a tableau of Paul Revere riding a white horse (on a treadmill) as figures of George Washington and Abe Lincoln appeared. President Wilson then reviewed a troop of continental soldiers (all female) as they did precision drills in front of a painted eagle. Next, the orchestra played the "Star-Spangled Banner" as a huge American flag unfolded above the audience. Finally, to close the act, Ziegfeld staged an outstanding optical illusion. A fleet of battleships appeared to be moving in the night through the sea toward the audience. The ships kept getting larger as they neared the footlights. Then, just as they reached the footlights, the scene ended.

In the humor category, Eddie Cantor sang "The Maiden's Prayer" and a very funny song called "That's the Kind of a Baby for Me." Walter Catlett was a hit as a country bumpkin who visited New York City and was cheated by everyone he met. He threatened to return to Missouri with a bad opinion of New York.

Will Rogers was at his comic best as he joked and did rope tricks. The crowd was also amused by Russell Vokes as a policeman who tried to get Don, an intoxicated dog, out of a bar and safely home.

And of course, the show was not complete without Fannie Brice. She was a hit singing Blanche Merrill's songs and imitating an exotic dancer, Rebecca, who was "Egyptian in everything but her nose."

ZIEGFELD FOLLIES OF 1918

NEW YORK RUN: June 18–September 14, 1918; New Amsterdam Theatre

Left, above: Dolores made her *Follies* debut in 1917 and went on to become one of Ziegfeld's most elegant showgirls. Here she is wearing a gown for her role in *Sally*. When the *Sally* tour ended in 1923, Dolores left the stage to marry a millionaire. Left, below: Dorothy Dickson and husband, Carl Hyson, danced in the 1917 and 1918 *Follies*. They also did exhibition ballroom dancing in the United States and abroad. After the couple divorced, Dickson stayed in London where she starred in musical comedies, including *Sally*, and, later, in dramas.

AUTHORS: Lines and lyrics by Rennold Wolf and Gene Buck; music by Louis A. Hirsch and Dave Stamper; interpolations by Irving Berlin and Victor Jacobi

STAGING: Ned Wayburn

PRINCIPALS: Eddie Cantor, Frank Carter, Dolores, the Fairbanks Twins, W. C. Fields, Frisco, Harry Kelly, Allyn King, Kay Laurell, Lillian Lorraine, Martha Mansfield, Marilyn Miller, Gus Minton, Bee Palmer, Ann Pennington, Billie Ritchie, Will Rogers, Savoy and Brennan

HIT SONG: "Oh! How I Hate to Get Up in the Morning" (Irving Berlin), an interpolation

NOTABLE NUMBERS: The curtain opened on a darkened stage to gradually reveal a huge revolving globe with the draped figure of Kay Laurell as the "Spirit of the Follies" poised on top. Laurell looked down on the warring worlds as Europe burned. Sylvia Ellias then introduced various Follies (the Folly of Dance, the Folly of Fame, etc.) via music and verse.

An interesting stage picture, "When I'm Looking at You," showed a boudoir containing a cut-out oval that represented an imaginary mirror. As one of the Fairbanks Twins danced in front of the frame, the other answered her movements on the opposite side. Lillian Lorraine sang the song while Marie Wallace simulated her movements.

Lorraine also appeared as an evening star. The center of the stage contained a staircase that led to a beautiful blue background. At the top of the staircase, one on each side, two large figures stood guard. A green light shone on the two figures while mauve light illuminated the stairs. Lorraine (in a silver lamé gown) and her thirty-two attendants (dressed as stars) moved up and down the stairs. The women's costumes were studded with tiny mirrors that reflected the light and looked like twinkling stars.

Wayburn's big production number, "Aviators' Parade," was part of the first-act finale. The stage was empty until a silk tent was pushed up through a trap door. One by one, forty-eight chorus girls, wearing gold aviator outfits and silver trench hats, emerged from the tent and alternately went right and left. After marching in precise formations, the women gradually disappeared the way they entered.

One of the most charming scenes featured Lillian Lorraine in "The Garden of Your Dreams." This was said to be Joseph Urban's best set, and the song was a hit as well. There was a huge Japanese bowl in the center of the stage, containing a Japanese garden complete with dwarf firs and a bridge over water. Lorraine, dressed in a kimono, crouched on a bridge while Frank Carter stood on nearby steps.

In the show's "Blue Devils" number, again featuring Lillian Lorraine, the women wore blue uniforms patterned after those of the Blue Devils, a French military unit. According to Muriel Harrison Merrill, who was in the scene, the number called for the women to lean out over the audience as they sang. Lillian Lorraine thought it was fun to black out some of her teeth for this number. When Ziegfeld found out about it, he came back stage and, in a

Left: Lillian Lorraine wears her costume from "The Blue Devils" number in 1918, her last year in the *Follies*. Opposite: Martha Mansfield was one of many Ziegfeld beauties who left the stage for films. She was only twenty-three when she died while filming a movie.

Right: These women made up the "Follies Salad" in the 1919 revue. Below: Because she was petite, Ray Dooley often played the role of a baby or a bratty child, as she did here in 1920. The comedian was in five editions of the *Ziegfeld Follies*: 1919 to 1921, 1925, and 1926 (*No Foolin'*).

scene unusual for him, "raised hell" in front of the other cast members.

This year's revue had many comedians, although the *Times* said it contained "no more than the legal amount of humor." One of the funniest scenes took place in a patent attorney's office and included W. C. Fields as a patent attorney, Frank Carter as his clerk, Eddie Cantor as the office boy, and Gus Minton and Harry Kelly as crazy inventors. Minton's invention was a gun that shot as many rabbits as the gun's owner desired, while Kelly invented a chair that killed anyone who sat in it. Fields also played a golfer with trick clubs, and Harry Kelly was a caddy who had squeaky shoes and who liked to tell riddles.

In her *Follies* debut, Marilyn Miller was outstanding in a variety of dances; in a beautiful silver ballet scene she was accompanied by twelve women. According to Miller's third husband, her talent lay in her ability to dance any kind of dance well, although she was not outstanding in any specific one.

The *New York Times* reviewer liked comedian Joe Frisco, formerly of the *Frolic*. The chorus tried to imitate his dance and hold cigars in their mouths at the same time—without screwing up their faces.

ZIEGFELD FOLLIES OF 1919

NEW YORK RUN: June 16–August 12, 1919 (closed due to the Actors Equity strike), and September 10–December 6, 1919; New Amsterdam Theatre

AUTHORS: Irving Berlin, Gene Buck, Rennold Wolf, and Dave Stamper; ballet by Victor Herbert

STAGING: Ned Wayburn

PRINCIPALS: DeLyle Alda, Eddie Cantor, Johnny and Ray Dooley, Eddie Dowling, Phil Dwyer, the Fairbanks Twins, Mary Hay, George LeMaire, Marilyn Miller, John Steele, Van and Schenck, Hazel Washburn, Bert Williams

HIT SONGS: The biggest hit and most enduring song was "A Pretty Girl Is Like a Melody" (Irving Berlin); many other songs were published from this edition, including "You Cannot Make Your Shimmy Shake on Tea" (Berlin, with help on lyrics from Rennold Wolf); "You'd Be Surprised" (Berlin); "I Want to See a Minstrel Show" (Berlin); "Mandy" (Berlin), an interpolation; "My Baby's Arms" (Joseph McCarthy/Harry Tierney); and "Tulip Time" (Gene Buck/Dave Stamper)

NOTABLE NUMBERS: In the opening number, Eddie Dowling appeared as a chef and prepared a "Follies Salad" while singing a song of the same name. As he called out the names of the ingredients, women representing those ingredients appeared: "Lettuce" (Mildred Sinclair), "Spice" (Marcelle Earle), "Oil" (Edith Hawes), "Sugar" (Kathryn Perry), "Paprika" (Lucille Levant—actually Doris Eaton), "Chicken" (Mary Hay), and "Salt and Pepper" (the Fairbanks Twins). The scene ended with the appearance of the Follies Girl of 1919, Florence Ware.

Eddie Cantor was well received in the hilarious skit "At the Osteopath's." Cantor played a sick patient who had to endure the

Fannie Brice, the blackface team of Moran and Mack, an unidentified man, and Paul Whiteman at the piano during a live 1928 radio broadcast from the Hotel Astor in New York. Brice and Moran and Mack were cast members in the 1920 *Follies;* the blackface team returned in 1926 for *No Foolin'.* The popular Whiteman and his orchestra were in the *Follies of 1923* and the last *Midnight Frolic* (1928).

Right: Florence O'Denishawn took her name from the Denishawn dancers, with whom she performed for several years. In the 1921 *Follies* she had one of the best numbers. O'Denishawn also appeared in Ziegfeld's *Rose Briar* before retiring in the mid-1920s after suffering an injury while performing. Below: Raymond Hitchcock as Louis XVI and Betty Carsdale as Marie Antoinette wear costumes by James Reynolds in "The Birthday of the Dauphin" scene in the 1921 *Follies*.

doctor's (George LeMaire) acrobatic ministrations.

One of the most memorable numbers was John Steele singing "A Pretty Girl Is Like a Melody," which Berlin later said was the best song ever written for a musical. He wrote the tune after Ziegfeld reviewed the dress rehearsal and said he wanted a song as the women descended the stairs. Although Ziegfeld had introduced the staircase lined with women back in 1916, it was only after this number in 1919 that the staircase became identified with Ziegfeld.

In another scene, Eddie Cantor, Bert Williams, and George LeMaire were blackface minstrels. Soon Van and Schenck, John Steele, and Eddie Dowling appeared on stage. Van and Schenck sang "Mandy," and Marilyn Miller did a soft shoe number while those around her tapped. There were ten "Mandys" headed by Lucille Levant and Mary Hay, dressed in pink satin like Miss Miller. The scene also included Ray Dooley as "Mandy," the "Dandys" (men), and the "Follies Pickaninnies." The entire group, dressed in pink, white, and silver, appeared on stage for the first-act finale.

In "The Circus Ballet," Marilyn Miller appeared atop a live horse—in a scene with a ringmaster, clowns, and bareback riders. But her big number was "Sweet Sixteen," performed against a backdrop of urns and floral bouquets designed by Joseph Urban.

Maurice and Walton performed a pantomime in a palace devoted to opium smoking. Maurice was a Chinaman with designs on Miss Walton who, in a drug-induced trance, danced almost nude. Their dancing was said to be the best in the show.

The applause for Ben Ali Haggin's two living pictures almost stopped the show. The first-act picture featured Jessie Reed as the New Folly accompanied by her twelve sisters. The second-act picture featured the Lady of Coventry atop a horse and her handmaidens, heralds, jester, and guards.

The petite Mary Hay appeared in a comic number with Phil Dwyer as her pet dog; the dog cried real tears and talked.

Some critics called this the best edition ever. Musically, it was. Bert Williams sang "You Cannot Make Your Shimmy Shake on Tea," a protest about Prohibition, and Eddie Cantor made a hit of "You'd Be Surprised." Together Cantor and Williams sang "I Want to See a Minstrel Show."

ZIEGFELD FOLLIES OF 1920

NEW YORK RUN: June 22–October 16, 1920; New Amsterdam Theatre

AUTHORS: Lyrics and music by Irving Berlin, Gene Buck, Dave Stamper, Joseph McCarthy, and Harry Tierney; special music by Victor Herbert

STAGING: Edward Royce

PRINCIPALS: DeLyle Alda, Fannie Brice, Lillian Broderick, Jack Donahue, Ray Dooley, Doris Eaton, Mary Eaton, W. C. Fields, Bernard Granville, Art Hickman's Orchestra, Margaret Irving, Moran and Mack, Carl Randall, Jessie Reed, John Steele,

Van and Schenck, Charles Winninger, Addison Young

HIT SONGS: "Girls of My Dreams" and "Tell Me, Little Gypsy" (Irving Berlin)

NOTABLE NUMBERS: In "The Family Ford," W. C. Fields played a father taking his family out for a ride in their brand-new Ford. (Fields actually drove a Ford automobile onto the stage.) The scene originally featured Fannie Brice as the mother and Ray Dooley as the child. In the skit, Fields tried to keep the car in perfect condition; however, while the car was stopped, a stranger came along and scratched a match on the hood to light his cigarette; then a blind man came down the road tapping his cane and broke a headlight. When Fields tried to crank up the car to leave, it would not start. He finally got the motor running, but as soon as he got into the car, the motor died. A few minutes later, the steering wheel came out, and the door fell off. Finally, the tires blew.

Fannie Brice was a hit with two humorous numbers. In "I'm a Vamp from East Broadway," she had an imaginary visit with a victim who described how Brice ruined his life. In "Poor Florodora Girl," Brice was the only one of six chorus girls who married for love—and the only one still in the chorus.

In the theater scene, a jealous Brice dragged Fields from the theater after accusing him of flirting with a chorus girl. The scene used over seventy people to create an authentic setting including an audience of actors that faced the real audience.

The critics liked Ray Dooley in the park scene. Dooley appeared in a baby carriage as a crying infant getting drunk on milk punch. Charles Winninger strolled through the park drinking and flirting while Dooley carried on.

ZIEGFELD FOLLIES OF 1921

NEW YORK RUN: June 21–October 1, 1921; Globe Theatre

AUTHORS: Lines and lyrics by Channing Pollock, Gene Buck, Willard Mack, Ralph Spence, and Bud DeSilva; music by Victor Herbert, Rudolf Friml, and Dave Stamper

DIRECTORS: Dialogue rehearsed by George Marion; orchestra directed by Frank Tours

PRINCIPALS: Fannie Brice, Margery Chapin, John Clarke, Ray Dooley, Mary Eaton, W. C. Fields, Raymond Hitchcock, Mary Lewis, Vera Michelena, Mary Milburn, Mitti and Tillio, Florence O'Denishawn, Charles O'Donnell, Jessie Reed, John Steele, Van and Schenck

HIT SONGS: "My Man" (English lyric, Channing Pollock; music, Maurice Yvain) and "Second Hand Rose" (Grant Clarke/ James Hanley), both interpolations

NOTABLE NUMBERS: Two scenes received particular praise in the press: "The Legend of the Cyclamen Tree" and "The Birthday of the Dauphin." In the "Legend" number, a twelfth-century Persian Princess accompanied by her courtiers and slaves received suitors in a walled courtyard. The entire party then moved to the desert where the cyclamen tree would—on

Barbara Stanwyck was fourteen when she made her Broadway debut as a *Follies* chorus girl. She achieved real stardom after she accompanied her then-husband, Frank Fay, to Hollywood in the early 1930s and appeared in movies and later on television.

certain occasions—come alive. Florence O'Denishawn as the tree was "rooted" to the floor but managed a graceful dance in which she moved only her torso and arms. The Persian costumes were purple, orange, yellow, and blue.

In the other scene, the dauphin watched from his special pavilion as the entire cast appeared in the Royal Garden of Versailles for his birthday. James Reynolds's period costumes in blues, yellows, shades of green, and pink taffeta were particularly striking.

Fannie Brice sang two numbers (interpolations) that were hits: "Second Hand Rose" and the French "Mon Homme," or "My Man." Brice's rendition of "My Man" surprised the audience because she usually sang only humorous numbers. It seemed strangely close to the mood of her unhappy marriage to Nicky Arnstein.

Brice, W. C. Fields, Raymond Hitchcock, and Ray Dooley appeared together in a skit (written by Fields) about a family loaded with picnic paraphernalia struggling to board a subway train for the country. Brice, Hitchcock, and Fields also amused the audience with their caricatures of Ethel, Lionel, and Jack Barrymore.

In one of the funniest prize fight skits, Brice impersonated a French boxer named Carpentier, and Dooley impersonated Jack Dempsey. The two exchanged blows in front of female trainers and an exclusively female audience. Fields and Hitchcock as announcer and referee were the only men in the scene.

Charles O'Donnell was featured in a humorous skit about a piano tuner. He never played a note, yet before he finished— ending up in a huge vase of flowers—the room was destroyed and everyone's nerves were wrecked.

In "The Professor," Fields played a minister who invited a magician (Hitchcock) to entertain his Sunday school class. The magician's bratty daughter (who else but Ray Dooley?) accompanied him. The magician had only one skill: he could change water into wine and wine into water. While the magician got drunk performing his trick, the minister juggled tennis balls. When prohibition agents appeared, they found only water.

One of the audience's favorite dance numbers featured Mitti and Tillio from Paris. Mitti's nudity had created international interest in their act. *Variety* said Mitti wore even less than expected; she "wore more on her hair than on the rest of her." Mitti was described as "athletic looking" in a cut-out cobweb outfit; the powerful Tillio effortlessly lifted and tossed her about.

ZIEGFELD FOLLIES OF 1922

NEW YORK RUN: June 5, 1922–June 23, 1923; New Amsterdam Theatre

AUTHORS: Written by Gene Buck, Ring Lardner, and Ralph Spence; music by Victor Herbert, Louis A. Hirsch, and Dave Stamper

STAGING: Ned Wayburn

PRINCIPALS: Mary Eaton, Gallagher and Shean, Alexander Gray, Gilda Gray, Evelyn Law, Mary Lewis, Martha Lorber, Lulu McConnell, Nervo and Knox, Al Ochs, Will Rogers, Muriel Stryker, the Tiller Girls, Andrew Tombes, Brandon Tynan

HIT SONG: "Oh! Mister Gallagher and Mister Shean" (Ed Gallagher and Al Shean)

NOTABLE NUMBERS: The most spectacular scene in this year's *Follies* was "Lace-Land." In the scene's first number, Mary Lewis was the lace maker. As she sang "Weaving My Dreams," five young women dressed in Dutch costumes posed around her. Then dancers representing lace articles (stockings, parasol, handkerchief, fan, bridal gown, and veil) appeared, and Mary Eaton led a ballet.

The costumes looked lace-colored until the women started dancing and the lights were lowered. Then the gowns glowed yellow and orange against a black curtain that was hung with glowing medallions. As the lights were blended, everything on the stage seemed to change. When all stage lights were turned off, the audience could see only the pattern of the laces and glowing medallions. At the scene's end, there were fifty-four female chorus members and eight soloists on stage.

The glowing radium effect was produced by a special paint that reportedly cost $185 per pound. Ziegfeld had heard of the paint in Paris, where he bought a mask that had been treated with it. The special paint had to be exposed to sunlight or powerful electric lights for ten minutes before the clothes were worn on stage. The original application cost $6,000 and had to be renewed several times during the run. Ziegfeld also paid a royalty for its use. This single scene was reported to cost $31,000 and to take one year to produce. However, it was so popular that it was carried over into the next year's *Follies*. Ned Wayburn staged the "Lace-Land" scene, and Charles LeMaire designed the costumes.

Designer James Reynolds and classical dancer Michael Fokine collaborated on two ballet scenes. Reynolds conceived and designed "Farljandio," which was set in a Sicilian mountain camp. Fokine staged the ballet for gypsy dancers wearing colorful red and yellow shawls. Muriel Stryker, as the bride, did a traditional gypsy wedding dance.

In the other scene, "Frolicking Gods," Fokine composed and produced the ballet, Joseph Urban created the art-museum set, and James Reynolds designed the Victorian costumes worn by the museum visitors. After the museum closed, the bronze and marble Greek statues came to life in skimpy costumes and jumped down from their pedestals to dance and cavort. They were joined in their merrymaking by a young couple who had accidentally been locked in the museum. At dawn the statues returned to their places while the disheveled lovers were seized by museum guards.

The first-act finale, "Bring on the Girls," was a big production number that opened with sixty-four chorus girls lined up on a golden staircase against a blue background. The women walked down the steps to the apron of the stage and then formed groups along the steps. Each group represented chorus girls from different historical periods—from the Black Crook Amazons to Ziegfeld Girls. The front of the stage opened, and the steps moved

Right: Brandon Tynan (left) as producer David Belasco and Will Rogers as an actress in a skit from the *Follies* about 1922. Below: Fannie Brice, Mae Daw, and William Roselle in the song-story "Mary Rose"; the scene was added several weeks after the 1923 edition opened and was one of the few serious numbers Brice ever performed. Opposite: Bert and Betty Wheeler had been a vaudeville team for eleven years before they made a hit in the 1923 *Follies*. However, they divorced shortly after their success, and Bert appeared solo for the first time in the 1924 edition.

downward so that they now led to the basement. The groups of women passed through golden gates and exited below.

For "It's Getting Dark on Old Broadway" (sung by Gilda Gray), the chorus girls wore white costumes and hats that glowed in the dark. Performed against a background of electric signs painted on a canvas drop of Longacre Square, the song employed unusual lighting effects. When the lights were turned down, the women's faces looked black. The number referred to the fact that blacks were moving beyond Harlem and closer to Broadway.

Critics liked Ring Lardner's baseball scene, "The Bull Pen." It featured two bush-league pitchers played by Andrew Tombes and Will Rogers; Al Ochs played a regular pitcher. The men exchanged quips in the bull pen as Tombes warmed up.

The show's finale depicted the stage door of the New Amsterdam Theatre. First, the show's principals came through the door one by one. Then some of the chorus girls came down a spiral staircase while others appeared at their dressing room windows. After the entire cast was assembled, the principals walked by and the audience applauded.

NOTES: The show grossed $10,000 the first night and $36–$37,000 the first week. Although it played to a bigger audience, earned more money, and enjoyed a longer run than any previous edition, twenty-seven weeks into the *Follies'* run Ziegfeld said he was still $9,000 short of his production cost. This did not include any deduction for lost interest on the money he invested. His pre-opening cost, according to an article in *Variety*, was $265,000. A cut in the top ticket price from $5 (previous year) to $4 meant a weekly loss of $4,500–$5,000. And he had the continuing expenses of cast and staff salaries.

Ziegfeld usually opened a new *Follies* as a summer attraction. But, since the 1922 show was so popular, he kept it running through most of 1923. Beginning June 15, 1923, he did add three Ben Ali Haggin tableaux and more cast members, including Ann Pennington, Ise Marvenga (a European singer), and new chorus girls. He called this revised show the "summer edition" and gave it a new edition number (seventeen) even though it was basically the 1922 show. Ziegfeld let the production run until September 15, 1923; it then left for Boston to begin its long road tour.

Chorus girl Lucile Layton Zinman said that until the Tiller Girls came along, chorus girls did not have to be great dancers or have a lot of training. She recalled the time the chorus did a pogo-stick number. The number had few dance steps; mostly the women jumped in time to the music as they crossed the stage on their pogo sticks. In Baltimore the stage had a slight pitch to it, and on one occasion two women bounced off the stage into the orchestra pit. Luckily, no one was hurt. (The opening program does not indicate that the 1922 show contained a pogo stick number. However, a 1921 *Frolic* had such a number. Since the *Follies* often added and dropped numbers before it toured, most likely this popular number was added just for the tour.)

Zinman said that Ziegfeld may have known the showgirls better than the chorus girls. But in the three and a half years that

she worked for him, Ziegfeld patted her on the head once and spoke to her only two or three times. There was almost an invisible curtain between Ziegfeld and the chorus girls. Zinman's salary ranged from an initial $50 a week up to $90. She said Ziegfeld actually paid slightly lower salaries in New York because women wanted the prestige of being a "Ziegfeld Girl." However, on the road, his salaries were higher than those of most producers.

ZIEGFELD FOLLIES OF 1922
Summer Edition
NEW YORK RUN: June 25–September 15, 1923; New Amsterdam Theatre
AUTHORS: Lyrics, Gene Buck; dialogue, Ralph Spence; sketches, Franklin Adams, Nate Salisbury, Emil Breitenfeld
STAGING: Ned Wayburn
PRINCIPALS: Eddie Cantor, Gallagher and Shean, Alexander Gray, Gilda Gray, Brooke Johns, Simeon Karavaeff, the Kelo Brothers, Evelyn Law, Ilse Marvenga, Will McGinty, Ann Pennington, the Tiller Girls, Andrew Tombes, Will West

ZIEGFELD FOLLIES OF 1923
NEW YORK RUN: October 20, 1923–May 10, 1924; New Amsterdam Theatre
AUTHORS: Lyrics by Gene Buck; music by Victor Herbert, Rudolf Friml, and Dave Stamper
STAGING: Ned Wayburn
PRINCIPALS: Lina Basquette, Fannie Brice, Marie Callahan, Eddie Cantor, Roy Cropper, Marie Dahm, Mae Daw, Harland Dixon, Mlle. Paulette Duval, the Empire Girls, Hilda Ferguson, Catherine Gallimore, Florentine Gosnova, Gertrude Hoffmann, Brooke Johns, Edna Leedom, Martha Lorber, Ann Pennington, Robert Quinault, William Roselle, Iris Rowe, Dave Stamper, Olga Steck, Arthur West, Bert and Betty Wheeler, Paul Whiteman's Orchestra, Alexander Yakovleff
NOTABLE NUMBERS: For his last *Follies* James Reynolds went all out in designing "The Legend of the Drums," which was set in Napoleonic times. The scene ended with a spectacular effect that simulated the burning of captured war drums. The scene featured dances by Lina Basquette and the Empire Girls.

In the "Maid of Gold" number, exotic dancer Muriel Stryker had her body coated with a special gold paint; however, after Stryker's physician warned her of the paint's hazards, the dancer wore a gold lamé dress. The other women in the number wore beautiful gowns designed by Erté.

Bert and Betty Wheeler were on stage only ten minutes but had one of the best-liked numbers. Wheeler sang an emotional "mammy song"—complete with tears running down his face—while eating a sandwich.

In the shadowgraph illusion, animated silhouettes were projected on the back of a white curtain by skillful contortions of fingers, hands, and arms. Special three-dimensional effects, intensified by expert lighting, could be seen only with the aid of "Fol-lies-Scope glasses" that had a red lens (right) and a green lens (left). The glasses came in each program, and if the patron wore them, the shadows seemed to leap across the orchestra pit. If a person looked at the ladder on stage, it appeared to pivot until it rested on the viewer's forehead. Next, in sequence, the following events seemed to occur: a man danced across the ladder and put his foot on each person's head; an organ grinder hurled a monkey that perched on the audience's heads; and a young woman undressed and flung all her clothes, including her undergarments, at each patron. The climax came when a huge insect leaped from the stage and spread his feet on everyone's hair, eliciting gasps of horror from the audience.

"The Harlequin's Doll" opened with miniature dolls seated on or near a settee (a pincushion on a dressing table). Robert Quinault as the Harlequin coaxed each doll to dance, but soon he became exasperated with the dolls' mechanical movements and threw them about. After considerable effort he persuaded a rag doll (Iris Rowe) to dance. The couple performed an exhilarating dance together until the Harlequin started swinging the doll with increasing speed and violence, and she fell apart. The Harlequin then laughed indifferently and leaped onto the settee to join the other dolls.

Ben Ali Haggin's picture, "La Marquise," received unanimous praise for its beauty. Most of the women, including Paulette Duval as The White Marquise, wore sumptuous gowns; however, one or two of the women reportedly had no clothes.

The ever-popular Fannie Brice performed several numbers; one of her best was in the Amateur Night skit in the Bowery. Ann Pennington and Brooke Johns were two other amateurs, but Brice won the lady's watch.

ZIEGFELD FOLLIES OF 1924
NEW YORK RUN: June 24–October 25, 1924; New Amsterdam Theatre
AUTHORS: Dialogue by William Anthony McGuire and Will Rogers; lyrics by Gene Buck and Joseph J. McCarthy; music by Victor Herbert, Raymond Hubbell, Dave Stamper, Harry Tierney, and Dr. Albert Szirmai
STAGING: Julian Mitchell
PRINCIPALS: Lina Basquette, Mae Daw, Gloria Dawn, the Empire Girls, Hilda Ferguson, Irving Fisher, Alf James, the Kelo Brothers, Lupino Lane, Evelyn Law, Edna Leedom, Tom Lewis, Martha Lorber, George Olsen's Band, Ann Pennington, Will Rogers, Phil Ryley, Vivienne Segal, the Tiller Girls, Brandon Tynan
HIT SONG: "Adoring You" (J. J. McCarthy/Harry Tierney)
NOTABLE NUMBERS: One of the show's most popular numbers featured the Tiller girls, a line of sixteen precision dancers from London. While the orchestra played Victor Herbert music, the Tiller Girls, using luminous ropes, skipped rope on a darkened stage.

Will Rogers's monologue was always popular. On opening

Opposite: Will Rogers distributes apples to female cast members from the 1924 *Follies;* Ann Pennington stands behind the crate, next to the woman in the feathered headdress. Rogers was well-liked by the cast because of his generosity as well as his pleasant disposition.

night Rogers said the difference between a good *Follies* and a bad *Follies* showed up in the gross receipts at the season's end; there was about a $1.80 difference.

In the final scene of Act One, Irving Fisher and Mae Daw sang, and the Empire and Tiller Girls danced. The scene included showgirls representing famous female historical figures—Eve, Brunhilde, Cleopatra, Gueneviere, Isabelle, etc. Wearing salmon- and rose-colored costumes designed by Ben Ali Haggin, the women descended a staircase and stood poised until the curtain came down.

ZIEGFELD FOLLIES OF 1924
Fall Edition
NEW YORK RUN: October 30, 1924–March 7, 1925; New Amsterdam Theatre
AUTHORS: Dialogue by William Anthony McGuire and Will Rogers; lyrics by Gene Buck and Joseph J. McCarthy; music by Victor Herbert, Raymond Hubbell, Dave Stamper, and Harry Tierney
STAGING: Julian Mitchell
PRINCIPALS: Greta Fayne, Peggy Fears, Irving Fisher, Alf James, the Kelo Brothers, Dorothy Knapp, Lupino Lane, Evelyn Law, Tom Lewis, the Lilliputians, Gladys Loftus, Martha Lorber, Mitti and Tillio, Al Ochs, George Olsen's Band, Ann Pennington, Will Rogers, Vivienne Segal, Jack Shannon, the Tiller Girls, Brandon Tynan

ZIEGFELD FOLLIES OF 1925
Spring Edition
NEW YORK RUN: March 10–July 4, 1925; New Amsterdam Theatre
AUTHORS: Dialogue by J. P. McEvoy, Will Rogers, and W.C. Fields; lyrics by Gene Buck; music by Raymond Hubbell, Dave Stamper, and Werner Janssen
STAGING: Julian Mitchell
PRINCIPALS: Ray Dooley, W. C. Fields, Irving Fisher, the Kelo Brothers, Dorothy Knapp, Marjorie Leet, Tom Lewis, Gladys Loftus, Martha Lorber, Clarence Nordstrom, Al Ochs, George Olsen's Band, Ann Pennington, Will Rogers, Vivienne Segal, Jack Shannon, the Tiller Girls, Brandon Tynan
NOTABLE NUMBERS: W. C. Fields and Ray Dooley appeared in several skits together, many from *The Comic Supplement*. J. P. McEvoy had created the character of Gertie for Dooley. In "The Drug Store" scene, Gertie came into the store where the owner (Fields) was spending all his time selling postage stamps, giving the time, and helping people with something in their eye—everything but earning money.

In "A Back Porch," Pa (Fields) was trying to nap on his back porch while Gertie and Ma (Martha Lorber)—plus the milkman, newsboy, bag man, fruit vendor, ice man, and scissors grinder—noisily went about their business. Pa, Ma, and Gertie

Above: Ray Dooley and W. C. Fields dance "The Waltz of Love" in the 1925 *Follies*. After this show Fields made a permanent move to Hollywood, where he concentrated on films and became an even bigger star. Opposite: Will Rogers (center, seated) in the "Country Store" scene from the 1925 *Follies*

appeared yet again in "A Road." Pa was driving the trio in his strange-looking car when a motor cop (Tom Lewis) yelled at them. The car responded by falling apart.

NOTE: Even though the show opened in 1925, Ziegfeld still considered it the nineteenth edition (the same edition number as both 1924 shows). Several scenes from the two 1924 editions were used as well as a few scenes from *The Comic Supplement*.

ZIEGFELD FOLLIES OF 1925
Summer Edition

NEW YORK RUN: July 6–September 19, 1925; New Amsterdam Theatre

AUTHORS: Dialogue by J. P. McEvoy, Will Rogers, and W. C. Fields; lyrics by Gene Buck; music by Raymond Hubbell, Dave Stamper, and Werner Janssen

STAGING: Julian Mitchell

PRINCIPALS: Lina Basquette, Bertha Belmore, Louise Brooks, Dare and Wall, Ray Dooley, W. C. Fields, Irving Fisher, Evelyn Goodwin, Marion Hurley, the Kelo Brothers, Dorothy Knapp, Edna Leedom, Gladys Loftus, Clarence Nordstom, Al Ochs, George Olsen's Band, Will Rogers, Jack Shannon, Vivienne Segal, Adelaide Seman, Brandon Tynan, Vangie Valentine

NOTABLE NUMBERS: In the opening scene, Dorothy Knapp and five other women climbed over the side of an ocean liner; Knapp then sang "Home Again," which was followed by the Tiller Girls doing an "Emigrant Dance."

While George Olsen's band played a jazz number, Ethel Shutta sang "Eddie Be Good" to twenty-four chorus girls who wore blackface makeup so they would look like Eddie Cantor.

One of the best skits featured Edna Leedom as a nagging wife and Fields as her husband; Fields tried to sleep while his wife complained.

NOTES: The edition numbering had gotten mixed up back in 1923. Ziegfeld had revised the popular 1922 *Follies* and let it run a second summer (1923), calling it the "summer edition." He also raised the edition number. In the fall, when the 1923 show opened, he had to give it a new number. Thus, two separate editions played on Broadway in a single year (1923). Later, Ziegfeld apparently had second thoughts about increasing the edition number for seasonal versions of the show. In 1924 and 1925, he presented seasonal variations but restricted himself to one edition number per year.

The 1926 revue opened on Broadway as *No Foolin'* but toured as the *Ziegfeld Follies*. Ziegfeld no doubt called the 1926 show the twentieth *Follies* because it was the twentieth *year* that a *Follies* had been presented. When the 1927 *Follies* opened, Ziegfeld advertised that show as being in its twenty-first consecutive year, which was possible only if the 1926 show was considered an edition of the *Follies*.

Above: This scene from the 1927 *Follies* is set in Florenz Ziegfeld's office. Andrew Tombes appeared as Ziegfeld and Helen Brown (center front) as Marilyn Miller.

Tombes was a *Follies* cast member from 1922 to 1927; in 1933 he went into movies. Opposite: Claire Luce aboard the ostrich she rode on stage in the 1927 *Follies*.

According to a newspaper clipping from the era, the ostrich chased W. C. Fields into the street after he plucked one of its feathers. (Fields was not in the 1927

show but still performed on Broadway when not making movies and may have visited the show.)

ZIEGFELD FOLLIES OF 1927

NEW YORK RUN: August 16, 1927–January 7, 1928; New Amsterdam Theatre

AUTHORS: Sketches by Harry Atteridge and Eddie Cantor; lyrics by Irving Berlin

STAGING: Dances by Sammy Lee; dialogue by Zeke Colvan; ballets by Albertina Rasch

PRINCIPALS: Franklyn Bauer, Helen Brown, the Brox Sisters, Eddie Cantor (featured), Peggy Chamberlain, Irene Delroy, Cliff Edwards (Ukele Ike), Ruth Etting, Fairchild and Rainger, Laura Foster, Les Ghezzi, Dan Healy, Ross Himes, the Ingenues, Claire Luce, Harry McNaughton, William Powers, the Albertina Rasch Girls, Phil Ryley, Andrew Tombes, Frances Upton

HIT SONGS: "Shaking the Blues Away" and "It All Belongs to Me" (Irving Berlin)

NOTABLE NUMBERS: In the opening number, sixteen shop girls who had been "glorified" practiced their dance steps in front of Ziegfeld (played by Andrew Tombes). After appearances by past stars (women impersonating Ann Pennington, Marilyn Miller, and Fannie Brice, among others), sixteen chorus boys who wanted to be glorified came on stage. In Act Two, the "glorified" chorus boys appeared as chorus girls dancing a ballet.

In "The Star's Double," Eddie Cantor parodied Hollywood's practice of using doubles (lower-salaried look-alikes in place of highly paid actors) for any dangerous scene. Just as he was about to be slugged by an irate husband—who had found Cantor with his wife—Cantor yelled for his double. He watched while the other actor took the punch.

For most gorgeous costumes, honors went to the "Ribbons and Bows" number. Irene Delroy sang, and nine women appeared as various ribbons, bows, and knots that adorned apparel. Finally, women dressed as blue bows came out to dance.

Delroy and Franklyn Bauer sang one of the revue's more popular tunes, "Maybe It's You," accompanied by the Ziegfeld Dancing Girls and the three Brox Sisters wearing rose-trimmed hoop skirts and floppy hats.

Ruth Etting sang "Shaking the Blues Away" in front of a beautiful Urban-designed backdrop depicting a cotton field and a white wooden house; Spanish moss hung from a cut drop. Etting was assisted by the Jazzbow Girls, the Albertina Rasch Dancers, the Banjo Ingenues, and Dan Healy. The Jazzbow Girls were dressed entirely in red: bandannas, stockings, shoes, and dresses. By the end of the number, there were nearly eighty people on stage.

In the first-act finale, "Melody Land," the lights went up and the curtains parted to reveal the Ingenues (a nineteen-member female orchestra) playing on center stage while two men (Fairchild and Rainger) and twelve women played pianos on the steps of a double staircase. The Military Dancing Girls were on hand while the Ingenues played Berlin's new "Stars and Stripes Forever." After an appearance by the Rasch Dancers, the principals came on stage dressed in white costumes with gold fringe and

Top: Ruth Etting and the Jazzbow Girls perform the "Shaking the Blues Away" number from the *1927 Follies*. The Rasch Dancers and the Banjo Ingenues are partially hidden behind the other women. Above: The 1927 revue's spectacular "Melody Land" scene featured the Ingenues, a female orchestra. Opposite: After Franklyn Bauer sang "The Rainbow of Girls," the Albertina Rasch Dancers, dressed in pastel colors under the dim lights, performed a ballet, "In the Clouds." The scene included several solo dancers and premiere danseuse Helen Brown.

Faith Bacon, shown here with her fans, was in the opening scene of the 1931 *Follies*.

gold feather hats and headdresses. Concurrently, the Ingenues were playing a medley of songs from the first act.

In Act Two, the Brox Sisters sang "Jungle Jingle," and Claire Luce, wearing a costume of ostrich feathers, entered a lush jungle riding a live ostrich (complete with rhinestone collar) to the center of the stage. She then slid off its back and performed an acrobatic dance with two huge fans; the chorus followed with an ensemble dance. However, the ostrich was tall and not easily controlled; one night the bird (with Luce on board) came running onto the stage but would not slow down. It kept going all the way to the street door, heading for its stable. Since Luce could not get off, she had to skip her number that night. (After the show, the ostrich was sold for $991.11.)

The Albertina Rasch Girls appeared in the same jungle, as did women in striking animal costumes representing a cobra, tiger, flamingo, giraffe, etc. To complete the scene Les Ghezzi, a team of two male dancers, appeared as apes and nearly stole the show as they danced on their hands.

ZIEGFELD FOLLIES OF 1931

NEW YORK RUN: July 1–November 21, 1931; Ziegfeld Theatre
AUTHORS: Music and sketches by Gene Buck, Mark Hellinger, J. P. Murray, Barry Trivers and Ben Oakland, Walter Donaldson, Dave Stamper, Mack Gordon and Harry Revel, and Dimitri Tiomkin
STAGING: Dances by Bobby Connolly; dialogue by Edward C. Lilley; Rasch Dancers' numbers by Albertina Rasch
PRINCIPALS: Faith Bacon, Ethel Borden, Milt and Frank Britton Band, Buck and Bubbles, Arthur Campbell, Albert Carroll, the Collette Sisters, Dorothy Dell, Ruth Etting, Gladys Glad, Cliff Hall, Hal LeRoy, Mitzi Mayfair, Grace Moore, Helen Morgan, Earl Oxford, Jack Pearl, Reri, Harry Richman
NOTABLE NUMBERS: The show's most spectacular number, the jungle scene, opened the second half. The scene started with a song by the male chorus; a tom-tom dance by the Albertina Rasch Dancers followed. Then came a head-on view of a herd of elephants, their trunks carrying scantily clad women.

The "Buckingham Palace" scene was a big number for the chorus. Women dressed as Scotch lassies performed an impressive rifle drill, and then Hal LeRoy and Mitzi Mayfair did a tap dance.

In a scene set at Rector's Restaurant in 1914, Ruth Etting imitated Nora Bayes and revived the old hit "Shine On, Harvest Moon."

The Brittons (Frank and Mitt) and their "gang," known for their crazy antics, broke musical instruments over each other's heads. Each night they smashed five violins, two cellos, and several bows—much to the audience's delight.

The Rasch Dancers performed a "Bolero" dance and a beautiful "Illusion in White" number in which they wore feathered costumes. Rasch's husband, Dimitri Tiomkin, composed the music for the number.

ZIEGFELD FOLLIES OF 1934

NEW YORK RUN: January 4–June 9, 1934; Winter Garden Theatre
AUTHORS: E. Y. Harburg, Fred Allen, Harry Tugend, H. I. Phillips, David Freedman, Vernon Duke, Arthur Swanstrom, Louis Alter, Samuel Pokrass, Ballard MacDonald, Joseph Meyer, Chris Taylor, James Hanley, Ann Runnell, Harold Atteridge, Robert Dolan, Dana Suesse, Billy Hill
STAGING: Bobby Connolly; dialogue staged by Edward C. Lilley
PRINCIPALS: John Adair, Eve Arden, Judith Barron, Betzi Beaton, Patricia Bowman, Fannie Brice, Jacques Cartier, Vilma and Buddy Ebsen, Jane Froman, Brice Hutchins, Vivian Janis, Everett Marshall, Georges Metaxa, Victor Morley, Jack Pepper, Cherry and June Preisser, Don Ross, the Sara Mildred Strauss Dancers, Oliver Wakefield
NOTABLE NUMBERS: Fannie Brice returned to the *Follies* this year and introduced her Baby Snooks character (created at a party in 1921); later she played this character on the radio. According to one review, Baby Snooks was "an infant whom her parents forgot to drown."

In addition to her Baby Snooks skit, Brice satirized female evangelist Aimee Semple McPherson ("Soul-Saving Sadie"); a nudist ("Sunshine Sara"); and Countess Dubinsky ("Sadie Salome"), a fan dancer from Minsky's burlesque.

Willie Howard did a funny reprise of "The Last Round-Up" using a Yiddish accent. He also played both the outgoing and incoming presidents in a Cuban revolution.

The dancing of Vilma and Buddy Ebsen drew a lot of attention. In their second-act number, "Stop That Clock," they were accompanied by women travelers and porters.
NOTE: The show cost between $125,000 and $150,000 to produce; this was less than the 1919 edition had cost ($175,000) when Ziegfeld was alive.

ZIEGFELD FOLLIES OF 1936

NEW YORK RUN: January 30–May 10, 1936; September 14–December 19, 1936; Winter Garden Theatre
AUTHORS: Lyrics by Ira Gershwin; music by Vernon Duke; sketches by David Freedman; dances by Robert Alton; ballets by George Balanchine; revised edition: sketches by Edward C. Lilley and Edward Dowling
STAGING: John Murray Anderson; the revised version was supervised by Harry Kaufman
PRINCIPALS: Eve Arden, Josephine Baker, Edgar Bergen, Fannie Brice (featured), the California Varsity Eight, Judy Canova, Harriet Hoctor, Bob Hope, John Hoysradt, Duke McHale, Rodney McLennan, the Nicholas Brothers, Gertrude Niesen, Hugh O'Connell, Cherry and June Preisser

ZIEGFELD FOLLIES OF 1943

NEW YORK RUN: April 1, 1943–July 22, 1944; Winter

Garden Theatre
AUTHORS: Sketches by Lester Lee, Jerry Seelan, Bud Pearson, Les White, Joseph Erens, Charles Sherman, Harry Young, Lester Lawrence, Baldwin Bergersen, Ray Golden, Sid Kuller, William Wells, and Harold Rome; lyrics by Jack Yellen; music by Ray Henderson
Director: John Murray Anderson; dances directed by Robert Alton
PRINCIPALS: Christine Ayers, Bill and Cora Baird, Milton Berle (featured), Imogen Carpenter, Jack Cole, Nadine Gae, the Jansleys, Ray Long, Jack McCauley, Jaye Martin, Ilona Massey (featured), Arthur Maxwell, Katherine Meskill, Dean Murphy, the Rhythmaires, Sue Ryan, Charles Senna, Arthur Treacher (featured), Tommy Wonder, Ben Yost's Vi-Kings

ZIEGFELD FOLLIES OF 1957

NEW YORK RUN: March 1–June 15, 1957; Winter Garden Theatre
AUTHORS: Sketches by Arnie Rosen, Coleman Jacoby, David Rogers, Alan Jeffreys, Maxwell Grant; music and lyrics by Jack Lawrence, Richard Myers, Howard Dietz, Sammy Fain, David Rogers, Colin Romoff, Dean Fuller, Marshall Barer, Carolyn Leigh, Philip Springer
DIRECTOR: John Kennedy; dances staged by Frank Wagner
PRINCIPALS: Beatrice Lillie (star billing), Billy DeWolfe (featured), Tony Franco, Harold Lang, Carol Lawrence, Bob and Larry Leslie, Micki Marlow, Jay Marshall, Jane Morgan, John Philip, Helen Wood

ZIEGFELD FROLIC (1922)

OPENING: January 10, 1922; Garrick Theatre, Philadelphia; the show was presented only on tour; there was no New York run.
AUTHORS: Music and lyrics by Gene Buck and Dave Stamper; dialogue initially by Ralph Spence, with Will Rogers added to the credits in February
STAGING: Leon Errol initially, with Ned Wayburn added to credits in February
PRINCIPALS: Annette Bade, Alexander Gray, the Lavarre Brothers, Jack McGowan, Lotta Miles, Will Rogers, Brandon Tynan, Arthur West, the White Sisters
NOTE: This show was not a typical *Frolic* in that it was neither a midnight show nor performed on the New Amsterdam Theatre Roof.

Ziegfeld Girls of 1920—*see* Ziegfeld Nine O'Clock Revue (1920)

ZIEGFELD MIDNIGHT FROLIC (1915)

OPENING: January 5, 1915; New Amsterdam Theatre Roof
AUTHORS: Lyrics by Gene Buck; music by Dave Stamper and Louis A. Hirsch
STAGING: Ned Wayburn
PRINCIPALS: Sybil Carmen, Ray Cox, Malvin Grindell, Muriel Hudson, Kay Laurell, Mlle. Morecan, Earl Oren, Charles Purcell, Helen Shipman, Will West
NOTABLE NUMBERS: In the opening number of the first *Frolic*, a man seated at one of the tables began singing "The Girl from My Hometown." During the song, young women representing various cities arose from tables and went to the center of the dance floor. The last woman was a country girl from the man's hometown.

The funniest scene was Will West's impersonation of Diamond Jim Brady doing the one-step. West was made up to look like Brady and had perfected Brady's mannerisms and dancing form. Brady and Lillian Russell sat at a ring-side table. Brady didn't mind the burlesque of his person or his dancing, but there was a limit when it came to his jewelry; Brady had a set of jewels for each day of the month, and he became upset when Ziegfeld satirized them.

But probably the most talked-about number was one in which the entire twenty-four-member chorus paraded across the glass walkway in beautiful dresses. The walkway was illuminated by red, white, and blue lights, and blowers were positioned along it to lift the women's skirts, which were made of strips of material that were easily blown about. The gentlemen below craned their necks to see, but Ziegfeld maintained decorum by having the dresses designed with full-length bloomers gathered at the knees and ankles.

ZIEGFELD MIDNIGHT FROLIC (1915)

OPENING: August 23, 1915; titled "Just Girls"; New Amsterdam Theatre Roof
AUTHORS: Lyrics by Gene Buck; music by Dave Stamper
STAGING: Leon Errol
PRINCIPALS: Sybil Carmen, Melville Ellis, Les Glorias, Muriel Hudson, Allyn King, Kay Laurell, Odette Myrtil, Earl Oren, Charles Purcell, Will Rogers

ZIEGFELD MIDNIGHT FROLIC (1916)

OPENING: January 24, 1916; New Amsterdam Theatre Roof
AUTHORS: Lyrics by Gene Buck; music by Dave Stamper
STAGING: Ned Wayburn
PRINCIPALS: Sybil Carmen, the Dolly Sisters, Paul Frawley, Paul Gordon, Marion Harris, Allyn King, Odette Myrtil, Will Rogers, Oscar Shaw, Genevieve Warner

ZIEGFELD MIDNIGHT FROLIC (1916)

OPENING: October 2, 1916; New Amsterdam Theatre Roof
AUTHORS: Lyrics by Gene Buck; music by Dave Stamper
STAGING: Ned Wayburn

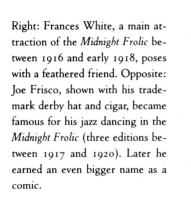

Right: Frances White, a main attraction of the *Midnight Frolic* between 1916 and early 1918, poses with a feathered friend. Opposite: Joe Frisco, shown with his trademark derby hat and cigar, became famous for his jazz dancing in the *Midnight Frolic* (three editions between 1917 and 1920). Later he earned an even bigger name as a comic.

PRINCIPALS: Peggy Brooks, Eddie Cantor, Sybil Carmen, Lucy Gillette, Lawrence Haynes, Bird Millman, Milo, William Rock, Olive Thomas, Frances White

ZIEGFELD MIDNIGHT FROLIC (1917)

OPENING: April 24, 1917; New Amsterdam Theatre Roof
AUTHORS: Lyrics by Gene Buck; music by Dave Stamper
STAGING: Ned Wayburn
PRINCIPALS: Sybil Carmen, Dane Claudius and Lillian Scarlet, Florence Lucille, John McGown, Ann Pennington, William Rock, Will Rogers, Dorothy St. Clair, Frances White

ZIEGFELD MIDNIGHT FROLIC (1917)

OPENING: December 29, 1917; New Amsterdam Theatre Roof
AUTHORS: Lyrics by Gene Buck; music by Leslie Stuart and Dave Stamper
STAGING: Ned Wayburn
PRINCIPALS: Frank Carter, Margie Cassidy, Dane Claudius and Lillian Scarlet, Ruby De Remer, Frisco, William Rock, Yvonne Shelton, Van and Schenck, Frances White, Lew Wilson
NOTABLE NUMBERS: Frank Carter, dressed in black and white and accompanied by eight women, opened the show singing "I'm Looking for the Gay White Way." As he sang, he carried a green lantern through the darkened auditorium. The Urban-designed background was a panorama of Broadway with electric signs. Ruby De Remer then appeared leading eight lantern-carrying women in the song "We are the Lights of Broadway." Later, Carter also sang "Beautiful Girl," while ten women impersonated heroines of the year's most popular plays.

In a novelty number, Frances White sang "Carmen Had Nothing on Me." Dressed as a Spanish dancer and followed by a group of toreadors and señoritas, White descended a flight of stairs and performed on the telescopic stage. Ned Wayburn's telescopic stage made its first appearance in this *Frolic* and was also used in Ruby De Remer's knitting number, "Every Girl Is Doing Her Bit." Gentlemen from the front row were invited to aid the women as they wound wool.

Frances White's "Gonzito" number (introduced in *Hitchy-Koo*) was the biggest hit of the show. White also wore rompers and sang her popular baby-talking "Mississippi" song introduced in 1916. Newcomer Joe Frisco's eccentric dancing earned three encores.

For the finale the chorus girls and principals were grouped at the front of stage, while a large, illuminated transparent shell occupied the rear of the stage. Behind the shell stood a young woman in flesh-colored tights holding the flag of France in her uplifted arm.

ZIEGFELD MIDNIGHT FROLIC (1918)

OPENING: April 24, 1918; New Amsterdam Theatre Roof

Right: Patriotic scenes such as this one were popular in 1918. Below: This photograph of cast members, including Will Rogers and Mary Hay (center), appears to be from the 1920 *Ziegfeld Nine O'Clock Revue*.

AUTHORS: Lyrics by Gene Buck; music by Dave Stamper
STAGING: Ned Wayburn
PRINCIPALS: Fannie Brice, Eddie Cantor, Frank Carter, Mabel Ferry, Frisco, Lillian Lorraine, Ann Pennington, Will Rogers, Yvonne Shelton
NOTABLE NUMBERS: Bird Millman, who had just come from an engagement with the Barnum and Bailey circus, did some electrifying stunts on her high wire.

During Yvonne Shelton's song "Try a Ring, Dear!" nine chorus girls carried racks of little canes and rings around the audience. Patrons who managed to toss a ring around a cane got to keep the cane.

Lillian Lorraine appeared on a flower-bedecked swing to sing "The Broadway Blues." In the darkness, the swing moved back and forth, accompanied by a ray from a star above her head.

Frisco performed his ingenious jazz dance on the telescopic stage, much to the audience's delight.

ZIEGFELD MIDNIGHT FROLIC (1918)

OPENING: December 9, 1918; New Amsterdam Theatre Roof
AUTHORS: Lyrics by Gene Buck; music by Dave Stamper
STAGING: Ned Wayburn
PRINCIPALS: Fannie Brice, Hal Hixon, Lillian Lorraine, Eve Lynn, Bird Millman, Lillian Mitchell, Bee Palmer, Julie Ross, Bert Williams

ZIEGFELD MIDNIGHT FROLIC (1919)

OPENING: October 2, 1919; New Amsterdam Theatre Roof
AUTHORS: Lyrics by Gene Buck; music by Dave Stamper
STAGING: Ned Wayburn
PRINCIPALS: Irene Barker, Fannie Brice, W. C. Fields, Hal Hixon, Allyn King, Keegan and Edwards, Ted Lewis, Martha Mansfield, Arthur Rose, Savoy and Brennan, Arthur Uttry, Frances White
NOTABLE NUMBERS: Margaret Irving and chorus sang "Surprise Package" while audience members pulled ribbons to unwrap a huge candy box. When the lid opened, out stepped Frances White. Each patron with a ribbon got a box of candy.

Arthur Uttry sang "Dearest," a song about beautiful jewels inspired by Cartier's. Seven jewels (showgirls) walked down a staircase in the order that their initial letter appeared in the title (D-iamond, E-merald, A-methyst, R-uby, dark E-merald, S-apphire, and T-opaz). For the climax Dolores made a dramatic entrance as the perfect jewel.

In the finale, Frances White sang "The World Is Going Shimmie Mad" as the entire cast participated in the wriggling. For the encore, first the stagehands and then the waiters joined the dance.

ZIEGFELD MIDNIGHT FROLIC (1920)

OPENING: March 15, 1920; New Amsterdam Theatre Roof

AUTHORS: Lyrics by Gene Buck; music by Dave Stamper
STAGING: Ned Wayburn
PRINCIPALS: Fannie Brice, Pauline Chambers, W. C. Fields, Frisco, John Price Jones, Allyn King, Lillian Leitzell, Lillian Lorraine, Sam Moore, Carl Randall, Mlle. Spinelli, Brandon Tynan

ZIEGFELD MIDNIGHT FROLIC (1920)

OPENING: September 2, 1920; New Amsterdam Theatre Roof
AUTHORS: Ballard MacDonald; music by Harry Carroll
STAGING: Edward Royce
PRINCIPALS: Annette Bade, Edythe Baker, Ruth Budd, Arline Chase, William and Gordon Dooley, Forest and Mason, Teddy Gerard, Herbert Hoey, Kathlene Martyn, Billy Mason, George and Dick Rath, Helen Shea, John Steele

ZIEGFELD MIDNIGHT FROLIC (1921)

OPENING: February 9, 1921; New Amsterdam Theatre Roof
AUTHORS: Ballard MacDonald; music by Harry Carroll
STAGING: Ed Royce
PRINCIPALS: Annette Bade, Edythe Baker, Virginia Bell, the Fairbanks Twins, Eleanor Griffith, Jack Hanley, Herbert Hoey, Bob LaSalle, Kathlene Martyn, Bird Millman, Anna Wheaton

ZIEGFELD MIDNIGHT FROLIC (1921)

OPENING: November 17, 1921; New Amsterdam Theatre Roof
AUTHORS: Lyrics by Gene Buck; music by Dave Stamper
STAGING: Leon Errol
PRINCIPALS: Althea, Dorothy Clarke, Leon Errol, Gloria Foy, Alf P. James, Kitty Kelly, Mary Lewis, Carl Randall, Will Rogers, Muriel Stryker

ZIEGFELD MIDNIGHT FROLIC (1928)

OPENING DATE: December 29, 1928
AUTHORS: Lyrics by Dorothy Fields; music by James McHugh
STAGING: Seymour Felix; later—Sammy Lee
TECHNICAL DIRECTOR: T. B. McDonald
PRINCIPALS: Charlotte Ayers, Maurice Chevalier (beginning February 1929), the Duncan Sisters, Paul Gregory, Irene Healy, Malinoff and Company, Helen Morgan, Lillian Roth, Paul Whiteman and his Orchestra (featured). According to a review of the opening-night performance, Eddie Cantor was in the show.

ZIEGFELD NINE O'CLOCK FROLIC (1918)

OPENING: December 9, 1918; New Amsterdam Theatre Roof
AUTHORS: Lyrics by Gene Buck; music by Dave Stamper
STAGING: Ned Wayburn

Above: The "Metropolitan Handicap" scene in the September 1920 *Midnight Frolic* presented women in racing silks riding fake horses; spectators dressed in fine clothes looked on. Opposite: Kathlene Martyn from England was a *Frolic* singer in 1920 and 1921; she then took over Mary Hay's role in *Sally* before moving to the *Follies*. Martyn worked for Ziegfeld through 1926.

PRINCIPALS: Delyle Alda, Holbrook Blinn, Fannie Brice, Bessie McCoy Davis, Evan Burrows Fontaine, Hal Hixon, Lillian Leitzell, Lillian Lorraine, Bee Palmer, Georgie Price, Yvonne Shelton, Bert Williams

NOTE: a double show was presented for the first time. The *Ziegfeld Nine O'Clock Frolic* was followed by the *Ziegfeld Midnight Frolic*.

ZIEGFELD NINE O'CLOCK FROLIC (1921)
OPENING: February 8, 1921; New Amsterdam Theatre Roof
AUTHORS: Ballard MacDonald; music by Harry Carroll
STAGING: Ed Royce
PRINCIPALS: Virginia Bell, the Fairbanks Twins, Frank Farnum, Eleanor Griffith, Jack Hanley, Herbert Hoey, Kathlene

Martyn, Oscar Shaw, Anna Wheaton, Princess White Deer

ZIEGFELD NINE O'CLOCK REVUE (1920)
OPENING: March 8, 1920; titled "Ziegfeld Girls of 1920"; New Amsterdam Theatre Roof
AUTHORS: Lyrics by Gene Buck; music by Dave Stamper
STAGING: Ned Wayburn
PRINCIPALS: William Blanche, Fannie Brice, the Cameron Sisters, Sybil Carmen, Eleanor Dell, Marcelle Earle, Peggy Eleanore, W. C. Fields, Thomas Handers, Mary Hay, Vanda Hoff, John Price Jones, Allyn King, Lillian Lorraine, Kathlene Martyn, Arthur Milliss, Kathryn Perry, Jessie Reed, Prince Royle, Princess Wah-letka, Florence Ware

HOW ONE SHOW CAME TOGETHER: ZIEGFELD FOLLIES OF 1917

❖

Backdrop used for the "American Eagle" scene in the *Follies of 1917*

Using our general knowledge of how Ziegfeld put together various shows, we have reconstructed a likely scenario of how Ziegfeld, his employees, and his suppliers produced a show, using as a model the 1917 *Follies*. Specific details about the show are drawn from Ned Wayburn's prompt book materials and from programs.

These are steps that Ziegfeld most likely followed in 1917, although in some cases the order may have varied.

CONCEIVE THE SHOW: Ziegfeld conceived the overall thrust and scene ideas sometime during the winter or early spring. He gathered ideas all year long, accumulating material samples, advertisements displaying dresses or accessories that he liked, and possibilities for scenes.

WORK INDIVIDUALLY WITH PRODUCTION HEADS: Once he had devised the general theme, Ziegfeld worked individually with the people in charge of sundry crews and with outside suppliers. In chatting with various people individually, he often sent them in divergent or even contradictory directions, with, for example, the authors discovering that Joseph Urban was working on a backdrop that did not mesh with the content Ziegfeld had asked them to develop.

In 1917, Ziegfeld worked with the following production people and suppliers:

Book and lyrics:	*Gene Buck and George V. Hobart*
Music:	*Raymond Hubbell, Dave Stamper, and Victor Herbert*
General stage director:	*Ned Wayburn*
Stage manager:	*William Schrode*
Wardrobe mistress:	*Ada Barclay*
Business manager:	*Sam Harrison*
Scenic decorations:	*Joseph Urban*
Scene construction:	*T. Bernard McDonald*
Electric effects:	*Ben Beerwald*
Properties:	*John Brunton*
Upholstery:	*Arnold Constable*
Costumes:	*Lady Duff-Gordon, Schneider-Anderson, Callot Seurs (Paris), Bendel*
Wigs:	*Hepner*
Shoes:	*Capezio*
Men's modern clothes:	*Finchley*
Uniforms:	*Ford and Russell Uniform Companies*
Stockings:	*Peck & Peck*
Tights:	*Siegman and Weil*
Men's uniforms:	*Dazian*

PRODUCTION CREW LEADERS DRAFT THEIR PORTIONS OF THE PLAN: It is not known how every one of the principal production people operated, but Joseph Urban did leave a record of his working methods for Ziegfeld shows. Most of his contribution consisted of skillfully painted and proportional "drops" and curtains combined with effective lighting. Urban used broken color: his artists applied color not in flat, mixed washes, but in suitable proportions of pure colors laid side by side in a method called "pointillage." Under the lights, the hues mixed and looked like one shade. As the different rays of light picked out and mixed the colors, they gained vitality. Changes of light could play upon the colors more freely, creating different effects. It was this element of light (not found in easel art), combined with the broken color, that produced such dramatic effects.

Urban's set designs were so superior to anyone else's because of his painstaking methods and great attention to detail.

Sketch ideas: First, Urban sketched his ideas, drawing everything to scale. He created a color key for his craftsmen, which he sent them along with his sketches and the measurements and instructions for the model.

Construct model: Next, the craftsmen, all of whom were trained in

Left: Control panel in the New Amsterdam Theatre where thirteen editions of the *Follies*, including the 1917 show, were staged. Above: Irving Fisher, Allyn King, and Thomas Richards in the "Arabian Night" scene from the *Follies of 1917*

Revised May 31st, 1917.

" ZIEGFELD FOLLIES OF 1917. "

COSTUME PLOT

A c t   I

Scene 1 - "An Arabian Night"- Allyn King (Lucille)
                               Peggy Hopkins

12 Lucille Arabian Maids.

1 - Miss Leeds	7 - Miss Osborne
2 - " Arthur	8 - " Dana
3 - " Tashman	9 - " Hale
4 - " Loftus	10 - " Lang
5 - " Browne	11 - " E. Whitney
6 - " Kern	12 - " MacKenzie

16 Arabian Dancers:

1 - Miss Carmen	9 - Miss Worth
2 - " Delmar	10 - " Perry
3 - " Barnett	11 - " Alexander
4 - " St. Clair	12 - " Dewey
5 - " Wallace	13 - " Earle
6 - " Markle	14 - " Eberts
7 - " Diana Allen	15 - " Walsh
8 - " Orange	16 - " Gardner

Solo Dancer - Miss Doris Lloyd - (Lucille)

"An Arabian Maid"- Miss Elvira Amazar (Prima Donna) (Lucille)

Scene 2 - "Purse Episode"- Miss Allyn King (modern.) (Lucille)
                            (Catlett, Hale, Ostrander, Vokes - Cop
                                                      Hicks - ")

Scene 3 - "Garden of Girls"(from Lucille)

1 - Miss Kern	- - - - - - -	Pansy
2 - " St. Clair		"Forget-me-not"
3 - " Doris Lloyd		Poppy
4 - " P. Hopkins		Cornflower (blue)
5 - " Delmar		Daisy
6 - " L. Tashman		Golden Rod
7 - " Wallace		Violet
8 - " Leeds		Lily
9 - " Browne		Orchid
10 - " Loftus		Rose

- 1 -

" ZIEGFELD FOLLIES OF 1917 "

FRONT LIGHT PLOT

A C T   I

SCENE 1 - Arabian Night.
    White spot on each Arabian Girl.
    "   "   "   announcer
    "   "   "   Mr. Richards
    "   "   "   My Arabian Maid
    "   "   "   Miss King
    "   "   "   Lloyd, dancer.
No.18 Amber Floods.
White on entrances of dancers.

SCENE 2 - Purse Episode
    White spot on Mr. Catlett
    "   "   " Miss King
No. 29 Blue floods.

SCENE 3 - Garden of Girls.
    White spot on dancer
    "   "   " Singer
    "   "   " each girl as they come from trap.
No.18 Floods - 35 blue spot on bubbles blind floods and white
                spot as capsule drop leaves the floor.

SCENE 4 - Episode of the Dog.
    White spot on dog
No. 29 Blue floods.

SCENE 5 - Tennis Episode
    2 No. 8 Straw spots - Characters
    "   8   " floods

SCENE 6 - Follies Rag
    White spot on Singer
    Come on with floods white when dancers enter

SCENE 7 - Grand Central
    1 white spot on Big Dancer
    " floods

Right: The costume plot for the first three scenes in Act One. Far right: Front light plot

European art studios (workshops), constructed a pasteboard model about a foot high. When every detail of the model was complete, they sent it to Urban.

Test model: Urban then used lighting to see whether the model met his conception of the scene. If it did, he approved the model; if it did not, he corrected the color, or rarely, the model's design.

Construct scenery: Once Urban approved the model, the studio work began. The craftsmen built the set, stretched the canvas, and painted scenery. Urban's men used the Continental method of painting the canvas on the floor and walking around on it. They could use longer or shorter brushes and get a firmness of touch and a view of the whole work—unobstructed by a scaffold—not possible the American way (hung vertically on the wall). Also, with the canvas on the floor, the artist could rub paint thoroughly into the canvas's surface.

Stage light rehearsals: When the scenery was complete, Urban would stage "light rehearsals" to be sure the desired effect could be achieved consistently. It was a difficult task for Urban to develop the proper lighting and keep it standard in the many theaters where the production toured.

Using these methods, Urban created scenery that often achieved a three-dimensional effect and a feeling of permanence. Like Ziegfeld, Urban did not spare expense. He used the best materials available. Moreover, he would not sacrifice an effect just to make it easier to move the set on the road.

CONFER WITH PRODUCTION CREW LEADERS: Once individual production chiefs such as Wayburn, Urban, and Buck finished their drafts, Ziegfeld conferred with them about the elements. This was often the point where they discovered the contradictions in Ziegfeld's orders.

INTEGRATE ELEMENTS INTO A WORKING LAY-OUT: Ziegfeld then integrated the elements into an overall working layout that listed the proposed scenes. A plan dated April 30, 1917 (six weeks before opening), had nine scenes in Act One and ten in Act Two. The show ended up with the same number of scenes (nineteen), but Ziegfeld had decided to run eleven in Act One and eight in Act Two. Some titles changed slightly (from "Telephone," for example, to "Episode of the Telephone Wires"), while others changed so drastically that it is no longer evident whether they were dropped or left intact with radically different titles.

CAST THE SHOW: Casting took place at different stages. Some of the principals would have been retained from the previous year through ongoing contracts; scenes would be written specifically for these performers. In other cases, principals would not be identified until just before rehearsals started in late April

```
" ZIEGFELD  FOLLIES  OF  1917 "
                _____

            SWITCHBOARD PLOT

Arabian Night:

    Blue fots full up.
     "   borders two circuits full up.
    Cue when first girls walk down stage amber foots 1/4 up.
     "   "  dancing girls enter - white foots 1/4 up.
    Special border blue full up.


SCENE 2 - Purse Episode
    White foots 3/4 up.
    Special border blue full up - Green 1/2


SCENE 3 - Garden of Girls
    Blue foots full up 2 & 3 border full blue
    Red   "   "   "   "   "   "    red
    Special border Blue
    Cue: when capsule drop flies out with the borders and foots


SCENE 4 - Episode of the Dog.
    White foots 3/4 up.
    Special border Green full.


SCENE 5 - Tennis Episode
    Foots white and amber
    2 & 3 border white
    Special border white


SCENE 6 - Follies Rag
    Blue foots and special border blue


SCENE 7 - Follies Rag - Kirchner Drop.
    Foots and special & 2 & 3 borders white


SCENE 8 - Nothing.
```

```
" ZIEGFELD   FOLLIES   OF   1917 "

            PROPERTY  PLOT
                A C T  I

Scene 1:        Brown ground cloth
                2  8' parrells for table
                3  Large flower vases
                2  Small    "     "
                2  Red tall vases
                6  Gold Cups
                6   "  Plates
                2  Pieces of prop fruit on each plate
                   Large gold table cover
                3  Taborette stools
                1  Kitchen chair (without back)
                6  Large gold cushions

Scene 2:        Man's wallet, Watch, Leather bag of coins
                Horse shoe pin
                Diamond Ring

Scene 3:        Some loose flowers for dancing girl
                Small basket with some seed in it
                1  Lily staff,
                1  Shepherd's crook
                1  Long stemmed silk rose
                2  Mechanical Bubbles
                2  Maskings for Bubbles
                1  Capsule drop

Scene 4:        Small board for "Don" to fall against
                Police signal box

Scene 5:        Tennis cloth down
                2  White benches
                1  Tennis net
                1  Small net
                1  Bananna
                   Rosin
                   Ball of dough
                   Crab net
                   Wooden masking to strike ball against
                   Brown canvas masking

Scene 6.        Rosin
```

Far left: Switchboard plot. Left: Props required for some of the early scenes

and early May. The final cuts for chorus members and showgirls often did not occur until well into the rehearsal phase. Ziegfeld, Buck, and Wayburn did most of the casting for the show. In 1917, Ziegfeld was still selecting the chorus girls himself. He did not like dyed hair and always told the chorus girls to get plenty of rest. He said that "the guys have paid plenty of money to see the show, and they don't want to see tired people."

REFINE MATERIAL: Meanwhile, with a final layout approved, writers and composers created drafts and then worked with Ziegfeld on refining the material. Using the working layout, Ziegfeld, the staff production chiefs, and the suppliers formulated plans, culminating in plot and inventory sheets that are pictured here.

CONDUCT PRELIMINARY REHEARSALS: Rehearsals often overlapped with other aspects such as the writing. When the *Follies* series first started, Ziegfeld was involved virtually from the beginning of the rehearsal each year. Later, in the mid-1920s, with more shows going, he intervened only after rehearsals were well under way.

In 1917, Ned Wayburn staged the *Follies*. In a *New York Sun* article dated June 10, 1917 (two days before the opening), Wayburn described a typical day. He arose at 7:00 A.M., dressed, ate breakfast, and was in his library by 8:00. On the way down-

town, he stopped at his office. From 10:30 A.M. until noon or 12:30, he directed rehearsals. He then conferred about the scenery, wardrobe, and other show matters. From 2:00 to 5:00 P.M., he rehearsed again, usually with five or six principals. After attending more conferences, he sometimes held evening rehearsals that often lasted from 8:00 to 10:00 P.M. and then generally visited one of the other shows on which he was working. Finally, his wife (a former dancer) would arrive to pick him up, and the couple would go for a drive so he could clear his head. After the drive, the Wayburns headed home and to bed.

Known for wearing a monogrammed sweater and a whistle around his neck, Wayburn was a tough taskmaster. Muriel Merrill recalled him telling people: "Walk a circle. I said a circle, not a pretzel! This is terrible." Then he would blow his whistle and say he wanted a particular girl out of the chorus and back on the ferry (to Staten Island).

The chorus generally rehearsed five hours a day—or longer as the opening neared. Once the dancers were familiar with Wayburn's directions, he had them march to the show's music. When the chorus knew the steps and could dance to the music, he worked on dramatic flair and the meaning of the action.

Through the rehearsal phase, Ziegfeld and his core of creative people continued changing the program and the details within scenes. Indecisiveness permeated Ziegfeld's work style, as

13 Arabian Girls:	Individual dresses - "Lucille Costumes" - flesh tights, pink satin shoes.
16 Arabian dancers:	Costumes of black chiffon trimmed gold snakes-headdress of gold and brown veils.
1 "Spirit of Garden"	Costume - dancing dress of different colored chiffon trimmed with flowers.
10 Flower Girls:	Poppy - Cornflower - Lilly - Forget-me-not - Daisy - Orchid - Golden Rod - Rose - Violet - Pansy.
2 "Bubbles":	Flesh silk combinations.
24 "Follies Rag" dancers:	Pink satin dresses and pants, trimmed swansdown and rhinestone ornaments, collar of rhinestones - hat of silver cloth, rose pink opera hose, pink satin shoes.
48 Continental Soldiers:	Blue and gold colored satin coats and pants. Black velvet hats - white silk hose, black pumps with steel buckles.
"North":	White net over green, with trimmings of white fur. Cap of white fur with yellow wing - white hose, white shoes.
"East":	Gray chiffon trimmed pink velvet and rhinestones. Silver cloth hat trimmed pink feathers.
"South":	White crepe, trimmed gold braid, forget-me-nots. Blue pantellettes, white bonnet.
"West":	Pink silk net with flower trimming, gold cloth, long pants - hat of rhinestones.
10 National costumes:	Belgium - Russia - Japan - Italy, Canada, Scotland, Ireland, England, France, America.
9 Grand Central Dancers:	White satin dresses, trimmed with black velvet - hats to match - Black hose and shoes.

"ZIEGFELD FOLLIES OF 1917"
(Cues to ring down and up
also bells for traps)

1. **ARABIAN SCENE:** Close in on last two bars of MissLloyd's dance.

2. **MADISON SQUARE:** (Purse) Take drop away on first note of "Spirit of the Garden" music and give one bell for warning for trap. On first note of Song give 2nd bell to open trap and then 3rd bell to bring trap up. On the first word of the last two lines of the first chorus give 4th bell to take down trap. After 4th bell only give a bell to take trap away but not until girls are off trap. After last girl is up give a bell for them to close trap. On the first note of the last chorus take away Bubble drop. In the middle of last chorus take up your Capsule drop and at end of chorus close in.

3. **SALOON:** (VOKES AND DOG) Take away drop after dog's exit through saloon door and take up drop on first note of Tennis music.

4. **TENNIS** (FIELDS) Close in Yellow C. when Fields and Catlett exit with net. Clear cloth and props and open curtains on first chorus of Follies Rag Song. After girls and Brice exit come in with your Blue Drop for encore. After encore take up your Blue Drop on first note of music going to Grand Central.

5. **GRAND CENTRAL:** Close in with Madison Square drop after Buck Dancers are on. Take up drop on first note of "Hello Dearie" Song.

6. **TELEPHONE:** (Hallor I.V. and on the 1st C.) Take up Tab. on Right. After Hallor and McGowan sing 2nd Chorus together bring tab down slow. Hallor sings 2nd and talks first chorus on last line of first chorus take up tab on left. Hallor and Richards sing last chorus together. Bring tab down slow at end of 2nd Chorus. Hallor exits, then come back with McGowan and they sing one chorus. On their exit close in Yellow Curtains.

Right: Costume list for the chorus girls and dancers. Far right: Curtain cues for stage crew. Opposite, left: A page from the script that leads into the "American Eagle" scene. Opposite, right: A review of the 1917 *Ziegfeld Follies* from *The Dramatic Mirror*

Eddie Cantor observed: "Zieggy's greatest difficulty was to make a decision. . . . Joseph Urban, his scenic creator, told me that Flo was like a man who gazed at a jewelry display in a window, could not decide which stones to buy, so he bought them all. Then, by a process of elimination, he kept two or three stones and threw the rest away." During the final weeks, Ziegfeld and Wayburn added night rehearsals. Scene rehearsals were incorporated the last few nights before opening, but by that point most changes involved refining details. The show usually ran four to five hours on tryout opening night in Atlantic City. (Beginning in 1922, out-of-town tryouts for the *Follies* were eliminated, because of the expense.)

CONDUCT DRESS REHEARSAL WITH ZIEGFELD PRESENT: When Wayburn had rehearsed the show to a certain point, Flo would arrive to begin his review. Eddie Cantor once described how Ziegfeld approached a dress rehearsal:

Ziegfeld removed his coat, and when Ziegfeld removes his coat the serious part of show business begins. He has often worked through a dress rehearsal for a span of twenty hours, starting at two in the afternoon and still going strong the next morning. The theater is empty and a solemn air pervades the darkened orchestra where only the glow of a lighted cigar betrays his presence. . . . Numbers are done over and over again. . . . Spots for certain special-ties are switched and musical cues adjusted. He complains that the finale is too drawn out and the scene in [Act] one, in front of the drop, does not give enough time for putting up the next set. He hardly interferes with the dialogue or comedy scenes, for he has no fixed ideas as to what the audience will like and waits for the public reaction on the road to draw his conclusions. If the costumes don't harmonize with a particular scene according to his notion, they are discarded as so much cloth and that's that. His main concern is ensemble effects and the sweeping impression of the whole. He begins to give instructions to the electricians for lighting of every scene and most of it sounds like deep Greek.

"Blue foots up on dimmer at start of overture," he says, "and white and amber foots up on dimmer at the end. Next scene, all lamps flood until finish, then dim down to blue and white one-quarter up and palm curtains open."

In this fashion are born those color moods which lend the final aura of splendor to the already lavish production.

GO INTO TRYOUTS: During tryouts Ziegfeld and key production people performed the required surgery that trimmed the show back to an acceptable running time—around three

(GEORGE WASHINGTON is revealed Right Center with vision lighting. Vision fades away after his speech)

George Washington

To be prepared for war is one of the most effectual ways of preserving peace.

(ABRAHAM LINCOLN is shown left center with vision lighting. Vision fades away. After this Chiffon drops are lifted in transparency style to reveal the American Eagle center. Then occurs the entrance of the 48 Continentals –(Girl-boy soldiers). Twenty-four from each side. They go through marching revolutions forming three interlocking stars after which they do the manual arms leading to the entrance of President Wilson, the Allies, the Army, Navy, etc., who all salute the American Flag and sing"The Star Spangled Banner."

CHANGE TO:

The Episode of the American Eagle

The March of the Continentals.

The Spirit of the North	Lilyan Tashman
The Spirit of the East	Gladys Loftus
The Spirit of the South	Mary Arthur
The Spirit of the West	Helen Barnes

Resources of the North " " East " " South " " West	By the Children

The Navy	Marion Fairbanks
The Army	Madeline Fairbanks
Belgium	Dorothy Leeds
Russia	Ethel Delmar
Japan	Cecile Markle
Italy	Edythe Whitney
Canada	May Carmen
Scotland	Margaret St. Clair
Ireland	Marie Wallace
England	Peggy Hopkins
France	Doris Lloyd
America	Allyn King

OUR FLAG

OUR NAVY

CURTAIN

NEW PLAYS IN NEW YORK

"ZIEGFELD FOLLIES"

Revue in Two Acts and Twenty Scenes; Book and Lyrics by George V. Hobart and Gene Buck; Music by Raymond Hubbell and Dave Stamper; Patriotic Finale by Victor Herbert.

Principals in cast: Bert Williams, Fannie Brice, Will Rogers, Walter Catlett, William C. Fields, Tom Richards, Irving Fisher, Eddie Cantor, Allyn King, Fred Heider, Russell Vokes, Peggy Hopkins, Helen Barnes, Marion Fairbanks and Madeline Fairbanks.

In the ladder scene she was the girl on the extreme right. She wore white silk trunks and yellow stockings. Vivacious, pretty and defiantly youthful, she was the supreme symbol of Ziegfeldian Folly as New York and the vastnesses beyond the Hudson River have come to know and appreciate it. Don Barclays may talk o' gin and beer, Bert Williamses may croon of domestic belligerency, Will Rogerses may even tell Ford jokes that are really funny, but we who are quartered safe out here in front will pass them up, in a manner of speaking, as essentially non-essentials in favor of that institution—girl.

And with girls this latest edition of the "Follies" is richly and decoratively supplied. Truly this man Ziegfeld has developed acute microscopia. He can detect and pick and hunt down beauty of face and figure to a degree that makes Marc Antony, Henry VIII and Brigham Young appear as indiscriminating college youths. Year after year the matrimonial or the motion picture mart garners the choicest of his crop, but year after year finds him dauntless and determined to show America's inexhaustibility in female beauty.

As the background to the lavish parade of girls, Mr. Ziegfeld has assembled a score of comedians and singers, some of whom appear to distinctive advantage as in the cases of Eddie Cantor and W. C. Fields, while others like Bert Williams are unfortunate in the material provided them. Appalling waste of talent is apparent in the manner in which the great colored comedian has been neglected in late years. Mr. Fields has a highly amusing scene on a tennis court, in which he is assisted most capably by Walter Catlett.

Fannie Brice provides a hilarious moment in a grotesque impersonation of an Egyptian dancer. Will Rogers talks of this and that the while he performs his familiar tricks with the lasso, and a genuine hit was scored by Officer Vokes's dog, Don, in an impersonation of a hopeless inebriate.

Pictorially, this year's "Follies" quite surpass all previous efforts. Joseph Urban, commissioned to design an Oriental setting, has outdone himself in his employment of colors and seemingly massive structures. But while in richness of tone and in suggestion of distance the setting is superb, it, nevertheless, obtrudes upon the players in the foreground. There is no personality definite and dominant enough to stand against it successfully, and therefore most of the fun and satire that had been contrived for the scene went for naught.

George V. Hobart has again furnished the framework of the "Follies," and it must be said that he went about his task too seriously. Here and there are amusing—vastly amusing moments —but they are provided chiefly by the respective players themselves. The best scene from the standpoint of fun represented the temporary makeshift character of Broadway in the vicinity of Times Square and showed Walter Corbett as a visitor from "St. Joe," succumbing in succession to certain well-recognized forms of outlawry. A scene in the Grand Central Station with Bert Williams as a versatile porter proved disappointing, though it did reveal the Fairbanks twins, of motion picture fame, as promising comediennes.

The dancing was arranged by Ned Wayburn and consisted of all varieties, from an ante-bellum buck and wing, performed by a score of people against an alluring background, which represented the Mississippi River by moonlight, to the modern "society" steps.

The music was indistinguishable, but served its purpose. Perhaps, the best number was a Chinese ragtime song, entitled "Chu Chu Chow." A patriotic finale, composed by Victor Herbert, showed skillful maneuvering on the part of the chorus, dressed to represent the forces of the United States passing in review before President Wilson.

---

hours. This revision phase could be chaotic. As the pressure of the New York opening mounted, rehearsals became more intense, occasionally going all night and into the next day.

The principals were acutely aware of the chaos as radical changes were being made (numbers cut and scenes added or dropped). However, chorus members escaped most of the frenzy. Ziegfeld, his director, and the stage manager made decisions among themselves. While many other producers allowed these strategy discussions to be conducted with the whole cast present, Ziegfeld's approach was good for morale because chorus members did not sense all of the "angst" about last-minute changes. By the time they heard of the changes, a new plan had been devised, which Wayburn then explained.

REHEARSE AS NEEDED AFTER THE RUN BEGINS: Once the show started its New York run, rehearsals were held only intermittently, when some phase of the performance deteriorated.

REFINE THE PRODUCTION BASED ON EXPERIENCE WITH AUDIENCES: Programs from different dates during the show's run indicate that changes continued even after the show opened; numbers were rearranged, and some were dropped as cast members left and were replaced.

Schneider-Anderson Co.
16-18 West 46th St.

New York June 13' 1917.

Sold to Ziegfeld Follies, Inc.,
214 West 42d Street, New York City.

48 Colonials	90.00	4320	00
48 Chinese Costumes	55.00	2640	00
18 Blk Silk Combinations	40.00	720	00
9 Cotton Costumes	85.00	765	00
9 Allies	185.00	1665	00
1 "		185	00
16 Orientals	95.00	1520	00
24 Ziegfeld Follies Rag	125.00	3000	00
9 Passenger Costumes	75.00	675	00
4 Costumes, East,West,South North	150.00	600	00
4 Children	30.00	120	00
2 Fan Bearers (Fairbanks Sisters)	55.00	110	00
1 Fan (Peacock)		12	00
1 " (Chinese Scene)		15	00
1 Egyptian Costume (Miss Brice)		125	00
1 Old Fashioned (Miss Brice)		85	00
1 Jet and spangled dress "Our Betters"Miss Brice		210	00
1 Silhouette Miss Maxwell pure silk tights & hat		40	00
1 Nurse costume Miss Hopkins		18	00
54 yds. Tarleton	.15 yd.	8	10
54 yds. Net for Silhouette Scene	2.00	108	00
3 yds. Pink Chiffon for Moon	1.75	5	25
1 Pink Feather		2	50
1 pr. chiffon fancy bloomers hemmed with lace, worn with Callot dress		15	00
		16963	85

A bill from the Schneider-Anderson Co., the maker of many Ziegfeld costumes

Famous as the *Follies* were, remarkably little production material remains available, particularly prompt books. One significant collection of production materials, from the University of Southern California, provides information on how the production crew organized its work. The following photos of prompt book material concentrate on the "Arabian Night" scene that opened and closed the show.

- Alphabetical list of chorus girls showing which scene each girl was to appear in and what her role was. This record allowed Wayburn to keep track of sixty-five chorus girls across nineteen scenes.

- Dance routines for several numbers including the "Ziegfeld Follies Rag."

- Costume inventories for principal ladies, principal men, chorus girls, and dancers. This list indicates that all of the principals had several costume changes, while Allyn King had seven costumes and six changes. The inventory for the chorus reveals why Ziegfeld's costume bills with Lucille and Schneider-Anderson ran so high. There were six different costume categories just for the "Arabian Night" scene, and one of those categories called for individual Lucille designs for twelve Arabian girls.

- Costume plot that was revised May 31. It shows the production taking shape because now there are names for the twelve maids and sixteen dancers.

- Cues on when to ring the curtain down and up indicate the detail work that it takes to coordinate the fine points in a production.

- Ziegfeld's attention to lighting is seen in the intricately detailed plans that are shown in these five sub-elements:

  ☐ Table of colors for the lights

  ☐ Front light plot

  ☐ Swinging bridge light plot

  ☐ Stage and truck lights plot

  ☐ Switchboard plot

- The Ziegfeld touch is evident in the property plot with its attention to specifics, calling for red vases and gold cups, plates, and cushions.

- Working script (dialogue and photo of eagle scene). The production crew also assembled prompt books with the script and photos of the backdrops related to each scene. The dialogue was in black text while the stage directions were typed in red. The photo at the beginning of each scene, such as this patriotic number with the painting of the American eagle, helped the crew visualize the scene.

ZIEGFELD SHOWS
A BRIEF CHRONOLOGY

SHOW TITLE	PERFORMANCE DATES	THEATER
A PARLOR MATCH	*September 21–October 31, 1896*	Herald Square
LA POUPÉE	*October 21–29, 1897*	Lyric
A GAY DECEIVER	*February 21–26, 1898*	Harlem Opera House (tour)
THE FRENCH MAID	*September 26–October 1, 1898*	Herald Square
THE TURTLE	*September 3, 1898–January 28, 1899* *April 23–29, 1899*	Manhattan Grand Opera House (tour)
MLLE. FIFI	*February 1–April 22, 1899* *April 24–29, 1899*	Manhattan Harlem Opera House (tour)
THE MANICURE	*April 24, 1899*	Manhattan
PAPA'S WIFE	*November 13, 1899–March 31, 1900*	Manhattan
THE LITTLE DUCHESS	*October 14, 1901–February 8, 1902* *February 10–15, 1902*	Casino Harlem Opera House (tour)
THE RED FEATHER	*November 9, 1903–January 2, 1904*	Lyric
MAM'SELLE NAPOLEON	*December 8, 1903–January 16, 1904*	Knickerbocker
HIGGLEDY-PIGGLEDY	*October 20, 1904–March 25, 1905*	Weber Music Hall
THE PARISIAN MODEL	*November 27, 1906–June 29, 1907*	Broadway
FOLLIES OF 1907 (1ST ED.)	*June 8–August 24, 1907* *August 26–September 14, 1907*	Jardin de Paris (New York Roof) Jardin de Paris (New York Roof)
THE SOUL KISS	*January 28–May 23, 1908*	New York
FOLLIES OF 1908 (2ND)	*June 15–September 5, 1908* *September 7–October 3, 1908*	Jardin de Paris (New York Roof) New York
MISS INNOCENCE	*November 30, 1908–May 1, 1909*	New York
FOLLIES OF 1909 (3RD)	*June 14–September 11, 1909*	Jardin de Paris (New York Roof)
FOLLIES OF 1910 (4TH)	*June 20–September 3, 1910*	Jardin de Paris (New York Roof)
THE PINK LADY	*March 13–December 9, 1911*	New Amsterdam
ZIEGFELD FOLLIES OF 1911 (5TH)	*June 26–September 2, 1911*	Jardin de Paris (New York Roof)
OVER THE RIVER	*January 8–April 20, 1912*	Globe
A WINSOME WIDOW	*April 11–September 7, 1912*	Moulin Rouge (New York)
ZIEGFELD FOLLIES OF 1912 (6TH)	*October 21, 1912–January 4, 1913*	Moulin Rouge (New York)

SHOW TITLE	PERFORMANCE DATES	THEATER
ZIEGFELD FOLLIES OF 1913 (7TH)	*June 16–September 6, 1913*	New Amsterdam
ZIEGFELD FOLLIES OF 1914 (8TH)	*June 1–September 5, 1914*	New Amsterdam
ZIEGFELD MIDNIGHT FROLIC	*January 5, 1915*	New Amsterdam Roof
ZIEGFELD FOLLIES OF 1915 (9TH)	*June 21–September 18, 1915*	New Amsterdam
ZIEGFELD MIDNIGHT FROLIC	*August 23, 1915*	New Amsterdam Roof
ZIEGFELD MIDNIGHT FROLIC	*January 24, 1916*	New Amsterdam Roof
ZIEGFELD FOLLIES OF 1916 (10TH)	*June 12–September 16, 1916*	New Amsterdam
ZIEGFELD MIDNIGHT FROLIC	*October 2, 1916*	New Amsterdam Roof
THE CENTURY GIRL	*November 6, 1916–April 28, 1917*	Century
MIDNIGHT REVUE	*January 18, 1917*	Cocoanut Grove (Century Roof)
ZIEGFELD MIDNIGHT FROLIC	*April 24, 1917*	New Amsterdam Roof
ZIEGFELD FOLLIES OF 1917 (11TH)	*June 12–September 16, 1917*	New Amsterdam
RESCUING ANGEL	*October 8–November 3, 1917*	Hudson
MISS 1917	*November 5, 1917–January 12, 1918*	Century
ZIEGFELD MIDNIGHT FROLIC	*December 29, 1917*	New Amsterdam Roof
ZIEGFELD MIDNIGHT FROLIC	*April 24, 1918*	New Amsterdam Roof
ZIEGFELD FOLLIES OF 1918 (12TH)	*June 18–September 14, 1918*	New Amsterdam
BY PIGEON POST	*November 25–December 14, 1918*	George M. Cohan
ZIEGFELD NINE O'CLOCK FROLIC	*December 9, 1918*	New Amsterdam Roof
ZIEGFELD MIDNIGHT FROLIC	*December 9, 1918*	New Amsterdam Roof
ZIEGFELD FOLLIES OF 1919 (13TH)	*June 16–August 12, 1919* *September 10–December 6, 1919*	New Amsterdam New Amsterdam
ZIEGFELD MIDNIGHT FROLIC	*October 2, 1919*	New Amsterdam Roof
CAESAR'S WIFE	*November 24, 1919–January 31, 1920*	Liberty
ZIEGFELD NINE O'CLOCK REVUE	*March 8, 1920*	New Amsterdam Roof
ZIEGFELD MIDNIGHT FROLIC	*March 15, 1920*	New Amsterdam Roof
ZIEGFELD MIDNIGHT FROLIC	*September 2, 1920*	New Amsterdam Roof
ZIEGFELD FOLLIES OF 1920 (14TH)	*June 22–October 16, 1920*	New Amsterdam
SALLY	*December 21, 1920–April 22, 1922*	New Amsterdam
ZIEGFELD NINE O'CLOCK FROLIC	*February 8, 1921*	New Amsterdam Roof
ZIEGFELD MIDNIGHT FROLIC	*February 9, 1921*	New Amsterdam Roof
ZIEGFELD FOLLIES OF 1921 (15TH)	*June 21–October 1, 1921*	Globe
THE INTIMATE STRANGERS	*November 7, 1921–January 21, 1922*	Henry Miller
ZIEGFELD MIDNIGHT FROLIC	*November 17, 1921*	New Amsterdam Roof
ZIEGFELD FROLIC	*January 10, 1922*	Tour only
ZIEGFELD FOLLIES OF 1922 (16TH)	*June 5, 1922–June 23, 1923*	New Amsterdam
ROSE BRIAR	*December 25, 1922–March 10, 1923*	Empire
ZIEGFELD FOLLIES OF 1923 (17TH, SUMMER)	*June 25–September 15, 1923*	New Amsterdam

SHOW TITLE	PERFORMANCE DATES	THEATER
ZIEGFELD FOLLIES OF 1923 (18TH)	*October 20, 1923–May 10, 1924*	New Amsterdam
KID BOOTS	*December 31, 1923–August 30, 1924*	Earl Carroll
	September 1, 1924–February 21, 1925	Selwyn
ZIEGFELD FOLLIES OF 1924 (19TH)	*June 24–October 25, 1924*	New Amsterdam
ZIEGFELD FOLLIES OF 1924 (19TH, FALL)	*October 30, 1924–March 7, 1925*	New Amsterdam
ANNIE DEAR	*November 4, 1924–January 31, 1925*	Times Square
THE COMIC SUPPLEMENT	*January 9–February 1925*	Tryouts
LOUIE THE 14TH	*March 3–December 5, 1925*	Cosmopolitan
ZIEGFELD FOLLIES OF 1925 (19TH)	*March 10–July 4, 1925*	New Amsterdam
ZIEGFELD FOLLIES OF 1925 (20TH, SUMMER)	*July 6–September 19, 1925*	New Amsterdam
NO FOOLIN' (ZIEGFELD AMERICAN REVUE OF 1926) TOUR NAME: ZIEGFELD FOLLIES OF 1926 (20TH ED.; ACTUALLY 20TH YEAR)	*June 24–September 25, 1926*	Globe
BETSY	*December 28, 1926–January 29, 1927*	New Amsterdam
RIO RITA	*February 2–December 24, 1927*	Ziegfeld
	December 26, 1927–March 10, 1928	Lyric
	March 12–April 7, 1928	Majestic
ZIEGFELD FOLLIES OF 1927 (21ST)	*August 16, 1927–January 7, 1928*	New Amsterdam
SHOW BOAT	*December 27, 1927–May 4, 1929*	Ziegfeld
ROSALIE	*January 10–October 27, 1928*	New Amsterdam
THE THREE MUSKETEERS	*March 13–December 22, 1928*	Lyric
WHOOPEE	*December 4, 1928–November 23, 1929*	New Amsterdam
ZIEGFELD MIDNIGHT FROLIC	*December 29, 1928*	New Amsterdam Roof
SHOW GIRL	*July 2–October 5, 1929*	Ziegfeld
BITTER SWEET	*November 5, 1929–February 15, 1930*	Ziegfeld
	February 17–March 22, 1930	Shubert
SIMPLE SIMON	*February 18–June 14, 1930*	Ziegfeld
SMILES	*November 18, 1930–January 10, 1931*	Ziegfeld
ZIEGFELD FOLLIES OF 1931 (NO EDITION NUMBER; 22ND YEAR OF SERIES)	*July 1–November 21, 1931*	Ziegfeld
HOT-CHA!	*March 8–June 18, 1932*	Ziegfeld
SHOW BOAT REVIVAL	*May 19–October 22, 1932*	Casino

Follies After Ziegfeld's Death

ZIEGFELD FOLLIES OF 1934	*January 4–June 9, 1934*	Winter Garden
ZIEGFELD FOLLIES OF 1936	*January 30–May 10, 1936*	Winter Garden
	September 14–December 19, 1936	Winter Garden
ZIEGFELD FOLLIES OF 1943	*April 1, 1943–July 22, 1944*	Winter Garden
ZIEGFELD FOLLIES OF 1957	*March 1–June 15, 1957*	Winter Garden

BIOGRAPHIES OF ZIEGFELD PEOPLE

❖ FRED AND ADELE ASTAIRE

were born Fred and Adele Austerlitz in Omaha, Nebraska—she in 1898 and he eighteen months later in 1899. He began to study ballet at age four, while Adele was already an accomplished dancer. Their mother took them to Ned Wayburn's dance school in New York, and by the time Fred was seven, he and his sister had an act.

The Astaires danced in vaudeville until their Broadway debut in *Over the Top* (1917). They starred in twenty Broadway musicals during the 1920s and appeared in *Smiles* and then in *Band Wagon* (1931), their last Broadway show together. In 1932, Adele retired to marry Lord Charles Cavendish, a wealthy member of the English aristocracy, who died shortly before World War II. In 1947, she married Kingman Douglas, who was from an old Chicago family. She died in 1981.

Fred teamed with *Follies* star Claire Luce in *Gay Divorce* (1932), his last stage musical. (The show was later made into a film and retitled *Gay Divorcée* starring Astaire and Ginger Rogers.) In 1933, he made his first picture, with Joan Crawford and Clark Gable. Astaire choreographed his own dance routines. From 1940 on, he became one of Hollywood's most famous names. In 1949, Astaire was given an honorary Oscar for his musical contributions. He received a Life Achievement Award in 1981 from the American Film Institute.

Astaire had two children and a stepson from his marriage (1933–54) to Phyllis Livingston Porter, who died in 1954. In 1980 (at age eighty-one) he married thirty-five-year-old former jockey Robyn Smith. He died in 1987.

❖ AUNT JEMIMA,

an Italian-American whose real name was Tess Gardella, was born in Pennsylvania around 1898. After her miner-father died, she moved to New York and sang at political rallies, dances, and Chinatown nightclubs before entering vaudeville, where she wore blackface and changed her name to Aunt Jemima. As a novice vaudevillian, she sang before the feature film started but was so popular that she had to ask the audience to stop applauding and watch the film.

Aunt Jemima appeared in George White's *Scandals* in 1921 and in 1922 played the Palace and the Hippodrome. In theater, she was best-known as Queenie in *Show Boat*. Aunt Jemima left *Show Boat* in 1930 to return to vaudeville. She died in January 1950.

❖ JAMES BARTON

was born in 1890 in Gloucester, New Jersey. He made his first stage appearance at age two in his parents' arms. At age four he debuted in vaudeville. Barton was in stock and repertory for several years before making his Broadway debut in *The Passing Show* (1919). He was the featured comedian in *No Foolin'*. After that show, Barton was in several revues and musicals and performed in vaudeville.

Famous for his drunk act, Barton had a gravel voice and a fighter's punched-in face. In 1934, he took over the role of Jeeter Lester in *Tobacco Road*, playing it for over five years. He had several failures before his success in the *Ice Man Cometh* (1946). Barton returned to musicals with *Paint Your Wagon* (1951) and was a character actor in several films. He died in 1962.

❖ LINA BASQUETTE

was born Lena Baskette in 1907 and grew up in California. As a young child, she studied with ballet masters. At age eight, she danced at the World's Fair in a Victrola advertisement. She attended a convent school through the tenth grade.

In 1916, Basquette was signed to a six-year contract with Universal Pictures to dance in a series of film featurettes. Billed as "The Baby Pavlova," she also appeared in feature films.

Basquette went to New York in 1923 to perform in a musical. When Mary Eaton left the 1923 *Ziegfeld Follies* to co-star in *Kid Boots*, the sixteen-year-old Basquette replaced her as featured dancer. Basquette danced in the 1924 *Follies* and in *Louie the 14th*. While still in *Louie*, she performed in the 1925 *Follies* for about a month before leaving to marry Sam Warner.

Warner and Basquette had a daughter in 1926, the year before Warner died. His twenty-year-old widow received little of his estate, and she allowed Harry Warner and his wife to become her child's guardians. The next fifteen years were a tumultuous time for Basquette. She failed in her efforts to regain custody of her daughter and attempted suicide. Basquette now had difficulty getting good film roles; she made *The Godless Girl* (1929) for Cecil B. DeMille as well as fifty other films, but few were notable.

Basquette had a son in 1934, at which time her then-husband, Teddy Hayes, authorized a tubal ligation while she was under anesthesia.

Basquette's film career ended in 1943. At age forty-two she started training Great Dane show dogs. She closed her kennels in 1975 and moved to Wheeling, West Virginia, where she still resides. Currently she writes a column for *Kennel Review* and is in demand as a professional dog-show judge. Basquette had seven husbands and numerous affairs but has lived alone for many years. Now in her eighties, she still drives to dog shows around the country.

❖ NORA BAYES,

born Leonora Goldberg in
1880, adopted an Irish name
when she began singing Irish
ballads. In 1899 she debuted in
Chicago vaudeville. Al Fields
was her partner and manager
until Bayes left him to team
with Jack Norworth, whom she
married (her second marriage)
in 1908; Bayes and Norworth
worked together until their
divorce in February 1913.
Ziegfeld hired Bayes for the
1907 *Follies* at a starting salary
of $75 a week. She was in and
out of vaudeville and the *Follies*
but appeared in every *Follies*
between 1907 and 1910 for a
portion of the run. In 1910
Bayes and Norworth appeared
in *The Jolly Bachelors*, where
Bayes introduced the song
"Has Anyone Here Seen
Kelly?" After her divorce from
Norworth, Bayes returned to
vaudeville and also appeared in
several musicals through the
early 1920s. A theater named in
her honor opened in 1918.

Her health began to
deteriorate in 1920, and she
became increasingly
temperamental, sometimes
telling stories about her
children instead of singing. Her
career slumped, but she made a
comeback. When she died in
1928, she was earning $5,000 a
week.

Bayes was known for her
ability to put over a song. One
of her many hits was "Shine
On, Harvest Moon," from the
Follies of 1908, a song whose
lyrics she and Norworth wrote.
Unfortunately, the two never
recorded this song, nor did
Bayes record any *Follies* songs.
She is famous for singing
Norworth's "Take Me Out to

Fannie Brice in a scene from the *Follies of 1910*.
She made her first *Follies* appearance that year and was a hit.

the Ball Game" and "Just Like
a Gypsy." Her rendition of
"Over There" was the biggest
seller during World War I.

Bayes wore extravagant
clothes and had a rivalry with
Eva Tanguay. Neither woman
would perform in a gown worth
less than $500, and their
dresses often cost $2,000 or
more. Bayes was married five

times and had three adopted
children. She died of cancer at
age forty-eight.

❖ IRVING BERLIN,

born Israel Baline on May 11,
1888, in a Russian ghetto, came
to the United States in 1892
and lived on New York's East
Side. When Berlin was eight,
his father died, so Berlin had to

quit school and work. At
fourteen he became a singing
waiter in the Bowery. He
earned little until he became
assistant to Blind Sol, a noted
Bowery singer. When Berlin
became well-known among the
area cafés, he left Blind Sol to
sing alone and to plug songs for
a music publisher. Berlin wrote
songs using an old battered
piano in one of the Bowery
cafés. Soon his compositions
began to earn money, and by
1912 he was becoming
recognized.

Berlin wrote music for
Ziegfeld's *Century Girl* and for
the *Follies* of 1919, 1920, and
1927. Years earlier his "By the
Light of the Silvery Moon" had
been interpolated in the *Follies
of 1909* and become a hit.
Likewise, many of his other
songs not written for the *Follies*
were popularized in that revue
series. Two of his biggest
Follies hits were "A Pretty Girl
Is Like a Melody" and
"Shaking the Blues Away."

Berlin produced *The
Music Box Revue* (1921–23 and
1925) with close friend Sam
Harris. After a creative "dry
spell," Berlin again began
turning out popular songs and
writing scores for Hollywood
films. Under a special
arrangement—which earned
him several million dollars—
Berlin's salary included a
percentage of the film's
earnings. The royalties for
"Cheek to Cheek" from *Top
Hat* (1935) gave him $250,000.

He also wrote songs for
Follow the Fleet (1936), *On the
Avenue* (1937), *Carefree* (1938),
and *Second Fiddle* (1939). He
composed "God Bless
America" for a 1917 show but
did not use it until World War
II, when it was voted best song

of 1940. He wrote and sang in *This Is the Army* (1942), which was later made into a movie. The show toured the war fronts, raising over $10 million for the Army Relief Fund. General Marshall awarded Berlin the Medal of Merit for his efforts.

Among his many hit compositions were "White Christmas," "Easter Parade," and "Blue Skies," first performed in Ziegfeld's *Betsy*. In 1947 *Annie Get Your Gun* netted Berlin $2,500 a week in royalties.

Berlin could not read or write music and played the piano only in F-sharp major, so he had a special piano made with a lever under the keyboard that enabled him to transpose into any key. Usually he would type the lyrics with one finger and then reread them until he got a melody. When the melody was ready, Berlin played it for his musical secretary who wrote it down. The secretary played the song—ten, twenty times, if necessary—as Berlin made revisions.

In 1912, Berlin married Dorothy Goetz, sister of Broadway producer Ray Goetz. Shortly after they married, Dorothy died of typhoid fever she had contracted on their honeymoon. Years later, Berlin fell in love with Ellin Mackay, heiress to $30 million. Her father, Clarence Mackay, head of the Postal Telegraph and member of the Social Register, threatened to disinherit his daughter if she married Berlin. Nevertheless, they wed on January 4, 1926.

When Berlin celebrated his one-hundredth birthday in 1988, he was still playing the piano and painting. His wife, a novelist and short story writer, died in August 1988; the couple had been married sixty-two years and had three daughters. Berlin lived in his New York City townhouse until his death at age 101 in September 1989.

❖ JULES BLEDSOE

was born in Waco, Texas, in 1898. He attended Central Texas College; Bishop College; Virginia Union University; and Columbia University. According to one source, Bledsoe went to Columbia to study medicine and was singing in the glee club when he was advised to turn professional. Bledsoe received a Bachelor of Music degree from the Chicago Musical College, formerly run by Ziegfeld's father, in 1918 and his Bachelor of Arts the following year. He studied voice in New York, Rome, and Paris and made his professional singing debut in 1924.

Bledsoe appeared in three Broadway shows and was a concert soloist in Boston before creating the role of Joe in *Show Boat*. In 1932 he was in the Cleveland production of *Voodoo King*. He then turned to grand opera, performing with the Metropolitan Opera, several European companies, and a number of Los Angeles opera groups. Additionally, he gave many concert-hall recitals and was in vaudeville for a time. He also composed music, including an African suite for violin and orchestra. During his career Bledsoe sang "Old Man River" more than 3,600 times. Shortly before his death, he had toured Army camps to promote war bonds. He died in 1943 after suffering a cerebral hemorrhage.

Elizabeth Brice was a principal singer in the 1912 and 1913 *Follies*.

❖ ELIZABETH BRICE

was born Bessie Shaler in Findlay, Ohio, around 1885. She grew up in Toledo, where she studied dance and elocution. She was a chorus girl in her first Broadway show, *The Chinese Honeymoon* (1906).

Brice danced and acted in several musicals between 1906 and 1910, including *The Motor Girl* (1909) and *The Jolly Bachelor* (1910). In 1910 she teamed with Charles King, and the two did exhibition ballroom dancing and musicals, including

A Winsome Widow and *Miss 1917.* Brice was also in the 1912 and 1913 *Ziegfeld Follies.* During World War I she entertained American troops in France. She retired in the early 1920s and died in 1965.

❖ FANNIE BRICE,

born Fannie Borach on New York's Lower East Side in 1891, made her stage debut at age fourteen in Brooklyn during amateur night at Keeney's Theater. She then worked in burlesque halls until 1910 when Ziegfeld asked to see her. When he asked Brice how old she was, she told him she was seventeen when she signed her current exclusive eight-year contract. Technically Brice's current contract was illegal, so Ziegfeld signed her for $75 a week the first year and $100 the next year. Brice was so excited about her contract that she showed it to everyone. After she wore out eight contracts showing it around, Ziegfeld refused to give her another one.

Brice performed in seven *Follies* between 1910 and 1923 (1910, 1911, 1916, 1917, 1921, 1922, and 1923) and in several *Midnight Frolic* editions (1915 to 1921). Brice was then in the *Music Box Revue* (1924) and toured in vaudeville (1925–26). She was also in a few Broadway shows and in movies, including *The Great Ziegfeld* (1936) and *The Ziegfeld Follies* (1946). Following Ziegfeld's death, Brice starred in the Shubert-produced *Ziegfeld Follies* (1934 and 1936). She first appeared as Baby Snooks in the 1934 *Follies.*

Brice's radio career started in 1932 but really took off in 1936, after she appeared as Baby Snooks. Her Baby Snooks character was on the radio almost continuously until 1948. In 1944 Brice got her own half-hour show on CBS and earned $6,000 a week.

Brice had her brief first marriage annulled. Then, from 1918 to 1927, she was married to Nicky Arnstein and had two children. In 1929 she married showman Billy Rose, whom she divorced nine years later. According to Billy Rose, Fannie told him "she married Frank White, the barber, because he smelled so good; she married Nicky Arnstein because he looked so good; and she married me because I thought so good." In the 1920s, Brice changed her name from "Fannie" to "Fanny." She eventually gave up performing for art collecting, dress designing, and interior decorating. She was fifty-nine when she died in 1951, five days after suffering a stroke. The films *Funny Girl* (1968) and *Funny Lady* (1975), both starring Barbra Streisand, were based on Brice's life.

❖ LOUISE BROOKS

was born Mary Louise Brooks in 1906 in a small Kansas town. The family moved to Wichita, where she took dance lessons. At age fifteen, Brooks went to New York to study dance with Ted Shawn, Ruth St. Denis, and Martha Graham. She went on tour with the Denishawn Dancers in late 1922 and danced with them until late 1924, when she became a chorus girl in *George White's Scandals.* She then danced in Ziegfeld's *Louie the 14th* when it opened in Washington, D.C. Brooks moved to the 1925 *Follies,* and in the summer edition did a specialty dance

with Lina Basquette. She stayed with the *Follies* until September and then went into the movie *The American Venus.* Although she dreamed of becoming a great dancer, Brooks signed a five-year movie contract with Paramount.

An iconoclast, Brooks was unpopular in Hollywood and did not bother to hide her dislike of the place. She became well-known for her silent films and made twenty-four movies, her best two in Germany. Brooks's last movie was *Overland Stage Raiders* (1938) with John Wayne; after that she left Hollywood because she could not get good roles and was bored with doing the same thing.

Brooks had numerous affairs with wealthy men but saved nothing and was often broke. Over the years she was in a successful dance act, ran a dance studio, and tried being a sales clerk but never stayed employed long. In the 1950s, Brooks began writing for film periodicals. She also devoted herself to painting. In 1982, she wrote the book *Lulu in Hollywood.*

From 1926 to 1928, Brooks was married to director Eddie Sutherland. She married wealthy Chicago playboy Deering Davis in 1933, but left him six months later. (They divorced in early 1938.) Brooks died of a heart attack in 1985, at age seventy-eight.

❖ GENE BUCK

was born in Detroit in 1885. When he was two years old, his father died, leaving the family poor. He attended the Detroit Academy of Art for two years before working as a bank messenger. Buck left the bank

to design sheet music covers for a stationery company. The covers had been in black and white until Buck started creating color poster-like covers. After creating over five thousand designs, Buck went blind for several months, apparently due to retinal ulcers. When he regained his sight, he went to New York. To earn money, he wrote jingles and jokes for weeklies and then decided to become a lyricist. He teamed with Dave Stamper for their first song, "Daddy Has a Sweetheart and Mother Is Her Name."

Buck's song was added to the *Follies of 1912.* He soon became Ziegfeld's right-hand man and talent scout. Buck was responsible for bringing Ed Wynn, Will Rogers, John Steele, and W. C. Fields to the *Follies,* but his biggest discovery was set designer Joseph Urban. Buck dragged Ziegfeld to the Park Theatre to see *The Garden of Paradise* (1914) even though the show was a flop so that the producer could see the beautiful scenery that Urban had designed.

While Buck worked under Ziegfeld, he collaborated with many composers, but Stamper was his most frequent associate. Some of Buck's most famous songs were "Hello, Frisco," "Tulip Time," "'Neath the South Sea Moon," and "Lovely Little Melody." Buck and Stamper wrote for most editions of the *Midnight Frolic* and for many *Follies.* Buck worked for Ziegfeld from 1911 through 1926 and then again in 1931. Between 1927 and 1931, he produced musicals; after 1931 he worked on ASCAP activities.

Buck was a co-founder of

the American Society of Composers, Authors, and Publishers (ASCAP) and was its president from 1924 to 1941. He was also president of the Catholic Actors Guild, a philanthropist, and frequent master of ceremonies and speaker for charity events. He was married and had two sons. He died in 1957 at age seventy-one.

❖ **BUCK AND BUBBLES**
were a black team who played the piano and tap danced. Buck (Ford Lee Washington) was nine and Bubbles (John W. Sublett) was thirteen when they teamed up in Louisville, Kentucky. After a few years together, they got their big break when a theater manager who had seen their act at a party asked them to replace a vaudeville act that had not gone over well. No blacks had ever performed on that stage, so the men wore burnt cork and gloves to conceal their race. When the vaudeville show ended, Buck and Bubbles were signed by a touring company. Buck was so young that his high school principal made Buck's mother name Bubbles his legal guardian before letting him out of school.

In 1919, Buck and Bubbles made their first New York appearance. They were such a hit that a few weeks later they were playing the Palace. The team soon became vaudeville headliners. (They appeared in blackface only in their hometown of Louisville.) In 1920, the team was in George White's *Scandals*.

According to Bubbles, around 1919 or 1920 they met with Ziegfeld and Gene Buck looking for work and were

asked if they were still under contract. When Bubbles said yes, they were told to come back when their contract was up. A dozen years later, they were principals in the 1931 *Follies*.

After the *Follies*, Buck and Bubbles returned to vaudeville and made occasional appearances at fairs and circuses. They were in *Blackbirds of 1930* and *Porgy and Bess* (1935), where Bubbles was a hit singing Gershwin's songs. (Bubbles also did some operettas.) Additionally, the team made three feature films and a series of shorts. Buck died in 1955. Bubbles continued to perform during the 1960s and died around 1980.

❖ **EDDIE CANTOR**
was born Isadore Iskowitch on New York's Lower East Side in 1892. As a teenager, Cantor did impersonations on amateur night and then joined a touring burlesque company. After the show folded, he returned to New York's Coney Island as a singing waiter in a restaurant where Jimmy Durante was the piano player.

Cantor first worked on Broadway as a general stage hand for a juggling team. He got a break when the act needed someone to carry a plate on stage. Cantor drew a laugh and was made a regular part of the act. He went on to vaudeville in 1912.

Ziegfeld hired Cantor for the *Midnight Frolic* in 1916. In 1917 Cantor debuted in the *Follies*. He was in the 1918 and 1919 *Follies* and in several more *Frolic* editions. After a falling out with Ziegfeld over the actors' strike in 1919, Cantor quit the *Follies*, but the two men

stayed in touch. Cantor made a surprise appearance in the *Follies of 1920* but left after the first week because he wanted better material.

Cantor returned to vaudeville in 1923. In June, he was added to the cast of the *Follies* summer edition. He also starred in the 1927 *Follies* and two hit musicals for Ziegfeld, *Kid Boots* and *Whoopee*. When Cantor started working for Ziegfeld his salary was $150 per week; later he made as much as $5,000 per week. In *Kid Boots* he earned 10 percent of the gross receipts.

During the 1920s, Cantor moved successfully from the stage to movies, making more than a dozen films. Radio, however, brought Cantor his biggest success. The first of the great vaudeville stars to make it in this medium, Cantor had appeared on radio as early as 1921; however, it was when he appeared on Rudy Vallee's *Fleischmann Hour* in 1931 that his radio career took off. Cantor soon got his own show, which aired until 1934. In 1935, he toured overseas and then started another radio show that ran until 1938. Although he was blacklisted in 1939 for calling United States officials Fascists, by the fall of 1940 his show was back on NBC. Cantor remained on the air until 1949. The next year he went on television with *The Colgate Comedy Hour*. He also wrote several books—about his life and career, about Ziegfeld, and about *Follies* stars.

Cantor was known for his charitable work; at the end of his radio broadcasts, he always plugged his favorite causes. In 1944, he raised $40 million in a twenty-four-hour marathon for

war bonds. He helped create the March of Dimes and was a leading spokesman in Jewish affairs. In 1956 Cantor received an Academy Award for "distinguished service to the film industry." President Johnson awarded him the United States Service Medal in 1964 for his humanitarian work.

He and his wife, Ida, married in 1914 and had five daughters. Cantor died in 1964 in Beverly Hills.

❖ **FRANK CARTER,**
born around 1888, was eight years old when he began passing out programs in a Kansas City vaudeville theater. If a child was needed in the last act of a show, Carter would sometimes get the part. He joined a carnival when he was sixteen and performed a daredevil act, diving ninety feet from the tent's main pole into a bathtub-size pool twice a day for over a year until he missed his mark and cracked his skull. After three weeks immobilized in the hospital, he recovered and rejoined the circus—as a ticket seller.

He barely eked out a living for the next couple of years. Then he went to Chicago where he got a job in a movie house. Carter would sing and dance at the end of each reel, often changing his act twenty times a day. After two weeks, at $12 a week, he realized he was drawing a bigger crowd than the movie was. He moved on to a one week's singing engagement that launched a new career. Carter worked his way into Hammerstein's vaudeville house and was later booked in London. He toured Europe and the Orient for four years. In 1914, he returned to the United States, where he toured the vaudeville circuit and performed in Shubert shows. While working at the Winter Garden Theatre, he met Marilyn Miller, who was nearly twelve years his junior.

Ziegfeld hired Carter for the *Midnight Frolic* in 1917 and 1918. Carter and Miller both appeared in the 1918 *Follies*, and their romance blossomed. The two married in May 1919, against Ziegfeld's wishes. After their marriage, Ziegfeld fired Carter from the 1919 *Follies* tryouts. Carter then went to work in *See Saw* (1919), a musical comedy he took on the road. After a performance in Wheeling, West Virginia, he left for Philadelphia to see his wife, who was on tour with the *Follies*. In Maryland his speeding car, a new Packard, missed a sharp curve, skidded into an embankment, and overturned. Carter died instantly of a skull fracture; he was thirty-two.

❖ CARUS, EMMA:

the daughter of a prima donna, singer/comedienne Carus was born in Berlin in 1879. At age six, she was singing in public. Although she was a talented singer, Carus turned to comedy because she was overweight and not particularly attractive. In 1894 Carus debuted on the New York stage in a musical comedy. Between 1900 and 1911 she was in several musical comedies. Carus was a featured singer in the *Follies of 1907* and also debuted in vaudeville that year. After 1915 Carus appeared only in vaudeville. She died in 1927.

❖ WALTER CATLETT

was born in San Francisco in 1889. After several years of working in troupes on the West Coast he began a long career as a vaudeville comedian. Between 1910 and 1930, he was in many musicals, often in "wise-guy" roles, wearing glasses and chomping a cigar.

Catlett was in only one edition of the *Follies* (1917) but appeared in Ziegfeld's *Miss 1917, Sally,* and *Rio Rita*. He left the stage for movies. He made over twenty films between 1924 and 1956, including *Bringing Up Baby* (1938), *Yankee Doodle Dandy* (1942), and *Look for the Silver Lining* (1949). He died in California in 1960.

❖ INA CLAIRE

was born Ina Fagan in Washington, D.C., in 1895. An expert dancer, she was in many amateur productions before entering vaudeville in 1905 as a singing mimic. In 1911, she debuted in musical comedy. She then played the lead in *The Quaker Girl* (1911) and in the London version of *The Girl from Utah* (1913). After several years in London, Claire returned to New York.

Claire danced and did impersonations in the *Follies* (1915 and 1916) and the *Midnight Frolic*. By 1916 she was earning $1,000 a week. Her first straight play, *Polly With a Past* (1917), got rave reviews. For nearly two years, she starred in *The Gold Digger* (1919). Between 1921 and 1928 she frequently appeared on Broadway in witty, sophisticated roles. She was the stage's top female comedian of her day and received a medal from The American Academy of Arts and Letters.

Claire made a movie in 1915 and was in several films in the 1930s and 1940s. In 1954, she retired. Claire was married three times: from 1919 to 1925 to a reporter; from 1929 to 1931 to film star John Gilbert, and from 1939 on to an attorney. She died in San Francisco in 1985.

❖ FORD DABNEY,

the long-time *Frolic* orchestra conductor, was born in Washington, D.C., in 1883 and studied music with his father and local white musicians. He was the official musician to the president of Haiti from 1904 to 1907. After returning to the United States, Dabney formed a quartet and then opened a theater for vaudeville acts. He moved to New York and, by 1913, was working with black band leader Jim Europe at Europe's Tempo Club. In 1914, Europe had started writing dance music for Irene and Vernon Castle. Before long Dabney also created several original dance numbers for them. In fact, Europe and Dabney were so prolific that on some sheet music, the publishers spelled their names backward so it would look as though several composers wrote it.

In 1915, Ziegfeld hired Dabney and his Syncopated Orchestra to play on the New Amsterdam Roof. Dabney continued to write most of the music he played, and he directed the orchestra for the *Ziegfeld Midnight Frolic* until September 1920, when Art Hickman's orchestra provided music for the opening of the new *Frolic*. When Hickman's engagement ended, Dabney's orchestra resumed the work. Max Hoffmann directed the orchestra for the *Midnight Frolic* that opened in February 1921; however, later that year Dabney returned to the *Frolic*, and his orchestra played until 1922, when the roof-garden entertainment was terminated.

After 1923, Dabney operated an entertainment bureau and played engagements in Florida and Newport, Rhode Island. He also wrote the musical score for the all-black Broadway show *Rang Tang* (1927). Dabney died in 1958 at age seventy-five.

❖ MARION DAVIES

was born Marion Douras in 1897 in Brooklyn. After leaving her convent school for the stage, she studied ballet, dance, and acting. Davies made her Broadway debut at age sixteen in a chorus line. She danced in revues and musicals and also modeled. Her only Ziegfeld shows were the 1916 *Follies* and *Miss 1917*. Later in 1917 she made her screen debut.

Davies met newspaper publisher and heir William Randolph Hearst while she was in the *Follies*. Hearst soon fell madly in love with Davies, eventually becoming her lover and patron. Determined to make her a star, he formed a studio, Cosmopolitan Pictures, to produce her films. Paramount released the studio's films between 1919 and 1923, losing as much as $7 million on them. In 1924, the Goldwyn Company took over Cosmopolitan and then merged to form M-G-M. Louis Mayer, recognizing the value of Hearst's newspaper connections, offered to pay Davies $10,000 a week and to finance Cosmopolitan films. Davies was given a fourteen-room bungalow on the M-G-M lot, where she entertained royalty and high society. Hearst's intense publicity campaign made Davies one of the most famous film stars.

Because she stuttered, Davies's career declined when sound pictures came into vogue. In 1934 Hearst broke with M-G-M because Davies was being bypassed for the best roles. Three years later, Hearst suffered financial setbacks. Davies loaned him $1 million, but he could no longer finance her movies, so her career ended.

By the time she retired, Davies had appeared in forty-five films, some good and some bad. She was an accomplished mimic and a talented comedian but was miscast in the fragile, innocent roles Hearst wanted for her. After leaving Hollywood, she became a successful business executive.

Hearst wanted to marry Davies, but his Catholic wife, mother of his five sons, refused to give him a divorce. Hearst and Davies shared many homes including a Beverly Hills mansion; a Santa Monica beach house with 110 rooms and fifty-five baths; and the famous San Simeon Castle. Orson Welles satirized the Hearst-Davies affair in *Citizen Kane* (1941), but in spite of a thirty-four-year age difference, their affair lasted until Hearst's death in 1951. Miss Davies then married Horace G. Brown. She died of cancer in 1961.

❖ **HAZEL DAWN,**
from Ogden, Utah, was born Hazel Tout in 1894, one of six children of a Mormon couple. The entire family moved to London so Dawn's sister could

During a rehearsal for *The Pink Lady* (1911), Hazel Dawn picked up one of the musicians' violins and started to play. Abe Erlanger heard her and added a violin number to the show.

study voice there. They stayed for twelve years, during which time Dawn took voice lessons and studied violin at London's Royal College of Music. She made her stage debut in London in 1909.

When Dawn was still a chorus member, Ivan Caryll, the orchestra director of her show, recommended her to Klaw and Erlanger for the part of Claudine in *The Gay Claudine* (which became *The Pink Lady.)* Dawn then went to New York (arriving New Year's Eve 1910) and auditioned. Her lead role in *The Pink Lady* propelled her to stardom.

For six years, Dawn played in farces for Al Woods. She also starred in musical comedies and revues through the mid-1920s. She played the title role in Ziegfeld's *The Century Girl* and a decade later toured with the *Ziegfeld Follies of 1926.* Dawn also made six films between 1914 and 1921.

In 1927 Dawn retired to marry a wealthy mining engineer. She made a brief return to Broadway in 1931. From 1935 until 1947, Dawn lived in Beverly Hills and raised her two children. She was widowed in 1941.

Dawn returned to New York in 1947 to launch her daughter's stage career. She made one film in 1946 and was on television twice in 1947. In the 1950s, she did public relations work for an advertising agency until retiring in the early 1960s. She died at age ninety-four in 1988. The mixed drink the "Pink Lady" was named after her, but since she was Mormon, she never tasted it.

❖ **MLLE. DAZIE** was born Daisy Peterkin in St. Louis in 1884. When she was eight, her family moved to Detroit to manage candy franchises in vaudeville theaters. Daisy studied ballet and debuted in vaudeville there while still a child. In 1905, she appeared in New York. After accepting an engagement in Paris, she became known as Mlle. Dazie.

When Mlle. Dazie returned to New York, it was as "The Girl in the Red Mask," a mysterious Russian dancer who did not speak English. For two years she performed at casinos and roof theaters wearing the mask at all times. She finally revealed her identity when she became premiere danseuse at Oscar Hammerstein's Manhattan Opera House. Ziegfeld then hired her for the *Follies;* she danced in the 1907 and 1908 editions. Her popularity increased, and after the *Follies,* she went on a European tour.

Mlle. Dazie returned to a varied career in the United States. She developed a pantomime act that she directed and performed in vaudeville, did exhibition ballroom dancing, appeared in Broadway revues and musical comedies, and performed character ballet roles in operettas. During the 1920s she starred in film serials. Mlle. Dazie died in 1952 at age sixty-seven.

❖ **The DOLLY TWINS,**
identical twins Janszieka (Jenny) and Roszika (Rose) Deutsch, were born in Hungary in 1892 but grew up in New York City. In 1909 they performed in vaudeville. The next year they appeared in Dillingham's *The Echo* (1910) with George White. Critics said they could not sing and rarely changed their dance routines; nevertheless, they became headliners in vaudeville, and their four-week run at the Palace was that theater's longest run for a sister act. Audiences were drawn in part by the sisters' many magnificent costumes.

The Dolly Twins danced several numbers in the *Follies* of 1911; Rose Dolly also appeared in the 1913 edition. Additionally, both twins appeared in Ziegfeld's *A Winsome Widow* and the early editions of the *Midnight Frolic.* In 1912, they appeared in *The Merry Countess* for the Shuberts. Rose was in *The Whirl of New York* (1914), while Jenny teamed with her then-husband Harry Fox. The Dolly Sisters made only one film, *The Million Dollar Dollies* (1917), which was the story of their lives. The twins were also in the national tour of *Oh, Look!* (1918).

Rose married a multimillionaire Canadian tobacco heir, but the two divorced. The sisters spent most of the 1920s in European music halls and became international stars. They bought a chateau in France where they entertained royalty and high society. Jenny gambled, winning millions of francs at the gaming tables and spending much of it on jewels. They retired in the late 1920s.

After retiring from the stage, Rose married a man from a wealthy Chicago family. She gave to charity and lived a relatively quiet life. Jenny had an affair with a World War I pilot but decided to marry H. Gordon Selfridge, owner of the London department store. While Jenny and her lover, the pilot, were returning to Paris from a last weekend fling, their speeding car crashed, and Jenny was nearly killed. Besides broken bones and internal injuries, she suffered numerous facial cuts and required major plastic surgery. She never fully recovered from the trauma of losing her beauty.

Jenny joined her sister and brother-in-law in Chicago where she married an attorney. In 1941, in a state of acute depression, she hanged herself. Rose died in 1970. George Jessel produced *The Dolly Sisters*, a 1945 film based on the twins' lives.

❖ **DOLORES** was born Kathleen Mary Rose in England, a farmer's daughter. She was an errand girl in Lucille's London salon when Lucille noticed her, trained her as a fashion model, and gave her the more exotic name of "Dolores." She came to New

York in 1914 with Lucille and was modeling gowns in a fashion show where Ziegfeld and Billie Burke saw her. Ziegfeld hired her at $75 per week even though she could not sing or dance.

Dolores debuted in the 1917 *Follies* in the "Episode of Chiffon." She was in *Miss 1917*, the 1918 *Follies*, and several editions of the *Midnight Frolic*. She is probably best remembered for her 1919 *Frolic* appearance as the white peacock.

Taller than the typical showgirl, Dolores had a regal bearing. In the *Follies*, she merely walked across the stage in beautiful costumes: for this, she earned up to $500 per week. After the 1919 *Frolic*, Dolores appeared in *Sally* for three years. Then in 1923 she sailed for Paris where she married Tudor Wilkinson, an American sportsman and multimillionaire. She died in 1975 at age eighty-three.

❖ **JACK DONAHUE**

was born in Charlestown, Massachusetts, in 1892. By age eleven he was dancing at house parties, and although he had no formal training, he started dancing in a medicine show when he was fourteen. When the proprietor failed to pay him, Donahue returned to school briefly; however, he soon left school for good, to dance between the acts of plays. He worked in burlesque before entering vaudeville, where he performed as a single until he met and married Alice Stewart. The couple danced together until she retired; Donahue then went back to performing solo.

Donahue was one of the best tap dancers of his time. He

debuted on Broadway in 1912 and appeared in *Hitchy-Koo of 1918*. His appearance in the 1920 *Follies* made him well known. Thereafter he alternated between vaudeville and musicals. By the time he co-starred with Marilyn Miller in Dillingham's *Sunny* (1925), he was highly paid. In *Rosalie*, Donahue played a comic role. He wanted to rid himself of the "hoofer" designation and become known as a comedian partly because dancing had become painful for him.

Donahue was in poor health from high blood pressure, heart disease, and a kidney problem, and his health deteriorated because of overwork. He ran a dance school in New York, wrote humorous magazine articles, and produced plays. Donahue co-wrote and starred in *Sons o' Guns* (1929) for a season and was on tour with that show when he died at age thirty-eight in 1930. He had a musical scheduled to open in New York the month he died.

❖ **RAY DOOLEY,**

born Rachel Dooley in Scotland in 1891, grew up in Philadelphia. As a child, Dooley appeared with the family minstrel act before entering vaudeville. By 1917 she debuted on Broadway in the *Passing Show of 1917*. In Raymond Hitchcock's *Hitchy-Koo of 1918*, the petite (five feet, one hundred pounds) Dooley appeared in a baby buggy because everyone else was too big for the part. Ziegfeld saw her and hired her to play babies and brats, preceding by several years Fannie Brice's similar Baby Snooks. Dooley was one of the

few female comedians to be a hit in the *Follies*; she was a cast member from 1919 to 1921 and in 1925 and 1926. She also appeared briefly with W. C. Fields in the unsuccessful *Comic Supplement*. Her brother Johnny was a principal in the 1919 *Follies*. Two other brothers, William and Gordon, appeared in a *Midnight Frolic*.

Dooley married Eddie Dowling about 1914. After she left the *Follies*, Dooley was in musical comedies, including several produced by her husband. She and her husband also toured vaudeville in 1931 and 1932. In 1935, Dooley retired to care for their son and daughter. She was living on Long Island when she died at the age of ninety-three.

❖ **BILLIE DOVE**

was born Lillian Bohny in New York City in 1903. At age fourteen she was an artist's model and movie extra at Fort Lee Studio in New Jersey. Ziegfeld saw her face on a magazine cover and sent for her but apparently decided she was too young for the *Follies*. In 1919 Dove, now sixteen, returned to Ziegfeld and was added to the 1919 *Follies*. She was also in the *Midnight Frolic* (1919–21) and danced for a short time in *Sally*.

After appearing in several Broadway shows, Dove started her movie career—courtesy of Billie Burke, who thought Flo was showing too much interest in Dove. There wasn't room enough in New York City for two women named "Billie," so in 1922 Dove abruptly arrived in Hollywood doing silent films. Her role opposite Douglas Fairbanks in *The Black Pirate* (1926) made her famous and led to a contract with First National Studio. Dove became a star and played many leading roles in musical comedies, melodramas, and westerns in the 1920s. After acting in more than forty-five films, Dove retired in 1932 when talkies began supplanting silent films. Her last role was in *Blondie of the Follies* (1932).

Dove was married to a movie director from 1923 to 1929 (divorced) and had a love affair with Howard Hughes. In 1933 she married millionaire rancher Robert Kenaston and had a son and a daughter. She was divorced from Kenaston in 1971.

❖ **EDDIE DOWLING**
was born Joseph Nelson Goucher in Rhode Island in 1894, the eleventh of fourteen children. After making his stage debut in Providence in 1909, he worked as a cabin boy on the Fall River Line and later on ocean liners. In England in 1911 he joined a boy's choir. Upon his return to Rhode Island, he became a song plugger for a local vaudeville theater; then he joined a vaudeville act and made his professional debut on stage. Dowling acted in a New England stock company and toured the vaudeville circuit before joining the 1918 *Follies* on tour. He was in the 1919 and 1920 editions, primarily as a singer and dancer.

After touring with a Broadway show in 1921, Dowling starred for three seasons in the musical *Sally, Irene, and Mary* (1922), which he co-authored. In 1926 and 1927, he co-authored shows for himself and Ray Dooley, whom he had married about 1914. In

1931 and 1932, Dowling and Dooley toured vaudeville. Dowling was also master of ceremonies for the "Ziegfeld Follies of the Air" (1932). The last musical he starred in was *Thumbs Up!* (1934), which he produced.

In 1940 and 1941, Dowling did radio shows before turning to straight plays. He acted in, directed, and/or produced the following Broadway plays: *Here Comes the Clown* (1938), the Pulitzer-prize winning *The Time of Your Life* (1939), *The Glass Menagerie* (1945), and *The Ice Man Cometh* (1946). Dowling won four New York Drama Critics Circle Awards. He also helped organize and was the first president of USO shows.

Dowling died in a nursing home in 1976 at age eighty-one.

❖ **MARIE DRESSLER**
was born Leila von Koerber in Canada in 1869. Homely and overweight, Dressler sought attention by clowning around. At age fourteen she joined a stock company. Her father disapproved, so Dressler took her aunt's name. Her first big break came when she played in *The Lady Slavey* (1896) for four years on the road until she became ill in Denver. Abe Erlanger did not believe that she was sick and was going to fire her. Dressler beat him to the punch and quit first. The vindictive and powerful Erlanger blacklisted her on Broadway for four years.

Dressler sang in Bowery cafés and became popular in burlesque and vaudeville. In 1904 Dressler appeared in *Higgledy-Piggledy* and then worked with Joe Weber for

several years. Beginning in 1910, Dressler starred in the farce *Tillie's Nightmare* for nearly five years. That role led to the film *Tillie's Punctured Romance* (1914) with Charlie Chaplin and two more Tillie films. In the 1910s, she also played vaudeville and did musical comedies, including *The Century Girl*.

Because she headed the chorus girls' division of the Actors' Equity Strike in 1919, Dressler was once again blacklisted. In 1927, she was preparing to go to Paris when she was offered a small film role. The part ignited her career. Her role in Garbo's first talkie, *Anna Christie* (1930), established Dressler as a character comedian. Between 1927 and 1933, she made seventeen films. Her role in *Min and Bill* (1930) opposite Wallace Beery won her an Academy Award for best actress. In 1934, at the height of her career, Dressler died of cancer. She was married twice but had no children.

❖ **IRENE DUNNE**
was born in Louisville, Kentucky, in 1898 and graduated from Loretta Academy there. She received a senior diploma from Florenz Ziegfeld, Sr.'s Chicago Musical College in 1919, earning a gold medal (second place) in vocal. In 1945, she received an honorary doctorate from the school. Dunne wanted to be an opera singer, which is apparently why she ignored the senior Ziegfeld's advice to look up his son in New York. After Dunne was turned down by the Met, she applied for a teaching certificate. Before receiving her certificate, she went to a road

show audition with her mother's friend. She was waiting in the theater when a man asked her whether she could sing. She was about to tell him she sang only classical music but instead decided to sing for him. She got the singing lead in the road show of *Irene* (1920). When the troupe returned to New York, Dunne had a teaching opportunity but decided to remain in musicals.

One day Dunne went to the New Amsterdam Theatre offices to meet an agent. She rode the elevator with Ziegfeld and several young women. While Dunne was in the agent's office, Ziegfeld's secretary came in looking for the girl in the blue dress and large hat. Dunne declined to see Ziegfeld because she had signed on for another show. When Norma Terris dropped out of the *Show Boat* tour in 1929, Ziegfeld remembered Dunne and sent for her—to play Magnolia. During the show's Chicago engagement, a film scout from RKO studio signed her to a film contract.

Dunne made her screen debut in 1930 and played leading ladies for the next twenty years. In 1931 she starred in *Cimarron* with Richard Dix and was nominated for an Academy Award as best actress. She also received Oscar nominations in 1936, 1937, 1939, and 1948 but never won. In 1936, she played Magnolia in the movie *Show Boat*.

Dunne's distinguished film career included more than forty movies—romances, melodrama, comedies, and musicals—in which she played dignified, intelligent, and independent women. She starred in *I Remember Mama*

This photograph of Irene Dunne as Magnolia was taken about 1929, when Dunne was touring in *Show Boat*. In Hollywood Dunne won the role of Sabra in *Cimarron* (1931) over fifty other actresses because she could not only look old but could also make her voice sound old, as she had demonstrated in *Show Boat*.

Ten-year-old Charles Eaton dressed as the dauphin in the *Ziegfeld Follies of 1921*. His brother, Joseph, and sister Mary were also in the revue that year.

(1948) and remained a star until she retired in 1952. She then appeared on television. A staunch Republican, she was devoted to political activity and was an alternate delegate to the United Nations in 1957.

Dunne was married to a dentist from 1928 until he died in 1965. They had one adopted daughter. Dunne lived in Los Angeles until her death in 1990.

❖ DORIS EATON

was born in 1904. She and her sister Mary attended Cora Shreve Dance School in Washington, D.C. One summer Doris, who was in eighth grade, was watching her older sister Pearl rehearse for the 1918 *Follies* when Ned Wayburn spotted her, asked if she danced, and hired her for the chorus. Since she was only fourteen, her mother accompanied her on tour. In the 1919 show, Doris progressed to specialty dancer and understudy for Marilyn Miller; finally, in 1920 she became a principal. Initially, she used a stage name (Lucille Levant) because she had dropped out of school. When she turned sixteen, she used her own name again.

After the *Follies*, Doris was in musicals and a revue. She was Al Jolson's leading lady in *Big Boy* (1926). She made a movie in England as well as one for RKO. In 1936, she started dancing with Arthur Murray Studios. Eaton obtained the Michigan franchise and opened the first Arthur Murray Studio outside New York—in Detroit (1938). She stayed with Murray until 1968.

Eaton and her husband now live on a working horse ranch in Oklahoma. In 1992 (at age eighty-eight), Doris graduated from Oklahoma University.

❖ JOSEPH and CHARLES EATON,

were born in Washington, D.C., Joseph in 1907 and Charles in 1911. Both boys (then aged fourteen and ten) were in the 1921 *Follies* in "The Birthday of the Dauphin" scene. Charles later appeared in Fox Studios' first talking picture and alternated work between New York and California. He was in the 1924 production of *Peter Pan* with Marilyn Miller and played the role of Andy Hardy in *Skidding*, the predecessor for the Andy Hardy film series. Like sister Doris, he worked for Arthur Murray Studios.

Joseph, on the other hand, continued his education after his *Follies* appearance. He graduated from the University of Pennsylvania, got a one-year contract writing for RKO, and served in World War II. After the war, he joined the Eaton dance-studio business and eventually became a Regional Director for Arthur Murray Dance Studios.

❖ MARY EATON,

born in Norfolk, Virginia, in 1901, moved with her family to Washington, D.C. She worked in a stock company for a time before appearing in the D.C. production of *The Blue Bird*.

When the Shubert brothers later decided to revive the show, they hired Eaton and her sisters (Pearl and Doris). The girls toured during 1914–15 and debuted in New York.

Eaton studied ballet in New York and was a solo dancer in *Follow Me* (1916) but had to leave the cast until she turned sixteen. In 1917 she was in *Over the Top* with the Astaires. Ziegfeld soon spotted her and groomed her as Marilyn Miller's successor. Eaton starred in the *Follies* for three years, from 1920 to 1922, as well as in *Kid Boots*. She went on to star in other Broadway musicals, her biggest hit being *Five O'Clock Girl* (1927). Eaton also made several movies, including *Cocoanuts* (1929) with the Marx Brothers and *Glorifying the American Girl* (1929).

Eaton was married to film director Millard Webb and then to rancher Charles Emery. When she died of a heart attack in 1948, she was married to actor Eddie Lawton.

❖ **PEARL EATON,**
born in 1898, worked in stock companies in Washington, D.C., with her sisters before going to New York, where she studied dance and appeared in many Ned Wayburn productions. Pearl was the first Eaton hired for the *Follies* (1918) and was a featured dancer in the *Ziegfeld Midnight Frolic*, appearing in editions between 1918 and 1920 and in the 1922 road show.

After working as Charles Dillingham's dance director, Pearl went to Hollywood and became a dance director for musical comedies. She married Oscar Levant's brother Harry.

❖ **LEON ERROL,**
a native of Sydney, Australia, was born in 1881. He left Sydney University and joined a repertory company and then a circus before moving to San Francisco to be a comedian and dancer and then heading for New York to do burlesque.

Errol debuted in the *Follies of 1911* in a pantomime skit with Bert Williams. From 1911 through 1915 he was a *Follies* cast member. He was also in *A Winsome Widow* and directed the *Follies* in 1914 and in 1915 with Julian Mitchell. Errol appeared in and staged numbers for *The Century Girl*, the *Midnight Revue* (1917), and the *Ziegfeld Frolic* (1922). He left Ziegfeld to co-direct *Words and Music* (1917) and to perform in the 1917 and 1918 editions of *Hitchy-Koo*.

Vaudeville beckoned in 1916, and by 1919 Errol headlined at the Palace. Because Errol was busy, Ziegfeld hired comedian Walter Catlett for *Sally*. When Errol became available, Ziegfeld had a second comic role written into the show for him. By 1925 when he starred in Ziegfeld's *Louie the 14th*, Errol was earning $1,800 per week. Errol co-directed a Broadway production in 1922 and acted in shows in 1927 and 1929. By then, however, films had become Errol's primary source of income.

Between 1924 and 1951, Errol acted in over sixty motion pictures, several of them with W. C. Fields. In the late 1930s and early 1940s, he played Lord Epping in the popular Mexican Spitfire series (eight films) with Lupe Velez. Between 1946 and 1951, he was in the Joe Palooka film series. He also appeared in many film shorts, often as a henpecked husband.

Errol was married to Stella Chatelaine from 1907 until her death in 1946. The couple danced together in *The Pink Lady* and in the *Follies* (1911–14). Errol was seventy when he died of a heart attack in Los Angeles in 1951.

❖ **RUTH ETTING**
was born in 1896 in David City, Nebraska. After high school she studied at Chicago's Academy of Fine Arts. In 1922, she married Martin "Moe" Snyder, a small-time gangster who managed her career. While Etting claimed that her stage debut was at the Marigold Garden Theater in 1925, other sources say she was on stage earlier. In the mid-1920s she was a popular torch singer in nightclubs and vaudeville houses in Chicago. She appeared in New York vaudeville with Paul Whiteman's orchestra.

Etting's records were popular, and she was promoted as the "Sweetheart of Columbia Records." After Irving Berlin heard one of her recordings, he had Ziegfeld send for her. She made a hit of Berlin's "Shaking the Blues Away" in the 1927 *Follies*. Etting's other hit songs in Ziegfeld shows included "Love Me, or Leave Me" from *Whoopee*; "Ten Cents a Dance" from *Simple Simon*; and the revival of Nora Bayes's "Shine On, Harvest Moon" from the 1931 *Follies*.

During the 1930s, Etting was on radio and in films. She made three feature films and more than thirty shorts for Warner Brothers (1928–36). Her career made a steady rise under Snyder's management, but she hated his possessiveness and jealousy. At age forty-two (in November 1937), Etting divorced Snyder and began seeing her arranger/accompanist, Myrl Alderman, who was thirty. The jealous Snyder shot Alderman, but Alderman survived. Alderman claimed he had secretly married Etting in Mexico in July 1938, but there were no records to document this. In December 1938, while Snyder was on trial, Alderman and Etting married in Las Vegas. Snyder went to jail for a year. Due to the damage the publicity caused her career—and possibly because the stage had lost its glamour for her after Ziegfeld died—she retired soon after her marriage.

During the 1940s, Etting made a comeback in nightclubs and on radio. In 1955, Doris Day and James Cagney starred in the movie *Love Me or Leave Me*, based on Etting's life. Etting and Alderman remained married until his death in 1968. Etting died in Colorado Springs in 1978.

❖ **The FAIRBANKS TWINS,**
Madeleine and Marion, were born in New York City in 1900. They debuted as children in a production of *The Blue Bird* (1910). They also danced for Ned Wayburn in some Lew Fields productions. After several Broadway shows, in 1912 they turned to films—first as the Biograph Kids in a serial and then as two of the Thankhouser Kids in serials and feature films. After making hundreds of films between 1913 and 1917, the Fairbanks Twins returned to New York. They were sixteen at the time of their *Follies* debut and always

Ruth Etting had a hit song in each of the four Ziegfeld shows in which she appeared: the 1927 and 1931 *Follies*, *Whoopee* (1928), and *Simple Simon* (1930). Her career waned after she became involved in a 1937 scandal in which her ex-husband shot her lover.

appeared on stage together. Ned Wayburn, now working for Ziegfeld, choreographed their routines. They danced in the *Follies* (1917–19), *The Century Girl*, and several editions of the *Frolic* until 1921. They then appeared in the *Passing Show of 1921, Two Little Girls in Blue* (1921), *Scandals* (1926), and other musicals.

❖ **W. C. FIELDS** was born Wilbur Claude Dukenfield in Philadelphia in 1880. At about age eleven he ran away from home. Fields taught himself to juggle and was hired to perform when he was about fourteen. Fields had apparently stuttered as a child so he initially talked little during his routine. Moreover, when he was touring

in foreign countries, it was easier not to speak so he would not have to keep learning a new language. Thus, he became known for his pantomime.

Fields soon became a vaudeville headliner. In 1901 he got top billing at the London Palace and the Paris *Folies-Bergère*. He debuted on Broadway in 1905 and in late May 1907 performed his juggling act for about two weeks at the newly opened Jardin de Paris managed by Flo Ziegfeld. Fields remained relatively unknown outside vaudeville until his 1915 *Follies* performance, which, combined with his appearances in the *Midnight Frolic*, greatly increased his popularity. Fields performed in the *Follies* over a ten-year span—1915–18, 1920, 1921, and 1925—often writing his own skits, including many pantomime routines. While working for Ziegfeld, he moved to speaking roles. His trademarks were a dead-pan expression and a totally bored look.

In 1922 Fields left Ziegfeld to perform in *George White's Scandals*. By 1923, he was in the musical comedy *Poppy* before going to Hollywood. Fields returned to New York to star in Ziegfeld's *A Comic Supplement*, but the show closed during tryouts. However, many of the sketches from that show became part of the 1925 *Follies*. After performing in the 1925 *Follies*, Fields moved to Hollywood permanently. Fields starred in silent films, but he was even more successful in sound pictures. His raspy voice enhanced his comic roles. For the most part, Fields played unlovable drunkards who were

frequently henpecked and who despised suckers, children, animals, and, of course, teetotalers. Fields wrote many of his screenplays. It was difficult for the public to separate his private and public personalities. He made about forty movies between 1924 and 1945.

Fields was a frequent guest on Edgar Bergen's radio show, where he feuded with wooden dummy Charlie McCarthy for six years. McCarthy asked Fields such questions as what that red thing on his face was—his nose or a tomato—or whether that was his nose or a new kind of flame thrower. Fields often responded by threatening McCarthy with a saw.

Fields married Harriet Hughes in 1900, but they separated after their son was born. Fields sent his wife and son a weekly check throughout his lifetime. While most people thought he was rude and self-centered, Fields could be caring and never approved of telling dirty jokes in mixed company. Although he had little formal schooling, he read widely.

Known for heavy drinking, Fields once told Eddie Cantor that when he donated blood, the doctor said he was very helpful—his blood contained so much alcohol they could use it to sterilize their instruments! Fields's fear of poverty caused him to stash large sums of money in banks all over the country. At one time, he said he had seven hundred bank accounts. When he died in 1946, only thirty accounts were found. He left $10,000 each to his wife and son and trust funds for his brother, sister, and a woman friend. The remainder of his estate was valued at $800,000.

❖ RUDOLF FRIML,

a Czechoslovakian composer, was born in 1879. He studied piano early and had his first composition published when he was ten. At fourteen he went to the Prague Conservatory, where he finished a six-year program in three years. He gave concerts throughout

Rudolf Friml composed music for four Ziegfeld shows; he was also a close personal friend of the Ziegfeld family. Here he appears with Patricia Ziegfeld's companion, "Blackie" (Marian Black), around 1920.

Europe and later became accompanist for violinist Jan Kubelik. In 1906 Friml settled in the United States, where he gave concerts and composed more than twenty operettas; his first successful one was *The Firefly* in 1912. Over the next ten years he wrote the scores

for many Broadway musicals. Ziegfeld shows for which he composed were the 1921 and 1923 *Follies, No Foolin',* and *The Three Musketeers.* Two of Friml's biggest hits were *Rose-Marie* in 1924 (550 performances) and *The Vagabond King* (1925).

In the 1930s, tastes changed, and his last two Broadway musicals failed. After 1934, he wrote for the movies with no great success. He then composed privately and gave piano concerts.

Friml was a friend of the Ziegfelds, visiting them frequently in the 1920s. He always practiced on a soundless keyboard that he took everywhere. Friml died in Hollywood in 1972.

❖ JOE FRISCO

(Louis Wilson Josephs) was born in Illinois in 1890. When he was a boy, his family moved to Dubuque, Iowa, where his dancing earned him local fame. In 1906, he headed to Chicago to pursue his dancing career. After performing in a two-man team, Frisco went solo and joined a musical chorus, using the single name Frisco, and developed his Frisco Dance. New York soon beckoned; by 1917 Frisco was a hit at Rector's. That December he started working in the *Frolic.* He was in two more *Frolics* (1918 and 1920) and one *Follies* (1918). Frisco's trademarks were his derby hat and a large cigar. Although he stuttered, his sharp wit made him a popular comedian. In the 1920s, he became a big star on Broadway and in vaudeville.

Although Frisco earned about $50,000 a year in the 1920s, he gambled much of it

away. As he was leaving the race track once, someone asked how he made out. Frisco replied, "I b-b-b-broke even, and boy, did I need the m-m-m-money!" When he was hospitalized for surgery, Frisco insisted his nurse be able to read *The Racing Form;* he even started a betting pool on how long his surgery would last. Frisco died of cancer in 1958.

❖ GALLAGHER AND SHEAN

were known for one song, "Oh! Mr. Gallagher and Mr. Shean." Al Shean was born in 1868 in Germany and entered vaudeville around 1890. He was with the Manhattan Comedy Four, a singing and comedy act, until 1900 when he teamed with Charles Warren. Ed Gallagher was born in San Francisco around 1873. He started out in burlesque as a straight man. For many years he was in a vaudeville comedy act with Joe Barett.

Gallagher and Shean teamed up around 1910 but split in 1914. For six years they were not on speaking terms; during this time Gallagher remained in vaudeville while Shean appeared in musicals. Shean also wrote some early routines for his nephews, the Marx Brothers.

Shean's sister (Minnie Marx) helped reunite Gallagher and Shean. They opened their new act in April 1920. In August 1921, they introduced "Oh! Mr. Gallagher and Mr. Shean" in a sketch called "Mr. Gallagher and Mr. Shean in Egypt." Thereafter, they performed the song before a painted backdrop showing Egyptian pyramids; Gallagher wore a straw hat and Shean

wore a fez. The song was the hit of the 1922 *Ziegfeld Follies;* as a featured act, they earned $1,500 a week.

After the summer *Follies,* they returned to vaudeville. They had top billing at the Palace, recorded their song, and were in a Shubert show and the *Greenwich Village Follies* (1924). While on tour with the 1925 edition of that show, they disagreed again and split up for good. Shean stayed with the *Greenwich Village Follies,* and Gallagher returned to vaudeville with a new partner.

Shean remained a solo act and was in Ziegfeld's *Betsy* (1926). He continued to perform his old song, playing both roles (changing voices and hats). Between 1934 and 1946 he was in many films. He died in New York City at age eighty-one (1949).

Gallagher's vaudeville career was prospering when a legal dispute arose over the authorship of the song he and Shean had made famous. To make matters worse, the Shuberts sued Gallagher, his third wife filed for divorce, and then Shean sued him. (Later his fourth wife also divorced him.) In 1925, Gallagher suffered a nervous breakdown; he never recovered. He was committed to a sanitarium in 1927 and died there in 1929 when he was fifty-six.

❖ ADELINE GENÉE,

born Anina Jensen in Denmark in 1878, studied dance with her aunt and uncle. She adopted her uncle's last name and made her stage debut at age ten. Genée danced with the Berlin Opera in 1896 and in 1897, at age nineteen, debuted at the Empire Theatre in London.

Over the next ten years, she danced in England and toured; she was the leading lady in twenty of the Empire Theatre's ballets. *The Soul Kiss* marked Genée's American debut. She spent five seasons in New York with her own company; she also danced at the Metropolitan Opera House and toured in vaudeville. Genée returned to England in 1910 and married. She gave up performing in 1917 to care for her ill husband. In 1932 she came out of retirement for a charity matinée and then danced a season in London in 1933.

In 1920 Genée was elected Founder President of the Association of Operatic Dancing in London; she served in that role until 1954, the year it became the Royal Academy of Dancing. Genée received many awards from the Danish government for her artistic contributions. In 1950 she was named Dame of the Order of the British Empire. She died in 1970 at age ninety-two.

❖ GEORGE GERSHWIN

was born Jacob Gershvin in Brooklyn, New York, in 1898. He began studying piano at age twelve. In 1914, he heard his first Jerome Kern song at his aunt's wedding. From then on he studied and imitated Kern's music. Gershwin worked as a piano demonstrator from ages fifteen to seventeen. He was a rehearsal pianist for Ziegfeld's *Miss 1917* when he met Kern.

The music for "Swanee" (lyrics by Irving Caesar) made Gershwin famous overnight. From 1920 to 1924 he wrote music for George White's *Scandals*. Beginning in 1924, he worked primarily with his brother, Ira. Gershwin

Composer George Gershwin wrote music for two Ziegfeld shows: *Rosalie* (1928) and *Show Girl* (1929).

composed music for two Ziegfeld shows, *Rosalie* and *Show Girl*, but his most popular songs, including "Fascinating Rhythm," "Oh, Lady Be Good," "I Got Rhythm," and "Summertime," were from his other musicals. In addition to musical scores, Gershwin wrote concert pieces: "Rhapsody in Blue," "An American in Paris,"

and "Piano Concerto in F." He wrote the film scores for *Shall We Dance* (1937) and the *Goldwyn Follies* (1938). Gershwin was thirty-eight when he died in 1937.

❖ PAULETTE GODDARD

was born Marian Goddard Levy on June 3, 1911. When she was

fifteen, her uncle got her an audition with Ziegfeld, who sent her to Florida to appear in *Ziegfeld's Palm Beach Girl.* Goddard stayed with the 1926 show in New York and on the road; she then appeared in the chorus of Ziegfeld's *Rio Rita* (1927).

Goddard quit Broadway while still in her teens to marry a wealthy North Carolina executive but left him when he refused to let her work. She then went to Hollywood where she played bit parts in films and was a member of a stock company. In 1932 she met Charlie Chaplin and signed an exclusive contract with him. She secretly married Chaplin in 1936. They appeared together in *Modern Times* (1936) and *The Great Dictator* (1940). The two divorced in 1942.

In the mid-1940s, Goddard earned a lot of money as a top star at Paramount. She married Burgess Meredith in 1944 and divorced him in 1950. Goddard's career began to decline rapidly in the late 1940s and ended by 1954. She married novelist Erich Maria Remarque in 1958, and the two lived in Europe until his death in 1970. Goddard made over fifty films in all. She died at the age of seventy-eight in Switzerland in 1990.

❖ BERNARD GRANVILLE

started his career in Chicago before becoming a singing/dancing star for the Shuberts. He left them to join the *Follies*. Besides the *Follies* (1912, 1915, 1916, and 1920), Granville was in several editions of the *Midnight Frolic, A Winsome Widow,* and *Miss 1917.* He also appeared in musical comedies, including *Louisiana Lou* (1911) with Sophie Tucker, *The Little Blue Devil* (1919) with Lillian Lorraine, and the New York production of *Castles in the Air* (1926). He married an entertainer and had a daughter who was a child film star. After retiring from the theater around 1931, Granville entered the insurance business. He died in 1936.

❖ GILDA GRAY

was born Marianne Michalski in Poland in 1901. After her parents were killed in the Polish uprising, Gray was adopted and escaped from Krakow just before the Russian invasion. Her family moved to the United States, and Gray made her professional debut as a dancer in Chicago. She allegedly created the "shimmy" in 1919 while working in a Wisconsin saloon. When the band swung into ragtime, she began to shake her body. When a customer asked the name of the dance, Gray shook her chemise and tried to pronounce the word. The man thought she was saying "shimmy," and the name stuck. Gray's employer was shocked at the dance and fired her.

Gray was working in Atlantic City as Mary Gray when Sophie Tucker saw her dance, told her that Mary was no name for a dancer, and suggested she call herself Gilda because of her golden hair. Gray danced in the 1922 *Follies* and *George White's Scandals* before touring Europe and then going to Hollywood. She acted and danced in six films between 1923 and 1936. She was also a singer, and at one time was reputed to be the world's

highest paid entertainer. Then, as many others did, she lost most of her savings in the stock market crash. During the Depression, her career declined. Poor health prevented her from making a comeback.

Gray was in Warsaw when Hitler invaded Poland. For a second time, she barely made it out of the country. Dressed in her nightclothes and fur coat, she caught the last flight to Paris. In 1949 Columbia produced the movie *Gilda* starring Rita Hayworth. Gray filed a $1 million lawsuit, claiming the movie was based on her life, but dropped the suit when a settlement was reached.

In 1956 Gray was featured on the television show "This Is Your Life." She was married and divorced three times and had one son. She lived in Hollywood with friends for the last six years of her life. She died of a heart attack at the age of fifty-eight in 1959.

❖ BEN ALI HAGGIN

(James Ben Ali Haggin, Jr.) was born in New York City. His father was a famous horseman and his grandfather owned a multimillion-dollar copper mine. Haggin studied art in Munich before returning home to become a well-known society portrait painter.

Ziegfeld hired Haggin to produce "living pictures" for the wealthy patrons of the 1917 *Midnight Frolic*. Ziegfeld had introduced the tableau to the *Follies* earlier, but he wanted something special. Haggin's tableaux were "copies" of famous paintings using live models. His models always stood perfectly still and were draped rather than dressed; some were almost nude. Just as

Joseph Urban did, Haggin used lighting to enhance the beauty of his pictures, but unlike Urban, who used darker, heavier colors, Haggin used light pastels, rose, and lavender.

From 1918 until 1926 (*No Foolin'*), Haggin's tableaux were regular attractions of both the *Follies* and the *Midnight Frolic*. Although the 1922 *Follies* lacked a Haggin tableau when the show opened, Ziegfeld added three for the summer season. Besides his tableaux, Haggin also designed costumes for several editions of the *Follies*.

Haggin and his family were close to the Ziegfelds in private life. Patty Ziegfeld was engaged briefly to Haggin's son. Haggin began a portrait of Billie and Patty but never completed it.

After he stopped working for Ziegfeld, Haggin continued amateur acting and occasionally designed a tableau for vaudeville. He produced and directed the Beaux Arts Ball from 1927 to 1933 and directed arrangements for the Metropolitan Opera Balls from 1933 to 1935. Haggin had been a member of the National Academy of Art since 1912 and was co-founder of the Society of Independent Artists. He was married three times and had four children. He died in 1951 at age sixty-nine.

❖ OSCAR HAMMERSTEIN II

was born in 1895 into a family of theater managers. His grandfather, Oscar Hammerstein I, managed theaters at the turn of the century and built a theater for the Manhattan Opera. His father, his uncle, and a son were

also in the business.

Beginning in 1917, Hammerstein managed New York theaters and wrote plays. He wrote the book and often the lyrics for more than thirty shows and films. He worked on *Wildflower* (1923) with Vincent Youmans, *Rose-Marie* (1923) with Rudolf Friml, *The Desert Song* (1926) with Sigmund Romberg, and, of course, *Show Boat*, which he wrote at age thirty-one, with Jerome Kern. Later, he teamed with Richard Rodgers for many hit shows: *Oklahoma* (1943), *South Pacific* (1949), *The King and I* (1951), *Flower Drum Song* (1958), and *The Sound of Music* (1959). From 1944 on he was a partner in Williamson Music Publishers. Hammerstein died in 1960.

❖ JOHN HARKRIDER

ran away from his Ft. Worth, Texas, home at fourteen (in 1915) to audition for the role of chariot driver in a DeMille film. Although he did not get the part, he eventually became a stunt double and later appeared in bit parts in many silent films. In the 1920s, Harkrider began designing costumes. He created costumes for pageants before moving on to operas and musicals.

Louise Brooks introduced Harkrider to Ziegfeld at the Astor Hotel. Harkrider first worked for Ziegfeld on *Palm Beach Nights* (1926), which later became *No Foolin'*. He designed costumes for the 1927 and 1931 *Follies*, the 1928 *Midnight Frolic*, and all of Ziegfeld's later shows: *Rio Rita*, *Show Boat*, *Rosalie*, *The Three Musketeers*, *Show Girl*, *Simple Simon*, and *Smiles*. For *Hot-Cha!* he designed Eleanor

Powell's costumes. Harkrider was also artistic director for *Simple Simon*; *Smiles*; and Hollywood's second color film, *Glorifying the American Girl* (1929), as well as costume designer for Samuel Goldwyn's *Whoopee!* (1930).

Not long after Ziegfeld's death, Harkrider moved to Hollywood to concentrate on films. Although his designs were spectacular, they were too expensive for most producers. He and William Anthony McGuire sold the idea of *The Great Ziegfeld* (1936) to Universal Studios. But when the project became too costly, Universal canceled it and sold it to M-G-M. At M-G-M Harkrider designed independently of the staff; he came up with the spectacular staircase scene for "The Most Beautiful Girl" number. The film won the Oscar for best picture that year.

For two years Harkrider was head of the New Universal art department. But, as elaborate musical films faded, so did Harkrider's career. He returned to designing musical pageants and an occasional Broadway show. From 1945 until 1962, he operated a casting agency. In 1962, he returned to Hollywood—as a location scout. At the time of his death, Harkrider was working on a mural, "Ziegfeldia," in honor of Flo Ziegfeld. Harkrider died in 1982 at eighty-one years of age.

❖ MARY HAY

(Mary Hay Caldwell) was born in Fort Bliss, Texas, in 1901, the daughter of an army general. Hay appeared in silent films before studying dance at the Los Angeles Denishawn

School. She moved to New York to study with Ned Wayburn. Hay debuted on Broadway in the *Ziegfeld Midnight Frolic* (1918) and appeared in the chorus of the 1919 *Follies*. She was soon so popular she was given parts in skits. Additionally, Hay was in Ziegfeld's *Nine O'Clock Revue* (1920) and *Sally*. After marrying matinée idol Richard Barthelmus in 1920, Hay left Broadway for two years.

Ned Wayburn teamed the petite Hay (almost four feet, ten inches) with the six-foot-tall Clifton Webb. The two danced together in *Sunny* (1925) and *The Treasure Girl* (1928). They went on to become a popular dance team in vaudeville and in music halls in Britain and Europe.

Besides Broadway shows, Hay co-starred in two Hollywood movies with Barthelmus before they divorced in 1927. (The couple had one daughter.) She retired from the stage in 1930 and married a wealthy British industrialist, but they, too, were divorced. Her third marriage was to Richard Hastings, whose father founded the Hastings School of Law at the University of California. Hay died in 1957 at the age fifty-six.

❖ VICTOR HERBERT

was born in Dublin in 1859. His father died when Herbert was an infant. His mother then married a German physician, and they moved to Stuttgart, Germany, where Herbert was educated. Musically precocious, he hummed tunes before he could talk. Eight weeks after starting cello lessons he was in his first concert.

Herbert joined the

Stuttgart Conservatory, where he composed and played cello. After a European tour, he became a member of the Royal Orchestra, where he met Augusta Foerster, an operatic soprano. They married in 1886 and soon thereafter left for the United States, where the New York Metropolitan Opera Company had engaged her as star soloist. Herbert played in the orchestra.

conducted the Pittsburgh Symphony Orchestra; he moved on to the Boston Symphony and then the New York Philharmonic Society. Finally Herbert organized his own band, which became very popular. In 1913 he co-founded the American Society of Composers, Authors, and Publishers (ASCAP).

When Herbert's comic operas became popular, he gave

Victor Herbert wrote music for ten Ziegfeld shows, including seven *Follies*.

He became a faculty member of the National Conservatory of Music in 1889 and also conducted. As leader of the 2nd Regiment Band of the New York City National Guard, he took the band on tour. From 1898 to 1904 he

up the cello. He wrote more than forty operettas, including *Babes in Toyland*, *Orange Blossoms*, and *My Golden Girl*. According to Ziegfeld, Herbert would sit in the office and work out a scene's music and the next day he would come in with the full orchestration. Although he disliked jazz, Herbert wrote beautiful pieces for Paul Whiteman's orchestra. Between 1916 and 1924, Herbert's music appeared in ten Ziegfeld shows: *The Century Girl, Miss 1917, Sally,* and seven *Ziegfeld Follies* (1917 and 1919–24). He died in May 1924 at age sixty-four, hours after he had finished composing a number for the Tiller Girls in the 1924 *Follies.*

❖ **HARRIET HOCTOR**

was born in Hoosick Falls, New York, around 1903. She studied dance in New York, Chicago, and London. Hoctor was an excellent ballerina at a time when ballet in the United States had little status as a performing art. Consequently, she danced in popular shows: vaudeville, musical comedies and revues, and presentation houses. She appeared at the Palace Theatre and Radio City Music Hall, as well as London's Hippodrome.

Hoctor made her professional debut in 1922 as part of the replacement cast in Ziegfeld's long-running *Sally.* She made her first vaudeville appearance that same year; she performed ballet solos with a dance act.

Hoctor was a featured soloist on Broadway in specialty numbers. From 1923 to 1925 she was in *Topsy and Eva,* where she introduced a backbend-on-point sequence, which became her trademark. As a member of the Albertina Rasch Dancers, she was premiere danseuse in three Ziegfeld productions: *The Three Musketeers, Show Girl,* and *Simple Simon.* In 1928 and 1929, she was voted "Prima Ballerina" in *Dance Magazine's* "all-American" poll. She was in

vaudeville in 1933 and 1934. From 1934 to 1937 she danced in films, including *The Great Ziegfeld* (1936) and *Shall We Dance?* (1937). Her only *Follies* appearance came in 1936. After Hoctor's last vaudeville appearance in 1940, she opened her own ballet school in Boston. From 1942 to 1943, she danced in revues at Billy Rose's Diamond Horseshoe nightclub; she also choreographed revues for Rose from 1943 to 1945. Hoctor operated and taught at her ballet schools in Massachusetts until the late 1960s. She was seventy-four when she died in 1977.

❖ **ALFRED CHENEY JOHNSTON**

was born in 1884, the son of a banker. From 1904 to 1908, he studied art at the National Academy of Design. Little is known about the next nine years in Johnston's life except that he married in 1909. Around 1917, a friend showed Ziegfeld a Johnston photograph. Ziegfeld liked it, invited him to see the *Follies,* and asked Johnston to become his official photographer. Johnston agreed on the condition that he get a credit line. Ziegfeld consented; Johnston was allowed to select and pose the women as he chose.

Johnston is best remembered for his creative use of drapes. Since he did not like most costumes of the era, he would have the women undress fully or partially and pose wearing a drape or a long strands of pearls. Ziegfeld never used Johnston photos of nude or bare-breasted women, and they were not shown publicly until after Johnston

Justine Johnstone made her Broadway debut when she was about sixteen and was in the *Follies* for two years (1915 and 1916). She appeared in musicals, nightclubs, and films until the 1920s. Famed for her beauty, she left show business to study medical pathology. In 1940 she was cited as one of the scientists behind the five-day cure for syphilis.

died. If a showgirl ever missed a photo session, Johnston never photographed her again. He soon earned an international reputation for his distinctive pictures. All of his theatrical photos—he said he photographed over 25,000 women—were shot in his studio except for one he took of the Barrymore brothers.

Johnston worked for Ziegfeld from about 1917 until Ziegfeld's death. By this time, stage and screen stars as well as society people were flocking to his studio and paying $500 to $1,200 for a sitting. In addition to theatrical work, Johnston did advertising photography on Madison Avenue for industrial firms and cigarette companies. Johnston is generally ranked

with the top photographers of the 1920s and 1930s.

In 1940, at age fifty-five, he abruptly stopped taking pictures professionally. He and his wife moved to a twenty-acre farm in Connecticut, where he took private photographs for many years in his barn-studio. He faithfully attended the annual Ziegfeld Girls' charity ball for many years. Johnston died at age eighty-seven in 1971.

❖ **JEROME KERN**

was born in New York City in 1885. His mother taught him to play the piano when he was five. In 1902, he enrolled at the New York College of Music but left the next year and went to Europe. While in England he became intrigued with musical comedy and began writing filler songs for Charles Frohman shows. He returned to New York in 1904 and became a rehearsal pianist and a song plugger for T. B. Harms, which published his songs.

Between 1904 and 1912, more than one hundred Kern songs were interpolated into thirty shows. Several Ziegfeld shows had his music: the 1912, 1915, and 1916 *Follies*; *A Winsome Widow*, with the interpolation "Call Me Flo"; *Miss 1917*; *Sally*; and *Show Boat*, his most important work. Kern's *The Girl from Utah* (1914) established his reputation. Between 1915 and 1918, he collaborated with P. G. Wodehouse, with whom he

Composer Jerome Kern's most famous work was *Show Boat* (1927); he also wrote music for other Ziegfeld book shows and for three *Follies*.

had worked in England, and Guy Bolton. The trio composed musicals for the Princess Theatre, a small three-hundred-seat theater with a twelve-piece orchestra. Some of Kern's hits during those years were *Nobody Home* (1915); *Oh, Boy!* (1917); *Leave It to Jane* (1917); and *Oh, Lady! Lady!* (1918). Kern also wrote *Sunny*

(1925) for Marilyn Miller and *Sweet Adeline* (1929) for Helen Morgan.

After *Show Boat*, Kern wrote more traditional musical comedies until 1939 and then moved to Beverly Hills where he wrote the scores for films. At Oscar Hammerstein's request, Kern wrote the music for "The Last Time I Saw Paris." The song was inserted in the 1941 movie *Lady, Be Good*, where it won an Academy Award. Kern is credited with writing more than one thousand songs that appeared in more than one hundred stage and film productions.

In 1910, Kern married an English woman, Eva Leale. When he started writing for films, the couple built a house in Beverly Hills. Kern went to New York in 1945 to help Hammerstein with another revival of *Show Boat*. While there, he suffered a heart attack and died.

❖ **ALLYN KING,**
born in 1900, was a singer who started working for Ziegfeld in 1915 in the *Midnight Frolic* (August) and was understudy for *Follies* star Ina Claire. She became a principal herself in the *Follies* (1916–18) and *Frolic* (1919 and 1920). Later, she starred in a Broadway musical. In 1927 King was forced to retire because she had gained too much weight.

After going on a self-imposed diet, King collapsed in her apartment. She suffered a nervous breakdown and spent two years in a sanitarium. After her release, King gained weight again. She became so depressed that her family would not let her go out alone. In 1930, when her

aunt (with whom King lived) left her New York apartment briefly, King jumped from a fifth-floor window into the courtyard below. She had fractured her skull, an arm, and a leg but remained conscious. She was expected to recover but suddenly took a turn for the worse and died the next day (at age thirty).

❖ **DENNIS KING**
was born Dennis Pratt in Coventry, England, in 1897. He was a call boy (calling cast members to the stage) at age fourteen. King, who adopted his mother's maiden name, debuted in *As You Like It* at age nineteen. He then acted in classical theater. He debuted on the London stage in 1919 and in New York in 1921. A baritone, he sang in numerous operettas, including *Rose-Marie* (1924), *The Vagabond King* (1925), *The Three Musketeers* (New York and London), the 1932 revival of *Show Boat* (he played Ravenal), *I Married an Angel* (1938), and *Music in the Air* (1951). He starred in several movies in the 1930s and later had supporting roles. In the 1940s, he was in Theatre Guild Productions. He was also on television and in summer theater.

After living in the United States for many years, King became a citizen in 1953. He married an actress and had two sons. The seventy-three-year-old King died of a heart condition in 1971.

❖ **BERT LAHR**
(Irving Lahrheim) was a native New Yorker born in 1895. He began his career with burlesque in 1910; by 1915 he had entered vaudeville. After

World War I, Lahr toured vaudeville with his wife. In 1927, he made his first Broadway appearance. The next year he achieved stardom with his comic role in *Hold Everything*.

Lahr made his movie debut in 1929. Between 1931 and 1967, he was featured in sixteen films. His most famous role was that of the Cowardly Lion in *The Wizard of Oz* (1939). During the 1930s, Lahr also appeared in many musical comedies, including *Hot-Cha!*, George White's *Music Hall Varieties* (1932), and *George White's Scandals of 1935*. After performing in *Waiting for Godot* (1956), Lahr was in only a few stage shows.

On stage Lahr was known for his rubber face and his caterwauling. Off stage he was always serious and constantly worried about his act. Lahr and his first wife were divorced in 1939; he remarried the next year. He died in 1967 while filming a movie.

❖ **KAY LAURELL,**
born Kay Leslie in Pittsburgh, was a telephone operator before joining the *Ziegfeld Follies* (1914, 1915, and 1918) and the *Midnight Frolic* (1915–18). Laurell was the first to volunteer when Ziegfeld asked for women to appear undraped in Ben Ali Haggin's tableau. In 1915 she appeared standing on a parapet wrapped in gauze and strapped to the muzzle of a cannon.

Hoping to become a serious actress and a member of high society, Laurell studied French, dancing, music, and elocution. She left the *Follies* for movies but stayed in Hollywood for only a few years (1919–21),

GRACE LA RUE

Singer/dancer Grace LaRue (1882-1956) began her career in vaudeville before debuting in musical comedies in 1906. She then alternated between musicals and vaudeville until the 1920s; she also appeared in two movies. LaRue was a principal singer in the 1907 and 1908 *Follies*. In 1912, she married former film star Hale Hamilton, and from then on the couple appeared together.

perhaps because she had casting difficulties. (Although Laurell was blonde, she played Native Americans in two films.) Laurell married Winnie Sheehan, general manager of Fox films, in 1916, but the two later divorced.

After leaving Hollywood, Laurell appeared briefly in vaudeville, performed with stock companies, starred in one Broadway show, and acted in films in New York. She then acted in Paris but never again achieved the fame she had in the *Follies*. Laurell died in 1927 in London. While one source said she was born in 1897, according to her family she was thirty-seven when she died.

❖ EVELYN LAW,

born in 1904, was the daughter of a U.S. naval lieutenant and his wife. As a child, Law was anemic and had a weak heart. She had always loved dancing, and when she was thirteen,

against a doctor's advice, her parents sent her to a dance master. Her physical condition, and her dancing, improved. Law became a pupil of Ned Wayburn's and debuted on stage in his *Two Little Girls in Blue* (1921). She then appeared in the *Ziegfeld Follies* (1922; 1924), *Louie the 14th*, and *Betsy*.

Law was known for high kicking. Many newspaper pictures show her foot touching the back of her head, but Law's trademark was a forward kick that reached ten inches above her head. In 1927 she danced at the famous Club Richmond and in 1928 was in the *Greenwich Village Follies*. She was a society dancer for many years and also appeared in films.

❖ LUCILE LAYTON

was born in New York in 1903. At age eleven she was in films with Mary Pickford. At eighteen, she was modeling. One Saturday night she accompanied an actress-friend to a benefit at the Plaza Hotel. Sam Kingston, Ziegfeld's business manager, was there. Layton's friend asked Kingston if he could get Lucile into the *Follies*. Kingston told her to audition next week.

On Monday Ned Wayburn called the showgirls first, and they took turns walking across the stage. Then he called the dancers, and they went up. Finally, Lucile was the only one sitting there. Sam Kingston turned to her and asked, "What are you?" She replied, "I don't know. Saturday night you told me to come here." "Well, what are you?" Again she replied, "I don't know." Then Ned Wayburn said, "I'll teach her"; Dave Stamper said he would

help her, too. With only three weeks of practice, she started in the 1921 *Midnight Frolic* as a dancer. After touring with the 1922 *Frolic*, Layton joined the 1922 *Follies* on the road.

When Layton married (and became Lucile Zinman), she retired from the stage and worked as an interior designer. She decorated Eddie Cantor's home but later broke off their friendship when Cantor told a friend not to worry about paying his decorating bill because Layton had money. In fact, Layton's husband, who had a seat on the New York stock exchange, had been wealthy but lost his money in the stock market crash. Layton currently lives in Yonkers, New York.

❖ CHARLES LEMAIRE

was born in Chicago circa 1897 and grew up in Salt Lake City. While in his teens, he teamed with one of his mother's boarders in a song-and-dance act. After a successful local run, they ventured to Chicago but could not find work, so they split up. LeMaire then headed for New York. Desperate for a job, he went into André-Sherri Costumes shop with the theatrical sketches that he drew for amusement. The owners were not interested in his sketches, but they did hire him to manage their shop. While employed at this shop, LeMaire learned French and studied costume design. He met important theatrical personalities, including Ziegfeld, who liked LeMaire's work and let him design a number in the 1920 *Frolic*. The number was such a hit that after the show, Ziegfeld introduced LeMaire as his protégé.

In 1921, when costume

designers were paid little, LeMaire charged Ziegfeld $1,000 for his sketches. LeMaire designed the beautiful "Lace-Land" costumes for the 1922 *Follies*. He also did costumes in the 1924 *Follies, Betsy, Rio Rita,* the *Midnight Frolic* (1928), and *Hot-Cha!*.

LeMaire was costume designer for many other Broadway shows in the 1920s and the early 1930s, including Hammerstein musicals, White's *Scandals,* and Earl Carroll's *Vanities*. While still in New York, LeMaire also designed wardrobes for three movies, created personal wardrobes for well-known women, and later had an exclusive shop. Additionally, he had a radio show, "Fashion Show on the Air," in which he discussed fashion trends and interviewed famous personalities.

LeMaire served in both world wars. In 1943 he became executive designer and director of the wardrobe department at Twentieth Century-Fox. For years he battled to have the film wardrobe designer included in the Academy Awards. He succeeded in 1949 and the next year won the first of three Academy Awards (he was nominated fifteen times) for his costumes for *All About Eve*. His designs also won Oscars for *The Robe* (1953) and *Love Is a Many-Splendored Thing* (1956). He was involved in over two hundred films, and his wardrobes set trends across the country.

LeMaire left show business to paint in 1960. He and his wife, Beatrice Goetz, exhibited their work in galleries and museums around the world. LeMaire died in 1985 at age eighty-eight.

Ziegfeld gave designer Charles LeMaire (seen here with former Ziegfeld showgirl Susan Fleming) his start in 1920 and employed him on and off for the next twelve years. After LeMaire turned to movies, his costumes won three Oscars.

❖ **HAL LEROY,**
born John LeRoy Schotte in 1914, grew up in Cincinnati and as a child tap-danced in amateur productions. He did so well that his mother took him to New York, where Ned Wayburn became his dance instructor. Wayburn got LeRoy his first professional job in *Hoboken Hoboes* (1928) when LeRoy was just fourteen. LeRoy was still sixteen when he became a principal in the *Ziegfeld Follies of 1931.* He appeared in several more Broadway shows and in vaudeville and then entered the movies, where he was in a number of musical shorts with Mitzi Mayfair and others. Beginning in 1933, he played the title role in the Harold Teen series. Besides feature films, LeRoy performed on television, in supper clubs, and in summer stock. He played Frank in the 1956 revival of *Show Boat.* When in his sixties, LeRoy was still dancing, though not professionally. LeRoy also produced, directed, and choreographed industrial shows. He died in 1985 at age seventy-one from complications following heart surgery.

❖ **LILLIAN LORRAINE**
was born Eulallean De Jacques in San Francisco in 1892. She appeared in and was understudy for Anna Held in *Miss Innocence* before her 1909 *Follies* debut. She was also in the 1910 edition and started the 1911 edition. Abe Erlanger did not like Lorraine and dropped her, along with Gene Buck's song "Daddy Has a Sweetheart and Mother Is Her Name," from the 1911 *Follies.* Later she made a hit of the song in vaudeville, and it sold more

than a million copies. She was in the 1912 *Follies* but then was not in the *Follies* again until 1918. She also appeared in Ziegfeld's *Over the River* and the *Ziegfeld Nine O'Clock Revue* (1919 and 1920) and the 1920 *Frolic.* Lorraine was really the first "Follies girl" to become a star.

When not in the *Follies,* Lorraine appeared in vaudeville or in musicals. Between 1906 and 1922 she was in more than a dozen Broadway shows. She had the lead role in two 1915 movies and was in other films. However, her heavy drinking sometimes interfered with her career.

It was widely known that Lorraine had an affair with Ziegfeld; when Anna Held sued for divorce in 1912, she cited Lorraine as a third party. Lillian also had several other affairs, including one with her chauffeur, whom she later charged with theft. She was in and out of bankruptcy court and had to sell her jewels. She was married at least two times. Although the *Follies* made her wealthy, Lorraine died poor in 1955 at age sixty-three.

❖ **CLAIRE LUCE**
was born in 1903 and raised in Rochester, New York. Since her foster mother was a dance teacher, Luce studied dance as a child. She started out as a cigarette girl, first in a Rochester restaurant and then a Broadway nightclub. The nightclub owner put Luce in the chorus of a show. From there she debuted on Broadway in *Little Jesse James* (1923). Apparently Luce also studied dance at the New York Denishawn School around this time.

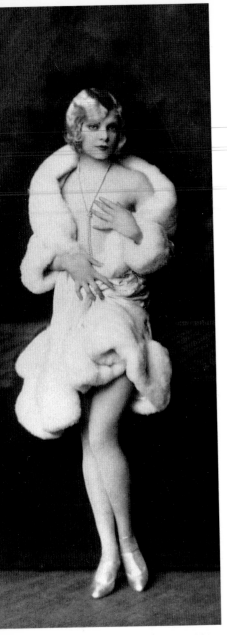

Claire Luce danced for Ziegfeld in 1926 and 1927. She later turned to drama and acted on Broadway and the London stage.

Luce was in the *Music Box Revue* (1924) and then replaced Mistinguett in *Casino de Paris* in 1925. She danced in Ziegfeld's *No Foolin'* and the *Follies of 1927*. Luce made her London debut in *Burlesque* (1928) before returning to New York. After Adele Astaire retired, Luce teamed with Fred Astaire in *Gay Divorce*, on Broadway (1932) and in London (1933).

Luce had signed a five-year movie contract with Fox in 1930 and made a film with Spencer Tracy that year. However, she left film when her millionaire husband was bitten by a mad dog and became ill. The couple (who had married in 1928) were divorced in 1934.

Luce took the role of Katherine in *The Taming of the Shrew* (1941) in London and toured in that show during World War II. After the war she acted in many classical dramas. In fact, Luce was the first American actress to play leading roles at the Shakespeare Memorial Theatre in Stratford-on-Avon. Luce continued acting when she returned to New York around 1947. She appeared in a one-woman dramatic show from 1956 to 1959. In the early 1960s, she was on television. Luce was also an accomplished painter and exhibited many of her works in galleries. Additionally, she recorded drama and poetry albums.

Luce died of cancer in 1989, just before her eighty-sixth birthday.

❖ LUCILLE

(Lady Duff-Gordon) was a London fashion designer. After Ziegfeld and his wife visited her shop, he hired her to design costumes for his shows. He also hired away several of her models, most notably Dolores. Lucille designed costumes for every *Follies* between 1915 and 1921 as well as for Ziegfeld's *The Century Girl, Miss 1917,* and *Sally*.

In her memoirs, Lucille wrote that she quarreled with Joseph Urban over lighting. He insisted they do it his way, but at dress rehearsal he always came to her and in a sulky voice told her to do it her way. Lucille also said that it was not unusual to find a note from Flo requesting sixty dresses for his new show—in ten days' time.

Lady Duff-Gordon made a small fortune designing dresses, but her fees were flexible. She might bill a millionaire's daughter $30,000 for a bridal gown but a struggling actress almost nothing. At one time, she had shops in London, Paris, New York, and Chicago and designed dresses for Irene Castle, Mary Pickford, many *Follies* stars, and numerous society women. After she sold her business to a big company, the shops went bankrupt.

Lady Duff-Gordon and her husband were on board the *Titanic* when it struck an iceberg; they escaped in a lifeboat with some of the crew.

❖ LULU MCCONNELL,

the daughter of a Kansas City dentist, acted in church socials and by age seventeen was traveling with a repertory company. As an adolescent she appeared in musicals; for years she did slapstick and farce in vaudeville. McConnell had a voice described as a "saw-blade." According to one story, when she was appearing at a theater in 1910, she was stricken with stage fright and could not speak. When she made rasping sounds, the audience broke into laughter. This incident established her as a comedian, and her gravel voice became her trademark. She married actor Grant Simpson, and the couple toured vaudeville together. McConnell appeared on the same bill as Anna Held, Eddie Cantor, Eva Tanguay, George Jessel, and Lillian Russell.

McConnell sang several songs in the 1922 *Follies*, the only edition in which she performed. She appeared in a number of other Broadway musicals during the 1920s and had a supporting role in one movie. But she is probably best known as a comic-panelist on the radio hit, "It Pays To Be Ignorant," a satire on quiz shows that ran for seven years (1942–49). McConnell was billed on the show as the "expert on imbecility." She died in 1962 at age seventy.

❖ BESSIE MCCOY

was born Elizabeth McAvoy about 1888. After a stint in vaudeville—she debuted in her step-father (Billy McCoy) and mother's act—she danced on Broadway. Ziegfeld saw her in the *Three Twins* (1908), where she introduced "The Yama Yama Man"; she wore a satin clown outfit and cone-shaped hat. The song was a hit, and McCoy became known as the Yama Yama Girl. She often sang in costumes similar to her clown outfit.

McCoy appeared in *The Echo* (1910) with George White and the Dolly Sisters before her *Follies* debut in 1911. When McCoy was in the *Follies*, author and war correspondent Richard Harding Davis sat in the same seat every night to watch her. In 1912, a few weeks after Davis and his wife divorced, Davis married McCoy. McCoy immediately retired from the stage and in 1915 had a daughter. In 1916 Davis died suddenly. McCoy returned to the stage in the Ziegfeld/Dillingham production, *Miss 1917*. She was also in the *Ziegfeld Midnight Frolic* (1918), the *Greenwich Village Follies* of 1919, and the *Midnight Whirl* (1919). She then retired permanently. McCoy was only forty-three when she died in France in 1931.

❖ J. P. MCEVOY

was the only child of an Irish mathematics professor who became a schoolteacher in Illinois. A child prodigy, McEvoy entered Notre Dame University at age thirteen. To earn tuition money, he worked as an office boy for a newspaper. When a critic could not attend a concert, McEvoy filled in and wrote his first piece. From then on he wrote news and sports stories and eventually became the sports editor. By the time he was seventeen, he had a job on a Chicago newspaper as a columnist. He was only in his early twenties when he was hired at *The Chicago Tribune*. When McEvoy headed to New York, he was offered several jobs, but for less money than he was making in Chicago. After a brief stint at *The New York American*, he returned to the *Tribune*, where he stayed seven years. McEvoy spent part of each season composing greeting-card verses and worked five years as editor and general manager of juvenile books.

McEvoy then began writing free-lance newspaper features. His family series, "The Potters," quickly became famous and was syndicated nationally. He wrote a Broadway play from "The Potters," which was later made into a motion picture starring W. C. Fields. For Ziegfeld, he

Bobby North (c. 1884-1976) entered show business at age twelve—singing in a theater gallery. He did whatever was needed to get a job—comedy, singing, dancing, or straight acting—but became known for his monologues and songs performed with a Yiddish accent. North was a principal in the *Follies of 1910* and had a successful vaudeville career, but he gave up performing in 1915. He later became a movie producer and was responsible for many major films.

worked on *The Comic Supplement*, the 1925 *Follies, No Foolin'*, and *Show Girl* (based on his own novel). McEvoy also wrote for television, radio, and the movies. He created three editions of the revue *Americana* (1926, 1927, and 1932) and for several years did the comic strip "Dixie Dugan." He was a roving editor at *Reader's Digest* for twenty years until his death.

McEvoy was married three times and had four children. He died at age sixty-three in 1958.

❖ MARTHA MANSFIELD,

born Martha Ehrlich in Mansfield, Ohio, lived in New York from the time she was fifteen. Mansfield was in one *Follies* (1918) as well as the *Midnight Frolic* (1918 and 1919) and the *Ziegfeld Nine O'Clock Revue* (1919). She made her first film in 1918 and soon left the musical stage for movies. After Olive Thomas died in 1920, David Selznick promoted Mansfield to stardom. She was John Barrymore's leading lady in *Dr. Jekyll and Mr. Hyde* (1921). Mansfield made eighteen movies before her death at age twenty-three. While she was in Texas filming *The Warrens of Virginia* (1924), her dress caught fire, and she died of burns.

❖ ROSE MARIE MARIELLA

was born in Africa and educated in Naples until age twelve. When she was thirteen, her family came to the United States. At fifteen, Mariella dropped out of school to help support her family. When her older sister married and her father died, Rose Marie was the sole support for her mother, herself, and three younger siblings.

Mariella was waiting tables at Child's Restaurant when one of Ziegfeld's associates spotted her. Mariella did not know who Ziegfeld was, but she finally agreed to see him. She would not ride in a cab with a stranger, so they went to Ziegfeld's office via the subway. Still wearing her waitress uniform, she was ushered in to see Ziegfeld. He told her to come closer and to raise her skirt so he could see

her legs. When she refused, Ziegfeld again told her to pick up her skirt. Finally she did, and Ziegfeld hired her. Mariella was twenty years old when she signed on as a showgirl. She immediately went into *Show Boat*. She and five other girls were chosen by Ziegfeld to be "glorified," and their "glorification" was publicized in the newspaper. Mariella stayed in *Show Boat* while it remained in New York, but she refused to tour, as she still had to support her family and could not afford to leave the city. Her refusal to travel meant she never appeared in the *Follies*, because they always toured. However, after *Show Boat*, she was in *Whoopee*, the *Midnight Frolic* (1928), *Show Girl, Smiles, Simple Simon*, and the 1932 revival of *Show Boat*.

When Ziegfeld died in 1932, Rose Marie found work at one of the movie studios on Long Island. She played the double for Claudette Colbert in several Paramount movies and did some independent shorts. She was a showgirl in the movie *The Great Ziegfeld* (1936).

When her movie career ended, Mariella modeled, was a receptionist, and eventually worked as a secretary for the Medical Society of the County of New York. Mariella was divorced twice and then widowed. She continues to live in New York.

❖ VERA MAXWELL,

a New York City native, was the daughter of a wealthy attorney. Her father refused to let her take dancing lessons, so Maxwell taught herself to dance by practicing before her bedroom mirror. When she was fourteen, her father lost his fortune. After a couple of years in near poverty, Maxwell left home and worked as a chorus girl in a traveling show. In 1908 she was in a Ned Wayburn feature act.

The first Ziegfeld show Maxwell appeared in was the touring version of the *Follies of 1909*. She was in the 1910 *Follies* when it opened on Broadway and remained with the revue through 1916, starting out as a dancer but later becoming a showgirl. She was also in *The Pink Lady, A Winsome Widow, The Century Girl*, and *Miss 1917*.

In addition to her work on Broadway, Maxwell toured vaudeville and concert halls with Wallace McCutcheon and John Jarrott, performing exhibition ballroom dancing. While she was in the *Follies*, she performed at the Palace Theatre, earning as much as $1,000 a week.

After ending her career as a showgirl, Maxwell opened cabarets in New York and Paris. She danced at openings and for special occasions before retiring in 1928. Following a long illness, Maxwell, who never married, died at age fifty-eight (1950).

❖ **MITZI MAYFAIR**
was born in Fulton, Kentucky, about 1910 and raised in St. Louis. She took dance instruction locally. Teamed with Hal LeRoy in the 1931 *Follies*, she was a hit. Between 1931 and 1934, Mayfair and LeRoy danced in a series of film shorts for Warner Brothers. Mayfair then got larger roles in Broadway shows between 1932 and 1936. She was in feature films from 1939 to the late 1940s. She performed

frequently for the USO during the war and appeared in variety shows and promotions for savings bonds.

❖ **MARILYN MILLER**
was born Mary Ellen Reynolds in Findlay, Ohio, around 1900. After making her stage debut at age four or five, she traveled internationally with her family's vaudeville act. In 1913, Lee Shubert discovered her in London and put her in *The Passing Show* (1914, 1915, and 1917 editions) and the *Show of Wonders* (1916). Ziegfeld signed her shortly after Billie Burke saw her at the Winter Garden.

Miller was an instant hit in the *Follies of 1918*. She was also in the *Midnight Frolic* that year. After the *Follies of 1919*, she starred in *Sally* for three years; in two more Ziegfeld musicals, *Rosalie* and *Smiles*; and in Dillingham's *Sunny* (1925). At the height of her stage career, she was earning $5,000 a week. She apparently earned even more in the movies—as much as $11,500 weekly for her last film, earning $3 million during her career.

Heavy drinking caused Miller's career to decline around 1930. In her last stage appearance, in *As Thousands Cheer* (1933), she sang Irving Berlin's hit "Easter Parade."

The five-foot, three-inch Miller was a slender, blue-eyed blonde. Although she was both pretty and talented, Ziegfeld thought it was her personality rather than her talent that made her a star. Despite a thirty-year age difference, Miller is alleged to have had an affair with Ziegfeld.

Ziegfeld opposed Miller's romance with *Follies* star, Frank

Carter, whom she married in 1919. A year later, Carter was killed in a car accident. Miller was devastated and began to party and drink heavily. She was married to Jack Pickford (1922–27) and was engaged several times. In 1934 she eloped with Chet O'Brien, a dancer and assistant stage manager. Miller was thirty-five when she died in Evansville, Indiana, in 1936, of complications from a sinus infection.

❖ **BIRD MILLMAN,**
born Jennadean Engelmann in 1895 in Colorado, was trained as a tightrope walker and dancer by her parents, who were circus aerialists. Millman joined their act, and in 1906, the Millman Trio began touring vaudeville. Millman was called "The Genée of the Air"; the family's act was later changed to Bird Millman and Company and toured vaudeville until 1924.

Millman also did her tightrope act on Broadway. She was in just one *Ziegfeld Follies* (1916) but appeared in many *Midnight Frolics*—two in 1915, two in 1916, three in 1918, the 1919 show, and the February 1921 edition. She was also in the *Greenwich Village Follies of 1921*.

Beginning in 1913, Millman worked five seasons for Barnum and Bailey Circus: 1913–15, 1917, and 1918. When the Ringling Brothers merged with Barnum and Bailey, she performed for that company in 1919 and 1920. After retiring from vaudeville in 1924, Millman moved to Colorado where she managed a ranch; she died there in 1940. In 1961 she was elected

posthumously to the American Circus Hall of Fame.

❖ **JULIAN MITCHELL,**
born in 1854 in Long Branch, New Jersey, started his career as a call boy before becoming a dancer. At age twenty Mitchell produced and danced in his own touring shows. In 1884, he became the principal director for producer Charles Hoyt.

When Mitchell went deaf, he turned to directing and choreography. To determine the music's rhythm he put his forehead or ear to the piano. He did several shows for Weber and Fields in which he established a beautiful chorus line. In 1903 Mitchell directed two of the year's biggest stage hits, *The Wizard of Oz* and *Babes in Toyland*. Mitchell first worked for Ziegfeld in 1906 when he staged *The Parisian Model*. He directed the chorus in the *Follies of 1907*, produced the *Follies'* ensemble numbers in 1908 and 1909, and staged the *Follies* from 1910 through 1913. His other Ziegfeld productions were *Miss Innocence, The Soul Kiss*, and *A Winsome Widow*. After Mitchell and Ziegfeld had a disagreement, he left the 1914 *Follies*. In 1915 Mitchell and Errol were *Follies* co-directors. Mitchell left the *Follies* in 1915, but he returned after a nine-year absence to stage the 1924 and 1925 *Follies* and Ziegfeld's *Comic Supplement*.

Mitchell directed or choreographed at least one Broadway show every year between 1896 and 1925, staging over eighty musicals in his career. The seventy-two-year-old Mitchell was assistant director for *No Foolin'*, but became ill and underwent surgery three weeks before the show's New York premiere. He died on opening day, June 24, 1926.

In 1894 Mitchell had married dancer Bessie Clayton, who was in the 1909 *Follies*. They divorced in 1924, after a long estrangement. They had one daughter.

❖ **HELEN MORGAN,**
born in 1900 in Danville, Illinois, was the daughter of a farmer and a teacher. After her father died, her mother moved them to Chicago. Morgan worked as a packer and then as a manicurist. She studied singing and dancing and by age eighteen was working in a small cabaret. She made her New York debut as part of the replacement cast in the chorus of *Sally*. When *Sally* closed, Morgan returned to Chicago to sing in a café.

In 1925 Morgan returned to New York to sing in a nightclub. Because the floor was small and crowded, she sat on the grand piano to be seen. From then on, she nearly always appeared perched on a piano. George White saw her perform and gave her a part in his *Scandals* (1925). When the star became ill opening night, Morgan took her place and was a hit. In the late 1920s, she appeared in vaudeville and sang in several nightclubs bearing her name. But it was her role as Julie in *Show Boat* that made her a star. She played Julie for three years and later re-created the role in the 1936 film version. In 1929 Morgan achieved further success in the Hammerstein/Kern musical *Sweet Adeline*. She was also in the 1928 *Ziegfeld Midnight Frolic* and the 1931 *Follies*. She

left Broadway to earn $2,500 a week in vaudeville.

Morgan appeared in a few films between 1929 and 1936. Her last nightclub went bankrupt in 1935. In 1941 she was set to appear in the Chicago production of *George White's Scandals* when she died of a recurring liver ailment, complicated by drinking.

Morgan had been married from 1933 to 1935 and had remarried shortly before her death. Although she had earned a fortune (as much as $117,000 one year), she died penniless. A television drama and a movie version of her life story appeared in 1957.

❖ **J. HAROLD MURRAY**
was born in Maine in 1891. He promoted songs for music publishers before entering vaudeville in 1918. After two successful years, Murray made his Broadway debut in *The Passing Show of 1921*. He did musical comedies during the 1920s, including Ziegfeld's *Rio Rita*, and made occasional appearances in vaudeville.

In 1929 Murray signed a film contract with Fox; he was in several movies in the early 1930s and made film shorts for Universal and RKO in 1937. He then returned to the East to do a radio show in the late 1930s. Murray left the entertainment field to go into business. He was president of the New England Brewing Company, maker of Murray's Beer. He died in Connecticut in 1940.

❖ **MAE MURRAY,**
originally Marie Koenig (from Portsmouth, Virginia), was born about 1889. She danced as a child and debuted on

Broadway as Vernon Castle's partner in *About Town* (1906). Her *Follies* appearances (1908, 1909, 1915, and 1920) and her role as a featured dancer in *Watch Your Step* (1914) made her famous. In 1914 Murray toured vaudeville with partner Clifton Webb.

Adolph Zukor saw Murray in the *Follies* (1915) and offered her a contract. She debuted on screen in 1916 and went on to become a big star in silent films. By most accounts, her best performance was opposite screen idol John Gilbert in *The Merry Widow* (1925). Although there were more talented actresses, Murray was beautiful and very graceful. She was one of the highest-paid stars of her era, earning an estimated $3 million during her career. Known as the nation's "number one glamour girl," she would come to the studio in her Rolls-Royce with a sable lap robe.

Murray's fourth husband, Prince David Mdivani, took over her career when they married. After quarreling with the M-G-M brass, Mdivani insisted Murray break her contract. Subsequently, Murray had difficulty getting parts. She acted in a couple of early talkies and returned to vaudeville in 1930. Although she made occasional television and nightclub appearances, her comeback attempts were largely unsuccessful. It did not help that she had a reputation for being difficult. Once, after losing a $300,000 lawsuit against a film studio, she slapped the company attorney. Another time she threw an inkwell at her own attorney when she did not like what he said.

Before long Murray was forgotten as an actress; however, her divorces, her unsuccessful custody battle for her son, and her bankruptcy continued to make news. Murray often went to charity balls where she had the orchestra play the theme from *The Merry Widow* and then danced by herself. Murray's 1959 biography sold poorly. In February 1964, she was found wandering the streets of St. Louis. She was penniless, so the Salvation Army paid her $13.20 hotel bill and flew her to California. Six months later, she suffered a stroke. In 1965, Murray, age seventy-five, died at the Motion Picture County Home in Woodland Hills, California.

❖ **EDNA MAY OLIVER**
(Ida May Nutter) was born in Malden, Massachusetts, in 1883. As a child she studied piano, dance, and voice and performed in amateur productions. At age fourteen, she left school and worked in a hat shop. In 1900, she joined a light opera company. She then toured as a pianist with a ladies' orchestra and worked in stock companies, developing her comic skills.

By 1917, Oliver was in the musical *Oh, Boy*. When she appeared in *Show Boat* ten years later, she was already a film actress, having debuted on screen in 1923. Oliver was the perfect Parthy Ann Hawks, with her long, aristocratic face and arrogant sniff. After *Show Boat*, she returned to films, making more than forty-five movies.

In the 1930s, Oliver played Aunt March in *Little Women* (1933), Aunt Betsy

Trotwood in *David Copperfield* (1934), and the nurse in *Romeo and Juliet* (1936). She was also in a *Tale of Two Cities* (1935), three mystery movies, *Pride and Prejudice* (1940), and *Lydia* (1941). She was nominated for an Oscar as best supporting actress for her role in *Drums Along the Mohawk* (1939).

After suffering from an intestinal ailment for over a year, Oliver died on her fifty-ninth birthday (1942). She had married in 1928 but divorced five years later and never remarried.

❖ **NONA OTERO,**
born in 1908, studied dance as a child and performed with an opera company for a year. When she was fifteen, she auditioned for Ziegfeld and joined the 1922 *Follies* as it was about to go on tour (fall 1923). Additionally, she was in the 1927 *Follies* and three Ziegfeld musicals: *Kid Boots, The Three Musketeers,* and *Show Girl.* In the Ziegfeld shows, Otero was a soloist with the famed Albertina Rasch Dancers and an understudy for many of the featured dancers.

Otero performed in vaudeville and danced in Broadway musicals, including *Band Wagon* (1931). For two years, she was in film musicals. She also danced at Grauman's Chinese Theater in Hollywood and at the Hollywood Rose Bowl.

After marrying in 1937, Otero retired from theatre and studied at the New York School of Interior Design and was a decorator for many years. For the last thirty years, she has been active in the Ziegfeld Club, a charitable organization. She lives in New York City.

❖ **ANN PENNINGTON**
was born in Camden, New Jersey, in 1894 and danced as an amateur in Philadelphia. Ned Wayburn was one of her dance instructors. She made her professional debut in the chorus of *The Red Widow* (1911). In 1913 she started her *Follies* career at $50 a week and was an immediate hit. Pennington became one of the era's most popular dancers. She was only 4 feet, 11½ inches tall (in heels), weighed 100 pounds, and wore a size 1½ shoe. Her nickname was Tiny. Pennington had long, dark hair and dimpled knees. She appeared in many *Follies:* 1913–16, 1918, 1923, 1924, and Spring 1925. She also danced in Ziegfeld's *Miss 1917* and several editions of the *Midnight Frolic.*

After the 1918 *Follies,* Pennington joined George White for his inaugural edition of the *Scandals;* she danced in five editions. She was earning $1,000 a week by 1920. In the 1926 *Scandals,* she danced and sang the "Black Bottom." Although it had been introduced the year before, Pennington is credited with popularizing the dance, which rivaled the Charleston.

Between 1916 and the 1930s, Pennington was in three feature films and more than a dozen shorts. During the early 1930s, she danced in musicals. In the 1940s she performed in a couple of road shows and in vaudeville; her last stage appearance was in 1946.

Pennington never married although she was engaged several times. When she was making movies on the West Coast, she lived in Los Angeles with her good friend Fannie Brice. Back in New York, she

lived alone, in a small room. She had been in a nursing home for some time before she died, in 1971, at age seventy-seven.

❖ **EVA PUCK**
was born in 1892 in Brooklyn. When she was three, she started dancing with her brother Harry in vaudeville. The two Pucks were a team until 1912, when Eva married a vaudeville manager and temporarily retired. After her marriage ended, Puck resumed dancing with her brother (1916–21). In 1921, she teamed with and wed Sammy White. Their act was popular in vaudeville, where White played the role of a dancing instructor trying to teach the not-very-bright Puck. The couple also performed a burlesque of grand opera and classical dancing. Additionally, Puck and White were successful in musical comedies. They were in the *Greenwich Village Follies* (1923), *Irene* (1924), and *The Girl Friend* (1926). In the latter show, the lead role was written for Puck. Puck and White danced in *Show Boat* and then returned to vaudeville as headliners. They ventured back to Broadway for the 1932 *Show Boat* revival. After Puck and White divorced, Puck retired. She died in 1979 at the age of eighty-six.

❖ **ALBERTINA RASCH**
was a Viennese dancer and choreographer who was born in 1891. She studied at the Imperial Theatre before coming to the States in 1912. Rasch danced with one of the Metropolitan Opera ballet companies at the Century Theatre and then founded her

own ballet company to generate more interest in ballet among Americans. She performed classical ballet in popular theaters and vaudeville houses in the 1920s and 1930s. Her career as a choreographer got a boost after her dancers appeared in *George White's Scandals* in 1925. Beginning in 1927 with *Rio Rita,* the Albertina Rasch Dancers appeared in several Ziegfeld productions—the *Follies* (1927 and 1931), *The Three Musketeers,* and *Show Girl.*

Rasch's presentations were unique to Broadway because she used trained ballet dancers, generally sixteen per show, who sometimes performed precision work.

In 1929, Rasch began choreographing Hollywood films but continued doing Broadway shows through 1945. One year, 1932, she choreographed eight Broadway shows and one London musical. Rasch married composer Dimitri Tiomkin in 1926; they had no children. She died in California at age seventy-six (1967) after a long illness.

❖ **JESSIE REED,**
born Jessie Rogers near Houston, was forced to leave elementary school to earn money, working first in a factory and then as waitress. In 1912, when she was fifteen, she married a blackface comedian who gave her a bit part in his act. When Reed was about sixteen, her only child was born. After her husband killed her lover, the couple divorced, and her ex-husband won custody of their daughter. Reed took her second husband's name. After divorcing him, she moved to New York and appeared with

Albertina Rasch started out as a dancer but became more famous for her choreography and for the group of dancers that performed under her direction. The Albertina Rasch Dancers first worked for Ziegfeld in *Rio Rita* (1927) and then performed in his *Follies* (1927 and 1931), *The Three Musketeers* (1928), and *Show Girl* (1929).

The Passing Show of 1918, where Ziegfeld saw her.

Reed made her *Follies* debut in 1919 as the *Follies* "Girl of the Year." Ziegfeld hired her at $125 per week, but soon she became the highest-paid chorus girl at $250 a week. Reed spent her earnings on furs, jewels, clothes, cars, and travel. She was in the *Follies* for five years (1919–23).

While in the *Follies,* Reed married a wealthy man from Cleveland whom she had met on a train. Two years later, after accepting his family's heirloom jewels and squandering his fortune, she divorced him. She also married a Chicago advertising executive in 1924 and the son of a wealthy publisher in 1928. This last marriage was her longest—four years.

Reed reportedly received a seven-carat diamond from one husband-to-be and a $37,000 wedding trip from another. For the last five years of her life, however, she was almost destitute. In 1935, she attempted a comeback in Chicago because she was facing eviction from her $5-per-week room. When the comeback failed, Reed became a nightclub hostess.

Reed's health was poor from years of heavy drinking. She was only forty-three and penniless when she died of pneumonia in 1940.

❖ **JAMES REYNOLDS**
was born in 1892 in Warrenton, Virginia. A set and costume designer, he created sets for *What's in a Name* (1920) and the *Greenwich Village Follies* (1920–23). His reputation soared when his beautiful costumes and sets appeared in the 1921, 1922, and 1923 *Ziegfeld Follies.* Reynolds worked on the *Music Box Revue* (1924) before becoming Charles Dillingham's artistic director in the mid-1920s. He designed the sets for *Sunny* (1925), *Crisscross* (1926), and *Oh, Please!* (1926). He worked on several other shows until he retired in the mid-1930s.

Jessie Reed was the highest-paid showgirl in her day, but she died penniless.

In addition to designing sets and costumes, Reynolds was an interior decorator in the United States and abroad. He also wrote, designed, and directed several ballets and dramas in Rome. In retirement, he painted, lectured, and wrote and illustrated his own travel books and ghost stories. Reynolds died in Italy in 1957.

❖ **HARRY RICHMAN,**
born in Cincinnati in 1895, was playing the piano in cafés there as early as 1907. In 1910, he

played the piano for Mae West and the Dolly Sisters. During the 1920s, he sang on the radio in New York City; he created the practice of payola when he offered to sing music publishers' songs for one dollar

Singer Harry Richman was one of the biggest names in New York, and his Club Richman was one of the city's top night spots.

each. In 1923, Richman put together a successful vaudeville act. He wore a top hat and tails and carried a cane, which soon became his trademarks. He achieved big-name status, and his Club Richman on Park Avenue was a top night spot in the 1920s.

In 1926 and 1928, Richman was in *George White's Scandals*. He was emcee for the 1931 *Ziegfeld Follies* and also performed in film. Richman composed and sang many of his own hits, including "Walking

My Baby Back Home" and his theme, "Putting on the Ritz."

Richman was married three times and had many affairs. He spent $30,000 on his wedding to his second wife, *Follies* showgirl Hazel Forbes. Richman said that he made and lost $13 million during his career (others said $7 million). In 1947, when Richman's voice began to give out, his career started to fade. He died in Los Angeles in 1972.

❖ **PAUL ROBESON,**
son of a runaway slave who became a minister and a teacher, was born in Princeton, New Jersey, in 1898. In 1915 he won a scholarship to Rutgers University; he was only the third black to attend the school. At Rutgers Robeson was an all-American in football and lettered in track, basketball, and baseball. He was also a member of the Phi Beta Kappa society. After graduating from Rutgers in 1919, he got a law degree from Columbia University. With the encouragement of his fiancée, Eslanda Goode, he went into the theater instead of practicing law. After he married Goode in 1921, Robeson's wife managed his career until her death in 1965.

Robeson first acted in a YMCA play before joining a group of Greenwich Village actors (including Eugene O'Neill), who sponsored Robeson's first concert in 1925. Robeson played Joe in the 1928 London production of *Show Boat*, in the 1932 Broadway revival, and in the 1936 movie; he played Othello in London (1930) and on Broadway (1943). After 1939, he lived mostly in Europe, where race was less of an issue. He was

Ziegfeld hired Sigmund Romberg (1887-1951) to compose the music for *Rosalie* (1928). When Romberg found out that Ziegfeld wanted the score in three weeks, he suggested that George Gershwin help him.

known internationally as a concert artist.

After his return to America, Robeson was active in black affairs and performed for many trade unions and organizations that the Attorney General's Office considered "subversive." Several times Congressional Committees questioned him about Communist Party activities, although he denied being a member. Because of his apparent "Communist sympathies," he was blacklisted; consequently his salary dropped from $100,000 in 1947 to

$6,000 in 1952. In 1950, the United States government canceled his passport for refusing to sign an oath that he was not a Communist. After he waged a long, costly legal battle, the government reinstated his passport in 1958.

Robeson became ill in 1961 while in East Germany. In 1963, he retired and returned to New York. He lived in a Harlem apartment for several years and then moved to Philadelphia to live with his sister. Robeson died at age seventy-eight (1976) of a stroke.

WILL ROGERS

was born in 1879 in Oolagah, Indian Territory (later Oklahoma). He was a poor student and preferred working on his father's prosperous ranch, where he became a cowhand at age fourteen. He continued this work in Argentina and then South Africa. In Africa he signed on as a trick roper with a Wild West Circus. He then toured Australia with a circus. Later he headed back to the States and performed his rope tricks in vaudeville. By 1905, he was in New York. While Rogers was doing his rope tricks, he started to talk and drew laughs. Thinking that the crowd was laughing at him, Rogers decided not to talk anymore. Other entertainers finally convinced him that the audience liked this addition to his act.

Rogers's funny, down-to-earth comments on current affairs and political leaders became so popular that Ziegfeld gave him complete control over his act. Rogers changed his material every night and never rehearsed his eight- to ten-minute act. During rehearsals he used his allotted time to joke about the cast, the show, or rehearsals. The cast loved him and hung around in the wings to hear his act. Rogers was the only Ziegfeld star who never had a written contract.

Rogers was in the *Follies* from 1916 to 1918, and again in 1922, 1924, and 1925. He was in several *Midnight Frolic* shows between 1915 and 1922. He starred in his first Hollywood movie in 1918 and made about a dozen films in the next two years. By 1921, he was back in the *Midnight Frolic* and

by 1922 returned to the *Follies*. In late 1922, Rogers produced three movies and went broke. He returned to the *Follies* in 1924 and earned up to $3,500 a week.

Rogers began accepting speaking engagements to pay off his movie-making debts and to support his family. In 1925 he left Ziegfeld permanently for a national lecture tour. He replaced Fred Stone in *Three Cheers* (1928) and had a successful radio show from 1933 to 1935. Additionally, Rogers wrote a newspaper column and several books. At the time of his death, he was appearing in movies (he had made twenty-one sound pictures and over fifty silent ones) and writing for newspapers.

Rogers married Betty Blake in 1908. They had three boys and a girl. (The youngest boy died of diphtheria at eighteen months of age.)

Rogers lived modestly and often gave money to charity and friends. According to Lucile Layton Zinman, who toured with Rogers in the 1922 *Follies,* Rogers usually knew which cast members had been playing poker with the road manager's wife, who always won. When the cast left the train early in the morning, Rogers would be leaning against one of the station's pillars with his hat pulled over one eye and his hands in his pockets. As dejected poker players passed by, he would say, "How much did she take you for?" The people would mumble that they had nothing left. Rogers would then pull his hand from his pocket and unobtrusively pass the person a fistful of bills. When the recipients of

Rogers's generosity checked later, they might find $40, $50, or $60. Rogers never counted the money and never asked about repayment; he just assumed people would pay it back when they could.

Ziegfeld appreciated Rogers's special talent and gave Will a shower in his dressing room—quite a luxury then. Ziegfeld also arranged for him to transport two horses (one of them his black roping pony, Dopey) in the scenery car while on tour.

Rogers loved flying. In 1935, he flew with Wiley Post to Alaska. Both men were killed when their plane crashed on August 15. Rogers was receiving $110,000 per film at the time of his death. He never invested in the stock market; instead, he put his money in life insurance, United States savings bonds, and real estate. At his death, Rogers's estate was valued at $2.3 million.

SAVOY AND BRENNAN

were a very popular comedy team. Bert Savoy was born Everett McKenzie in Boston around 1888. He worked in a freak museum and a carnival before becoming a chorus boy. He later became a female impersonator in the Yukon and Alaska. He left Alaska for Chicago where he married a showgirl in 1904. (They divorced in 1922.)

Jay Brennan was born around 1883 and also became a chorus boy. The two met in 1913 on a streetcar. At the time, both men were unemployed, so they formed a new act. The tall, handsome Brennan played the straight man, while Savoy was the

female impersonator. By 1916 they were playing the Palace for $1,500 a week; that same year they debuted in the *Ziegfeld Follies*. Savoy and Brennan were also in the 1918 *Follies* and several editions of the *Midnight Frolic* as well as the *Greenwich Village Follies* (1920–22).

In June 1923, Savoy and a vaudeville associate were walking on a Long Island beach when a thunderstorm arose. They were both struck by lightning and killed.

After Savoy's death, Jay Brennan teamed with Stanley Rogers in a similar and successful vaudeville act. In 1929 Brennan went solo in the musical revue *Fioreta* with Leon Errol and Fannie Brice. He and Rogers reunited at the Palace the next year. In the mid-1930s, Brennan became a script writer and dialogue director for films. He performed until 1945. A life-long bachelor, Brennan died in 1961 at the reported age of seventy-eight.

VIVIENNE SEGAL

was born in Philadelphia in 1897 to a wealthy physician and his wife. She went to private schools and had private tutors. Because her father made large contributions to cultural and theatrical organizations, Segal started her career in Philadelphia in good roles. In 1914, she debuted as the lead in *Carmen* and followed with a role in *Faust*. In *The Blue Paradise* (1915), she sang only a duet, but the show was a hit so she received much attention.

Segal first worked for Ziegfeld in *Miss 1917*. She was in the 1924 and 1925 *Follies* before accepting a principal role in *The Three Musketeers*.

Between 1930 and 1934, Segal made several films and then retired. She was married twice.

❖ ETHEL SHUTTA,

born in 1896, was only five when she made her first stage appearance dancing the Cake Walk in Madison Square Garden. In 1901, Shutta was in a revival of *Uncle Tom's Cabin*. For years she performed with her parents in carnivals, burlesque shows, and vaudeville.

Shutta's first Broadway appearance was in *The Passing Show of 1922*. She was in *Louie the 14th* and the 1925 *Ziegfeld Follies*. Later she sang in *Whoopee*—the Broadway show and the movie. Shutta met and married band leader George Olsen while both were in the *Follies*. She toured as a vocalist with Olsen's orchestra and in musicals. After Shutta and Olsen were divorced, Shutta remarried. She continued to entertain extensively in nightclubs and cabarets. She was on "The Jack Benny Show" (radio) in 1932–33 and appeared on television. As late as 1971 she performed at the Winter Garden. Shutta was seventy-nine when she died in 1976.

❖ HARRY B. SMITH

was born in Buffalo in 1860 and grew up in Chicago. As a child, he put on shows in the family's barn or attic and acted in amateur productions with his friends. At fifteen he became a billing clerk for a wholesale drug firm. When a relative left him a little money, Smith began acting in the Chicago Church Choir Company, making loans to the manager in return for acting parts. When that

company foundered, Smith spent two years with a burlesque company. He eventually returned to Chicago where he became drama and music critic for the *Chicago Tribune* and wrote articles for other newspapers. Smith founded a weekly comic and society paper that he ran for two years before he began writing for the stage. After writing burlesque, he teamed up with Reginald De Koven to write comic operas. *Robin Hood* (1891) was their first success.

Smith was the primary sketch writer for the early *Follies* (1907–10 and 1912). He also contributed material to five book shows produced by Ziegfeld: *Papa's Wife, The Little Duchess, The Parisian Model, Miss Innocence,* and *The Soul Kiss.*

Smith produced lyrics and librettos for 123 Broadway musicals. By his own count, Smith wrote 300 librettos and the lyrics for 6,000 songs, making him the most prolific librettist and lyricist in the history of the American theatre.

Rennold Wolf, who co-authored the 1915 *Follies*, tells of the time he was at a prominent producer's apartment when the producer telephoned Smith requesting three new stanzas and new choruses for a waltz number. He wanted the new lyrics by the following week. Smith told the man to send his secretary over and he would have the lyrics ready for him. The secretary returned in about ten minutes with three new stanzas of eight lines each. Even more remarkable, according to Wolf, the lyrics were "amusing and ingeniously rhymed."

Smith worked hard so he

Between 1912 and 1931, Dave Stamper composed songs for fourteen *Follies* and fourteen editions of the *Midnight Frolic.*

would have money for collecting rare literary works and Napoleona. He enjoyed reading and studied French and German. He was married to prima donna Irene Bentley. Smith died in 1936.

❖ DAVE STAMPER

attended public schools in New York City, where he was born in 1883. He taught himself to play the piano, and at age seventeen, left school to work in a Coney Island dance hall. Next Stamper was a staff pianist and song plugger for music publishers. At age twenty he toured vaudeville as a piano accompanist; he worked four years with Nora Bayes and Jack Norworth. During World War I, Stamper went to London and wrote music for *Zig Zag* and *Box of Tricks.*

Stamper started his Broadway career with Ziegfeld in 1912. From then until 1931, Stamper wrote songs for the *Follies* (1912–17, 1919, 1921–27, 1931) and the *Midnight Frolic* (fourteen editions), usually teaming with Gene Buck. Additionally, he composed music for *Lovely Lady* (1927) and *Take the Air* (1927). He also wrote the score for the

sound film *Married in Hollywood.*

When Ziegfeld died, Stamper's career on Broadway essentially ended. He was married to *Follies* star Edna Leedom. He died in 1963 at age seventy-nine.

❖ BARBARA STANWYCK,

born Ruby Stevens in Brooklyn (1907), was orphaned when she was four. Her older sister, a dancer, raised her with the help of relatives and friends. Stanwyck quit school and performed unskilled jobs while teaching herself to dance. A month before her fifteenth birthday she debuted in the 1922 *Ziegfeld Follies*, using a stage name because she was underage. She toured with the *Follies* in 1923 and early 1924 before moving on to *Keep Kool* (1924). After a few more revues, she started in the chorus of *The Noose* (1926) but was promoted to a lead role, at which point she changed her name to Stanwyck.

Stanwyck danced in her first movie, *Broadway Nights* (1927), a silent film made in New York. She did another Broadway show and then married vaudevillian Frank Fay in 1928. When Fay began working for Warner Brothers, Stanwyck accompanied him to Hollywood. She worked for Columbia and Warner Studios before signing a contract with RKO Studio that let her freelance. She became a box office star in roles of independent, ruthless, sophisticated women.

Stanwyck made over eighty films and was nominated for Academy Awards for her roles in *Stella Dallas* (1937), *Ball of Fire* (1942), *Double*

Indemnity (1944), and *Sorry, Wrong Number* (1948). In 1982 she was awarded an honorary Oscar.

Beginning in 1954, Stanwyck was a guest on many television shows. She had her own series in 1960–61 and starred on "The Big Valley" from 1965 to 1969. Later she made guest appearances on television; she was in "The Thorn Birds" (1983) and on "The Colbys" for one season (1986). Stanwyck won three Emmy awards for her performances.

Stanwyck and Frank Fay adopted a son before divorcing in 1935. From 1939 to 1951, Stanwyck was married to actor Robert Taylor. She died at age eighty-two of heart failure in 1990.

❖ EVA TANGUAY

was born in 1878 in Marbleton, Quebec, and raised in Massachusetts. She did stock theater and Broadway plays and was acclaimed as the youngest star on the American stage. In the early 1900s, she achieved fame in vaudeville, becoming one of vaudeville's biggest hits and highest-paid performers. By 1910 Tanguay was earning $3,500 a week and by 1916, $10,000 per week.

Tanguay sang risqué songs that other stars could not get by with or would not even try. Her most famous song was "I Don't Care." She had frizzy, blonde hair and wore outrageous costumes on stage, many of them feathered. She shocked audiences when she first appeared on stage in white tights, but they soon became her trademark.

The tempestuous Tanguay frequently feuded with

agents who wanted her to share billing. She got into fights and often walked out on engagements. She paid fines with the $1,000 bills she carried. One booking agent required her to post a $5,000 bond to ensure she showed up for work.

Tanguay had rivalries with other stars including Nora Bayes and Gertrude Hoffmann. Tanguay admitted that she could not sing or dance and was not beautiful. She said she owed her success to the exploitation of her personality, which was said to be the most dynamic in vaudeville.

In 1909 Tanguay replaced Nora Bayes in the *Follies* (Tanguay's only *Follies*), doing her racy Salome number, which had caused an uproar in vaudeville the year before. Though Tanguay later became famous for musical comedy, she was first and foremost a vaudevillian, having performed there for twenty-five years. When vaudeville died in the 1930s, Tanguay retired to Los Angeles. She was a recluse until her death in 1947. On her sixty-eighth birthday, just before her death, Tanguay gave an interview but would only talk through the screen on her bedroom window.

❖ NORMA TERRIS

was born Norma Cook in Chicago, Illinois, in 1900 or 1902. She spent much of her childhood with her grandparents in Columbus, Kansas, because her father, who managed movie theaters, moved frequently. As a young child, Norma learned to mimic people and to play the piano and sing.

When she was about seventeen, while living in

Chicago, Norma started going out with a wealthy forty-nine-year-old divorced man who offered to send her to school. Her father objected to the relationship and killed the man. Norma was required to testify at her father's murder trial. The trial was front-page news in Chicago (early 1919) and generated a lot of undesirable publicity.

When the trial ended, Norma and her mother had to find jobs. For a time, Norma sold cosmetics and worked at a telegraph office, but people eventually recognized her, so she moved to Long Island. There she studied for the stage with a cousin, Lucille (Mrs. Sidney) Drew, as well as Gertrude Hoffmann; she also studied ballet.

Terris made her Broadway debut in the chorus of the *Ziegfeld Midnight Frolic* (September 1920), using the name Norma Allison. Next she appeared in the *Ziegfeld Nine O'Clock Revue* (1921). In 1921, Terris married Max Hoffmann, Jr. The couple toured vaudeville as "Junior and Terris." The two divorced about five years later.

Terris returned to New York and soon appeared in musicals. She got a break when she played the lead in George M. Cohan's *Little Nellie Kelly* on tour (1923–24). She toured in another show (1924–25) and then returned to Broadway in 1926. She was in a Shubert revue (earning $600 a week) when Ziegfeld saw her. Although she had a five-year contract with Shubert, she was released from it after arbitration before Actors' Equity so she could play Magnolia in *Show Boat*.

Ziegfeld gave Terris her original *Show Boat* contract in July 1927. They were in back of the Ziegfeld Theatre during the run of *Rio Rita* when Ziegfeld took out a piece of paper and wrote the contract by hand. When he asked Terris what salary she wanted, she said $1,000 per week. He offered her $900 per week with a raise if the show was successful. After opening night, Ziegfeld raised her salary to $1,000. (Later it went up to $1,250 a week.)

Terris began touring with *Show Boat* but left the show before it reached Chicago (Irene Dunne replaced her). Most people thought she left to sign a film contract with Fox; actually, she was afraid that someone in Chicago would recognize her as Norma Cook and that the scandal would ruin her career. Because Terris deserted the *Show Boat* tour, for years she had difficulty getting other parts on Broadway.

In 1929, Terris signed a three-movie contract for $50,000 per picture. She disliked making movies and left Hollywood after completing two pictures. In 1932, Ziegfeld hired her back to recreate her role of Magnolia (and Kim) in the revival of *Show Boat*. For ten years in the 1930s and 1940s, Terris was a star of the Municipal Opera Company of St. Louis. She also acted with various stock companies.

Terris became a patron of the Goodspeed Opera in Connecticut, where she occasionally performed. She helped remodel a knitting-needle factory into the Norma Terris Theater.

In August 1929, during the run of *Show Boat*, Terris

married Ziegfeld's close friend Dr. Jerome Wagner; they remained married until his death in 1955. She then lived with J. Harold Preston for thirty-two years, until they parted ways in 1986. In 1987 Terris married Albert D. Firestone, a long-time friend. Terris lived with her husband on their four-hundred-acre estate in Lyme, Connecticut, and in Palm Beach, Florida, until she died in November 1989.

❖ OLIVE THOMAS

(Olive Elaine Duffy) was born in Pennsylvania in 1898. Her father's death left the family poor. When Olive was ten, her mother remarried, and they moved near Pittsburgh. Thomas quit school at age fourteen to become a $3-per-week salesgirl. At sixteen, hoping for a life of wealth, she married a businessman. Before long Thomas and a childhood friend left for New York where Thomas became a model. She divorced her husband in 1915.

Thomas was hired for the *Follies* at a starting salary of $75 per week. She appeared in the *Frolic* (1915 and 1916) and the *Follies* (1915). Although she did not have major roles, she soon became famous for her beauty. In 1916 she made her first movie. One source said Thomas was rehearsing for the 1917 *Follies* when she broke off what had been an intimate relationship with Ziegfeld. At any rate, she was not in the *Follies* that year. She left the stage entirely for better money in film. Between 1916 and 1920, Thomas made nine films, earning a fortune.

Thomas was nineteen when she met Jack Pickford.

The couple married a few months later, in 1917. They had a stormy marriage. Thomas had decided to divorce Pickford, but the couple reconciled shortly before sailing to Paris. After a night of partying, Thomas and Pickford returned to their hotel, and she took several poisonous tablets, apparently mistaking them for sleeping pills. (How this occurred remained a mystery since the bottle was clearly marked.) Thomas lost her vision and speech and lingered in agony for five days before she slipped into a coma and died peacefully on September 10, 1920. Her jewels and cars were auctioned off for $30,000.

❖ FRANK TINNEY,

born in Philadelphia in 1878, made his stage debut wearing blackface at age four. In Texas, where his mother took him to perform, an agent spotted Tinney and brought him to New York for big-time vaudeville. He became one of the most famous blackface comics in vaudeville, performing until 1920. Tinney rarely used dialect but was known for his corny jokes, his confidences to the audience, and his chats with the orchestra.

By January 1913, the actor was earning $1,000 a week. He alternated between vaudeville and musical comedy, where he starred in several shows between 1912 and 1926. Tinney first worked for Ziegfeld in 1912 in *A Winsome Widow*. Other Ziegfeld productions in which Tinney performed were the 1913 *Follies*, *The Century Girl*, the *Midnight Frolic*, and the 1920 *Follies*. Tinney appeared at the Palace in London several times.

For his 1919 appearance, he was the highest paid American actor up to that time—earning $2,250 per week. He was one of the stars of the *Music Box Revue of 1923*.

Although he had a wife and child, Tinney had many affairs, including a highly publicized one with *Follies* star Imogene Wilson. In a 1924 scandal, Wilson accused Tinney of beating her and sued him; Tinney was never indicted, but the publicity hurt his career and cost him many friends. His wife divorced him and later had him arrested for nonpayment of alimony. In 1926 Tinney suffered a nervous breakdown and retired from the stage. Although he had earned millions of dollars, he was penniless. He died in a Long Island Veterans Hospital in 1940.

❖ SOPHIE TUCKER

(Sonia Kalish) was born in Russia in 1884 and started singing in the family restaurant as a child in Hartford, Connecticut. She was married briefly to Louis Tuck, from whom she took her stage name. In 1906 she started performing in vaudeville. Marc Klaw saw her on the burlesque circuit and hired her for the *Follies*. Ziegfeld was irked at Klaw for not consulting him, especially after he saw Sophie. Far from being a beautiful and graceful "Follies girl," Tucker was large and awkward.

Just before the Atlantic City opening, Ziegfeld demanded a new number about Teddy Roosevelt's recent African hunting expedition. When Harry B. Smith said they had no one to sing it, Ziegfeld turned to Sophie. The

composers worked all night writing "It's Moving Day in Jungle Town." Tucker, dressed as a leopard while she sang her number, was the hit of the show. She received a standing ovation opening night in Atlantic City.

Nora Bayes was jealous of Tucker's success and threatened to leave the show unless Tucker was fired. After consulting with Erlanger and Julian Mitchell, Ziegfeld announced at the next rehearsal that Tucker would do only one song; when the show opened in New York, Tucker appeared in only one scene, and Bayes got her other songs. Later in the run, Bayes left the show and was replaced by Eva Tanguay. Tanguay demanded Tucker's "Jungle Queen" number and most of Bayes's numbers, so Tucker was dropped from the show. Years later, when Tucker became famous, Ziegfeld said that he could not afford her.

Tucker returned to vaudeville where she eventually reached headliner status. She performed at the Palace in 1914. She had a big, brassy voice and was billed as "the last of the red-hot Mamas." Beginning in 1918, Tucker sang in restaurants and cabarets, where she introduced the song "A Good Man Is Hard to Find." In the 1920s, she returned to vaudeville, and between 1919 and 1941, she was in six Broadway musicals. In her later years Tucker sang mostly in nightclubs. She performed until shortly before her death in 1966.

❖ JOSEPH URBAN

was born in 1872 in Vienna, where he studied art and architecture. His designs won medals at international expositions. About 1904, Urban assisted with the Austrian Pavilion at the St. Louis Fair; he then began designing sets for the Boston Opera Company and with that company visited Paris in 1914. Urban was stranded in Italy when George Tyler brought him to America to design scenery for the *Garden of Paradise*. The show's run was brief, but critics raved about the scenery. Gene Buck took Ziegfeld to see the show and persuaded him to hire Urban.

Urban worked for Ziegfeld from 1914 until 1931. He took ten weeks to design his first *Follies* (1915) and received $5,000 for the sketches and the painting. In later *Follies*, Urban received $30,000 for sketches alone. Urban painted some scenes for every show that Flo did after 1914 except *Betsy*. When *Betsy* started off poorly, the superstitious Ziegfeld called upon Urban to paint the last scene in Act Two; but it was too late to save the show.

An artist of incredible versatility, Urban also illustrated children's books and designed sets for other Broadway shows, including George White's *Scandals*, and for the films that William Randolph Hearst produced for Marion Davies. As artistic director of the Metropolitan Opera, he designed fifty-five of its productions. Moreover, he designed several private mansions and public buildings, including a palace, the Ziegfeld Theatre, and the Paramount Theatre in Palm Beach.

The Viennese designer brought beauty and taste to the stage. He turned out consistently beautiful Broadway sets for more than seventeen years, and his work influenced future set designs. Apparently his consistency caused critics to take his talent for granted because his sets for *Music in the Air* (1932) and *Melody* (1933) received only passing attention. The latter production, by George White, was Urban's final Broadway show. He died in New York City in 1933.

❖ **VAN AND SCHENCK**
(August van Glone and Joe Schenck) were both born in Brooklyn. The two met in public school and worked as trolley car operators before becoming performers. They entered vaudeville separately but teamed up in 1910. At first Schenck played the piano while Van sang. When Schenck's voice improved, he started singing tenor while Van sang baritone. They specialized in Yiddish or Italian dialect songs, many of which Van wrote. By 1916 the two men were fairly well known in vaudeville. That same year Ziegfeld hired them for *The Century Girl*. In 1917 they began appearing in the *Midnight Frolic* and were in *Miss 1917*. Then in April 1918, they had a difference with Ziegfeld and quit; however, they returned to his employment in the 1919 *Follies* and sang their biggest hit, "Mandy." They stayed with the *Follies* through 1921.

Van and Schenck appeared on a radio show in 1923, in nightclubs, in several M-G-M musical shorts, and in a 1930 feature film. They were one of vaudeville's most popular singing teams and played the Palace three or four times a year—the last time in early June 1930. Later that month,

Joe Schenck died (at age thirty-nine) of a heart attack. Gus Van was at his side. The two men had remained friends since their school days and lived only a block from each other.

After Schenck's death, Van performed alone—in vaudeville, film shorts, and one movie (a supporting role)—through the 1940s. He was president of the American Guild of Variety Artists and was made a life member in 1949. Van retired to Miami, Florida, where he died in 1968, at age eighty, after being hit by a car.

❖ **ALBERTO VARGAS**
became well-known for his portraits of *Follies* stars. The Peruvian artist was born Joaquin Alberto Vargas y Chavez in 1896. The son of a famous photographer, the young Vargas learned that art from his father. In 1911 he went to Zurich to study photography, and he began an apprenticeship in 1915 at a Geneva studio. Vargas was to begin work at Sarony Studios in London, but wartime restrictions kept him in Paris. He decided to head home via New York but immediately fell in love with New York City and remained there.

Vargas, for the first time in his life without family financial support, worked in a studio retouching photographs; then he went to work for Butterick Patterns. In 1917, he began selling freelance work and by 1919 was drawing only women. Sam Kingston, Ziegfeld's general manager, saw his work in a window display and asked Vargas to bring his samples to Ziegfeld's office.

Ziegfeld liked Vargas's drawings and hired him to paint cast portraits for the theater lobby at $200 per painting. Vargas worked for Ziegfeld from 1919 to 1931, painting at least twelve portraits for each edition of the *Follies* during those years and for *Show Boat*.

During the 1920s, because of his work for Ziegfeld, Vargas got other commissions. But after Ziegfeld's death in 1932, his career slumped; he did some magazine covers and his wife modeled to support them. After painting some movie-star portraits in 1934, he worked in the art departments at Fox and Warner Studios. His Hollywood career ended after he was blacklisted for joining a 1939 artists' strike.

Jobless, Vargas returned to New York and in 1940, signed a contract with *Esquire* magazine; eventually 180 Vargas paintings appeared there. In the late 1950s, Vargas created the Vargas Girl for *Playboy* magazine. Over a period of sixteen years, he created 152 paintings for *Playboy*.

Vargas was married to Anna Mae Clift, a former showgirl and model who frequently posed for him. They never had children. Vargas died in 1983 at age eighty-seven.

❖ **LUPE VELEZ,**
born in Mexico in 1908, was educated in a San Antonio convent. She danced on the Mexican stage and in Hollywood nightclub revues. Velez started out in silent films in a 1927 movie playing opposite Douglas Fairbanks. She was very photogenic but had a heavy accent and could

not handle dialogue very well. While drama was not her forte, Velez achieved moderate success in the 1930s playing funny, temperamental leading ladies. She made a few Spanish films but earned more money in Hollywood. She was in Ziegfeld's *Hot-Cha!* in 1932. In the late 1930s and early 1940s, she co-starred with Leon Errol in eight Mexican Spitfire movies for RKO Studio.

Velez's personal life was volatile; she had many affairs, including one with Gary Cooper. In 1933, she married swimmer/actor Johnny Weissmuller. The couple often quarreled in public and divorced in 1938. In December 1944, two weeks after an affair ended, the pregnant and unmarried Velez committed suicide. After having her hair and makeup done, she swallowed a bottle of pills.

❖ NED WAYBURN

was born in Pittsburgh in 1871 and raised in Chicago. After high school, he attended a manual training school where he learned wood-working and mechanical drawing. While he worked for his father, who manufactured heavy machinery, and as a draftsman in a real-estate firm, Ned played piano in social clubs on the side. After his father lost his business, Wayburn took his act to vaudeville. He learned dancing and then became a stage manager. In 1901, he began choreographing and directing musicals. Wayburn is credited with inventing tap dancing in 1903. By 1915, he had his own dance studio and employment agency. At one time he had the names, addresses, and measurements of 8,300 chorus

girls. He continued to run his dance studio during the years he worked for Ziegfeld. In fact, many of his students were *Follies* girls.

Ziegfeld hired Wayburn to stage the first *Frolic* (January 1915). Altogether Wayburn staged eleven of the first sixteen roof shows and came in to liven up the 1922 touring show (originally staged by Leon Errol). He also staged the *Follies* from 1916 through 1919 and again in 1922 and 1923, *Miss 1917,* several numbers in *The Century Girl,* and *No Foolin'.*

Wayburn distinguished chorus members by their height and proportion, scale of movement, and the ability to perform all five standard techniques (soft-shoe; tap and stepping; acrobatics; modern Americanized ballet; and exhibition ballroom). He divided his list of chorus girls into classes. Class A were the statuesque showgirls. Class B were those between chorus and showgirl. Class C were the well-drilled girls who were proficient in all kinds of routines. And Class D were the more delicate girls who were used for lighter, decorative numbers. The girls were subdivided further into those who would not leave New York and those who would take any engagement.

A prolific director, Wayburn staged sixty shows in Chicago and New York alone during his thirty-year career. He was interested in creating pleasant-looking yet fast-paced scenes. In 1925, he wrote the book, *The Art of Stage Dancing.* Wayburn died in 1942.

❖ BERT WHEELER,

born in Patterson, New Jersey,

in 1895, was the son of a bookmaker. He dropped out of grammar school and started his show-business career at age thirteen, playing bit parts in the theater before learning to dance. After he broke an ankle, he turned to comedy. At age eighteen, Wheeler married a showgirl, Betty Wheeler, and the two toured vaudeville for eleven years. They sang and danced together in the 1923 *Follies* but later divorced. The slightly chubby Wheeler was only five-feet, five-inches tall, had wavy brown hair and blue eyes. He often sat on the edge of the stage eating a sandwich or an apple, injecting monologue and pantomime between bites. During his act, he would impart backstage gossip. Later, he added a crying bit where he would wipe his eyes with his sandwich and chew his handkerchief.

After a few seasons in radio, Wheeler played a comic role in Ziegfeld's *Rio Rita* with Robert Woolsey. Wheeler and Woolsey became a team, acting in the 1929 film version of the musical and several feature films for RKO before splitting briefly in 1932. They soon reunited and were in nearly two dozen movies until Woolsey's death in 1938. Wheeler was in only two films after Woolsey died. He returned to vaudeville and was on the radio and early television (1955). At age sixty-eight he was performing in nightclubs, frequently appearing in drag as an elderly lady with an abusive son. Wheeler was married and divorced four times. His last years were spent in near poverty. He died from emphysema at age seventy-two in 1968.

❖ FRANCES WHITE

was born about 1898 in Seattle, Washington. She began her career as a singer in Los Angeles. She was a San Francisco chorus girl when dancer William Rock spotted her in 1916. Rock's former partner had just gone solo, so he teamed with White. The two were an immediate hit in vaudeville, with White becoming the star.

Rock and White did their vaudeville dance in the *Follies* of 1916. She is better remembered, however, as a star of *Ziegfeld Midnight Frolic.* During 1916 and 1917, she was female lead in several roof shows. In December 1917, she signed a contract that paid $2,000 a week for her *Frolic* appearances. White stayed in the *Frolic* until April 1918, when Ziegfeld added Ann Pennington. Jealous of Pennington, White abruptly quit the show.

Rock and White danced together until they completed a 1919 engagement in London. White then returned to the *Ziegfeld Midnight Frolic* (October 1919) but got poor reviews. After leaving the *Frolic,* she performed in vaudeville as a single until her career waned. When she was about forty, she stopped performing altogether.

White was married to Frank Fay, a famous vaudeville comedian (later Barbara Stanwyck's husband). After the couple separated in 1917, White would purchase a front-row seat where Fay was performing so she could make faces at him during the show. Nevertheless, when White went to jail for failure to pay a $3.50 taxi fare, Fay came to her aid.

A couple of years later, White sued him for back alimony. She died in Los Angeles in 1969 at age seventy-one.

❖ SAMMY WHITE,

born in 1895, first performed in vaudeville in a blackface act with Lew Clayton (later Jimmy Durante's partner); then J. J. Shubert booked them for the *Show of Wonders* (1918) and the *Passing Show* (1918–21). After the team split up in 1921, White married Eva Puck and became her dance partner. The couple performed in vaudeville and musical comedies. White's most famous role was that of Frank in *Show Boat* and its 1932 revival. After his marriage to Eva Puck ended, White turned to the movies. He did specialties in the 1930s; in 1936 he played opposite Marion Davies in *Cain and Mabel* (1936). White did frequent revivals of *Show Boat* and performed on television. In the 1950s, he returned to films as a character actor, playing Spencer Tracy's partner, Barney, in *Pat and Mike* (1952). His last movie was *The Helen Morgan Story* (1957). White was sixty-five when he died in 1960.

❖ PAUL WHITEMAN,

son of a school music supervisor and a singer, was born in Denver in 1890. When he was seven, his father made him play the violin and even locked him in a room to practice. Later Whiteman played viola in the Denver Symphony and violin in the San Francisco People's Symphony. After a stint as a band master in the navy, Whiteman organized a dance orchestra in 1919 and introduced "symphonic jazz."

He brought his orchestra to New York in 1920. The next year he was offered $2,500 a week to appear at the Palace vaudeville house. Eventually he became the most famous band leader in vaudeville.

Whiteman's one *Follies* appearance was in 1923, and his orchestra played in the 1928 revival of the *Midnight Frolic*. He and his orchestra also were in the *Scandals* and toured Europe. His 1924 national concert tour popularized his music and established his reputation.

Whiteman organized fifty bands around the country to operate under his name. From 1927 to 1930, Bing Crosby, Al Rinker, and Harry Barris toured with Whiteman as The Rhythm Boys.

Whiteman starred in seven films and had a replacement radio show in the summer of 1943; the show's theme was "Rhapsody in Blue," which he had commissioned Gershwin to write in 1924. Whiteman was musical director for the Blue Network (later ABC) and performed on the "Philco Radio Hall of Fame" for nearly seven years. In the 1950s, he was on television.

The jovial and portly (six feet, three hundred pounds) Whiteman had a flair for showmanship; once he conducted his orchestra from a white horse at the Hippodrome. He was a popular entertainer at society galas and had several hit records. His recording of "Three O'Clock in the Morning" sold 3.4 million copies and earned him a fortune.

Whiteman was married four times and had four children. He owned hundreds

of cars and was director of the Daytona Speedway. He died of a heart attack at age seventy-seven in 1967.

❖ ANNABELLE WHITFORD

was born in Chicago in 1878 and became known simply as Annabelle. While still a teenager, she became a popular vaudeville and music-hall attraction with her Serpentine dance, in which she wore yards of silk material. She danced at the Columbian Exposition in 1893; in 1894, Thomas Edison photographed her in her butterfly costume. *Annabelle's Butterfly Dance* was seen in kinetoscope peepshows and later, with the advent of projection, on screen. Annabelle became the very first motion-picture star; at the time, the $40 fee to movie houses made this the highest priced feature film in the world.

Annabelle also became famous as the girl *not* at Seeley's dinner. In late 1896, when she was seventeen, she refused to dance at William Seeley's bachelor dinner party. Annabelle's step-father told the police Seeley had wanted Annabelle to dance and then to take off her dress. The police raided the party, and the resulting publicity propelled Annabelle to even greater fame. She worked as a specialty dancer for several years at roof gardens and became famous on Broadway and appeared in Ziegfeld's *Follies* from 1907 through 1911. In 1912 she retired from the stage to become the wife of Dr. E. J. Buchan of Chicago. Whitford died in 1961 at age eighty-three.

❖ BERT WILLIAMS

was born in the West Indies in 1874, the grandson of a Danish consul. The family moved to San Pedro, California, and Williams graduated from high school and studied civil engineering before he and three friends toured California playing Hawaiian music. He then turned to minstrel shows, one of the few entertainment areas open to black performers. Like all minstrel show actors, Williams had to wear blackface. He also had to learn the American Negro dialect and slapstick humor.

In 1895 Williams formed a vaudeville team with George Walker; six months later they were headliners. From 1902 to 1905 the two starred in the all-black Broadway comedy *In Dahomey*. They remained a team until Walker's retirement in 1909. Williams performed briefly with Walker's wife and then returned to vaudeville as a single.

It was in the *Follies* that Williams introduced the song "Nobody"; he sang the song for seven years. He tried to drop it, but audiences always wanted to hear it. Williams was a regular in the *Follies* for ten years (1910–19), missing only the 1913 and 1918 editions. He performed in some of the funniest scenes in the *Follies*, usually with Leon Errol.

Williams was known for his sense of timing and his pantomime. Although he wanted to do serious drama, he was apprehensive about his success for two reasons. First, he had become so associated with comedy that he did not know if audiences would accept him in a serious role; and, second, racial barriers were still

Bert Williams was in eight editions of the *Follies* between 1910 and 1919.

difficult to overcome. Williams was the only black performer the Keith vaudeville circuit would book on a white bill in Washington, D.C. While Williams helped the white public accept black actors outside the South, some white vaudevillians still refused to appear with him. Even at the height of his fame, Williams could live in a good New York hotel only if he used the rear elevator. Once when Williams went bicycle riding, the local sheriff confiscated the bike, assuming that because Williams

was black, the actor had stolen it.

After the 1919 edition, Williams left the *Follies*. He financed and appeared in his own revue, *Broadway Brevities of 1920*, written and produced by George LeMaire, a former *Follies* cast member. Later he signed with the Shuberts.

Williams was a loner who discouraged personal relationships. Being from the West Indies, he did not identify with Harlem blacks. Around August or September of 1900, Williams had apparently

married Lottie Cole Thompson; she had been married before and was several years older than Williams. Lottie performed with Williams until he became a *Follies* star; she then retired. They never had children.

Williams was a heavy drinker and a chain smoker. As early as 1911 he had developed a weak heart and problems with his feet due to poor circulation. In later years he was chronically depressed. His health deteriorated seriously in 1921. While touring in a Shubert show in Detroit, Williams caught a cold and developed pneumonia. He refused to cancel the show because it would put the other actors out of work. He collapsed during a performance and was taken home to New York, where he died March 4, 1922.

❖ IMOGENE "BUBBLES" WILSON

was born Mary Imogene Robertson about 1905 in Kentucky, where she grew up in an orphanage before becoming a model in New York. Ziegfeld saw a painting of her and hired her for the *Follies*. As Imogene Wilson, she was in the 1923 and 1924 editions.

Wilson had a highly publicized affair with *Follies* comedian Frank Tinney, during which he allegedly beat her. In 1924, Wilson accused Tinney of assault and sued him for $100,000. The scandal prompted Ziegfeld to dismiss her from the *Follies*. Wilson then followed Tinney to Europe, where the couple ended their relationship.

In Berlin, Wilson appeared in several German movies (beginning in 1925) as

Mary or Imogene Robertson. Wilson left Europe and headed for Hollywood. As Mary Nolan she became a leading lady in about twenty late silent and early talking films.

Apparently Wilson could not lead a quiet life. She sued a producer for $500,000 for beating her and was involved in a number of damage suits. Before long her career faded; she retired in 1932. At age thirty-one, ill and penniless, she lived in the Actors' Fund Home in New York, appearing for a time in cheap roadhouses. When her health improved, she returned to Hollywood to live with her sister.

Wilson spent a year writing her memoirs. She had just sold her story to a publishing house and a national magazine and was negotiating for movie rights when she died, at age forty-two. Wilson had been hospitalized for malnutrition; at her death she weighed only ninety pounds. An obituary noted that Wilson was so popular in 1922 that a reporter commented that "only two people in America would bring every reporter in New York to the docks to see them off. One is the President. The other is Imogene (Bubbles) Wilson."

❖ CHARLES WINNINGER,

born in Athens, Wisconsin (1884), performed in vaudeville for many years. In 1916 he began playing character roles in films between his vaudeville engagements. He appeared in the 1920 *Follies* and played Captain Andy in *Show Boat* (1927–30). Winninger acted in approximately seventeen films including *Show Boat* (1936) and

The Ziegfeld Girl (1941). In 1932, he began playing Captain Henry on NBC radio's variety hour, produced in New York and patterned after the Broadway musical. It became the country's top-ranked variety hour. Winninger left the show in 1934, after a disagreement with the producers. He died in Palm Springs, California, in 1969.

❖ ED WYNN

was born Isaiah Edwin Leopold in Philadelphia (1886), the son of a wealthy hat manufacturer. At age sixteen Wynn left school to play in a repertory company. After he and Jack Lewis performed their act at a benefit, they were booked into vaudeville, where they played for ninety-eight weeks. Wynn broke with Lewis in 1904 to headline under his own name, doing two shows a day for eight years. In vaudeville he was known for his lisp, his fluttering hands, his outlandish puns and costumes, and his crazy inventions; he was called "The Perfect Fool."

In 1910, Wynn made his legitimate stage debut in *The Deacon and the Lady*. In 1913 he quit vaudeville, and in 1914 he joined the *Follies*. After the 1915 *Follies*, Wynn joined the Shuberts' *The Passing Show* (1916). In addition to Shubert revues, Wynn performed in musicals. When he started out in New York, Wynn lived in a boarding house on West Forty-fourth Street in a room that cost $2.50 a week. Seventeen years later, after the site became the Forty-fourth Street Theatre, he played there for $1,750 a week.

Because he was active in the Equity strike, Ziegfeld and the Shuberts blacklisted Wynn, forcing him to produce his own show, *Ed Wynn Carnival* (1920). His first film, in 1927, failed. In 1930, Ziegfeld produced *Simple Simon* for Wynn, but that show, too, was unsuccessful.

Later Wynn did his "Perfect Fool" act on radio; he was the first radio comedian to appear in full costume and makeup. In 1932, he was approached by Texaco to star in his own radio show. Initially he turned down the offer because his act relied on visual material and props, but he finally accepted—for a reported $5,000 a week. He became a national figure as "The Fire Chief" and was on the air from 1932 until 1935 and again in 1936–37. He once said that he spent $750,000 publicizing himself as "The Perfect Fool," but almost overnight it was forgotten and he was known as "The Fire Chief."

In the 1950s, Wynn became a character actor in movies, playing eccentric old men. He made several films: *The Great Man* (1956), *Marjorie Morningstar* (1958), *Diary of Anne Frank* (1959), *The Absent-Minded Professor* (1960), *Mary Poppins* (1964), *Dear Brigette* (1964), and *The Greatest Story Ever Told* (1965). His serious role in "Requiem for a Heavyweight," an early television drama, astounded critics who thought he could do only comedy.

Wynn and his first wife (Hilda Keenan) were divorced in 1937. They had one son, actor Keenan Wynn. His second marriage lasted from 1937 to 1939. He married a third time—for nine years—in 1946. Wynn died in 1966.

Ed Wynn around the time he joined the *Follies*; Wynn is wearing the panama hat, which he could make into twenty-eight different shapes, that he wore on stage for eleven years. After Ziegfeld told him the hat was all he could do, Wynn never wore it again.

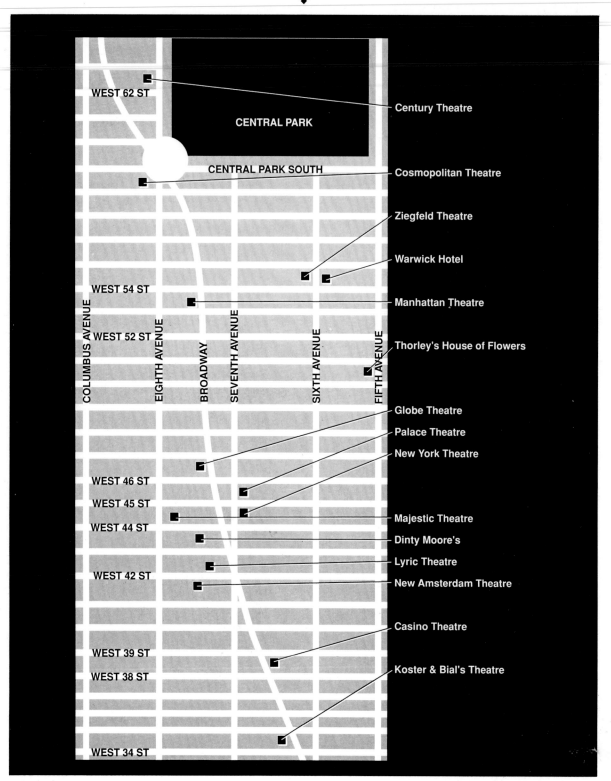

WEST 62 ST

CENTRAL PARK

CENTRAL PARK SOUTH

Century Theatre

Cosmopolitan Theatre

Ziegfeld Theatre

Warwick Hotel

WEST 54 ST

Manhattan Theatre

COLUMBUS AVENUE

EIGHTH AVENUE

BROADWAY

SEVENTH AVENUE

WEST 52 ST

SIXTH AVENUE

FIFTH AVENUE

Thorley's House of Flowers

Globe Theatre

Palace Theatre

New York Theatre

WEST 46 ST

WEST 45 ST

Majestic Theatre

WEST 44 ST

Dinty Moore's

Lyric Theatre

WEST 42 ST

New Amsterdam Theatre

Casino Theatre

WEST 39 ST

WEST 38 ST

Koster & Bial's Theatre

WEST 34 ST

NOTES

Numbers preceding note entries refer to page numbers. For the sake of brevity, the following abbreviations are used in the notes for the much repeated persons and sources:

Abbreviation	Full Name
BB	Billie Burke
BB + page number	Billie Burke, *With a Feather on My Nose* (New York: Appleton-Century-Crofts), 1949.
BS	Bernard Sobel
CM	*Collier's Magazine*
CMC	Chicago Musical College
CT	*Chicago Tribune*
CYC	Cecily Youmans Collins Collection
DM	*The Dance Magazine*
FZ	Florenz Ziegfeld, Jr.
IAM	Institute of the American Musical
LAHE	*Los Angeles Herald Examiner*
LC	Liane Carrera, *Anna Held and Flo Ziegfeld*. Tr. Guy Daniels (Hicksville, New York: Exposition, 1979).
LCE	Liane Carrera estate
MCNY	Museum of the City of New York
NYP	New York Public Library, Lincoln Center Theatre Collection
NY-Surr	New York State Surrogate Court
NYT	*New York Times*
PZS	Patricia Ziegfeld Stephenson
PZS-I	Patricia Ziegfeld Stephenson interview
PZ + page number	Patricia Ziegfeld, *The Ziegfelds' Girl* (Boston: Little, Brown, 1964).
PZSC	Patricia Ziegfeld Stephenson Collection
SA	Shubert Archive

ACT I
Chapter 1

12 how he accomplished it: BB, pp. 242–43.

13 passion to his son: 1886–87 CMC catalogue.

13 public and private concerts: 1886–87 CMC catalogue; and Peter Felix Ganz, "Chicago Musical College, 1867–1967: An Historical Sketch," unpublished manuscript. Chicago.

13 a year or two: Ibid.

13 in Roles's home: Charles Higham file at the University of Southern California Film and Television archive.

13 Napoleon's marshall of France: PZ, p. 33.

13 the Methodist Episcopal Church: Higham file at USC.

13 Catholic Holy Name Cathedral: Ganz ms.

14 Musical Academy, in 1867: Ibid.

14 just six years later: Ibid.

14 office at 610 Michigan: *Chicago Tribune*, October 13, 1871.

14 Fifty thousand people attended: Ganz ms.

14 had nine hundred pupils: Ibid.

16 state in the Union: 1878–79 CMC catalogue.

16 to send their daughters: Ganz ms.

16 for light and ventilation: PZS-I.

16 retelling of his childhood: PZS-I.

16 to avoid failing any subjects: Vincent Kiraly, "The Golden Olden Days with Florenz Ziegfeld," unpublished biography. Patricia Ziegfeld Stephenson private collection. Los Angeles.

16 "the cook, I believe": Chicago Public Library—Special Collections, Neighborhood file, Brown School reminiscences, Billie Burke letter of February 28, 1952, to Margaret Jackson.

16 he got into mischief: PZS-I.

17 this rich European cuisine: BB, p. 162.

17 "artists of that day": Louis Falk, *Across the Little Space: The Life Story of Dr. Louis Falk* (Chicago: Bauman, 1933), pp. 85–87.

17 above New York theaters: Stephen Burge Johnson, *The Roof Gardens of Broadway Theatres* (Ann Arbor, Michigan: UMI Research Press, 1985), pp. 5–7.

17 the Illinois National Guard: *Musical Courier*, 1923, p. 32.

18 story is probably apocryphal: Donald Russell, *The Lives and Legends of Buffalo Bill* (Norman: University of Oklahoma, 1960), pp. 310–18; and Walter Havighurst, *Annie Oakley of the Wild West* (New

York: MacMillan, 1954), pp. 30–50.

18 "Buffalo Bill's Wild West Show": Kenyo Nicholson, ed., *Revues: A Book of Short Sketches*. Preface by Florenz Ziegfeld. (New York: Appleton, 1929), p. v.

18 the board of directors: 1887–88 CMC catalogue.

18 leader of Chicago cotillions: Kiraly ms.

18 "fabulously wealthy Pullman family": BB, p. 136.

19 to which he would belong: Kiraly ms.; and *DM*, October 1929, pp. 16–17.

19 at the train station: Ganz ms.

20 "fully confessed in Europe": *CT*, February 24, 1892.

20 1992 value of $450,000: The Consumer Price Index (CPI) method, the most conservative of three available means, was used to translate figures. Salary and rent comparisons translate into $700,000 and $1.5 million, respectively.

20 at the World's Fair: 1890–91 CMC catalogue.

20 fantasy land for Fair patrons: Ezra Schabas, *Theodore Thomas* (Urbana: University of Illinois Press, 1989), p. 196.

21 "impracticable and luxuriously expensive": *The Inter Ocean*, October 29, 1893.

21 from 110,000 to 138,000:

Chicago Record's History of the World's Fair.

21 total was $8.3 million: Ibid.

Chapter 2

22 Strauss's "Blue Danube" waltz: Program, May 3, 1893.

22 to liven the program: *DM*, October 1929, p. 58; Florenz Ziegfeld, Jr., "What Becomes of the *Ziegfeld Follies* Girls," *Pictorial Review*, 26 (May 1925), pp. 12–13.

22 the "pre-eminent operetta house": Johnson, p. 16.

22 light opera and musical comedies: Ibid., p. 23.

22 a sophisticated European flavor: Ibid., pp. 26–27.

23 at the propitious moment: Ibid., p. 34.

23 $5,000 on Sandow: FZ, *Pictorial Review*, pp. 12–13.

23 packed house in London: Eugen Sandow, "My Reminiscences," *Strand* (March 1910), pp. 164–68.

23 "better...cooler than a roof garden": *CT*, July 29, 1893.

23 in those early days: *CT*.

23 plank on his chest: *DM*, October 1929, p. 58.

23 Tartajada, a Spanish dancer: *CT*, October 15, 1893.

23 in his dressing room: *DM*, October 1929, p. 58.

23–24 week's receipts were $32,000: FZ, *Pictorial Review*, pp. 12–13.

24 "packed to the doors": *CT*, August 6, 1893.

24 "music hall amusement enterprise": *CT*, September 24, 1893.

24 Europe on family business: *CT*, October 29, 1893.

24 the Battery D building: *New York Clipper*, November 18 and 25, 1893.

24 jobs from the Fair disappeared: Schabas, p. 214.

24 and sign with him: *CT*, November 5, 1893.

26 following the World's Fair: Unidentified 1914 newspaper clipping, NYP.

26 between the animal and Sandow: Unidentified 1914 newspaper clipping, NYP.

26 "or any other century": May 23, 1894.

26 displayed by the brute: *San Francisco Chronicle*, May 23, 1894.

27 "the menu—his keeper": Sandow, *Strand*, p. 170.

27 "where he fell, dazed": Ibid., p. 171.

27 turned the tables successfully: Eugen Sandow, *Strength and How To Obtain It* (London: Gale & Polden, No year [ca. 1899]), pp. 137–38.

27 and doing a backflip: Kemp Niver, *Early Motion Pictures* (Washington, D.C.: Library of Congress, 1985), p. 286.

27 stage director, and electrician: Program from the Boston Theatre, week of April 29, 1895.

28 "talked and written about": *Cleveland Plain Dealer*, January 27, 1895.

28 "Miss Josephine Subel, vocalist": *CT*, October 6, 1895.

28 "air of naughtiness": Lewis A. Erenberg, *Steppin' Out: New York Nightlife* (Westport, Connecticut: Greenwood, 1981), p. 52.

28 including men of society: Ibid., pp. 41, 51.

28 to meet their mistresses: Ibid., pp. 52–53.

29 the Palace in London: *DM*, November 1929, p. 18.

29 a Yiddish theater company: LC, pp. 29–31.

29 Adler for five years: Ibid., p. 35.

29 in Germany and Russia: Chicago Public Library—Special Collections, Scrapbook PP1, Box 3.

29 radically reduced his allowance: LC, p. 59.

29 susceptible to Ziegfeld's lure: Ibid., pp. 79–81.

29 "that pleases women most": *DM*, November 1929, p. 19.

Chapter 3

30 "sustained applause broke

322

31 out": *DM*, November 1929, p. 20.

31 "take zee beauty bath": Ibid.

31 "were wretched bores": BB, pp. 143–44.

33 last act of the farce: Charles Higham, *Ziegfeld* (Chicago: Regnery, 1972), p. 46.

33 "play of its time": Unidentified 1914 newspaper clipping, NYP.

34 "Nights in New York City": *CT*, November 18, 1900.

34 "illusion of her innocence": *CT*, November 25, 1900.

35 back in New York: Higham, pp. 51–52.

35 project still lost money: *CM*, January 20, 1934, p. 22.

35 "stage could be desired": *Chicago Record-Herald*, May 29, 1904.

36 beginning in September: Joseph and June Csida, *American Entertainment* (New York: Billboard, 1978), p. 121.

36 in the same show: Dressler, *My Own Story* (Boston: Little, Brown, 1934), p. 207.

36 clashed almost immediately: LC, pp. 109–10.

36 "was hastily broken off": *DM*, November 1929, p. 55.

36 role to twenty lines: LC, pp. 110–11.

36 all around the Continent: *Cleveland Plain Dealer*, October 28, 1906.

36 Nice, Biarritz, and Trouville: *CM*, January 20, 1934, p. 22.

36 in fact, legally responsible: LC, pp. 103–4.

37 Shubert houses were available: Contract, March 21, 1905, SA.

37 in the booking industry: Mary C. Henderson, *Theater in America* (New York: Abrams, 1986), p. 25.

37 and the successful scripts: *New York Sun*, March 7, 1930; and Kendall, *The Golden Age of New Orleans Theatre* (Baton Rouge: Louisiana State University Press, 1952), pp. 587–89.

37 owed Lee Shubert $1,299: *NYT*, January 9, 1909.

38 "of its alleged suggestiveness": *DM*, November 1929, p. 55.

38 "vulgar rubbish": *Chicago Record-Herald*, November 8, 1906.

38 "Make My Eyes Behave": *CT*, November 11, 1906.

38 "do not know me": *Cleveland Plain Dealer*, October 26, 1906.

39 "have not been recovered": *Detroit Free Press*, October 31, 1906.

39 tried for the theft: Higham, pp. 58–62.

Chapter 4

40 the Syndicate for bookings: *New York Sun*, March 7, 1930.

40 or controlled almost fifty: Kendall, p. 589.

40 begun working with Erlanger: *New York Sun*, June 15, 1936.

40 theaters across the country: Michael Roach interview.

40 earning $200 a week: Eddie Cantor and David Freedman, *Ziegfeld: The Great Glorifier* (New York: A. H. King, 1934), p. 41.

41 was much commented upon: *Ladies Home Journal*, March 1923, p. 17.

41 number in those days: PZS-I.

41 "disorder of their appearance": *Follies of 1907* script, p. 3; MCNY.

41 "Beds extra'": Ibid., p. 5.

41 "direct and boisterous": *DM*, December 1929, p. 33.

43 "a plot was unearthed": *NYT*, July 4, 1907.

43 before proceeding to Chicago: Unidentified interview, 1927 newspaper feature, NYP.

43 "raw, common, and noisy": *CT*, November 18, 1907.

43 "flight of a bird": *NYT*, January 29, 1908.

43 "ten thousand dollars a toe": *DM*, December 1929, p. 34.

44 Borowski, and Leopold Auer: Ganz ms.

44 with her mother permanently: LC, p. 111.

44 Liane back to Paris: Ibid., p. 137.

44 in France and England: Ibid., p. 113.

44 "as the law allows": *CT*, November 23, 1908.

45 "in an inside pocket": *New York Telegraph*, September 28 or 29, 1908.

45 one of Flo Ziegfeld: Dr. Alexander Hegedus interview.

45 mother in the "memoirs": Hegedus interview.

46 "girl was Lillian Lorraine": *Green Book Magazine*, January 1912.

46 than to her intelligence: PZS-I; Nils Hanson letter, October 1, 1992.

46 he owed $20,000 more: *NYT*, May 27, 1909.

46 and John D. Rockefeller: *Follies of 1909* script, Act Two, pp. 2–3, MCNY.

47 the opening night audience: Higham, p. 76.

47 "do in my employ": *NYT*, December 4, 1909.

48 titled *The Silver Star*: *DM*, December, 1929, p. 34.

49 owed her an apology: Norman Katkov, *The Fabulous Fanny: The Story of Fanny Brice* (New York: Knopf, 1953), pp. 67–69.

49 cut material was restored: Douglas Gilbert, *American Vaudeville: Its Life and Times* (New York: McGraw-Hill, 1940), pp. 284–85.

49 "what an artist he was": FZ, *Ladies Home Journal*, June 1923, p. 23.

49 his contract with Ziegfeld: Ann Charters, *Nobody: the Story of Bert Williams* (New York: Macmillan, 1970), p. 132.

Chapter 5

50 "title of our play": *Theatre Arts*, October 1959, p. 94.

50 did not implicate her: Nils Hanson research on *Denver Post* clippings about grand-jury and trial events; Gene Fowler, *Timber line* (New York: Covici, Friede, 1933), pp. 291–305.

50 or unhook eyes: *New York Review*, July 8, 1911.

51 $5,000 on the number: *DM*, December 1929, p. 54.

51 defy Erlanger: *CM*, January 27, 1934, p. 45.

51 "to any one else": *CT*, September 5, 1911.

52 "medley of changing color": *NYT*, April 12, 1912.

52 "of the spectacular shows": *CT*, March 9, 1913.

53 corespondents, including Lillian Lorraine: *NYT*, April 23, 1912.

53 from two years earlier: *NYT*, October 4, 1912.

53 a reconciliation was possible: Higham, p. 87.

53 several occasions, for example: Elsie Johnson interview. Nils Hanson Collection, New York.

53 news of the wedding: *New York Review*, March 30, 1912.

53 knowledge of a divorce: *New York Telegraph*, March 29, 1912.

53 given up on marriage: Unidentified newspaper, April 3, 1912; Hanson Collection.

53 had never married Lorraine: *San Francisco Morning Telegraph*, April 4, 1912; Hanson Collection.

53 Lorraine and Gresheimer "remarried": Unidentified newspaper, May 7, 1912; Hanson Collection.

53 round of unwelcome publicity: *New York World*, June 30, 1913.

54 pictures of showgirls: PZS-I.

54 "trying to emulate today": Joel Laubenthal ms. on the New Amsterdam Theatre, MCNY.

54 costume into evening clothes: BB, pp. 155–56.

55 love at first sight: Ibid., pp. 118–19.

55 Billy Burke and Blanche Hodkinson: PZS-I.

55 Treasury Department in Washington: BB, pp. 3, 6, 8.

55 her father touring constantly: Ibid., p. 11.

55 there for a while: Ibid.

55 interrupted her formal schooling: Ibid., pp. 17–18.

55 singing "coon songs": Ibid., pp. 24–25.

55 *The School Girl*'s co-producer: Ibid., pp. 27–28.

55 the Barrymores, and Maxine Elliott: Ibid., pp. 53–54.

55 the Astors, the Goulds: Ibid., pp. 69–71.

55 producers in the world: Ibid., p. 62.

56 until the spring: *Hastings News*, March 1, 1912.

56 "very careful with a nickel": PZS-I.

56 she worked for Frohman: *DM*, January 1930, p. 40.

56 "on falling in love": BB, p. 120.

56 "good meal ticket": PZS-I.

56 Kiraly to pass notes: *CM*, January 27, 1934, p. 25.

56 fruit and pink champagne: BB, p. 122.

57 career faster than Frohman: Ibid., p. 123.

57 Alice at the switchboard: PZS-I.

57 "lurking in the bushes": BB, p. 125.

57 on April 11, 1914: *DM*, January 1930, p. 40.

58 mistook for bootleg liquor: PZS-I; and BB, p. 148.

58 "would freeze to death": BB, p. 146.

58 royalties for *Miss Innocence*: *New York Review*, April 23, 1914.

58 to stage an opening: SA, May 27, 1914.

59 brushed, polished and groomed: *New York Evening Mail*, June 13, 1914.

59 traveling to stay home: Roach interview.

60 was his latest infatuation: BB, p. 164.

60 taking to his bed: PZS-I.

61 "word left for 'love'": BB to FZ, December 18, 1914, PZSC.

61 "my darling. Hope better": BB to FZ, December 18, 1914, PZSC.

61 "proud of you. Love, Baby." BB to FZ, December 19, 1914, PZSC.

61 marriage by working less: BB, pp. 170–71.

Chapter 6

63 or the dance floor: Johnson, p. 152.

64 adoration of your, Baby 5:15 P.M.: BB to FZ, January 6, 1915, PZSC.

64 "in a cute way": FZ to "Captain," undated, MCNY.

64 Urban's color and lighting: *DM*, January 1930, p. 42.

64 "...It succeeded": *DM*, January 1930, p. 42.

68 for the *Frolic*'s revival: *NYT*, December 30, 1929.

69 outstanding publicity—for free: Jesse Lasky and Don Weldon, *I Blow My Own Horn* (Garden City, New York: Doubleday, 1957), p. 225.

69 of freedom and pleasure: Erenberg, p. 209.

70 and hold a man: Ibid., pp. 218–19.

70 could remain in charge: Ibid., pp. 217–18.

70 controlled these beautiful women: Ibid., pp. 219–20.

71 it'd worked: Cantor ms. on Ziegfeld, UCLA Special Collections.

Chapter 7

72 "did not bounce": Randolph Carter's Gretl Urban interview.

73 "like them, was startling": Ibid.

73 "and hence effective collision": Ibid.

73 "was written that afternoon": *NYT*, September 22, 1919.

73 three-quarters of the performance!: *Green Book*, September, 1915, pp. 388–403.

73–74 "would stop the performance": J. P. McEvoy, "He Knew What They Wanted." *Saturday Evening Post*, September 10, 1932, pp. 10–11.

74 "'as long as I can'": *Cleveland Leader*, November 14, 1915.

75 bungalow on Catalina Island: Higham, p. 112.

75 had produced twenty-five films: Niver.

75 to be with Flo: BB, pp. 170–71.

76 film to that point: Higham, p. 116.

76 and avoid long hours: Ibid.

76 "dared not penetrate": Cantor ms., UCLA.

76 "people without taste": Marilyn Cantor Baker interview.

76 let him keep it: Natalie Cantor Clary interview.

76 father and son might: Baker interview.

77 Karsavina for the opening: FZ to Dillingham, March 17, 1916, MCNY.

77 won an infringement case: *NYT*, April 20, 1916.

77 friend in the audience: PZS-I.

78 allow him to recover: *NYT*, June 22, 1916.

78 when she became ill: LC, p. 159.

78 sent her a long telegram: *CM*, January 13, 1934, p. 50.

78 "Mother's Big Blue Eyes": PZS-I.

78 residence at Burkeley Crest: BB, p. 178.

79 stagehands, and many others: *Theatre Magazine*, January 1917, p. 12.

Chapter 8

80 "'best head waiter I ever had'": *New York Telegraph*, January 20, 1917.

81 "and little to affront": *CT*, December 24, 1917.

81 "a soul-stirring finale?": *Newark Star Eagle*, October 15, 1917.

82 "amusing and charming" production: *New York Evening Post*, November 6, 1917.

82 be like *Miss 1917*: *New York Tribune*, November 6, 1917.

82 "assets of only $63,871": Gerald Bordman, *Jerome Kern: His Life and Music* (New York: Oxford University Press, 1980), p. 161.

83 stress on the arrangement: *New York Telegram*, March 7, 1930.

83 with Sam Goldwyn: Scott Berg, *Goldwyn: A Biography* (New York: Knopf, 1989), p. 85.

84 at the box office: June 13, 1918.

84 with reproaches from conservatives: PZS-I; and Roach interview.

84 on September 2, 1918: *NYT*, July 31, 1918.

85 would pay the penalty: *Variety*, May 31, 1918.

85 "on behalf of American soldiers": *Variety*, June 7, 1918.

85 "a cortège of thousands": Cantor and Freedman, *Ziegfeld*, p. 92.

85 worth several million dollars: American estate inventory, September 30, 1920, undated Paris effects inventory, LCE Collection.

Chapter 9

86 "of their stage experience": Eddie Cantor and David Freedman, *My Life Is in Your Hands* (New York: Harper, 1928), p. 206.

87 soiling their costumes: Muriel Harrison Merrill interview.

87 for the blood spilled: Roach interview.

87 total of four nights: Alfred Harding, *The Revolt of the Actors* (New York: Morrow, 1929), pp. 5–7.

87 There was no appeal: Ibid., pp. 8–9.

88 accept a standard contract: Ibid., p. 15.

88 theater owners and bookers: Ibid., p. 19.

88 was formally announced: Ibid., p. 53.

88 joined the PMA's ranks: Ibid., p. 72.

88 refused to recognize Equity: Ibid., pp. 75–76.

88 a show named *Lightnin'*: Ibid., p. 79.

88 member of the PMA: Ibid., pp. 83–84.

89 being a PMA member: Ibid., pp. 105–6.

89 to help with expenses: *New York Call*, August 13, 1919.

89 "ourselves with the actors": *NYT*, August 14, 1919.

89 theaters on Broadway were dark: Harding, p. 172.

89 ceased production about August 18: Ibid., p. 150; Roach interview.

89 simply ignored Hendrick's ruling: Ibid., p. 188.

90 resumed production on September 10: Ibid., pp. 235–39.

90 "to have a standard": Baker interview.

90 "fresh in his mind": Cantor and Freedman, *My Life*, p. 211.

91 Volstead Act was passed: PZS-I.

91 Billie do the work: Ibid.

91 went to Los Angeles: Ibid.

91 and Ina Claire: Baral typescript, Ziegfeld people in films, *Variety*, January 3, 1979, NYP.

Chapter 10

92 of the social season: BB, p. 213.

92 was to become *Sally*: Bordman, *Kern*, p. 203.

92 accident site, that morning: *Variety Obituaries*, May 14, 1920.

93 and Bayes as well: SA.

93 his Winter Garden show: J. J. Shubert to FZ, May 11, 1920, SA.

93 "offers in your behalf": FZ to J. J. Shubert, May 12, 1920, SA.

94 got out of bed: Doris Eaton interview.

95 and always commanded attention: Dana O'Connell interview.

95 "that now I will": 1920 *Follies* file, FZ to Hirsch, October 16, 1920, NYP.

95 action and not dialogue: 1920 *Follies* file, Hirsch to FZ, October 16, 1920, NYP.

95 hours before she died: *NYT*, September 7, 11, and 12, 1920.

95 became a public spectacle: *NYT*, September 29, 1920.

96 or changed Kern's score: Warner file, Wisconsin State Historical Society.

96 electrifying to the audience: FZ to Herbert, December 14, 1920, LCE.

96 and F. S. Golding: *Clipper*, December 15, 1920.

97 a "socko" moment: PZS-I.

98 "that beautiful that angry": PZS-I; and PZ, pp. 183–86.

98 so extroverted and flamboyant: Lawrence Bergreen, *As Thousands Cheer: The Life of Irving Berlin* (New York: Viking, 1990), p. 65.

99 except Captain Gray: PZS-I; and Delia Leonard, unpublished memoir on the Ziegfelds, PZSC.

99 "It was rather tasty": PZS-I.

99 mousse, ice cream, strawberries: Ibid.

99 or paddling a canoe: Ibid.

99 no show was running: Ibid.

99 Hastings ahead of him: Ibid.

99 another entry. She won: Ibid.

100 single-minded, almost a passion: Ibid.

100 away too long–Baby: BB to FZ, ca. 1920, LCE.

100 them resuming their affair: January 1921.

100 New Year's Day, 1922: Warner file.

101 move it to London: *NYT*, May 19, 1921.

101 for flasks was intolerable: July 1, 1921.

101 the Chicago Musical College: *CT*, August 8, 1921.

101 part as a flapper: Berg, p. 134.

101 interfering with a performance: PZS-I.

101 become a six-*month* break: *NYT*, November 19, 1921.

101 "my first real opportunity": November 18, 1921.

101 covered extra performances: *NYT*, December 27, 1921.

Chapter 11

102 "to play for her": BB, p. 202.

102 "on a summer evening": *Life*, June 29, 1922, p. 18.

103 restored to the treasury: *NYT*, June 20, 1922.

103 "my two beloved ones": FZ to BB, July 10, 1922, PZSC.

103 "get a pony wagon?": FZ to PZS, June 26, 1922, PZSC.

103 free of ulterior motives: PZS-I.

103 berths in the navy: *NYT*, May 28, 1922.

104 "out of it tomorrow": *NYT*, July 10, 1922.

104 threw up her hands: *NYT*, July 24, 1922.

104 from across the room: BB, pp. 209–12.

104 her mother wear it: PZS-I.

104 sat puffing his cigar: BB, pp. 172–73.

104 "grin" on his face: PZS-I.

104 Her eyes were blue: Ibid.

104 "knew you'd been hugged": Ibid.

105 "played with great force": Ibid.

105 check on his sister: Ibid.

105 came out to Detroit: Willis Buhl interview.

105 named Colonel William Thompson: PZS-I.

105 weeks of show rehearsals: Ibid.

106 that they had purchased: Ibid.

106 to maintain Burkeley Crest: BB, pp. 220–21.

106 passageway to the kitchen: PZ, pp. 50–51.

106 beds contained 17,000 blooms: *Hastings News*, August 15, 1932.

107 goldfish—they were bad luck!: PZS-I.

107 and fixings plus candy: Leonard ms., p. 8.

107 the film for her: Ibid, p. 11.

108 had solid-gold appointments: John Harkrider and James Patrick, "Life Story," Harkrider's unpublished autobiography. Nantucket, Massachusetts.

108 according to Patty: PZ, p. 58.

108 "quite an affair": Carter/G. Urban interview.

108 invitation to Sunday dinner: PZS-I; and Baker interview.

108 no tolerance for stupidity: PZS-I.

109 "must have—personality": *Palm Beach Post*, October 21, 1924.

109 Ziegfeld liked it, though: PZS-I.

109 he did like mysteries: Ibid.

109 shipped it to Palm Beach: PZS-I.

109 "happier at another school": PZ, pp. 79–80.

109 "want to shrivel up": PZS-I.

109 Ziegfeld's secretary since 1912, Higham, p. 190.

110 appropriate for Ziegfeld's staff: Harkrider and Patrick.

110 "They got her out": Unidentified news clipping, Golden interview, IAM.

110 ask a spelling question: Ibid.

110 to his financial records: NY-Surr Records, June 5, 1934.

110 "am I running here?": Higham, pp. 151–52.

110 clutter on his desk: Golden, IAM.

111 "you tonight. Devotedly, Baby": BB to FZ, February 3, 1923, LCE.

111 "are married to me": BB to FZ, February 4, 1923, LCE.

111–12 My devoted love always. Bill: BB to FZ, February 21, 1923, LCE.

112 "Cheer up, darling. Love, Billie": BB to FZ, February 18, 1923, LCE.

112 "tension she lives under": BB to FZ, February 24, 1923, LCE.

112 have dared tell you: BB to FZ, February 11, 1923, LCE.

112 labor for the *Follies:* Elsie Sloan Farley to FZ, February 28, 1923, LCE.

112 $3,000 (March 15–31, 1923): Cox and Stevens to FZ, February 17, 1923, LCE.

112 the deck/engine room consummables: March 2, 1923 contract, LCE.

113 to see you. Devotedly, Billie: BB to FZ, February 28, 1923, LCE.

113 present when he died: CT, May 21, 1923.

113 "Very sincerely yours, Ziegfeld": FZ to Rogers, June 2, 1923, Will Rogers Memorial.

113 a very strong start: *Variety,* November 1, 1923.

114 to renew her contract: *NYT,* December 18, 1923.

114 Eaton in *Kid Boots*: *NYT,* December 19, 1923.

114 success in Shubert shows: Eddie Cantor, *Take My Life* (Garden City: Doubleday, 1957), p. 127.

115 "catch him at it": PZS-I.

115 "treating me like a son": Cantor ms., UCLA.

115 grossed $35,000 in Boston: February 28, 1925, books, Boston/Colonial, NYP.

115 "men of the day": BB to FZ, undated, LCE.

Chapter 12

116 New Amsterdam Roof Theatre: Unsigned stockholder legal document for Ziegfeld Follies, Inc., February 29, 1924, LCE.

116 and they were late: *NYT,* August 16, 1924.

116 in a closed shop: *NYT,* April 22, 1924.

116 Equity in mid-May 1924: Harding, p. 466.

117 "Answer quick": FZ to Rogers, August 29, 1923, Rogers Memorial.

117 nearly seventy years later: Jimmy Rogers interview.

117 partitions made of blankets: PZS-I.

117 and Ziegfeld's valet, Sidney: PZ, pp. 101–3.

117 for the assembled masses: Leonard ms.

117–18 "and growing a beard": PZ, p. 106.

118 "water was 'oomph' degrees": PZS-I.

118 "for weeks to meet": Ibid.

118 regular in theater circles: 1931 unidentified newspaper clipping, Norma Terris Estate.

118 Terris, were like family: PZS-I.

118 film version of *Sally*: October 15, 1924, Warner file.

118 two-thousand-seat theater in Chicago: *CT,* November 2, 1924.

119 to be enjoyed by her: Kiraly ms.

119 Geddes's sets were masterpieces: *Life,* April 2, 1925, p. 22.

119 *Old Army Game* (1926): Ronald J. Fields, *W. C. Fields: A Life on Film* (New York: St. Martins', 1984), p. 39.

119 "made a commendable start": *Washington Times,* January 21, 1925.

120 "things would be different": Bernard Sobel, "This Was Ziegfeld," *American Mercury,* 60 (January 1945), p. 100.

121 street from the Warwick: *DM,* January 1930, p. 63.

121 spring and summer editions: Lina Basquette interview.

122 "connection to Ziegfeld's office": Ibid.

122 "at his own stuff": *Saturday Evening Post,* September 10, 1932, pp. 10–11.

122 for dance direction—$150: *1925 Follies* file, NYP.

122 "your reviews since then?": Harkrider and Patrick.

122 series of film projects: *NYT,* June 16, 1925.

123 was delayed for years: FZ to Lasky, October 23, 1925, NYP.

123 got his gambling "fix": PZ, pp. 157–71.

123 on unsnarling the mess: *NYT*, September 1, 1925.

123 more than $3 million: Frank N. Magill, *Magill's Survey of Cinema: Silent Films* (Englewood Cliffs, New Jersey: Salem, 1982), pp. 202–3.

123 and A. J. Drexel Biddle, Jr.: *NYT*, October 27, 1925.

Chapter 13

124 "in the United States": James Knott, *Palm Beach Revisited: Historical Vignettes of Palm Beach County* (No city: Self-published, 1987), p. 4.

124 "was rich, rich, rich": Ibid. p. 8.

124 "'very much down here'": Ibid., p. 6.

124 white-gloved waiters in attendance: Theodore Pratt, *That Was Palm Beach* (St. Petersburg, Florida: Great Outdoors, 1968), pp. 19–20.

124 modest place by comparison: PZS-I.

124 "to read and write": Ibid.

125 Palm Beach to that time: *NYT*, February 24, 1922.

125 out of the water: PZS-I.

125 for her epicurean taste: Leonard ms.

125 with fresh coconut icing: PZ, p. 121.

125 "assisted to their cars": Leonard ms.

125 and Mrs. Roach's cakes: PZS-I.

125 "to be yelled at": Ibid.

126 a magnificent ten-gallon hat: *Palm Beach Life*, March 12, 1929; and PZS-I.

126 commercial shops, and offices: Historical registry papers, Historical Society of Palm Beach County.

127 as much as Ziegfeld: PZS-I.

128 money off those opportunities: Ector Munn interview.

128 "with the Western Union": BB to FZ, January 15, 1923, LCE.

128 "hope you are benefited": BB to FZ, January 18, 1923, LCE.

128 "Palm Beach lost its zipperoo": Kilpatrick in Knott, *Revisited*, p. 6.

128 without being closed down once: Pratt, p. 48.

128 dressed in evening clothes: Ibid., p. 41.

128 his patrons and himself: Knott, *Revisited*, p. 78.

128 "signifying 'Beach Club'": Cleveland Amory, *The Last Resorts* (New York: Harper and Brothers, 1952), p. 347.

128 "of the croupiers' sticks": Pratt, p. 49.

129 crying over Ziegfeld's gambling: BB, p. 215.

129 moved to Palm Beach: Unidentified Palm Beach newspaper, January 26, 1926; Historical Society of Palm Beach.

129 Friml and Ned Wayburn: *Palm Beach Independent*, January 15, 1926.

129 and lost around $30,000: *Ziegfeld Revue of 1926* file, NYP.

129 his reputation on Broadway: Harkrider and Patrick.

130 "'well better pay off'": Ibid.

130 "I have ever done": Ibid.

130 "the ocean coming in": *Palm Beach Post*, March 4, 1989.

130 "the season to date": *Palm Beach Independent*, January 15, 1926.

130 "and during their performances": *Palm Beach Post*, January 26, 1926.

130 "San Quentin Quail": PZS-I.

131 years of bitter wrangling: *NYT*, July 17, 1926.

131 they invested as partners: Saul Baron testimony, NY-Surr, July 19, 1934.

Chapter 14

132 April and September 1926: Miles Kreuger, *Show Boat: The Story of a Classic American Musical* (New York: Oxford University Press, 1977), p. 12.

132 in the United States: *NYT*, May 9, 1926.

132 irreplaceable keepsakes: *NYT*, June 23, 1926.

133 "...I am through": FZ to Bernard Sobel, June 19, 1926, NYP.

133 the Suppression of Vice: *NYT*, June 26 and 29, 1926.

133 "beautiful and more popular": *NYT*, July 21, 1926.

133 strike, so be it: *NYT*, July 24, 1926.

133 not to walk out: *NYT*, July 29, 1926.

133 sold 320,000 copies: Kreuger, p. 12.

133 introduce him to Edna Ferber: Ibid., p. 18.

134 seek work elsewhere: Ibid., pp. 19–25.

134 "be made in Hollywood": Lasky to FZ, November 4, 1926, NYP.

134 and a radio broadcast: *NYT*, November 7, 1926.

134 patrons, reflected his personality: *NYT*, December 10, 1926.

134 29 feet by 21 feet: Theater Historical Society.

134 balcony off his office: Sobel, p. 100.

134 he rarely used it: PZS-I.

135 at the New Amsterdam: Ibid.

135 and a music library: Theatre Historical Society.

135 played with Patty Ziegfeld: PZS-I.

135 equipment for the stage: Ibid.

135 Billie went into town: Ibid.

136 "Ravenal and Magnolia": Kreuger, p. 20.

136 "of his nine-year-old daughter": Richard Rodgers, *Musical Stages: An Autobiography* (New York: Random House, 1975), pp. 92–93, 95.

136 "would occasionally take over": Ibid., p. 96.

136 and lost about $107,000: *Betsy* file, NYP.

137 "have more important business": Harkrider and Patrick.

137 disliked Fields intensely: Higham, p. 165.

137 it impaired his work: PZS-I.

138 in the business office: Gloria Sharpe Rudes, Annabelle Whitney Reals interviews.

138 "operate to his advantage." Sobel, p. 97.

138 Joan of Arc around 1926: PZS-I.

138 in the entertainment industry: Ibid.

138 make him an asset: Ibid.

139 introduced Kern to her: Edna Ferber, *A Peculiar Treasure* (Cleveland: World, 1947), pp. 304–5.

139 life on the set miserable: Harkrider and Patrick.

139 his very own Joe Urban: Randolph Carter, *Joseph Urban* (New York: Abbeville, 1992), pp. 238–39.

140 portico and gray pillars: *Boston Transcript*, December 30, 1926.

140 shawls and velvet dresses: Ibid.

140 net profit was $243,069.31: *Rio Rita* file, NYP.

141 for the $1,400 memento: *NYT*, July 22, 1927.

141 account in Billie's name: PZS-I.

141 about $450 a week: Sam Kingston to BB, March 14, 1927, PZSC.

141 Ziegfeld was overworked: *NYT*, February 6, 1927.

141 1927 until September 15: *NYT*, February 7, 1927.

141 for the April premiere: Kreuger, p. 26.

141 ... Answer. Flo: FZ to Kern: March 3, 1927, NYP.

141 for her in October: *NYT*, February 22, 1927.

141 a $17,819 costume bill: *NYT*, March 31, 1927.

142 Mexican Seaboard Oil stock: Higham, p. 178.

142 "'kisses, your father, Flo'": *CM*, February 3, 1934, p. 19.

143 "you have everything. Flo': Eddie Cantor, *As I Remember Them* (New York: Duell, Sloan, and Pearce, 1963), p. 27.

143 My devoted love—Baby: BB to FZ, undated (ca. 1926), LCE.

143 "art his full devotion": BB, p. 207.

143 on Broadway at once: *The Great Ziegfeld*, Universal.

Chapter 15

144 "droppings from a cow": Harkrider and Patrick.

144 interfere in staging concerns: Ibid.

144 music from the outset: PZS-I.

145 "'show at eleven o'clock'": Terris to Jack O'Brien, May 23, 1971, Terris Estate.

145 life of its own: Kreuger, pp. 26–27.

145 "get out. Go home!": Ferber, p. 317.

145 "coming over the shoulder": Ferber, November 18, 1927, PZSC.

146 "thought I looked gorgeous": Terris, "*Show Boat* Remembered"; Terris Estate.

146 "I didn't write it": Ferber, November 18, 1927, PZSC.

146 "Don't neglect evening papers": FZ to BS: Dec 22, 1927, NYP.

147 "duet emerged more clearly": Ferber, p. 318.

147 "off to the storehouse": *NYT*, January 8, 1928.

147 were well developed: Ethan Mordden, "'Show Boat' Crosses Over," *New Yorker*, July 3, 1989, pp. 79–82.

148 hands on the money: PZS-I.

148 "costumes for the audience": *NYT*, January 11, 1928.

149 the current vulgar revues: *NYT*, February 23.

149 on the boards simultaneously: *NYT*, March 29, 1928.

149 cards in their hands: Higham, p. 190.

149 "sufficient to halt it": Harkrider and Patrick.

149 "of legs and knees": *NYT*, March 25, 1928.

149 "calls, cables or telegrams": *Los Angeles Herald Examiner*, March 17, 1928.

150 gave him book credit: *NYT*, March 22, 1928.

150 production for Billie Burke: *NYT*, August 6, 1928.

150 "steel and railroad magnate": *LAHE*, September 12, 1928.

150 that said "99.44% pure": PZS-I.

150 progress when tryouts began: Higham, pp. 194–95.

150 A review of the Pittsburgh opening reported that there were six Indian princesses on horses, while a review of the New York opening said five.

150 costumes won rave reviews: Harkrider and Patrick.

150 girls fainted on stage: Clary interview.

150 returned just in time: Higham, pp. 194–95.

151 he would do next: Clary interview.

151 Net profit was $34,000: *Whoopee* file, NYP.

151 "Will phone you. Love, Flo": FZ to BB, November 7, 1928, PZSC.

151 the Drury Lane Theatre: *LAHE*, November 18, 1928.

151 came to an end: *Midnight Frolic* file, NYP.

151 an obsessive workaholic pattern: Higham, p. 188.

Chapter 16

152 profits over $125,000: Kreuger, p. 83.

153 and a wider screen: *NYT*, June 14, 1929.

153 to open with *Rio Rita*: *NYT*, January 29, 1929.

153 "I may be wrong": *Show Girl* file, July 3, 1929, NYP.

153 The audiences loved it: Higham, pp. 197–98.

154 "in you this afternoon": July 15, 1929, CYC.

154 the order to sell: PZS-I.

154 was testifying in court: Randolph Carter, *The World of Flo Ziegfeld* (New York: Praeger, 1974), p. 150.

154 designed for *Show Girl*, Higham, p. 201.

155 his step was uncertain: BB, pp. 221–22.

155 the market was shaky: William K. Klingaman, *1929: The Year of the Great Crash* (New York: Harper & Row, 1989), pp. 116, 152–53, 198–200.

155 "crumbling before my eyes": PZS-I.

155 except Sidney and Delia: Ibid.

156 novice in making films: Ibid.

156 an exaggerated British accent: Ibid.

156 and they celebrated lavishly: Higham, pp. 200–201.

156 up to the job: Rodgers, p. 131.

156 became her signature tune: Ibid., p. 132.

156 "complete nervous breakdown": *LAHE*, March 5, 1930.

156 were selected for Ziegfeld: FZ to BS, March 3, 1930, NYP.

157 back of Goldwyn's estate: PZS-I.

157 Nita Naldi, and others: BB, pp. 217–18.

157 to Marion Davies's sister: PZS-I.

157 "cash for cachet": Berg, p. 197.

157 "produced for the stage": Berg, March 5, 1930 telegram, p. 199.

157 "Daddy on the effect": PZ, p. 202.

157 Goldwyn about hiring Billie: Berg, pp. 197–207.

157 was still going strong: *NYT*, April 14, 1930.

158 showmen from legitimate theater: *NYT*, August 23, 1930.

158 "must have it now?": FZ to W. A. McGuire, July 11, 1930, NYP.

158 fired the errant McGuire: Higham, p. 206.

158 his materials and services: Gerald Bordman, *Days to Be Happy, Years to Be Sad* (New York: Oxford University Press, 1982), pp. 132–37.

158 "cheque for 200,000 dollars": FZ to Ring Lardner, November 9, 1930, PZSC.

158 "wishes in the matter": November 17, 1930, CYC.

158 "on drinking parties constantly": November 18, 1930, CYC.

158 a musical director's capabilities: November 18, 1930, CYC.

158 Youmans write additional songs: November 20, 1930, CYC.

158 "the above numbers forthwith": November 28, 1930, CYC.

159 an already troubled show: PZS-I; and Higham, p. 208.

159 had the ending altered: Bordman, *Days*, p. 134.

159 money to buy coal: Sobel, p. 101.

160 easy or pleasant adjustment: Golden file, IAM; and Higham, pp. 210–11.

160 would revive the series: *NYT*, April 3, 1931.

160 "beautiful to be photographed": 1931 *Follies* file, June 13, 1931, NYP.

160 "New York print it": FZ to BS, February 16, 1932, NYP.

160 "he means this. Sidney": 1931 *Follies* file, June 26, 1931, NYP.

160 "like phoning every hour": FZ to BB, June 19, 1931, PZSC.

160 "again, it's a contract": *NYT*, August 16, 1931.

161 "Your devoted Joe": Urban to BB, July 4, 1931, PZSC.

161 "without repeated bows": BB, pp. 230.

161 $721 worth of flower bulbs: *NYT*, July 18, 1931.

161 $4,000—one week's salary: *NYT*, July 21, 1931.

161 "Flo ever embarked upon": Gene Buck to BB, July 27, 1931, PZSC.

161 with *The Vinegar Tree*: BB to PZS, October 6, 1931, PZSC.

161 "Hollywood of all places": FZ to BB, November 11, 1931, PZSC.

Chapter 17

162 Take care of Mother: FZ to PZS, Winter 1932, PZSC.

162 to be done about it: Higham, pp. 211–12.

162 be at the opening: FZ to BB, March 5, 1932, PZSC.

163 "All that beauty": Harkrider and Patrick.

163 I was the debtor: LeMaire to Baral, October 29, 1972, NYP.

163 sky and picturesque architecture: *NYT*, March 9, 1932.

163 "Let's get proper pacing": Sobel, p. 97.

163 lost more than $115,000: *Hot-Cha!* file, NYP.

163 just before show time: O. O. McIntyre column, undated, NYP.

164 aired *Show Boat* music: Kreuger, Appendix F.

164 "he was ever angry": BB, p. 152.

164 always called him "Ziegfield": "Ziegfeld Follies of the Air," April 3, 1932.

165 at length—for four pages: FZ to BB, April 5, 1932, PZSC.

165 "to sing a song": FZ to BB, April 9, 1932, PZSC.

165 "All my love, Daddy": FZ to BB, April 24, 1932, PZSC.

165 "of the window yet": FZ to PZS & BB, May 9, 1932, PZSC.

165 "behave in any theater": Ferber, p. 306.

166 money had come from: Norma Terris interview.

166 attendance day and night: *NYT*, June 24, 1932.

166 give me the chance: Golden file, IAM.

166 bring Flo to California: PZS-I; and BB, p. 234.

166 make the trip more comfortable: Buhl interview.

166 to about $65,000 today: BB, p. 237.

166 keep *Show Boat* in business: Ibid.

167 Hospital in serious condition: *LAHE*, July 18, 1932.

167 was weak, had improved: *NYT*, July 19, 1932.

167 "speedy recovery. Best, Schnozzle": Durante to FZ, July 21, 1932, PZSC.

167 to change their rules: Golden file, IAM.

167 was on the mend: PZS-I.

168 shortly after he died: *New York Herald Tribune*, July 24, 1932.

168 was page-one news: PZS-I.

168 as if in a dream: Ibid.

168 "no peer on Broadway": Baker interview.

168 "of a dear friend": Hearst to BB, July 23, 1932, PZSC.

168 Thalberg, and Walter Wanger: *LAHE*, July 25, 1932.

168 verge of a collapse: *Los Angeles Times*, July 25, 1932.

169 eyes out. Yours, Will Rogers: *NYT*, July 24, 1932.

169 "people he worked for": Rogers interview.

169 his turbulent last days: Ibid.

169 live by his imagination: Buck to BB, August 6, 1932, PZSC.

Chapter 18

170 control of financial problems: *NYT*, July 24, 1932.

170 of Ziegfeld's numerous debts: *NYT*, August 17, 1932.

170 or even household goods: NY-Surr, April 10, 1934.

170 at more than $500,000: NY-Surr, February 27, 1935.

171 "qualify as executor thereunder": NY-Surr, February 27, 1933.

171 citation—all to no avail: NY-Surr, March–April 1933.

171 be admitted to probate: NY-Surr, May 29, 1933.

171 made from the loanouts: BB, p. 249.

171 Sheriff's sale for $2,500: *NYT*, December 29, 1932.

171 on the Ziegfeld Theatre: *NYT*, February 2, 1933.

171 stage for live theater: *NYT*, April 18, 1933.

171 to complete the number: Higham, p. 225; and *NYT*, April 22, 1933.

171 3 percent of the gross: BB and Erlanger representative to Producing Associates, May 16, 1933, SA.

172 the *Ziegfeld Follies* name: *NYT*, August 28, 1934.

172 assets of only $108,000: *New York Herald Tribune*, August 31, 1934.

172 the Internal Revenue Service: NY-Surr.

173 received a $17,500 settlement: NY-Surr, December 8, 1937.

173 and Sigmund Romberg: *New York World Telegram*, October 15, 1937.

173 "Ziegfeld or Ziegfeld Follies": *New York World Telegram*, October 15, 1937.

173 grand total of $42,000: *LAHE*, April 22, 1940.

Epilogue

176 "they influenced those events": *Publishers Weekly*, April 13, 1990, p. 47.

176 "...or Charles Frohman were": Anna Sosenko interview.

176 found the right combination: Ibid.

177 and the turkey trot: Rosaline Stone, "The Ziegfeld Follies: A Study of Theatrical Opulence from 1907–1931" (Denver University, 1985), p. 78.

179 who were considered "wicked": Erenberg, pp. 214–15.

180 helped perpetuate blackface routines: Roach interview.

181 and after *Show Boat*: Miles Kreuger interview.

184 "work to the...dream": Faulkner in *The Writer's Chapbook*, ed. George Plimpton (New York: Viking, 1989), p. 128.

184 could make it happen: Sosenko interview.

ACT II

Shows

221 "are the light-hearted mosquitos": *Follies of 1908* script, version 2, Act I, Scene 2, MCNY.

225 opened, and Luce emerged: Nona Otero interview.

228 "floated about the stage": *Vogue*, April 1, 1927, p. 132.

232 at least *two* nightgowns: Terris interview.

237 "of fire" and "electrifying": *NYT*, November 11, 1928.

238 Errol "muffed it": Gerald Bordman, *American Musical Theatre: A Chronicle* (Expanded Edition) (New York: Oxford, 1986), p. 268.

238 "Oats, Nicodemus, OATS": Charters, pp. 119–20.

239 "to find the audience": *Follies of 1912* script, Act One, Scene One, p. 3, MCNY.

239 tariff reform, and Cuba: *Follies of 1912* script, Act Two, Scene Five, pp. 31–35, MCNY.

241 disgust of the loser: Gilbert, *American Vaudeville*, p. 286.

248 in any specific one: Chet O'Brien interview.

252 and tossed her about: *Variety*, June 24, 1921, p. 17.

257 those of most producers: Lucile Zinman interview.

257 horror from the audience: *NYT*, December 23, 1923.

265 her number that night: Otero interview.

266 when Ziegfeld satirized them: *New Yorker*, October 17, 1931, p. 23.

Case Study

277 "to see tired people": Merrill interview.

278 "threw the rest away": *CM*, January 20, 1934, p. 26.

278 changes involved refining details: Doris Eaton interview.

278 the already lavish production: Cantor and Freedman, *My Life*, pp. 244–45.

279 "angst" about last-minute changes: Charles Eaton interview.

Biographies

287 "I thought so good": Katkov, p. 215.

296 "I need the m-m-m-money!": *NYT*, February 18, 1958.

298 pastels, rose, and lavender: Zinman interview.

304 do it her way: Lady Lucille Duff-Gordon, *Discretions and Indiscretions* (London: Jarrolds, 1932), p. 245.

305 live in New York: Rosemarie Mariella interview.

306 $3 million during her career: O'Brien interview.

311 back when they could: Zinman interview.

311 car while on tour: Rogers, pp. 138–39.

314 was large and awkward: Higham, pp. 75–76.

315 sketches and the painter: Cantor and Freedman, *Ziegfeld*, p. 129.

318 "is Imogene (Bubbles) Wilson": *NYT*, November 1, 1948.

319 as "The Fire Chief": Gilbert, *American Vaudeville*, p. 253.

❖ BIBLIOGRAPHY ❖

BOOKS

Amory, Cleveland. *The Last Resorts.* New York: Harper and Brothers, 1952.

Asbury, Herbert. *Gem of the Prairie.* Garden City, New York: Garden City, 1942.

Badrig, Robert H. *Florenz Ziegfeld: Twentieth-Century Showman.* Charlottesville, New York: Sam Har, 1972.

Baral, Robert. *Revue: A Nostalgic Reprise of the Great Broadway Period.* New York: Fleet, 1962.

Berg, Scott. *Goldwyn: A Biography.* New York: Knopf, 1989.

Bergreen, Lawrence. *As Thousands Cheer: The Life of Irving Berlin.* New York: Viking, 1990.

Bordman, Gerald. *American Musical Theatre: A Chronicle.* (Expanded ed.). New York: Oxford, 1986.

————. *Jerome Kern: His Life and Music.* New York: Oxford University Press, 1980.

————. *Days to Be Happy, Years to Be Sad.* New York: Oxford University Press, 1982.

Burke, Billie. *With a Feather on My Nose.* New York: Appleton-Century-Crofts, 1949.

Burke, John. *Duet in Diamonds.* New York: Putnam, 1972.

Cantor, Eddie. *As I Remember Them.* New York: Duell, Sloan, and Pearce, 1963.

————. *Take My Life.* Garden City, New York: Doubleday, 1957.

————. *The Way I See It.* Englewood Cliffs, New Jersey: Prentice-Hall, 1959.

Cantor, Eddie, and David Freedman. *My Life Is in Your Hands.* New York: Harper, 1928.

————. *Ziegfeld: The Great Glorifier.* New York: A. H. King, 1934.

Carrera, Liane. *Anna Held and Flo Ziegfeld.* Tr. Guy Daniels. Hicksville, New York: Exposition, 1979.

Carter, Randolph. *Joseph Urban.* New York: Abbeville, 1992.

————. *The World of Flo Ziegfeld.* New York: Praeger, 1974.

Charters, Ann. *Nobody: The Story of Bert Williams.* New York: Macmillan, 1970.

Chicago Record's History of the World's Fair. Chicago: Chicago Daily News, 1893.

Chujoy, Anatole, and P. W. Manchester, eds. *The Dance Encyclopedia.* Rev. ed. New York: Simon & Schuster, 1967.

Cohen-Stratyner, Barbara. *Biographical Dictionary of Dance.* New York: Schirmer Books, 1982.

Day, Donald, ed. *The Autobiography of Will Rogers.* Boston: Houghton Mifflin, 1949.

————. *Will Rogers: A Biography.* New York: David McKay, 1962.

Draper, David F. "Costumes for The Ziegfeld Follies: 1907–1931." M.A. Thesis, University of Texas at Austin, 1972.

Duff-Gordon, Lady Lucille. *Discretions and Indiscretions.* London: Jarrolds, 1932.

Dunning, John. *Tune in Yesterday.* Englewood Cliffs, New Jersey: Prentice-Hall, 1976.

Duval, Katherine. *Ziegfeld: The Man and His Women.* No City: Paradise Books, 1978.

Erenberg, Lewis A. *Steppin' Out: New York Nightlife.* Westport, Connecticut: Greenwood, 1981.

Ewen, David. *New Complete Book of the American Musical Theater.* New York: Holt, Rinehart, and Winston, 1970.

————. *The Story of America's Musical Theater.* Philadelphia: Chilton, 1968.

Falk, Louis. *Across the Little Space: The Life Story of Dr. Louis Falk.* Chicago: Bauman, 1933.

Farnsworth, Marjorie. *Ziegfeld Follies: A History in Text and Pictures.* New York: Putnam, 1956.

Ferber, Edna. *A Peculiar Treasure.* Cleveland: World, 1947.

Fields, Ronald J. *W. C. Fields: A Life on Film.* New York: St. Martins', 1984.

Fowler, Gene. *Timber line.* New York: Covici, Friede, 1933.

Franklin, Joe. *Joe Franklin's Encyclopedia of Comedians.* Secaucus, New Jersey: Citadel Press, 1979.

Gilbert, Douglas. *American Vaudeville: Its Life and Times.* New York: McGraw-Hill, 1940.

————. *Encyclopedia of the Musical Theatre.* New York: Dodd, Mead, 1976.

Halliwell, Leslie. *Halliwell's Filmgoer's Companion.* 8th ed. New York: Scribner's, 1984.

————. *Halliwell's Film Guide.* 5th ed. New York: Scribner's, 1985.

Harding, Alfred. *The Revolt of the Actors.* New York: Morrow, 1929.

Havighurst, Walter. *Annie Oakley of the Wild West.* New York: MacMillan, 1954.

Henderson, Mary C. *Theater in America.* New York: Abrams, 1986.

Higham, Charles. *Ziegfeld.* Chicago: Regnery, 1972.

Johnson, Stephen Burge. *The Roof Gardens of Broadway Theatres*. Ann Arbor, Michigan: UMI Research Press, 1985.

Katkov, Norman. *The Fabulous Fanny: The Story of Fanny Brice*. New York: Knopf, 1953.

Klingaman, William K. *1929: The Year of the Great Crash*. New York: Harper & Row, 1989.

Knott, James. *Palm Beach Revisited: Historical Vignettes of Palm Beach County*. No city: Self-published, 1987.

————. *Palm Beach Revisited II: Historical Vignettes of Palm Beach County*. No city: Self-published, 1988.

Kreuger, Miles. *Show Boat: The Story of a Classic American Musical*. New York: Oxford University Press, 1977.

McNamara, Brooks. *The Shuberts of Broadway*. New York: Oxford University Press, 1990.

Magill, Frank N. *Magill's Survey of Cinema: Silent Films*. Englewood Cliffs, New Jersey: Salem, 1982.

Maschio, Geraldine. "The *Ziegfeld Follies*." University of Wisconsin, 1981.

Morell, Parker. *Lillian Russell: The Era of Plush*. New York: Random House, 1940.

Nathan, George. *The Theatre, the Drama, the Girls*. New York: Knopf, 1921.

New York Times Biographical Service. New York: Arno Press, 1964–1984.

Nicholson, Kenyo, ed. *Revues: A Book of Short Sketches*. Preface by Florenz Ziegfeld. New York: Appleton, 1929.

Niver, Kemp. *Early Motion Pictures*. Washington, D.C.: Library of Congress, 1985.

Pratt, Theodore. *That Was Palm Beach*. St. Petersburg, Florida: Great Outdoors, 1968.

Raffe, W. G., assisted by M. E. Purdon, eds. *Dictionary of the Dance*. New York: Barnes, 1964.

Raggan, David. *Who's Who in Hollywood, 1900–1976*. New Rochelle, New York: Arlington House, 1976.

Ramsaye, Terry. *A Million and One Nights*. New York: Simon & Schuster, 1984.

Rigdon, Walter, ed. *The Biographical Encyclopedia and Who's Who of American Theatre*. New York: Heinman, 1966.

Rodgers, Richard. *Musical Stages: An Autobiography*. New York: Random House, 1975.

Rogers, Betty Blake. *Will Rogers: His Wife's Story*. New York: Bobbs Merrill, 1941.

Russell, Donald. *The Lives and Legends of Buffalo Bill*. Norman: University of Oklahoma, 1960.

Sandow, Eugene. *Strength and How To Obtain It*. London: Gale & Polden, No year [c. 1899].

Sayers, Isabelle S. *Annie Oakley and Buffalo Bill's Wild West*. New York: Dover, 1981.

Schabas, Ezra. *Theodore Thomas*. Urbana: University of Illinois Press, 1989.

Slide, Anthony. *The Vaudevillians: A Dictionary of Vaudeville Performers*. Westport, Connecticut: Arlington, 1981.

Southern, Eileen. *The Musical Black Americans: A History*. 2nd ed. New York: Norton, 1983.

Stone, Rosaline. "The Ziegfeld Follies: A Study of Theatrical Opulence from 1907–1931." Denver University, 1985.

Swanberg, W. A. *Citizen Hearst*. New York: Scribner's, 1961.

Taylor, Robert Lewis. *W. C. Fields: His Follies and Fortunes*. Garden City, New York: Doubleday, 1949.

This Fabulous Century 1910–1920. New York: Time Books, 1975.

Unterbrink, Mary. *Funny Women: American Comediennes, 1860–1985*. Jefferson, North Carolina: McFarland, 1987.

Urban, Joseph. *Theatres*. Boston: Theatre Arts, 1929.

Vargas, Alberto, and Reid Austin. *Vargas*. New York: Harmony Books, 1978.

Variety Obituaries. Vols. 1905–1986. New York: Garland, 1988.

Wodehouse, P. G., and Guy Bolton. *Bring on the Girls*. New York: Simon & Schuster, 1953.

Ziegfeld, Patricia. *The Ziegfelds' Girl: Confessions of an Abnormally Happy Childhood*. Boston: Little, Brown, 1964.

UNPUBLISHED AND ARCHIVAL MATERIAL

Baral, Robert/Ziegfeld Club. New York Public Library—Lincoln Center Theatre. Uncatalogued collection: photos, unpublished manuscripts, news clippings, correspondence, and programs.

Burke, Billie. University of Southern California Cinema–Television Library. Los Angeles. Newsclips, photos, unpublished scripts.

Chicago Musical College. Roosevelt University Music Library. Chicago. Catalogues, ledgers, memorabilia.

Clough, Matilda Golden. Institute of the American Musical. Los Angeles. Newsclips, photos, correspondence.

Dawn, Hazel, and Norma Terris. Institute of the American Musical. Los Angeles. Radio interview.

Fields, W. C. Fields family private collection. Los Angeles. Scrapbooks.

Ganz, Peter Felix. "Chicago Musical College, 1867–1967: An Historical Sketch." Roosevelt University Music Library. Chicago. Unpublished manuscript.

Harkrider, John, and James Patrick. "Life Story." James Patrick private collection. Nantucket, Massachusetts. Harkrider's unpublished autobiography.

Held, Anna. New York Public Library—Lincoln Center Theatre. Photos, papers, memorabilia.

Kiraly, Vincent. "The Golden Olden Days with Florenz Ziegfeld." Patricia Ziegfeld Stephenson private collection. Los Angeles. Unpublished biography.

Leonard, Delia. Patricia Ziegfeld Stephenson private collection. Los Angeles. Unpublished memoir on the Ziegfelds.

Locke, Robinson Scrapbooks. New York Public Library—Lincoln Center Theatre. Billie Burke, Anna

Held, Lillian Lorraine, Claire Luce, Florenz Ziegfeld.

Lorimar Picture Research Library. Lorimar Studios. Los Angeles. Photos and correspondence.

Lorraine, Lillian. Nils Hanson private collection. New York. Papers, newsclips, photos.

Terris, Norma. Albert Firestone private collection. Lyme, Connecticut. Unpublished papers and photos.

Vinton, Doris. Joe Adamson private collection. Los Angeles. Unpublished interview.

Wayburn, Ned. University of Southern California Cinema–Television Library. Los Angeles. Newsclips, photos, unpublished scripts.

Warner Bros. Wisconsin State Historical Society. Madison. Financial records.

Youmans, Vincent. Cecily Youmans Collins private collection. New York City. Legal papers and correspondence.

Ziegfeld, Florenz, Jr. Historical Society of Palm Beach County. Palm Beach. Newsclips and photos.

———. Museum of the City of New York. New York. Papers, photos, scripts, memorabilia.

———. New York Public Library—Lincoln Center Theatre. Papers, photos, and memorabilia.

———. New York State Surrogate Court. White Plains.

———. Patricia Ziegfeld Stephenson private collection. Los Angeles. Photos, letters, and memorabilia.

———. Shubert Archives. New York. Papers and photos.

———. Theatre Historical Society. Chicago. Architectural records and newsclips.

———. Will Rogers Memorial. Claremore, Oklahoma. Papers and photos.

ARTICLES

Austen, Roger. "Flo Ziegfeld's Blond Bodybuilder." *California Library Magazine,* June 4, 1978, 31–33.

Cantor, Eddie and David Freeman. "Ziegfeld and His Follies." *Collier's,* January 13–February 10, 1934.

Churchill, Allen. "Them As Has 'Em, Wears 'Em." *Diners' Club Magazine,* July 1962, 16–18, 33–35.

Cohen-Stratyner, Barbara. "Welcome to 'Laceland'." *Musical Theater in America.* Ed. Glenn Loney. Westport, Connecticut: Greenwood, 1984, 315–21.

Kaye, Joseph. "Master of the 'Follies'." *The Dance Magazine,* October–December 1929 and January 1930.

Lardner, Ring. "A Day with Conrad Green." *Best Short Stories of Ring Lardner.* New York: Scribner's, 1957, 127–38.

McEvoy, J. P. "He Knew What They Wanted." *Saturday Evening Post,* September 10, 1932, 10–11, 51–52.

Morehouse, Ward. "The Ziegfeld Follies—A Formula with Class." *Theatre Arts,* May 1956, 66–69, 87.

Pollack, Channing. "Building the *Follies.*" *Green Book,* September 1915, 388–403.

Sandow, Eugen. "My Reminiscences." *Strand,* March 1910, 164–72.

Seldes, Gilbert. "Profile: Glorifier." *The New Yorker,* July 25, 1931, 18–22 and August 1, 1931, 18–22.

Sobel, Bernard. "This Was Ziegfeld." *American Mercury,* January 1945, 96–102.

Wolf, Rennold. "Billie Burke, Married and at Home." *Green Book,* November 1914, 830, 843–54.

———. "How the *Follies* Are Written." *New York Times,* September 22, 1919.

Ziegfeld, Florenz, Jr. "Beauty, the Fashions and the *Follies*." *Ladies Home Journal*, March 1923, 16–17+.

———. "How I Pick Beauties." *Theatre Magazine*, September 1919, 158–60.

———. "How I Pick My Beauties." *Green Book*, February 1914, 212–18.

———. "Picking Out Pretty Girls for the Stage." *American Magazine*, December 1919, 34–37, 119–27.

———. "What Becomes of the *Ziegfeld Follies* Girls." *Pictorial Review*, May 1925, 12–13.

———. "Why I Produce the Kind of Shows I Do." *The Green Book Album*, January 1912, 172–77.

AUDIO

"American Musical Theater: Shows, Songs, and Stars." Vol. 1. CD. Smithsonian and CBS Records, RD 036 A 20854, 1989.

"Follies, Scandals & Other Diversions: from Ziegfeld to the Shuberts." LP. New World Records, NW215, 1977.

"Rio Rita." LP. Monmouth Evergreen, MES 7058, [No date: 1975?].

"Show Boat." CD. EMI Records, 3 Vols., CDS 7 49108 2, 1988.

"Stars of the Ziegfeld Follies." LP. Pelican, LP 102, 1972.

"This Is Your Life: Billie Burke." NBC Radio. February 1 and February 8, 1950.

Urban, Gretl. Unpublished interview on Joseph Urban (by Randolph Carter). Columbia University.

"Whoopee." LP. Smithsonian and RCA, R012/DPM1 0349, 1978.

"Ziegfeld." LP. Friends of the Theatre & Music Collection of the Museum of the City of New York, New York.

"Ziegfeld Follies." LP. Veritas, VM 107, 1967.

"Ziegfeld Follies of 1919." LP. Smithsonian American Musical Theater Series/CBS, R009/P14272, 1977.

"Ziegfeld Follies of the Air." April 3–June 26, 1932. CBS Radio.

FILMS

"Flo Ziegfeld and His 1931 *Follies* Beauties." Blackhawk Films, 1931. "Movieland," Tape 1, CS530, UCLA Film Archive. Also contains other Ziegfeld shorts.

Funny Girl. Columbia, 1968.

Glorifying the American Girl. Paramount, 1929.

The Great Ziegfeld. MGM, 1936.

Kid Boots. Paramount, 1926.

Movietone News Collection. Twentieth-Century Fox, New York, segments that aired; University of South Carolina, outtakes.

"Prologue," *Show Boat.* Universal, 1929, with sound footage of Bledsoe, Morgan, Gardella singing their signature songs.

Rio Rita. MGM, 1929 and 1942.

Sally. First National/Warner Bros., 1929—sound; Warner Bros., 1925—silent.

Show Boat. Universal, 1929— sound; Universal, 1936—sound; MGM, 1951—sound; Criterion Videodisc, 1989.

Whoopee! Samuel Goldwyn (United Artists), 1930.

Ziegfeld Follies. MGM, 1946.

Ziegfeld Girl. MGM, 1941.

"Ziegfeld: The Man and His Women." Columbia Pictures produced for NBC Television, 1978.

SCRIPTS OF ZIEGFELD PRODUCTIONS

Institute of the American Musical, Los Angeles: "Pink Lady."

Lincoln Center—Theatre, New York Public Library, New York (typescripts): "Annie Dear," "Betsy," "Bitter Sweet," "Caesar's Wife," "The Intimate Strangers," "Kid Boots," "Louis the XIV," "Parlor Match," "Rescuing Angel," "Rio Rita," "Sally," "Show Boat" (1927; 1932), "Show Girl," "Simple Simon," "Three Musketeers," "Whoopee."

Museum of the City of New York, New York (typescripts): "Follies" scripts for 1907–10, 1912.

University of Southern California, Los Angeles (typescripts): "Century Girl" (Act I), "Midnight Frolic" ("Lobby" scene), "Miss 1917" (partial—60 pp.), "Nine O'Clock Revue," "Miss 1920," "Ziegfeld Follies" scripts for 1916–19, 1923.

INDEX

Chicago Musical College, 14, 15, 16–21, 23, 24, 44, 72, 101, 286, 292; income from, 17, 20, 24; locations, 14, 16

Chorus, *33*, 34, *51*, 59, 63, 64, *64*, 65, 67, 70, 86–87, 89, 95, 133, 147, *148, 170*, 174, 180, *214*, 219, *220*, 221, 230, 237, 243, 244, 247, 248, 252, 254, 257, 260, 263, 265, 266, 269, 271, 277–80, 293, 297, 299, 306, 307, 309, 313, 316; significance of, 34, 35, 41, 43, 59, 69–70, 102, *102*, 121, 179

Chorus Equity, 89

Chu Chin Chow (play), 88

Claire, Ina (Ina Fagan), 73, 77, 91, *197*, 241, 243, 244, 289

Clarion, Laura, *231*

Clark, Bobby, 172

Clayton, Bessie, 221, 307

Clayton, Jackson, and Durante, 153, 232

Clayton, Lew, 317

Close, Justice Frederick P., 161

Clough, Goldie. *See* Golden, Matilda

Club de Montmartre, *127*

Cochran, Charles B., 218

Cocoanut Grove (Century Theatre Roof), 80, 224, 282

Coffey, William S., 170, 172, 173

Cole, Jack, 174, 266

Collins, Jose, 54, 239, *239*

Columbian Exposition. *See* World's Fair

Colvan, Zeke, 230, 232, 263

Comic Supplement, The, 119, *119*, 121, 219, 258, 260, 283, 291, 295, 305, 306

composers, *178*

Connolly, Bobby, 223, 232, 265

Conrad, Con, 219

Constable, Arnold, 274

Conway, Charles, 174

Cook, Charles Emerson, 227

Cornell, Olive, 116

Cosmopolitan Theatre (New York City), 120, 121, 223

cost of shows, 35, 58, 83, 101, 113, 114, 115, 119, 121, 148, 151, 163, 252, 265

Coward, Noël, 98, *154*, 156, 218

Curry, Dan, 138, 158, 165, 166

D

Dabney, Ford, 62, *62*, 125, 131, 289

Dahm, Marie, 257

Dahomey dancers, 230

Dale, Margaret, 148, 218, 229

Daly, Anna, 81

Dancing Ducks of Denmark incident, 19

Danse de Follies, 59, 62

"Darktown Poker Club" (1914 *Follies*), 241

D'Arle, Yvonne, *144*, 234, 236

Davies, Marion (Marion Douras), *74*, 77, 91, 135, 157, 168, 224, 244, 289–90, 315

Davis, Deering, 287

Davis, Owen, 236

Davis, Richard Harding, 304

Daw, Mae, *254*, 257–58

Dawn, Hazel (Hazel Tout), 50, *193*, 219, 227, 290

Day, Edith, 232

Dazian, 274

Dazie, Mlle. (Daisy Peterkin), 41, 44, 219, 221, 290

Deagon, Arthur, 44, 46, 221, 241

"Dearest" (*Midnight Frolic*, 1919), 271

De Koven, Reginald, 223, 227, 312

De Remer, Ruby, 269

Derwent, Clarence, *144*, 234

DeSilva, Bud, 198, 251

De Wolfe, Billie, 174

Dickson, Dorothy, *245*

Dietz, Howard, 266

Dillingham, Charles, 50, *51*, 66, 71, 75, 80, 84, 96, 176, 181, 294, 309; career of, 51–52, 79, 80, 89, 172, 219, 223, 224, 227; relationship with Ziegfeld, 51–52, 76, 78, 79, 80, 82, 84, 92, 102, 120

Dinarzade, *222*

Dingle, Tom, *51*, 237–38

Dinner at Eight (film), 174

Ditrichstein, Leo, 224, 236

Dix, Kathryn, 110

Dolan, Robert, 265

Dolly Twins, Jenny and Rose, *51*, 237, 239, 266, 290–91

Dolores (Kathleen Mary Rose), 65, 66, *82*, 83, 222, *222*, 229–30, 245, *245*, 247, 271, 291, 304

Donahue, Jack, 84, 93, 148, *148*, 229, 250, 291

Donaldson, Walter, 204

Dooley, Johnny, 86, *87*, 89, 248, 291

Dooley, Ray, 86, *87*, 89, 93, 122, *128*, 164, 219, 225, 248, *248*, 250, 251, 252, 258, *258*, 260, 291, 292

Dooley, William and Gordon, 67, 271, 291

Douglas, Kingman, 284

Dove, Billie (Lillian Bohny), 86, *86*, 91, 104, 291

Dowling, Eddie (Joseph Nelson Goucher), 86, *87*, 88–89, 163, 171, 248, 250, 265, 291, 292

Dressler, Marie (Leila von Koerber), 36, 79, 89, 219, 223, 292

Drew, John, 55

Duff-Gordon, Lady. *See* Lucille

Duke, Vernon, 265

Dumanoir and Carre, 224

Dumas, Alexandre, 149, 234

Duncan, Isadora, 126

Duncan Sisters, 271

Dunne, Irene, 173, 232, 292–93, *293*, 313

Durante, Jimmy, 153, *153*, 167, 181, 232, 288

DuSouchet, H. A., 227

Duval, Paulette, 257

Dwyer, Phil, 88–89, 241, 248, 250

"Dying Swan, The" (1916 *Follies*), 244

E

Earl Carroll's Vanities (revue), 90, 302

Earle, Marcelle, 248, 272

"Hello, Honey" (1913 *Follies*), 239
Henderson, Ray, 223, 266
Hendrick, Justice, 89
Henwood, Frank, 50
Hepburn, Katharine, 168
Hepner (wig maker), 274
Herbert, Joseph W., 223, 224
Herbert, Victor I, 78, 81, 82, 96,
    113–14, 176, 219, 224,
    229, 245, 248, 250, 251,
    252, 257, 258, 274,
    299–300, *299*
Hershfield, Harry, *119*
Hickman, Art, 93, 131, 250, 289
Higgledy-Piggledy, 33, 36, 222, 281,
    292; tour of, 36
High culture, 18, 47, 68, 158
Hill, Billy, 265
Hill, J. Leubrie, 59
Hines, Elizabeth, 141, 230
Hirsch, Louis A., 75, 241, 243, 247,
    252, 266
Hitchcock, Raymond, *72*, 84, *250*,
    251–52, 291
Hitchy-Koo, 84, 269, 291, 294
Hobart, George V., 227, 237, 239,
    241, 243, 244, 274
Hoctor, Harriet, *149*, 172, 232,
    232–33, 234, 265, 300
Hoey, Herbert, 271, 272
Hoey, William, 29–30, 227
Hoff, Vanda, 67, 272
Hoffman, Gertrude, 38, 80, 224,
    227, 257, 313
Hoffmann, Max, 37, 78, 227, 289
Hoffmann, Max, Jr., 313
"Hold Me in Your Loving Arms"
    (1915 *Follies*), 241

"Homeland" (*Louie the 14th*), 201
Hope, Bob, 172, *172*, 265
Hopkins, Peggy, 91, 245
Horne, Lena, 174
Hot-Cha!, 162–63, *162–63*, 223,
    283; tour of, 162
Hotel Ansonia (New York City),
    40, *41*, 44, 47, 78
Howard, Tom, 234
Howland, Jobyna, 223
Hoyt, Charles, 237, 306
Hoyt, Julia, 229
Hoyt, Vonnie, *219*
Hubbell, Raymond, 237, 238, 239,
    241, 244, 257, 258, 260,
    274
Hughes, Harriet, 295
Hughes, Howard, 166, 292
Hunter, Glenn, *94*
Hutton, Edward, 124, *125*, 126,
    129, 154–55, 157
Hutton, Marjorie Meriweather, 76,
    124, 126
Hyson, Carl, 245, *245*

I

"If a Table at Rector's Could Talk"
    (1913 *Follies*), 239
"I Just Can't Make My Eyes
    Behave" (*A Parisian
    Model*), 38, *189*
"I'll See You Again" (*Bitter Sweet*),
    218
"I'm With You" (1931 *Follies*), 211
Ince, Thomas, 75
"In Florida among the Palms" (*No
    Foolin'*), 210
Injunction. *See* lawsuit

"In the Shade of the Alamo" (1925
    Follies), 211
Intimate Strangers, The, *94*, 98, 101,
    223, 282; tour of, 101
"It All Belongs to Me" (1927
    Follies), 263
"It's Delightful to Be Married" (*A
    Parlor Match*), 38
"It's Getting Dark on Old
    Broadway" (1922 *Follies*),
    254
"I Want Someone to Make a Fuss
    Over Me" (*Midnight Frolic*,
    January 1915), 63
"I Want to See a Minstrel Show"
    (1919 *Follies*), 248, 250

J

Jackson, Bee, *128*
Jackson, Joe, 80, 224
Jacobi, Victor, 247
Jacoby, Coleman, 266
Janis, Elsie, 52, 79, 219, 244
Janssen, Werner, 258, 260
Jardin de Paris (New York Theatre
    Roof), 40, 51, 219, 221,
    237, 281, 295
Jazz Age, the, 57, 84, 131, 181, 184
Jazzbow Girls, 263, *263*
Jeffreys, Alan, 266
Jerry (play), 60; tour of, 60
"Joan of Arc" (unproduced play),
    138, 150
Johnston, Alfred Cheney, 83
Johnstone, Justine, *300*
Jolson, Al, 153, 237, 293
Jones, Allen, 173, 232
Jubilee Singers, 147, 230

Judels, Charles, 238
"Jungle Jingle" (1927 *Follies*), 265

K

Kahn, Gus, 232, 236
Kahn, Otto, 77, 129, 153
Kainer, Ludwig, 117
Karsavina, Tamara, 77
Keeler, Ruby, 153–54, *153*, 157,
    232, 237
Keenan, Hilda, 319
Kellerman, Annette, 73
Kelly, Ethel Amorita, 54, 239
Kelly, Harry, *82*, 219, 221, 247, 248
Kenaston, Robert, 292
Kennedy, Helen, 168
Kennedy, John, 266
Kennedy, Joseph P., 128
Kern, Jerome, 82, 92, 95–96, 108,
    133, 134, 135, 138–39,
    141, 144–45, 148, 152,
    173, 176, 198, 224, 229,
    230, 232, 243, 297–98,
    300–301, *301*, 307
Kid Boots, 73, 92, 98, 112, 114–15,
    114–15, 123, 223, 283;
    tour of, 115
Kilpatrick, James, 124
Kinetoscope, 27, 317
King, Allyn, 67, 245, 247, 266, 271,
    272, *275*, 280, 301
King, Dennis (Dennis Pratt), *144*,
    145, *149*, *150*, 165, 232,
    234, 301
Kingsley, Walter, *136*
Kingston, Sam, 30, *30*, 110, 122,
    136, 141, 302, 315
Kiraly, Victor, 56, 119

PHOTOGRAPH CREDITS

The authors and publishers wish to thank the following institutions, collectors, photographers, and all others who have graciously consented to the reproduction of their photographs. Numerals refer to page numbers.

Courtesy of the Academy of Motion Picture Arts and Sciences and Turner Entertainment Company: 175. Reprinted from *Architectural Record*, May 1927, © 1927 McGraw-Hill, Inc. All rights reserved. Reproduced with the permission of the publisher: 202. Courtesy of Bert and Richard Morgan Studio. Copy photographer Quentin Schwinn: 127 top middle. The Bettmann Archive: 12 bottom; 32; 92 middle; 107 left; 111 left; 113 right; 136 right; 153 top middle; 154 top; 249. Billie Burke Collection, USC Cinema–Television Library and Archives of Performing Arts: 72 right. Billy Rose Theatre Collection, New York Public Library: 2; 40 top left; 42 left; 43 right; 55 left; 63 left; 64 top left; 65 middle right; 74 right; 86 right and top left; 93 right; 94 right; 118 bottom left; 120 left and right; 132 top left; 135 all; 137 left; 148 top right and top left; 153 left; 183; 187; 213 top right; 217; 228; 229 bottom; 230 left; 235 left; 236; 240; 241 right; 248 top; 250 left; 254 bottom; 260; 261; 262; 263 top; 264; 285; 309 right. Billy Rose Theatre Collection, New York Public Library. Copy photographer Jonathan Wallen: 30 top left, bottom left, and top right; 31 top right; 33 left; 40 top right; 41 left; 42 middle right; 43 middle; 45; 50 right and bottom left; 51 left and top right; 55 middle; 64 right; 65 left and bottom right; 66 bottom left; 67 right and left; 72 left; 73 bottom right, left, and top right; 80 right; 81 top right and bottom right; 82 top left; 83 middle and right; 87 all; 92 left and right; 102 left and right; 103 left; 111 middle; 117 bottom right; 118 top left; 119 middle and right; 128 left, right, and top left; 134; 136 top left; 146 left and right; 148 bottom left; 151 right; 153 top right; 154 left; 155; 163 right and middle; 170 right; 178; 188 left; 190; 191 right; 192 right; 193 bottom left and top right; 197; 200; 207 left; 218 all; 219 right, top left, and bottom left; 220 bottom and top; 225; 229 top; 231 top; 232; 233; 237; 238 top and bottom; 239 left and right; 241 top left and bottom left; 242 left; 244 top and bottom; 245 top and bottom; 246; 248 bottom; 250 right; 251; 253 top and bottom; 255; 269; 272; 273; 275 right; 279 right; 286; 290; 295; 297; 299–305; 310 right and left; 312; 319. Billy Rose Theatre Collection, New York Public Library, and Alfred J. Frueh. Copy photographer Jonathan Wallen: 144 left. Chicago Historical Society: 22 left; 152 left; 186. Chicago Public Library Special Collections Department: 12 top left; 22 right; 213 bottom right. Circus World Museum of Baraboo Wisconsin: 64 bottom left. Cleveland Public Library: 153 bottom right; 163 left; 243; 247; 293 left; 318. Cleveland Public Library. Copy photographer Quentin Schwinn: 50 top left; 62 top left; 114–15; 239 top. Robert Cushman Collection, Los Angeles: 88; 188 right; 189; 191 bottom left; 193 bottom right; 198 right; 210 all; 211 all but middle right and bottom left; 214 top left, bottom left, and bottom right; 215; 216. Collection Charles Eaton, Detroit. Copy photographer Quentin Schwinn: 43 left; 293 right. Courtesy the W. C. Fields family. Copy photographer Richard Thompson: 119 left; 258. Courtesy Albert D. Firestone: 117 top middle; 231 bottom. Courtesy Albert D. Firestone. Copy photographer Jonathan Wallen: 230 right. Courtesy of Nona Otero Friedman. Copy photographer Quentin Schwinn: 66 top left; 103 middle; 149; 150 bottom; 309 left. Harry N. Abrams, Inc.: 194. The Harry Ransom Humanities Research Center, The University of Texas at Austin: 42 bottom right; 43 left; 63 top right; 80 left; 82 bottom left; 118 right; 136 top middle; 144 top; 145 bottom right; 150 top; 162; 195 left and right; 211 middle right; 222 top; 226; 235 right; 242 right; 263 bottom; 270 top. Harvard Theatre Collection: 41 top right; 81 left; 94 left. Historical Society of Palm Beach County: 124 left and right; 125 middle and right; 126 bottom left, top left, and top right; 127 top left, bottom left, top right, and middle right. The Institute of the American Musical: 112 left. Collection David A. Jasen, Flushing, New York. Copy photographer Quentin Schwinn: 211 bottom left. Joseph Urban Collection, Rare Book and Manuscript Library, Columbia University, New York: 185; 195; 196 left; 203; 204 top; 205; 212 top and bottom. Photo by A. C. Langmuir, courtesy Hastings Historical Society: 108 left; 109 left. Collection Gene London, New York. Copy photographer Quentin Schwinn: 137 bottom right; 191 top left; 198 left; 199; 201; 205; 206; 214 top right. Lorimar Picture Research Library: 52 right; 53; 62 right; 93 left and middle; 132 left and right; 133 right; 267; 275 left. Museum of the City of New York, The Leonard Hassam Bogart Collection: 41 bottom right. Museum of the City of New York, The Theater Collection: 55 middle; 66 right; 75; 82 right; 254 top; 268. Museum of the City of New York, The Theater Collection. Photo from the *New York Star*, 1909: 40 bottom left. Museum of the City of New York, The Theater Collection, Photograph by Wurts: 133 left. Museum of the City of New York, The Theater Collection, Watercolor by Charles LeMaire: 213 left. Ole Olsen Collection, USC Cinema–Television Library and Archives of Performing Arts. Copy photographer Richard Thompson: 274; 276 left and right; 277 both; 278 left and right; 279 left. Roosevelt University, Chicago: 12 top right; 23 left; 113 left. Roosevelt University, Chicago. Copy photographer Danguole Variakojis: 15.

Courtesy the Samuel Goldwyn Company and the Wisconsin Center for Film and Theater Research: 151 left. The Shubert Archive: 170 left; 171; 172. Collection Patricia Ziegfeld Stephenson, Los Angeles. Copy photographer Richard Thompson: 13 right; 25 top; 33 top right; 51 bottom right; 54 left and right; 62 bottom left; 72 middle; 74 left; 86 bottom left; 103 right; 106 right; 107 right; 108; 109 right; 110 right; 111 right; 112 right; 116 all; 117 left and top right; 121; 124 middle; 126 top, second from right; 129; 137 top right; 145 left; 152 right; 192 left; 193 top left; 196 right; 280; 207 right; 296. Collection Patricia Ziegfeld Stephenson, Los Angeles. Copy photographer Quentin Schwinn: 136 bottom left. Theatre Historical Society of America Archives: 52 left and middle. Painting by Thomas Torrenti, courtesy Albert D. Firestone: 204 bottom; 208. Courtesy Rosemarie M. Volcano: 164. Will Rogers Memorial, Claremore, Oklahoma: 63 bottom right; 110 left; 125 left; 127 bottom right; 256; 259; 270 bottom. Wisconsin Center for Film and Theater Research: 13 left; 23 right; 24; 176. Photograph by Paulette Ziegfeld: 209. Collection Richard and Paulette Ziegfeld. Copy photographer Quentin Schwinn: 12 top middle; 25 bottom; 30 top middle; 31 top left, top middle, and bottom right; 33 bottom right; 41 middle right; 42 top; 65 top right; 106 left; 145 middle and top right; 222 bottom; 234. Collection Richard and Paulette Ziegfeld. Graphic by Charles Cooper: 320.